EMPIRE AT WAR

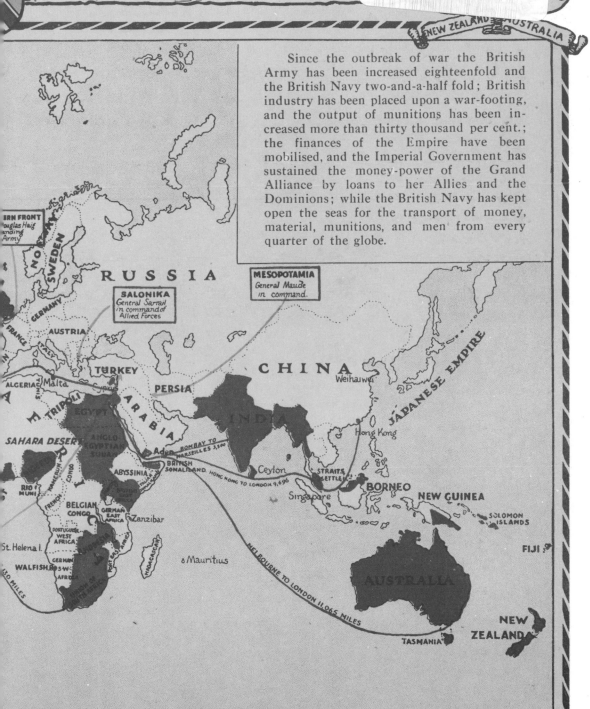

Since the outbreak of war the British Army has been increased eighteenfold and the British Navy two-and-a-half fold; British industry has been placed upon a war-footing, and the output of munitions has been increased more than thirty thousand per cent.; the finances of the Empire have been mobilised, and the Imperial Government has sustained the money-power of the Grand Alliance by loans to her Allies and the Dominions; while the British Navy has kept open the seas for the transport of money, material, munitions, and men from every quarter of the globe.

NEW ZEALAND AUSTRALIA

ERN FRONT
ouglas Haig
anding
Army

RUSSIA

MESOPOTAMIA
General Maude
in command.

SALONIKA
General Sarrail
in command of
Allied Forces

SWEDEN

NO

GERMANY

AUSTRIA

FRANCE

TURKEY

CHINA

Weihaiwei

JAPANESE EMPIRE

ALGERIA Malta

PERSIA

ARABIA

INDIA

Hong Kong

TRIPOLI

EGYPT

ANGLO
EGYPTIAN
SUDAN

Aden

BOMBAY TO
MARSEILLES 3,300

Ceylon

STRAITS
SETTLE

SAHARA DESERT

BRITISH
SOMALILAND

HONG KONG TO LONDON 9,690

BORNEO

NEW GUINEA

ABYSSINIA

Singapore

RIO
MUNI

FRENCH CONGO

GERMAN
EAST
AFRICA

Zanzibar

SOLOMON
ISLANDS

BELGIAN
CONGO

PORTUGUESE
WEST
AFRICA

St. Helena I.

GERMAN
S.W.
AFRICA

MADAGASCAR

Mauritius

MELBOURNE TO LONDON 11,065 MILES

AUSTRALIA

FIJI

WALFISH B

UNION OF SOUTH AFRICA

30 MILES

TASMANIA

NEW
ZEALAND

HOMES & THEIR BATTLEFIELDS

INDIA
AVEN LIGHT OUR

The Soldier's War
1914-18

△3.　▽4.

△1.　▽2.

PETER H. LIDDLE
THE SOLDIER'S WAR
1914-18

BLANDFORD PRESS
LONDON   NEW YORK   SYDNEY

1. A Royal Fusilier officer pauses for a photograph on his way up to a sniper position in the spring of 1915. Note his rifle, a non-standard weapon modified for personal use, fitted with a Ross telescope sight. (Captain K. W. Brewster)

2. Conventional breakfast in an unconventional setting. A Middlesex Yeomanryman rises and shines at Moascar Camp near Ismailia in 1915. (E. H. Dixon)

3. 18 September 1918. In clearing the ground in front of the main Hindenburg Line, British troops were to encounter stiff opposition, particularly at Epehy, but artillery dominance and the use of great numbers of machine-guns laying down a curtain of fire were now offering some protection to attacking troops. ('Realistic Travels' Photo Series/P.H.L. Archives)

4. Fallen in action. Captain Andrews of the 4th Battalion, the Duke of Wellington's Regiment, is laid to rest by members of his unit in 1915. (Lieutenant Colonel J. Walker)

First published in Great Britain, 1988 by Blandford
Press Ltd., Artillery House, Artillery Row, London
SW1P 1RT.

Distributed in the USA by Sterling Publishing Co. Inc.,
2 Park Avenue, New York, NY 10016.

Distributed in Australia by Capricorn Link (Australia)
Pty. Ltd., P.O. Box 665, Lane Cove, New South
Wales 2066, Australia.

British Library Cataloguing in Publication Data
Liddle, Peter, *1934 –*
    The Soldier's War, 1914–1918
    1. World War 1. Army operations by Great Britain. Army –
    Biographies
    I. Title
    940.4′81′41
    ISBN 0–7137–1892–7

Typeset by Ronset Typesetters Ltd, Darwen, Lancashire.
Printed and bound by the Bath Press, Avon.

Jacket photograph by Albert E. Snell.

Contents

Rifleman Alan Liddle, 16th Battalion, King's Royal Rifles, taken prisoner 23 April 1917, brother to Private Richard Mordey Liddle, 1st Battalion, Coldstream Guards, killed 15 September 1916 and to Gunner Harry Liddle, Royal Field Artillery. (A. Liddle)

Foreword

There is undoubtedly a growing interest, especially among the young, in what it must have been like to have had to serve in the 1914-18 war. There are very few left to give an account of their experiences, but the distinguished historian Peter Liddle has spent years building up a vast collection, housed at the Sunderland Polytechnic, of memorabilia from which he has drawn to write a trilogy, *The Sailor's War 1914-18*, *The Airman's War 1914-18* and now *The Soldier's War 1914-18*. The collection is built up from personal diaries and letters from the various fronts, largely of junior officers and other ranks. The book tells not only what it felt like taking part in the great battles of the war, but also experiences in the many 'side shows' quite unknown to most people.

As one who fought as a young officer in a Highland regiment at Loos, The Somme, Arras, Passchendaele and the 1918 Advance to Victory, I am honoured to have been asked to read the draft and write this Foreword for *The Soldiers' War 1914-18*. What struck me first was the enormous amount of work Peter Liddle has put in to produce the material for this book. It must comprise the largest and most important collection of 1914-18 memorabilia in private hands. Then I looked to see if I could find anything that did not ring true. I could find no fault there. The author has obviously made a point of discarding anything that looked suspect. This strict adherence to the truth in my view greatly enhances the value of the book.

Amid all the strain and horrors of battle there were, of course, many instances of a lighter nature, and we had our opinions of the French and the raw Americans. But what did they think of us? When the Americans first arrived in France in 1918 I was detailed to go and 'ease in' the 119th Infantry Regiment. This regiment consisted of three battalions and ancillary troops and services. I had one day to lecture to the officers in a local Town Hall. The subject being the Division in the attack, I thought I had done rather well. The commanding Colonel, a huge man who must have been in his sixties and who sported a cavalry sabre and two pearl-handled revolvers heaved himself from his seat and said 'I want you all to thank the Scottish major for his verra interesting lecture. But I'd have youse guys remember the British have been trying these methods for four years and they ain't done much good!'

I strongly recommend this book. It preserves much intimate history that might have been lost for ever.

General Sir Philip Christison,

BT, GBE, KBE, CB, DSO, MC AND BAR.

Preface and Acknowledgements

Following upon *The Sailor's War 1914-18* (Blandford, 1985) and the *Airman's War 1916-18* (Blandford, 1987), this book draws upon the letters, diaries, photographs, sketches and recollections of the regimental officers, the NCOs and the men in the ranks to illustrate, together with relevant official documentation, the varied essence of life as a soldier on active service in the Great War. In the main the source material consulted has not been used in any previous publication and in almost all cases it comes from my 1914-18 Personal Experience Archives which are still currently housed within Sunderland Polytechnic and which continue to grow as more families generously present papers and souvenirs. The cross-reference cataloguing system which highlights special interest contained within the letters or diaries of every man among the thousands documented in these archives has enabled me to select extracts which reflect many aspects of specialist duty, of personal experience and reaction to that experience, and extracts too which reveal attitudes or opinions held by the soldier on active service. By this means and in an awareness of the danger of delusion arising from the making of unreasonable generalisations out of particular examples, an attempt has been made to convey what it was like to be in battle, to be holding the line or in reserve, to be in a rest or a base camp, or to be on active service on a front far distant from the home country.

The most senior view point offered, and this quite exceptionally, will be that of a lieutenant colonel in command of a battalion of approximately 850 men, but far more usually it will be the perspective of those 850 men, the captains or lieutenants in command of their companies of 250, the subalterns with their platoons of 60 and the non-commissioned officers, ranging from the authority of the regimental sergeant major to the most newly-promoted lance corporal, and then of the private soldiers themselves.

The structure of the book allows for a consideration of different aspects of soldiering service as an infantryman, gunner, sapper or trooper and with certain specialities such as tunnelling or signalling.

Matters which would have been common to all are considered, such as transportation, rations, health as well as a focus upon those who became casualties. The many-sided question of the maintenance of morale is explored and, within the overall structure of the book, a sense of progress in time has been preserved so that the reader can sense both the transformation in the nature of the British Army as year followed year and also the laying down of the semi-rigid framework of Western Front soldiering which clamped itself upon the earlier months of movement and was not released until, for a variety of reasons, movement returned to the entrenched mass armies in the ebb and flow of the final year of the war.

It would be a strange book on soldiers of the Great War which did not deal in some depth with battle experiences and such a commanding guide line will not be broken in this book. In contemporary and in retrospective evidence, what has to be done before and during battle, what this calls for in personal courage and self-control, the interdependence of a man on those around him and that of the officer and his men, what is seen, felt and experienced, will certainly be considered, but soldiering was about more than such experience, searing and indeed final as it may have been. In accordance with this, every effort will be made to provide the reader with a verifiable sense of being with the men in all aspects of their soldiering. Daily routine, food, latrines, recreation, entertainment, discipline, health, leave, humour, promotion and many other aspects of service have their place, together with the fateful eventuality of being wounded or taken prisoner. What emerges is the undeniable reality of a personal experience archive: the indestructable individuality of the individual; but, in looking at the way a man expressed his acceptance or otherwise of his particular lot, it has been the intention to paint with the brushstroke of the Impressionist a picture which is also truly representative. Selection of material allows of course for as much subjectivity as in the original expression of opinion, but in building up a cross-reference system to illustrate what a man recorded about his war, I do not believe I have allowed preconceptions to close some avenues of sentiment and direct concentration upon others.

The Western Front must dominate the book due to its primacy of significance to the British military effort, but consideration will also be given to the distinctive differences of soldiering in Macedonia or Mesopotamia or in campaigns and garrison duties in more remote locations. The changing of the seasons, the ebb, flow or stagnation of a campaign, and the differences imposed by varied topographical conditions on one Front will all feature, thus avoiding temptation to generalise. For example, I have tried not to write of the heat of the Jordanean plain without some reference to the icy sleet and chilling temperatures in the night-marching of the mountain passes for the raids on Amman. Similarly I have not dwelt upon the malarial misfortunes and desultory shelling or patrolling on long months of relative quiet on the Struma Front in Macedonia without reference to the desperately difficult conditions faced in the fiercely contested assaults made on the Bulgarian heights or indeed to the different tactical methods adopted in the fighting for the villages in the plain.

I shall not make here, as I did in *The Sailor's War*, a statement about the critical examination required in judging the academic utility of letters, diaries or recollections. I feel that it can be taken as understood that personal experience documentation, as in the case of all historical evidence, needs careful scrutiny and the source material here has been rigorously considered before use in this book. One factor which distinguishes this book from *The Airman's War* is that evidence from non-commissioned sources is much greater in volume and there should be no doubt that the voice of the man in the ranks is heard, however much it may be maintained that it is the subaltern whose relatively more frequent and more descriptive pen charted the circumstance of the time and whose work has then survived in domestic security the destructive broomsweeps of house moves and changed family circumstance.

This book is dedicated first to the memory of my own father, Alan Liddle, (King's Royal Rifles) captured on the Western Front in 1917 and to my respected but unknown uncle, Richard Mordey Liddle, a Coldstream Guardsman killed at Flers on 15 September 1916, and then it is offered in the hope that it may be a worthy tribute to the memory of all the men whose soldier service is documented in my archives. The author remembers too, brothers, sisters, sons, daughters and grandchildren who, in the twenty-four years of my work, have so gener-

ously contributed long-treasured documentation and souvenirs that they may be preserved under my care. Especially do I thank those men from whose papers and related material extracts have been selected for this book; their names are listed separately as well as shown in the text, the end notes or the caption to accompany each illustration. I hope that this book may be the catalyst to draw in further 1914-18 material and if this were to be the case then all the more must I bear in mind those who made the book possible. For more than a generation, soldiers of the Great War have been helping me in my work and as I consider the form of expression of my thanks, many well-remembered faces come to mind, many distinctively handwritten envelopes, many voices on tape or telephone. Am I to select five or ten or twenty for special mention here when so many more could have been mentioned? What about the many known only through the fascination of original papers sent to me by supportive families? No, I take proper and not cowardly or slovenly refuge in offering a quiet assurance that no man and no family from whom help has been received could ever feel that such help was not valued whether the gift were one of papers or of time, thought and labour.

Acknowledgement is due, I must add, to the Controller of the Public Record Office for permission to quote from papers held at Kew and to the authors and publishers of a number of books which have increased my understanding and from which, on occasion, I have quoted.

In turning to those who have helped actually to produce this book and at the same time to assist me in the running of the archives, I record first Charlie Ward, a good friend whose death in 1986 saddened all who came to know him by his positive presence in the archives over fifteen years. Into the breach Maureen Hine has stepped with quiet grace. With family papers already here, Mrs Hine has been 'at home' from the start and generously she has undertaken a regular commitment which has ensured that the backlog of important 'office practice' work is kept under control. The advice of Squadron Leader Nobby Clark was always at hand and the meticulous photographic research of Kevin Kelly was quite simply invaluable while Bill Lawson in Ponteland, Barrie Herbert in the Isle of Wight, Mrs Rosemary Healing in Woking, Colin and Morag Bailey in Middlesbrough, the Reverend Major John Croft in Somerset, Hall Beken in East Anglia, Gervase Phillips in Knutsford, Stuart Stott in Hythe, Liz Ward in Welton, Eric Gourley near Paisley, Gaynor Greenwood in Lancaster, and Harry Siepmann in London have skilfully processed letters, diaries and recollections before they were taken into the archives, or have tape-recorded men and women for me. I have been particularly fortunate in that research work for the selection of suitable material for certain areas of this book was facilitated by Sunderland Polytechnic students engaged on their own 1914–18 dissertations. My thanks and re-affirmed good wishes are offered to Simon Jones, Andrew Read, Andrew Dorman, Robert Leedham and Lisa Butler. My unimaginably untidy manuscript has again been typed by Kathleen Barnes and Birgitta Scott, the final typing completed by Carol Gardner, and I have benefited enormously from the sound advice from first-hand 1914–18 soldiering experience of Sir Thomas Harley and Major General Ashton Wade in checking the text as it developed. The photographs were painstakingly copied by Albert Snell, Gwennyth Gibson and David Beaumont.

During the months in which the book has been on the stocks I have been able emotionally and physically to cope with this work, that of the archives, of my lectureship duties and most critically the anxiety over achieving the preservation of my archival collections in perpetuity by reason of the loving support of my wife, Louise. Her sunshine has always finally broken through the lowering clouds of frustration as progress towards resolution of the future of the archives has continued to be so wearisomely slow.

Peter H. Liddle, F.R.Hist.S.,
DIPITY COTTAGE,
LIME STREET,
WALDRIDGE FELL,
CHESTER-LE-STREET,
COUNTY DURHAM.

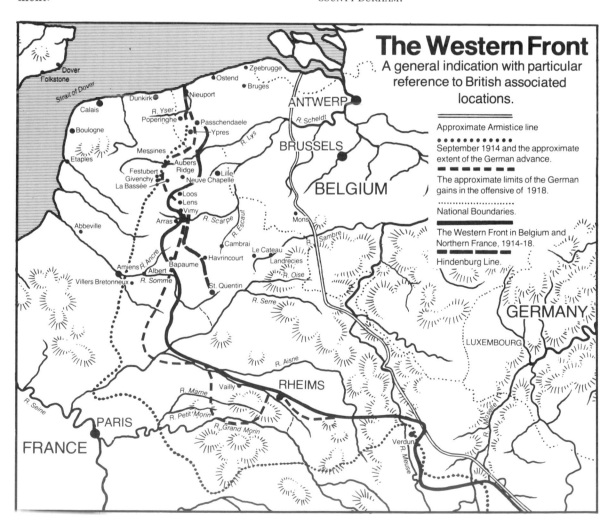

Introduction: From the Army of a Nation to a Nation in Arms

The first two chapters in this book will emphasize the degree of professional excellence with which soldiers of the British Expeditionary Force met the challenge of European warfare in 1914-15, their numerical inadequacy and the fact that the nature of the new warfare on the Continent and the small numbers of men in the BEF tragically diminished the significance of having troops of such high quality. Such were the demands of the new warfare that from its manhood, the nation had to develop armed forces on a transformedly huge scale. Behind the pre-1914 regular soldiers and their reservists called back to the colours from civilian life, stood the part-timers, the Territorials from diverse backgrounds who for various reasons left the butcher's shop, the business world or the classroom for a once-weekly night of army drill and a fortnight's summer camp. When some military knowledge had been grasped by these men, their wide range of background ensured that a rich potential of intelligence and leadership was at the disposal of their country. It was invaluable from late 1914 but of course not enough. The inexorable nature of the war raised insatiable manpower demands. Neither the remarkable surge of voluntary enlistment in 1914, nor the tangible official pressure of the Derby Scheme in 1915, which asked for registration of readiness to serve when called, could answer the national emergency. Allies and enemy had not needed the onset of war to require their young manhood to serve and from early in 1916 a British Coalition Government expressed an overwhelming Parliamentary and public opinion consensus in following suit. Conscription became law. The pictures in these crudely delineated stages in a country girding its loins for war are completed by the voluntary service of women. The Women's Army Auxilliary Corps gathered together several strands of female readiness to serve and with their presence in France in 1917 it can then truly be said that the nation was in arms.[1]

It may be dubious to put forward an individual pre-1914 regular soldier as representative of his fellows or similarly for a Territorial mobilized in August 1914, a New Army recruit of September 1914, a conscript of 1916 and a newly enlisted 1918 member of the WAAC, because so many factors might distinguish that person from those whom he or she might otherwise properly represent. Motivation, individual aptitudes or relevant skills, social background, and military rank, are merely some of the variables but an attempt should be made to show that Britain put into the field four different armies during the First World War: the regular, the territorial, the volunteer for the duration and the conscript, and then there was the WAAC too. This organic growth by stages simply had to be reflected by changes in the character of the Army. If we were to look briefly at someone in the ranks within each layer of growth we might be able to glimpse features which would distinguish him and his platoon from that of a subsequent platoon of later origin.

Born in 1889 and brought up in the West Country first by foster-parents and then by his real parents, Edward Humphries had enlisted in 1906. His widowed mother moved to London in 1903. He had drifted away from her and, more summarily, from a number of jobs in hotels and clubs until, inspired by the tales of an old soldier working with him in the Constitutional Club, he had falsified his age by two years and embarked upon soldiering. His swollen tonsils precluded acceptance by the army, but did not disqualify him from the Militia, soon to be renamed the Special Reserve under the Haldane Army Reforms. In the regulation three months of footdrill and parades, route marches and field days with the 5th Battalion, The Rifle Brigade, heel-balling and polishing his boots and black leather equipment till they shone like patent leather, Humphries was educated into Army life. His health had improved and he immediately attested his readiness for the Regular Army and was enlisted into the Royal Scots – '7 years with the Colours and 5 in the Reserve, or if the man completes his seven years' service with the Colours while beyond the seas, then for a further period, not exceeding one year, with the Colours and the remainder of the 12 years in the Reserve.'

Of the ten men who had accepted their shilling

1907. Lance Corporal F. S. Hudson (Ox and Bucks Light Infantry) on his barrack room bed with his 'bed space' in inspection order, blankets folded, equipment hung in place, two Army chests one acquired from a soldier who had served in India. Above him is displayed a range of personal souvenirs. Hudson reads the *Alton Gazette* – his future lies in transfer to the Royal Garrison Artillery, service in India, the Seige of Kut and years of Turkish captivity. (F. S. Hudson)

and food and accommodation while the necessary adminstration procedures were undertaken before entrainment for Edinburgh, only one turned up with Humphries at Euston Station. Apparently the Recruiting Sergeant supervising the departure was 'disappointed but not surprised'.

From arrival at Glencorse Barracks, Penecuik near Edinburgh, the recruits were left in no doubt of the ancient, proud lineage of the Royal Scots, the oldest regiment of infantry in the British Army – 'Pontius Pilate's Bodyguard' in military parlance. Its battle honours emblazoned on the Regimental Colour were a record of national history. 'Our daily training consisted of a long succession of parades devoted to footdrill, squad and Company formation drill, arms drill, musketry (both slow and rapid fire) gymnastics and education which invariably included a lecture on the fine history of our regiment.' All

recruits had to attend 'School parades' until they had obtained their 3rd Class Certificate of Education, a level accepted by Humphries as 'very elementary' and one improved upon by a goodlier measure of the 'bun Wallahs' – those investing in food and tea, than by the 'Canteen Wallahs' who sank their money in the wet canteen.

Humphries was posted to the 1st battalion Royal Scots stationed at Shornecliffe in Kent and undertook training as a regimental signaller reaching, via blistered hands, the necessary proficiency in Morse code by flags, large and small, heliograph, Begbie Lamp, and Semaphore.

All infantry regiments commenced their yearly programme in the spring with company training, then brigade and divisional exercises followed in succession. When the Royal Scots embarked on a long march to Winchester for Army manoeuvres in the autumn, Humphries enthusiasm for army life was at a low ebb, but money he had saved to escape the monotony by desertion was lost at Crown and Anchor. Some keenness returned as he secured a marksman's proficiency pay and performed well in the 1907 Battalion Cup for Shooting Aim Endurance.

In the barracks, all sorts of competitive games were improvised: 'balancing a barrack table on our chins, weight-lifting iron trestles, flying long jumps over three beds, wrestling or boxing and many varieties of feats of strength with our rifles'. In all periods of free time, practising kicking a football past self-confident goalkeepers occupied many soldiers and then, after exhaustion of high-spirited energy, the ever-present cards and gambling came into their own.

In December 1908 the battalion embarked for its tour of duty in India – to Ranikhet a march of four days and a three-day train journey from Bombay. At Ranikhet, a wooded hilly region, each day except Thursday (a free day) various parades occupied about six hours. Hill climbing was an officially encouraged relaxation taken up by many, and obviously improved physical fitness. India gave space for training on a scale and with variety not known in the United Kingdom. 'Signal schemes were devised involving less than fifty men scattered over an area of a hundred square miles and we were kept at it until we became hardened and self-reliant soldiers.' Humphries might well have added that his regiment had immeasurably increased its proficient professionalism and was ready for its 1909 'Kitchener Test' of a forced march of at least fifteen miles, an attack at night, the defence of an outpost and a battle of manoeuvre over a large area matched

against the regiment whose men proudly proclaimed themselves 'The Kings of the Hills', the King's Royal Rifles. With flying colours and a victory in battle, the Royal Scots passed their test.

The regiment's Winter Station was at Bareilly on the Northern plains of India, a huge tented encampment utilizing the European Pattern Marquees which comfortably offered space for movement between the eight beds, eight barrack-room boxes for personal kit and the rifle rack. At Bareilly, the routine of battalion training, ceremonial parades and brigade manoeuvres, was enlivened by the annual sports and from this station in 1911, Humphries left for Fategarh and a voluntary transfer to an Indian Divisional Signal Company with the prospect of 'a new life, increased responsibility and maybe a better chance of promotion'. It was the first occasion in which 'other ranks' of the British and Indian Army were linked together to work in the same unit and within the forty-four British 'other ranks' almost twenty different regiments were represented. There were eighty-eight Indian 'other ranks' and so one can presume that the number of Indian Army regiments was correspondingly larger.

Humphries' account of the manner by which his new unit, No. 32 Divisional Signal Company of the Indian Army, was worked up to efficiency is as

Regular Army manoeuvres between Royston and Cambridge 1913. A Maxim gun section makes sure of cover while still allowing a field of fire for the two guns. The Maxim machine-gun was to be superseded by the Vickers during the war. (Lieutenant Colonel R. W. Oldfield)

impressive as it is fascinating and through the story of this soldier can be seen something of the ordinary extra-ordinariness of the pre-war regular soldier.[2] Routine, drill, repetition, discipline, physical fitness, competition, unit pride are the elements reflected in all original or recollected accounts by such men. In the early 1980s, Harry Easton, a former Trooper of the 9th Lancers, recalled without hesitation the words of command of sword and lance drill in the first decade of the twentieth century, and over an almost comparable length of time, Stanley Waldron remembered the words learned to teach him his RFA trumpet calls.[3 & 4] It may be charged that this was ill-fitting preparation for a war of modern technology, but a breathing space had to be fought for in 1914-15 and thankfully the Regulars of the BEF earned it by their adaptable proficiency in their trade.

Naturally no such standard of soldiering could be met by the men of the Territorial Force, but a former rifleman of the 5th City of London Regiment, Territorial Force, H. G. R. Williams, has made it quite clear that they had much to offer. He had been a member of Aldenham School's Officer Training Corps and when Williams was leaving school in 1910, the master in charge of the Corps had seen each leaver and stressed his duty to join the Territorials: 'so that the elements of military training we had acquired should not be wasted'. Williams wrote that in any case all his fellows were aware of the German challenge. 'We all saw war coming and I felt it was up to us to do something about it.' This meant that it was quite simply: 'the thing to do' to join the Territorials.

For Williams, and for others from all walks of life who felt the call of Territorial service, it meant that after work, once a week on a weekday evening, they reported to their Battalion or Squadron drill hall for drill and a lecture. From time to time in the summer months there were weekend training schemes and then, the high spot of the year, the two-week Summer Camp. Attendance of this was compulsory for at least one week unless an exceptional reason were put forward. At Easter, too, there was special musketry training which for the London Rifle Brigade took place either at Bisley or Hythe.

The Territorial Force came into existence in 1908 as a modernized amalgamation of the previous Volunteer Forces. It was organized along Regular Army lines but regionally and, where possible, grafted on to the existing local regiments. Artillery,

Engineers, Cavalry, Infantry and Medical Service units were to be in fourteen infantry divisions and fourteen cavalry (yeomanry) brigades in such a way that they could undertake training, fully to prepare them for Home Defence and, after six months intensive training, could mobilize for service overseas. There were some differences, most notably in the Territorials retaining the older Long Lee Enfield rifles while the regulars had the Short Lee Enfield, but in principle so complementary was the organization that, to some, it still seems a major missed opportunity that Kitchener, as Secretary of State for War, did not use the Territorial Force as the base from which to initiate the huge expansion of the British armed forces which, to his credit, he saw to be immediately essential when war broke out.[5]

Pre-1914 Territorial Force battalion commanding officers were usually ex-regulars and there were Regular Army Sergeant Instructors, and of course the Regimental Sergeant Major himself was from the same stock. Enlistment was for four years and Williams clearly saw his obligations as: first, to support the Regular Army and the Royal Navy in

Pre-war Territorials. Seemingly no traverses, but a useful initiation into what would become accustomed work on the Gallipoli Peninsular for these sappers of the 42nd East Lancashire Division wearing their training overalls. (H. Lyson)

repelling the anticipated invasion, and then to act in the Garrison of the Country on the departure of the Expeditionary Force to France. In 1910 he attested that he would become: 'liable to be embodied' – in a case of: 'imminent national danger or great emergency' and that he would be liable to serve: 'in any place in the United Kingdom without further agreement but not in any place outside the United Kingdom unless you voluntarily undertake to do so'.

The account left by H. G. R. Williams of his pre-1914 training reflects a rather different pride in the distinctive Rifle Brigade from that shown by Humphries in the Royal Scots. Of course a Rifleman could trace the origins of his regiment back more than a hundred years but there is something of the Territorial's fresh enthusiasm of personal conviction lighting up Williams's account rather than the requirement of upholding the pre-eminence of Pontius Pilate's Bodyguard due to an imposition of regimental pride imprinted upon the raw recruit fundamentally as a part of his training sanctified by the centuries. In August 1914, Williams could not be and was not a professionally ready soldier but to add to the experience of his drills, markmanship, assaults at arms and camps at Lulworth for example, there had been regimental dinners and concerts which had assisted in the development of unit esprit de corps, something which grew not merely from the regiment with its traditions, but from the fusion of the personal commitment of so many men sufficiently keen to devote so much of their time to military training.

It is not insignificant to note that at the 1913 camp at Perham Down on Salisbury Plain, the 5th City of London Regiment had their first instruction in the use of the entrenching tool. In day time, supposedly under fire, prone figures scooped holes and threw up personal parapets; at night, with pick and shovel, proper trenches with parapets were dug. The men spent a day and a night in this trench. They cooked their own food there, this trenchwork being but a tiny illustration of the need for some caution in repeating the old adage of Britain always having prepared for the 'last war'.

In the summer of 1914, the battalion had been encamped at Eastbourne for little more than two hours when it was ordered precipitately to pack up and return to London, the men being sent to their homes to await mobilization. Some learned by pasted-up notices as early as the evening of 3 August that they had to report to their HQ forthwith, others learned by first post on the morrow. Their civilian status was ended. In gold sovereigns Williams received £5 'bounty on embodiment' and in due

'While England sleeps', 1914. The Officer in Command of the First Northumbrian Brigade, R.F.A. Territorial Force has, one presumes, fulfilled his responsibilities, read his paper, smoked his cigar and now can rest at peace with the world. (Major H. Pybus)

course sufficient was the individual response of readiness to serve overseas that the future integrity of the unit for active service was assured. This was important in the preservation of the essential character of a Territorial unit. It thus could continue to be a truer reflection of the 'Nation in Arms' than the Regular Army – local bankclerks and men in business and commerce in the Newcastle Commercials, brewers, shipyard and forge workers and pitmen in the 7th Durhams, farmers and farm workers in the 5th Suffolks. Officers and men were so regionally and occupationally bound together that even before active service these new important elements in morale were integral factors in a unit's estimate of its own worth.

When one considers for a moment the numerical inadequacy of the BEF before it suffered its first casualty and then the patent unreadiness of the New Army, any debate on the quality of the Territorial soldier must begin with an acceptance that the Territorial was the only currency available when military manpower expenditure was essential. H. G. R. Williams was one of approximately 268,000 officers and men in August 1914 who were to give a distinctive colouring to the British Army as citizen soldiers. Army ways and civilian perceptions had already come into sufficient contact to make more smooth the transition into full-time soldiering.[6] In motivation, in speed and completeness of the total change of his way of life, the circumstances for the New Army recruit would be altogether more highly coloured, intense and not without some danger of disillusionment.

On 7 August 1914, Kitchener made his first appeal – it was for volunteers between the ages of 19 and 30 and for: 'General Service for a period of three years, or until the war is concluded'. Later appeals extended the age limit at its upper end, called for married men to enlist and relaxed the stringent minimum height requirement. Although a medical examination of remarkably varying thoroughness concerning sight, teeth, heart, lungs and feet provided a sieve through which some failed to pass, the response was still phenomenal – nearly 300,000 in August and almost 463,000 in September. Administratively the Army could not have been

On the very day of the outbreak of war, this straightforward appeal to 'old boys' of St. Dunstan's College was sent out inviting them to match National duty with the honour of the school by enlisting in the local Territorial regiment with other former scholars. (Captain A. B. Rowlerson)

S? DUNSTAN'S COLLEGE.
CATFORD. S.E.

Dear Sir   Aug. 4th. 1914

In this hour of National crisis may I call on your services and ask that you will at once enlist in the Old Boy's Company?

It will be a splendid record if this School can send a full company of old boys who are ready to take their place in England's Home Defence Army.

This appeal is made to you in every confidence that you are not only ready to do all you can to assist your Country in its hour of need, but that you will also appreciate the very special claims that your old school has upon you.

The 20th. Battn. London Regiment Headquarters are at Holly Hedge House, Blackheath, where either I myself, or an officer in charge will be ready at all times to enrol your name or give full information.

                    yours faithfully,

                    F. C. Bentley,

                    O. C., "G Company",

                    20th. Battn. The London Regt.

expected to cope, it did not, and yet it had to. As every class, every occupation, every region, responded, there remained but one element missing in the call to arms – statutory compulsion.

When considering motivation for enlistment into the Army from August to December 1914, account must be taken of the opportunity of adventure, employment, perceived improvement in living conditions, the encouragement of friends and the pressure of society, but there remains an overwhelming consensus in all forms of personal documentation, of patriotism, of King and Country, including of course the Homeland – the Mother Country for so many in Dominions and Colonies. 'I thought the Country worth living in, was worth fighting for,' is a sentiment expressed in one form or another in countless memoirs but in most of them there is evidence too of different strands of emotion being naturally woven into the thread of a decision scarcely needing consideration, indeed, however paradoxically, an 'involuntary' volunteering. 'My reason was a simple one, at my age and in my circumstances and in the atmosphere of patriotic enthusiasm, I would have been ashamed not to join and my parents would have been ashamed of me if I had not done so. Secondary reasons were that several of my friends were joining the same regiment, also I had decided I did not want to be a Civil Engineer. It seemed likely to be a dull sort of profession.'[7] C. N. Barclay came from no traditionally military family and if his judgement of the reaction of his parents were to have been correct there would be many households with, at least initially, a different response. W. G. Bentley describes his parents as being 'stunned . . . but seeing how determined I was to serve as a soldier they began to accept it and I sensed were even proud of me'.[8]

Volunteers would not of course understand what active military service would entail, and many parents in 1914 could comfort themselves with the widespread belief that it would 'soon be over' and thus their son at least would be spared exposure to danger.

D. J. Price has written of his motivation. 'I was intensely patriotic. My work was not unpleasant but I knew I wouldn't miss it. My thought of joining was instantaneous. I was terribly keen to go, afraid to miss any of it. I'd had a very happy youth but no doubt looked for adventure.' He admitted that: 'I never thought of the responsibility I had to my mother.' In fact Price was a big lad of sixteen but he claimed nineteen and was accepted. 'My mother was deeply dismayed,' but both she and the firm where he was serving his apprenticeship in the wholesale textile trade came to accept his decision and took no steps to expose its illegality.[9]

For some it was a moral issue and not one of conventional patriotism. A. L. Robins believed that he was one of many for whom the conflict was between might and right. 'Certain things had happened and were continuing to happen that were wrong, and could not be allowed to continue. Gallant little Belgium might well be overdone and become somewhat of a joke, but behind it all was the feeling that something that was very wrong ought to be stopped.[10]

The account left by a man from Warrington on holiday in Scarborough, F. O. Stansfield, is illuminatingly different from that of Price or Robins; it is that of a man who finds the sandy ground of normality slipping from under his feet, of his attempt to grasp at something stable and not changing before his eyes and of his failure. He and a friend had at first cancelled their hotel booking, proceeding to the station amid the turmoil of Territorials and reservists hurrying off, of anxiety and excitement everywhere, grey naval vessels having been glimpsed steaming north, even, it was said, some gunfire out to sea. Thinking better of their own precipitate departure, they returned to their hotel to complete their holiday. On their return to Warrington they saw the Warrington Territorials cooped up in their Drill Hall and its precincts, dramatic war news was being received and Stansfield's office work was half-heartedly resumed. The flood tide was too strong: 'A friend got his orders to leave for his unit and, seeing him off from Bank Quay Station: unsettled me more than ever'. On 3 September Stansfield and his friend Arthur Lee responded to Lord Derby's announced intention of forming a 'Pal's Brigade' of the Kings Liverpool Regiment and thus in Liverpool, as in so many industrial centres of Britain, the powerful magnet of a local identity acted upon the direction of intent of the nation's young manhood in responding to the call of King and Country, doing so in close company with friends and workmates.[11] The regional and occupational character of the New Army was not invariable, but in the regiments associated with Barnsley and Leeds, Oldham and Manchester or the mining villages of County Durham, the Scottish, Irish or Welsh character of some great cities, the kinship of local railway company employment, the rural unity of some of the battalions of the County Regiments, the commercial companionship of those on the Stock Exchange or insurance or banking, the University fellowship of others, Boy's Brigade friendships and sporting associations, a specially attractive identity was forged. Eighty-three such battalions were formed before the end of the year. Clive Hughes, in Beckett and Simpson's valuable book *A Nation in Arms*, maintains that: 'By area, the north was most successful, Lancashire and Cheshire producing twenty-four local battalions, Yorkshire fifteen, the north-east fifteen and Cumbria one. The London area raised twenty-three battalions though

August 1914 in Britain. It might be in any town in Britain, but in fact it is Bristol. A column of volunteers marches behind the Mayor's carriage. (Madge Angus)

Canadians in and around Winnipeg respond to the Mother Country's call. The recruiting staff of a battalion enlisting men for overseas service, pose outside their office and under a banner which clearly calls for nothing less than action from all men of a suitable – or 'nearly suitable' – age. Eventually 640,000 Canadians donned uniform, 400,000 serving overseas and 57,000 paying the supreme sacrifice. (Dr. Dorothy N. Findlay)

many were University and Public School or similar formations appealing nationwide.'[12]

Stansfield enlisted at St George's Hall, Liverpool. The surrender of civilian status was abrupt. 'We were ordered to strip, bundle our clothes together on the floor and pass through an inner door. We found ourselves in a great long corridor with scores and scores of naked men sitting on either side.' It was draughty, the wait was lengthy and he slowly shuffled his way along until called into a large room where four or five doctors with weighing machines and other paraphernalia put him through the usual tests. 'Cough, "say 99" etc., and we were given a chit and sent on our way back to our clothes by another route. Having dressed, we were led before an officer who swore us in, gave each of us the King's shilling and told us to go home and await calling-up orders.'

The Orders came within a week to assemble at the Liverpool Transport Depot in Tramway Road, Aigburth. A thousand men in their civilian clothes were divided up into platoons of sixty or more by twelve NCOs, some in khaki but some in the uniform of Commissionaires. This being achieved, the platoons were dismissed and ordered to parade in Sefton Park at 9 a.m. on the following Monday. On that day the platoons were divided into sections and drill was begun. The journey back to Warrington was tedious after the end of drill in the late afternoon, and after a week of tired travelling Stansfield

and his friend applied for and got billets in separate houses in streets off Smithdown Road. After six weeks, Sefton Park was left for Lord Derby's estate, Knowsley Park, where the huts awaiting them lacked complete roofs or glass for the windows or stoves but appropriately introduced them to mud following heavy rain. Mattresses were not immediately available, the bare boards of the flooring were. In a cold wet and windy November the open washhouses did not encourage cleanliness, but they did presumably provide the problems of the latrine: 'a pole stretched horizontally over tubs'. A sense of balance was mandatory in avoiding disaster, but Stansfield did not know that those billeted upon infant school premises were finding balance on infant toilets no less a problem.

Unappetizing food was made still less acceptable when it was discovered that food in the canteen, which could be supplementarily bought, was from the same Liverpool caterer. Still the men were hungry, the strenuous training from 6 a.m. reveille to 6 p.m. encouraging them to get used to their fare.

The first official issue of clothing was of army boots with every man being paid ten shillings as compensation for having, so far, worn his own. Some weeks later, when uniforms were issued (dungarees having been worn for digging exercises on the Knowsley estate) thirty shillings was given as compensation for the use of one's own civilian clothes. The recruits' terracing of some sloping land was professionally surveyed and the proper amount paid by Lord Derby into the Regimental Funds. 'He was a great sport. We bore his badge, the Eagle and the Child (The Constipated Duck as we called it) and later at a ceremonial parade at the hall, he presented each of us individually with a silver badge.'

Stansfield recorded typhoid injections, but not the issue of rifles and then, an inspection by Kitchener in February 1915. In April, the Liverpool Pals left for Belton Park near Grantham where the whole 30th New Army Division was assembled. Here training was much more advanced and horses and mules newly arrived from South America were broken in. The men were now palpably feeling that: 'we were no longer amateur soldiers but members of a Division being trained for active service'. A different sort of frustration was being felt, not one associated with army administrative inadequacy but with not being 'out at the front'. An issue of a Brigade magazine contained a drawing of a woman and child standing at the entrance of the camp and old men with beards staggering around the camp carrying dixies. It bore the caption of the boy asking his mother, 'Which hut is Grandpa in?' The magazine was thereupon surpressed, the Liverpool Pals being destined more immediately for Salisbury Plain rather than for France. However, from Larkhill Camp in October 1915, every effort was made to prepare the men for the future. 'Thursday was to be a Divisional Day. It poured with rain and was very cold. The scheme was that the Liverpools had to drive the Manchesters out of their lines of trenches. General Paget looked on and the affair was very realistic. At a fixed time 10,000 appeared from nowhere as 5,000 Liverpools rushed out of their trenches across no man's land through entanglements, etc. and into the enemy's trenches where 5,000 Manchesters were waiting for them. There was a terrific row caused by rifles and machine-guns firing "blank" and small sandbags played the role of bombs and were very effective too! There were a good many "casualties" (including our Captain) due to the trenches being wide and the ground slippery and a 6-foot drop in between. The pouring rain added to the realism of the whole thing. It was very exciting and we quite forgot our many discomforts until it was all over and we returned to camp exhausted and like drowned rats.' The men were less than a month from France and would soon be in a position to compare their 'Divisional Day' with the real thing.[13]

November 1914: Knowsley Park near Liverpool. Lord Derby presents to the uniformed Liverpool Pals a silver badge of his family crest 'The Eagle and Child'. (F. Hindle).

Yeovil, August 1914. These Territorials, troopers of the West Somerset Yeomanry, intend to to start the war on a full stomach. Corporal Wood (in front) then kneeling L to R, Troopers White, King, Denziloe, Bevis and Corporal Dunn with Trooper Watts at the back already in action with his beer, are about to enjoy roast hare, being carved by Denziloe. Bread, jam and cake are to follow. (Sir Geoffrey King)

The Liverpool Pals route-marching to fitness. (E. W. Willmer)

Attention is well drawn in *A Nation in Arms*[14] to the failure of the Army properly to provide for the recruiting avalanche. Some good examples are given of quite serious disturbances, in one case initiated by the womenfolk of the men concerned. There is abundant evidence of a degree of disenchantment in the letters of men from the village of Dyrham in Gloucestershire writing to their Rector, the Reverend Wynter Blathwayt. An Albert Ball wrote that: 'I likes Taunton very much but there is so many down here we don't get nothing to eat hardly,' but this and the fact that his mother was upset at his going had to be accepted because he wanted to: 'serve my country the same as every young chap ought to do.'[15] George Crew, also at Taunton, was less ready to accept things: 'I am very sorry to have to tell you it is very rough here. In fact it is disgraceful. There are over a thousand in the barracks and there is only room for 250 so we have lodgings for which we have to pay ourselves – of course we can't do that for long as we have not got an income and up to now there is no likelihood of our getting any so we shall have to rough it with the rest if things don't alter soon. It must be experienced to be believed, it is past explaining.' Crew did go on to explain the mealtime rush which left those not in the forefront going without. 'There is plenty of food here if it was dealt out properly but some get two or three shares and the rest have none. . . . There are hundreds of young

fellows including ourselves that if they had only known what they had to put up with would never have came.' Perhaps Crew then remembered that the Rector's concern for the men might be moved to disapproval that such sentiments should be expressed because he added: 'If others can stand it, I suppose we can do the same for our country's sake – we are determined that we shall do our duty in spite of all obstacles and prove ourselves worthy of being called soldiers of the King,' but he still added that the kindly people of Taunton were disgusted with the reputation of their barracks and called it appropriately: 'Kitchener's prison.'[16]

Crew was correct in drawing attention to bad administration. The situation at Taunton was certainly not unique. The circumstances which gave rise to difficulty were national and they were unprecedented. Crew was also expressing with undeniable reason, an individual's prerogative to grumble; life in the Army would provide no reason to close down that human privilege. The character of the New Army was in essence that of the youth of the Nation. In romantic perception patriotism and griping may not seem to go together but we are dealing with the nature of man.

By no means incidentally, disease and bad weather would intrude malevolently into the conditions under which the New Army proceeded with its late autumn and winter training – those troops in tented accommodation on Salisbury Plain and in particular the Canadian Expeditionary Force were to suffer cruelly.

One further point might be made about the New Army. A West Country recruit stationed in Northumberland might well be truly representative in writing of the local people being very difficult to understand – 'They have a peculiar way of talking,' but the Nation was getting to know itself in a way hitherto inexperienced. Across geographical distance and class distinction, the bridges of direct communication were being built, a gift of the tragic circumstance of war.

With compulsion adding its ingredient to the developing Nation in Arms, we must be cautious about discriminating against the conscript as if he were by definition to be the man who had hitherto held back from enlistment, not feeling either the high motivation of the enthusiastic patriot early in the war or the later more stoic readiness to 'do one's bit' as harsh realities enlightened public ignorance of the nature of modern war. However many men above the age of voluntary enlistment did come within that category, from 1916 men newly arriving at the age of compulsory enlistment were not given the opportunity to display loyalty to King and Country, the state required their service. Some, in

varying degree, would of course be reluctant soldiers and a very small number of men, the conscientious objectors whose appeals for exemption had been refused, would have a distinctively special character to their reluctance. They were never to consider themselves soldiers no matter what the regimental nomenclature, as for example the Non-Combatant Corps, they unwillingly bore.[17]

In January 1916, the First Military Service Act conscripted all single men and childless widowers between 18 and 41. Successive acts closed some of the loopholes which had allowed exemption on various grounds and an act in April 1918 included the age group below 50 and provided for an extension to 56.

Under the circumstances of compulsion, the conscript may seem precluded from the possession of high motivation and thus his large-scale entry into the Army would patently diminish its quality while raising its numbers. A good deal has been written on this to explain the spring 1918 defeats, the withdrawals and on occasion demoralization. This author feels that if one were to dwell at length upon the inadequacies in physique, morale and training of those troops forced into retreat from 21 March 1918, it is going to be a more difficult problem explaining their achievements from August to the Armistice except in terms of their battle experience. As it takes two to tango, so it is in war and while it is quite proper searchingly to examine one side in a conflict, that surely is not self-sufficient and investigation

Nothing less than the utmost ferocity and correct technique will satisfy the eagle-eyed Sergeant Cobley supervising this bayonet charge by men of the 12th Battalion, Northumberland Fusiliers. The chalk of the Chiltern Hills shows clearly in the upcast from the trench. (Sir Roderic Hill)

From what commercial use has the 25th Cyclist Battalion of the London Regiment requisitioned this vehicle? On the reverse of this picture postcard the sender, Private Sims, has written, somewhat alarmingly, 'On Saturday we are going off on a 50 mile race'. The cyclists had been on a week of manoeuvres ('a lot of work and no rest') and he was looking forward to being able to get home after the race. (G. W. Sims; (de Grolian papers))

Ceremonial review before proceeding overseas in 1915. Lord Kitchener, mounted on a white horse, honours the 61st Division Territorials at Chelmsford who have now built up their proficiency to readiness for active service. (L. B. Stanley)

Men of the 2/21st London Regiment in the marquee canteen at Hockerill Camp early in the War. Draught and bottled beer make this quite evidently a 'wet' canteen. (H. H. Frost)

6 October 1914: no uniforms yet for a New Army Field Ambulance but macabre evidence of their training! The 2/1st West Lancashire Field Ambulance, RAMC pose in front of their stretchers – the skull of the skull and crossbones smokes a pipe and, at the back, a femur or a prodigious tibia is raised on high. (A. Pickthall)

"FULL MARCHING ORDER"
WHAT YOUR KIT FEELS LIKE
AFTER TEN MILES !

The postcard artist celebrated for his naughty seaside scenes symbolically depicts the War Department burden of equipment carried by the soldier on the march. (Brigadier G. T. Wards)

Absent without leave. The 3rd Battalion, Sherwood Foresters were encamped on the seafront at Sunderland. Private Allen, hankering after the attractions of his Midlands home, had taken unofficial leave to enjoy them. The Military Police, to forestall such intentions by anyone, patrolled the main railway stations and Allen was apprehended at Nottingham and charged as above. (P.H.L. Archives)

Headquarters Gymnasium Aldershot

The necessary expansion of organised fitness training for recruits into the army, offered opportunity for men to volunteer for acceptance as Physical Training Instructors. Here at the Regular Army Headquarters Gymnasium, Aldershot, 'Would-be' PTIs perform under the eagle eye of the white-sweatered Staff Instructors. This postcard was sent by Lance Corporal T. E. Stirk of the King's Own Yorkshire Light Infantry, a member of the '11th Class, 35th Course' in July 1917. (T. E. Stirk)

must take place on 'the other side of the hill' to account for defeat as well as for victory.

It is difficult scientifically to delineate what effect compulsion had on the character of new units enlisted and the old units brought up to strength by new drafts. Occasional disparaging remarks by officers on such new drafts might well be drawn from pride in, and an understanding of, a diminished platoon or company so that the new element, as it found its feet, was almost certainly doing so at a disadvantage in the eyes of its commanding officer. It is clear that as the regular soldier showed an understandable reluctance to consider the Territorial to be of equivalent worth and the Territorial judged the Kitchener man similarly, so would the conscript be judged.

When the conscript felt as strongly conscious of his status as did Harry Innes, a private in the 14th Battalion Royal Fusiliers, his letters would reflect a sense of being out of place. 'Although the men in my hut are on the whole so common, yet beyond a mechanical habit of swearing which sends me into fits of laughter, there is no indecency or obscenity. They are always willing to help and are grateful for a cigarette. There is no thieving and as no new drafts will be coming in for a fortnight at least, I feel secure for the present. Nevertheless I shall get a padlock for my kit. Do not forget this is all for the good of the country – we shall be much happier if I am spared, not but that I should have preferred far and away to have been able to stay at home.'

In another letter, also written in February 1916, he felt it: 'hardest of all that none of my best friends have had to go . . . I hope you have cheered up. I am sure you would not like to feel that our family is doing less than others in the cause of freedom.' Innes, for all his unmilitary instincts, was to show amusement at his more advanced stage of training readiness than that of some newly arrived subalterns whose competence in drill instruction was tested upon Innes's battalion and furthermore he acknowledged to his mother that his khaki uniform enabled them both to: 'retain our self-respect. We can say to anyone, we are doing our share'.[17A] Measured by this common denominator, he and an unknown number of the more sensitive, introspective conscripts were nor necessarily beyond the pale in being turned into effective soldiers but if, by chance, their influence were dominant in a particular unit, then less confidently may we look for evidence of that same regimental or local pride which characterized earlier bodies of men.

The final seal on the fully national identity of the Army in the First World War was that of the enrolment of women into a Women's Army Auxiliary Corps in March 1917, the first women actually being sent to France in the following month and the Corps taking on the title of Queen Mary's Army Auxiliary Corps in April 1918. The roots of the WAAC lay with the Women's Legion which had from August 1915 provided substitute labour for the Army in the form of cooks, cookery instructors, waitresses and, in February 1917, as drivers. At the Armistice, just short of 40,000 women were in the WAAC, a small number to set beside a total of more than 3,750,000 soldiers, but it might well be judged that the social and military conventions which had delayed the formation of the Corps were against the national interest. The clear evidence of the keenness of women from all backgrounds to play their part in the war effort, urged on by wide-ranging motivation which had the central focus of the country's need, had seen them voluntarily fulfil many new roles in everyday life, well beyond the more publicized work in industry and in the Voluntary Aid Detachment. A disciplined enthusiasm for uniformed service had been displayed in the years immediately before the war by the First Aid Nursing Yeomanry and then by the non-nursing orientation of the Women's Legion.

The full particulars of Terms and Conditions of Service in the WAAC indicated that service was for the duration of the war though if the war were to end in less than a year from the date of enlistment, the liability was for a year. Women could enrol for Home Service if over eighteen or for Home or Overseas Service as required if they were over twenty. The classes of employment included clerical work, typing, accountancy and, perhaps surprisingly, 'librarians'. It is interesting to note that pay in France was at a rate of of £1.17s.6d. for a shorthand typist, but in London she would get £1.19s.6d. Pay outside London was at the same rate as in France.

Cooks, waitresses, housemaids, pantry maids, laundresses, wine waitresses were paid at a rate of £26 per annum as were the intriguing classifications of vegetable women and the by-product women. Qualified driver mechanics received £1.15s. per week, considerably higher than the pay for storehouse women, packers, sewers and general unskilled labour but the opportunities and the pay differences were legion, no rate of pay having been yet detailed for telephonists and telegraphists when the rates

given above had already been fixed. Assistant forewomen and forewomen corresponded to the Army NCO rank and with no commissioned rank yet possible for women, 'officer' authority was exercised by Controllers and Administrators.

WAACs in the United Kingdom and in France were housed in hostels or official quarters provided by the Army and, with exceptions, board, lodging and washing brought a 14s. per week deduction in pay. Whatever the bureaucratic details, there was a tangible excitement for women in being in military uniformed participation in the war effort – perhaps a degree of romantic excitement trimmed as it was for the happily married women because she could not serve overseas on the same front as her husband. Before enrolment, a recruit had to pass her selection board interview and medical examination and sign her acceptance of the fact that a serious breach of her contract would render her: 'Liable on conviction by a Court of Summary Jurisdiction to be sentenced to imprisonment with or without hard labour for a term not exceeding six months, or to a fine not exceeding £100 or to both such imprisonment and fine.' Having signed such a declaration, Daisy Philp, as an assistant forewoman, served in France, her WAAC pay book indicating that she was paid: 'in the Field'.[18]

WAAC service in France was at one of the great base depots or on the lines of communication, the expressed but unprovable essence of such service being that a soldier was thus released to go 'up the line'. To a similarly ideal state of discipline the Army Adjutant General issued his first instructions to members of the Corps. 'All grades of the Corps are forbidden to enter any café or estaminet; to attend any places of public entertainment; or to be absent from any meal except when on duty, without the written permission of a Controller or Administrator.' Smoking on duty or in public places and thoroughfares was forbidden and: 'the consumption of alcohol will not be permitted, except under medical advice'. Without a pass or unless on duty, all military camps and barracks were out of bounds and of course: 'Persons not belonging to the Corps will not be admitted into Women's Army Auxiliary Corps camps or hostels except on duty or with a pass signed by the Chief Controller, or by one of the administrators in charge of the hostel or camp.'[19] The degree to which such stringent orders were broken and then the remarkably low percentage of pregnancies resultant from some illicit assignation and the disciplinary measures taken in consequence, are nicely dealt with in *Service with the Army*, written by the Chief Controller in France at the time, Helen Gwynne-Vaughan.[20]

In a letter to her friend working in munitions, a fledgling WAAC at Larkhill acknowledged that irregular happenings were not confined to France. 'We are always getting frightened, a few nights ago, about twelve o'clock in the night, one of the girls woke up and found a man in her room, of course we sleep 3 in a room so she started screaming and woke the others up. He soon went out I can tell you but we don't know how he came in because the gates were locked ages before that – but we all think that he came in after the one that is getting her discharge.' Life at Larkhill for this girl was not however all fear and fluffed feathers because in the same letter she wrote of going to dances two or three times a week

Role Reversal, 1918. The artist here suggests that marriage proposals by women will be the end result of the employment of WAACs to substitute for men currently engaged in work on the lines of communication, in base camps in France or indeed in the United Kingdom. This postcard was sent to a group of WAACs serving in France and the sender, 'One of the lads', wrote 'Look at this girls and do your best'. (N. Steer)

and of hockey with soldiers who provided sticks and jerseys.[21]

Dorothy Loveday's letters to her former head-mistress paint a somewhat depressing picture of her first days in the new Corps, general lateness of the commencement of all activities, alterations in the regulations and conditions of service, too many women for some types of work, insufficient for others. 'There seem to be too many drivers at present. There is supposed to be friction between the Flying Corps and the WAACs about them. I may be sent to do a test on a machine I have never seen and know nothing about. I asked originally whether I should have a course of instruction and was told that I should but it seems I am put down by the Selection board as a competent driver so I have to be.' In single file the girls waited for their meals: 'Its very slow especially if you keep your place as most of the people who are educated think its their natural right to thrust themselves in and get served first.'

Drill, route marching and lectures filled each day, and though Miss Loveday was able to 'go home every day for tea', she hated the inefficiency typified for her by the incorrect feet position of the woman drilling them. She felt 'trapped', and to add to her distaste she found that there was a: 'lot of thieving and nothing is safe unless locked up and even then some suitcases have been broken into'.

A talk by the Chaplain General was no inspiration. 'It really was lamentable, insulting the intelligence of a child of 10. I suppose most clergymen do talk drivel to girls but it beat anything I have ever heard.' 13539 Loveday got to France early in February 1918 but alas she found sloppiness and muddle there too and worse still, the 'age long abuse of having men in command of women'. At the garage from which she collected her vehicle, there was an 'atmosphere of women being considered a nuisance'. As this particular WAAC was having trouble in coping with double declutching she was particularly vulnerable and wished there were 'a Pelman system for getting one's nerve back'.

An area of work which Miss Loveday did find impressive was the office organization of the vehicle depot. Everything was tabulated or charted and easily located. The officer in command here earned her respect though he had so strong a personality that he 'blots out my intelligence the moment he speaks to me'. Her own meticulous attention to detail and capacity in drawing charts of road accidents involving army vehicles, encouraged the CO to keep her in his office where she fully appreciated that she was not releasing a man to go up the line, she was only 'nursing his hobby'.[22]

Despite periods of hectic activity as a clerk in Motor Transport depots in Abbeville and Calais, Nora Steer's 1918 diary entries substantiate the demobilization message she would in due course receive that she should look back on her service to King and Country 'as a very pleasant memory'. Four days before the opening of the German offensive, office work in the depot at Abbeville had finished at 11.30 a.m. and she had a 'game of hockey and footer'. After lunch she and the other girls had taken rugs out onto the lawn and 'had a lazy afternoon . . . Met Alf after tea and went into the woods. Climbed up the hill and sat on the top. Lost our way in coming down and struggled through the dense branches. Set Alf down to the church and returned to camp'. Now that particular day was a Sunday which would seem to explain the leisure time but on Wednesday 20 March, she had shopped with other girls and met Alf in town. It is not clear whether he were to have been with her for a meal in the Café de la Paix but they certainly met again in the evening and he 'set me home'. In two senses the idyll was to end: Alf had to go up the line or at least was moved and then the impact of the German push was felt in the depot because: 'Something in wind. In bath when Miss Joiner called me to go back to work. All men called back too. Went to depot and worked till 10 p.m. as hard as we could go. Came back, had supper and packed our clothes. Everybody excited. Rumours were to go to Calais in morning. Heard guns all night again.' In the morning they were paraded and informed by Miss Clowes, Senior Controller, that if they were to go it would be in an 'orderly' fashion. Mrs Gwynne-Vaughan, the Senior Controller, came to make a 'speech' to them too, but not until Saturday 30 March were they evacuated. They had seen plenty of evidence of the retreat, floods of civilian refugees from Amiens and of wounded soldiers for whom the women's beds had to be conceded. At Calais they: 'found a hut to sleep in and dossed on floor très fatigué'. However things were to look up; not only were the Germans being slowed but on Sunday 31 March, Miss Steer found Calais: 'a lovely old place – six of us went out and all got an Aussie. Be and I had a car ride with our two. First since I left home.'[23]

Reaction among the soldiers to the presence of WAACs in what had hitherto been by definition, the man's world of the Army, varied. One may presume that Alf's life was enriched and, more grudgingly, the CO of the vehicle depot where 13539 Loveday worked, may have confessed to a measure of satisfaction but an officer in the Northumberland Fusiliers found no improvement in telephonic lines

Women's Army Auxiliary Corps in France. It was to be expected that even in a nationally structured unit, friendships would flourish not least on regional grounds. On the reverse of this photograph the signatures show that Nan Moor came from Jarrow, Kitty Stones from Durham City, Nora Steer from Sunderland, B. Bracey from Bradford and Vi Fidler from Doncaster, but there was also a Scot, A. Fairgrieve and a Welsh girl, M. M. Llewellyn. (N. Steer)

of communication. 'You should just hear us trying to telephone to anyone at the Base Exchange. They are manned by shrill-voiced WAACs whose one eternal cry is "Finished, please, finished" and they cut you off before you have time to speak! Thank heavens they are no nearer. The war's bad enough without women screaming all round you.'[24] Even if the more kindly judgement of Captain Green (2/5 West Yorks) were to seem a little patronising (especially in view of the fact that some WAACs were to be killed and others badly wounded by air raids in France), it was accurate and shrewdly assessed that a valuable new element had been added to the composition of the British Army. From an officer's club at the Base he wrote that the WAACs: 'do the waiting and the attendance and general run about the place. They are dressed in khaki frocks and look very picturesque and delightfully English. In other departments, they drive motor buses, do signal office work, attend to gardens and nearly all the jobs which can be done by women instead of men. It is a good idea, frees more men for the line and gives the Tommies good female company when Tommies get down here.' Green's observations may stand as one measure of the transformation in the nature of the British Army as a result of its experience of the Great War.[25]

1

To War: 1914 in France and Flanders

Soldiers of the BEF arriving in France from 12 August were welcomed by at least one newspaper, *L'Avenir*[1] with alternate columns in English: 'The arrival of the English is to all French hearts a stimulating and a comfort. The presence of English soldiers among us enjoys every French.' With unusual generosity a tribute was paid to the English who: 'with the tenacity of their race and the cold heroism of Wellington, boat down Napoleon in the plain Waterloo and proclaimed the liberty of peoples.' The disembarkation had been observed of: 'English soldiers who are going to shed blood near ours', and then, somewhat enigmatically: 'The history of english army is full of glorious pages, and is worth of french's.'

With no more than a passing nod to the irony of such a welcome to troops whose actual role within the French military plan had been almost derisively neglected, one can sense that even the hardened Regular soldiers must have been touched by the quayside, road and railside welcome they received from the French people. An artillery subaltern wrote home of the Le Havre arrival of his unit from Dublin and of the singing crowds answered by the British troops with 'Songs of Araby', 'It's a long way to Tipperary' and a mouth organ rendition of the 'Marseillaise' which brought storms of cheers. Horses, guns and limbers were expertly slung ashore from French-operated cranes, coffee was offered and then, marching through the cobbled streets of Le Havre at 3 a.m., the rattling progress drew out nightdressed townsfolk onto their balconies. After breakfast at their rest camp, they were besieged by crowds of civilians intensely interested in everything and admiring the equipment and horses. The civilians: 'quickly, especially the fair sex, made friends with our men, and I noticed many cap badges and buttons were missing.'[2] An ASC officer wrote to his father that it was: 'difficult to pay in shops'[3] and a Corporal of the South Wales Borderers laconically noted that: 'The people go mad over us. Fairly idolize us. Plenty of milk and eggs of course, taking full advantage of it. Natives distribute eatables and wine and water. They are very acceptable. They (the natives) are very excitable and hysterical poor devils.'[4] To what extent the enthusiasm of the 'poor devils' encouraged infringement of Kitchener's stern admonition to avoid any excesses is difficult to establish. 'In this new experience you may find temptation in wine and women. You must entirely resist both temptations and, while treating all women with perfect courtesy you should avoid any intimacy.'[5]

Approximately 80,000 officers and men of the BEF were landed from 12 August and over the next few days, and it is a number to be compared with the 1,500,000 German troops committed to the Western attack of the Schlieffen Plan and the 1,000,000 men of France's Plan XVII. Further divisions were to be added to the BEF later in August, September and in October (including four divisions of Regular Indian troops), but one need go little further than these comparative statistics to grasp that until the British figure was transformed in relation to its ally and its enemy, the initiative in no sense could lie with Britain in determining policy, objectives and methods in the struggle to repel the invader.

By foot on pavé roads and by train, the two Corps of the BEF were moved through northern France to cross the Belgian Frontier and take up position on the left of the French on a line covered by the Mons-Condé Canal. Whatever attacking intent were to have been behind the Allied decision to align the BEF on the left of the French Fifth Army as the French moved forward to deal with the Northern threat to the concept of their own plan, it may appropriately be said to have become wholly 'bouleversé' by the actual circumstances of the weight of the German attack and then the withdrawal of the French from their alignment with the BEF. Of this of course the British soldier knew nothing; what he did know was that it was: 'Scorching hot. Heat unbearable.' That even though they were: 'supposed to be resting', they kept: 'grinding at it in the way of musketry training'.[6] The musketry would stand them in good stead but what would not, was the blistered feet suffered by so many and particularly by the unfit reservists as mile after weary mile of uneven cobbles found weaknesses in arches and ankles as well as puffing up unhardened skin for chafing and blisters. Diversion from such discomforts took the form of false alarms of imminent action, rumours of the catching and summary shooting of spies, but there can be little doubt that even before the first action in defence of the Mons-Condé line, officers and men must have been very tired. A private in the 2nd Battalion Sussex Regiment recorded in his diary for 22 August: 'Reveille at 3.30 and marched off at 5.15 a.m. Hot day and trying for the march which was full of halts and slow or hundreds would have dropped.' For the following day the battalion set off before dawn and: 'Marched to Mons. Very cautious march. Refugees swarmed past all day and gave me my first glimpse of war.'[7]

On 21 August a Squadron of the 4th Dragoon Guards had the distinction of the first British encounter with the enemy and three days later 2nd Lieutenant R. J. F. Chance of this regiment was to be required for immediate action when in fact the horses of his troop were grazing near Audregnies. 'We quite serene till a few shells drop near on houses – no idea that enemy near or in large numbers. Move out of village into hellish fire and ordered to charge. Do so, first down a black road which raised dust. Can't see a yard in front and "Spitfire" jumped two dead horses just in time. Jolly thick hail of bullets and shells dropping everywhere. Reach farmhouse where Squadron rallies. Can't get at enemy because of wire and impractical ground. We get out somehow. Gallagher missing. 10 left in my troop. Hit on collar badge. Out at last and we get away to Bavai demoralized.'[8]

British infantry were occupied on 22 August preparing positions from which they could defend the line of the Mons-Condé Canal – earth parapets were thrown up by sweating soldiers, outpost positons dug to defend bridgeheads while sappers cleared fields of fire by cutting gaps in hedges. Additionally the sappers tried to persuade the infantry to throw up parapets nearer to the recommended height of three feet six inches and positioned demolition charges for those same bridges to be defended. A sapper officer has recalled that in his sector in the one building across the canal which was to be made into a strong point, a modern red brick house, the owner had obviously been a collector of watches and all the watches were put into a couple of sandbags while loop holes were hacked out of his house upstairs and downstairs to make firing positions. Only four coils of barbed wire were held by the sappers so a scavenging party was sent out to the nearby town of St Ghislain to try to buy more. Knife-rest obstacles for road-blocks were being hastily made and the sapper officer, K. B. Godsell, remembered the dejection of the two Lance Corporals in charge of the tool-cart – their insistence on signed orders and receipts having been countermanded because of their slowness to issue the urgently needed implements.

In the industrial area of the canal, slag heaps were used for artillery observation, and 18-pdr guns on occasion were actually firing through loop-holed factory or coalyard walls. Godsell has recalled the first German ranging shells and then suddenly the coalyard where his local 18-pdrs were positioned: 'became a seething cauldron and the slag heap

Eastern suburbs of Mons, 21 August 1914. Troopers of the 15th King's Hussars, acting as scouts for the divisional cavalry, attempt to secure information from civilians as to any sighting of the Germans. Note the cavalry sword (1908 Pattern Mark I) with a picketing rope and peg attached to it, the rifle and the horse's eye and trooper's neck protection against flies and sun respectively, and the egg held by one of the soldiers. (R. Chant)

looked like an active volcano. Anything on the slag heap was just blown off. The row and the dust and bits flying about were almost unimaginable.'[9] As nearby buildings were hit, women who had waited till the very last moment hurried away from being householders into becoming frightened refugees pushing over-laden handcarts or prams and carrying or dragging children who could not understand what had so suddenly transformed their world. The visual image of these poor people was not merely recorded at the time in diaries but stayed with many into their old age, lasting evidence of the intriguingly latent sentimentality of the unsentimental Regular soldier.

Infantry were ordered to retain but a minimum of kit even great coats being discarded. They were issued with extra ammunition, ordered to direct aimed fire on any targets presenting themselves, hold the bridges for as long as possible and then fall back as the bridges were demolished, collecting rations where they had been dumped by the road-side.[10] A private in the 1st Bn Cameronians remembers the digging of trenches as his battalion fell back to their first position, the trenches being camouflaged with root crops.[11] Reaching Le Cateau, the Cameronians were billeted in the railway station, and on high ground outside this town a delaying action was fought where the 15 rounds per minute of the British musketry in battle established so formidable a reputation. The effectiveness with which the retirement was covered against the overwhelming numbers and artillery strength of the Germans was possible only through the physical and moral resilience of the troops who stuck at their task even when, as R. C. Money's field message book diary indicates for the Cameronians who reached a camp at Ollezy in the evening of 27 August 'The troops were well-nigh exhausted: Straggling dreadful. Men played out. We had been marching continuously since leaving Le Cateau at 6 a.m. the previous day.'[12]

More immediately destructive than the distant slowly advancing grey waves of enemy infantry, was the German shelling. The 1st Bn Dorset Regiment outside Wasmes near Mons had dug and occupied trenches by a coalmine. At 3.15 a.m. 24 August they suddenly came under very heavy shellfire. They got the wounded away but their transport was shelled while retiring through Wasmes. 'Sudden appearance of enemy's cavalry. Transport's helplessness. Lt. Margett's wounded in shoulder. Sgt. Kelly reported killed, loss of ammunition cart and supply waggon with day's rations. German artillery surround village.' The diary of this private soldier then pays an unaffected tribute to senior command leadership.

The retirement of the BEF continues, 29 August 1914. Having arrived at Pontoise at about 2 a.m. an unexpected pleasure for Cameronian officers is to find their servants have also arrived with equipment and stores for a breakfast and, even more surprisingly, there is mail awaiting the battalion. The following officers appear in this picture: Hobkirk (stripped), Davidson (RAMC Armlet) and Becher, Lee, Newman, Ferry and Minchin. (Major General R. C. Money)

'Brigadier General O.C. 15th Brigade leads his men away from village at 3 p.m. safely and retires for about 5 kils and placed [them] in an orchard to await stragglers.' Furthermore, a section of HQ staff is stationed at a street corner to give forwarning if the enemy cavalry were to appear. This diary, which also records the retirement 'constantly pursued by enemy's aeroplanes', has a splendid illustration of regimental priorities in that the CO, having sent ahead for food for his men, orders the rescue of drums and flutes which had been left at the village of Ors on the march up to their forward position.[13]

The 1st Bn, the Duke of Cornwall's Light Infantry, had been at Sardon on the canal and had set up their outposts and dug themselves in to wait for the Germans who appeared on 23 August in small patrols, but then at 4 p.m.: 'They arrived in a large solid mass on the road we were holding on the far side of the canal and proceeded to march up to a point we had carefully ranged on. . . . They deployed quickly on either side of the road and came on quickly.' The advanced companies of the regiment had been ordered to retire in the face of a strong attack, and withdrawal began. The canal bridge was blown, a stand was made at the neighbouring river bridge and then that was blown too, after which retirement to the village, not inappropriately named Dour, was carried out. 'I can't quite describe my feelings through this show, but I somehow don't believe it dispelled the odd idea that we were on some big sort of manoeuvres, which had idiotically been with me since we started from the Curragh. The burst and hum of the shrapnel surprised me and the bullets made me duck my head – I won't say I was not frightened, I'm sure I was but I don't think I knew it.' This officer, Captain A. N. Acland, Adjutant to his battalion, continued in his letter to his wife to describe their nearly being outflanked outside Le Cateau, of having his horse shot under him as he was: 'ass enough to ride one of the CO's horses along the firing line with an order', and most graphically, of the utter physical weariness of the retreat. 'At every halt we *all* slept. The men were so dead asleep that we officers had to shake them to wake them. For many miles Hammans and I walked arm in arm to keep us from rolling too much like drunken men.'[14]

A stand by the II Corps was made at Le Cateau on 26–27 August and while the Corps suffered considerable losses it can be maintained that the Germans were too close and the Corps was in too disordered a state to do anything but stand. No incident illustrates the confusion and drama of Le Cateau more vividly than the events associated with the surrender of Gordon Highlanders on 27 August. An account of the surrender has survived in the papers of a subaltern in the Gordons but circumspection requires

The date of this photograph is unknown. It was taken from a German soldier captured in 1918 and shows a column of Scottish and French POWs marching through an unknown town once the scene of heavy fighting. The number of spectators suggests that the parade may have been staged to impress (or depress) them. The well-armed German escort, includes a mounted cavalryman complete with lance. This and other features, like the German 'Pickelhauben' helmets, the absence of British steel helmets, British and French troops together and the cleared-up rubble, suggests an early date in the war. (T. H. Newsome)

his anonymity. In the early morning of 27 August, well before daylight, a mixed column of troops from the Scottish regiments on retirement, halted when firing was heard ahead of them. The subaltern who has left this account ordered his own men to line the sides of the road with loaded rifles and fixed bayonets while he hurried to the front of the column. A body of men whose officers claimed to be French was intermingled with the Scots and suspicious of the French accent of one, the Gordon officer shouted out that the troops were German. Immediately the officer whose men were so suddenly identified grappled with the senior British officer in command of the column, Colonel W. E. Gordon, VC. As they rolled on the ground, the subaltern relates that he joined in, freed Gordon, captured the German, shot another and used his revolver butt on the face of a third. The German troops who had claimed to be French were now firing at close range but of course in darkness. The Gordon officer managed to get to his men and ordered a bayonet charge up the road. It forced the Germans back, some entering a house at the side of the road. 'Together with Lt. Lyon we entered the house and forced open the first door on the right inside. Two Germans levelling their rifles I shot dead immediately, another jumped from behind a door with a rifle at Lt. Lyon who grappled with him.' In this scuffle Lyon was badly wounded but the Gordon officer shot his assailant. 'The door of the room was then slammed from inside. I decided not to try again single-handed and the Germans inside refused to come out. I therefore went outside and got three or four men to fire through the windows which made the Germans inside bolt; standing at the door I shot both as they came out.' When organizing fire on the Germans outside the house the officer heard an

31

After the cavalry and horse artillery action to defend Nery during the misty morning of 1 September 1914, the 11th Hussars had pursued the German Cavalry units' withdrawal and had captured 78 prisoners. Here the Queen's Bays (The Queen's Dragoon Guards) are escorting the mixed regimental bag of prisoners, at least one, second from right, being a Death's Head Hussar. (Major General R. C. Money)

order to cease fire. He ordered his men to disregard this but he went to investigate. He learned that the order had come from his own regimental CO but was not being followed by Colonel Gordon himself whose rank of brevet colonel gave him command of a mixed column even though he was not in command of his battalion. In such disarray the opportunity for the continuation of independent offensive action melted away and a general surrender into captivity was the result.[15]

Cavalry, infantry, sappers and gunners became intermixed on the retirement and particular problems were faced by the latter in withdrawing their guns from positions in danger of being overrun. On the morning of 24 August, 80th Battery RFA awoke to find that there were no infantry between them and the advancing enemy only a few hundred yards off. Immediate retirement to Dour, and then to Wasmes was necessary and of this a young subaltern recalled his Colonel seated outside a house writing out new orders, ignoring the plea of a distracted householder who wanted the chair locked in his house before he fled. Reaching his battery, he found it in action firing

over open sights at a target of massed German infantry near a slag heap approximately 2,400 yards away. The officer, 2nd Lt Rory Macleod, was ordered to take his section to a new position to support the withdrawal of the 2nd Bn King's Own Yorkshire Light Infantry and, as they trotted through Petit Wasmes, shellfire shattered cobbles and bricks sending fragments flying in all directions, the noise and the smoke adding to the fright of the horses. As they fell back, they used buckets at each halt to water the horses from wayside streams, collecting stooks of corn from the fields for fodder and fruit from orchards for their men or for the infantry. Keeping tiredness at bay was difficult but for this battery and others in the II Corps a temporary halt came at Le Cateau.[16]

In the stand here, German fire upon the 4.5-inch howitzers of the 37th Battery RFA was sufficiently heavy for the drivers with their horses to be sent to the rear. Here they were still under fire but on being ordered to return to the gun positions to withdraw the guns there were only sufficient unwounded horses to rescue four of the six howitzers. With these guns safe, Driver Fred Luke remembered Captain Reynolds calling for volunteers to make an attempt to get the apparently abandoned guns out. 'Drain, Coby and myself volunteered along with one other team. We walked the horses with limbers along the road to the guns and as we reached to within 300 yards we started to gallop. The Germans were now only a hundred yards or so away and, seeing what we were after, opened fire by machine-gun and rifle fire. One team of horses was shot down, but our team managed to come through with only Driver Coby being killed, a few flesh wounds on some horses and bullet holes in gun wheels.' Captain Reynolds was so near to Coby when he was hit that he was able to grab Coby's whip to urge on the horses. Luke, the wheel driver, was responsible for the exceptionally skilled turn of his team on the hard dry ground of the harvested corn field where the two guns were positioned. The turn left his limber hook right beside the trail eye of the gun so that even with just three men at the gun, limbering up could be done in seconds for the dash away. Soldierly composure under extreme danger was shown by many gunners at Le Cateau and the courage of Drain and Luke and of Captain Reynolds was so closely observed that the subsequent Victoria Cross awards had indeed been personally as well as representatively earned.[17]

Inherent flaws in the Schlieffen Plan, the sterling resistance it met and the errors of German High Command allowed for the end of the retreat and the Allied counter-attack into the newly presented flank of the German advance and a gap between two of their armies. The personal dramas taking place at points where the British order to concede no further ground combined with the last flickerings of the German advance on the British, as opposed to the French sector, are well reflected in the experience of 2nd Lt Charles Lloyd of the 2nd Battalion, Coldstream Guards. Two platoons were ordered to eliminate an enemy machine-gun post positioned at the edge of a wood. Each platoon gave covering fire to the other and then in turn advanced across open but fenced ground to the wood. When the Company Commander was wounded two hundred yards from the objective, Lloyd had to assume command. About eighty yards from the position to be attacked, he gave further orders but his voice could not be heard over the enemy machine-gun fire cracking like whips over their heads. 'The situation could scarcely be more difficult, and I find myself in completely open ground with fifty men's lives on my hands. We obviously cannot stay where we are. If we do we shall be shot to pieces. To go back is unthinkable in view of the orders. . . . The only thing to do is to get out in front to a point where both platoons can seen me and signify the charge as best I can. Accordingly I walk out diagonally to my left (the second platoon was on his left) and when everyone can seen me, wave my stick towards the enemy and shout "charge".'[18] With no man faltering in his response, the whole line charged forward with a roar and white flags appeared in the enemy position before half the distance to be charged had been covered. While fearful numbers of 'Charles Lloyds' and their men were to be killed in 1914 and indeed throughout the war, a peculiarly twisted cynicism would be needed to deny that in this little incident a substantial truth is revealed about officer responsiblity and officer/man relationships which stood the awful test of France and Belgium in 1914–18.

Accounts in September graphically document the changing circumstances of the war. A Lance Corporal who, on 6 September, had written: 'People can't realise the horrors of war. . . . Roll on Peace say everyone of us', and rather extraordinarily, 'Why did I leave my mother's apron-strings?' was to write in his diary two days later, on having been informed that the enemy had been checked and his unit was to change direction and head due east, 'Trekked straight across the country for 10 miles driving them in front of us: their pursuit is headlong for they are leaving a lot of stores and ammunition behind: even their wounded are neglected. Poor devils are starving, very few look happy but when they see how we are treating them what a difference of expression is on their faces the reason being that their officers had told them that we would commit all manner of atrocities on them.' The Corporal, W. A. Wilson of the South Wales Borderers, is not representative of the Regular soldier whose testimony is much less emotionally responsive to prevailing circumstances, but what he saw of German 'wanton destruction and brutality' can have left few unmoved. 'Flat on a window sill was a dear little kiddie stabbed through the back, the grandparents and mother being treated the same.'[19]

In the fluidity of these early weeks of action it may be presumed that there would remain some opportunity for mounted action, but even as early as 8 September, Major John Crabbe of the distinguished cavalry regiment, The Royal Scots Greys, took his men on foot into Rebais to liberate it and free some troopers who had been ambushed and captured there. He led his men along a watercourse flanked by undergrowth and trees, right up into the centre of the village despite the channel narrowing into a veritable tunnel filled with nettles and trees. Crabbe reluctantly decided that he had to split his small detachment to outflank the position where he adjudged the Germans to be holding their prisoners. Village lanes at right angles to the watercourse facilitated these tactics while Crabbe himself, with eight troopers, reached the end of the ditch which led into a garden and then took his men through this garden and through a house, the front door of which opened onto the main square. Opening the door cautiously, he was warned by a grimace from a face at the closed window of the house across the square. Peering round the door to the right he saw a mass of horses led by a few Germans. Letting his men regain their breath, Crabbe outlined his own plan of ambush. He and his trumpeter would retire through the house and cross gardens at the back to block a main road out of the square and then, as the first detachments broke into the square and those from the house dashed out too, the horses of the German cavalrymen could be stampeded and the men killed or captured. The surprise attack was frustrated by Crabbe's being seen first and fired at but, with the noise and firing of the Scots Greys' incursion into the square, the German troopers galloped hastily out leaving two wounded men, some dead horses and forty-seven lances, the latter an indication of the measure of surprise achieved.[20]

The Germans chose to halt their retirement on the heights about the River Aisne. Pursuit of them might perhaps have been pressed more vigorously, but the BEF had been hard hit, its units were very tired and its numbers demonstrably insufficient decisively to hit the enemy on their withdrawal. The Germans, unlike the British, had a goodly supply of tools and materials for the construction of defensive positions, and weapons for use from such positions. Their geographical advantage above the river which fronted an Allied advance was itself formidable. For such an attack, demolished bridges would have to be repaired, pontoons would have to be placed and fixed and all the while the sappers concerned would be under fire. The crossing of the broad river would itself have to be done under fire as would the deployment from the bridgeheads into almost immediate assault. The thirteenth and fourteenth of September were days which required special qualities from officers, NCOs and men. An HLI officer was surely understating matters in writing of the crossing and sheltering under trees being 'very trying' as the shells whistled over for half an hour before they were ordered to move off.[21] At Vailly, a brigade of cavalry had first crossed an undestroyed canal bridge and then, at a careful walk, a pontoon bridge replace-

Scottish nails in the coffin lid of the Schlieffen Plan: 10 September 1914 and 'D' Company, 1st Battalion, the Cameronians cross the Marne at La Ferté sous Jouarre following up the German retirement. Sitting contemplatively on the near pontoon is Lieutenant G. N. Macready, 7th Field Company, Royal Engineers. (Major General R. C. Money)

Brewing up, not far behind the lines. The goatskin jacket was an Army issue which may help to date this picture to the first winter of the war. Note the trench waders – not the easiest of equipment to take off. (Captain E. L. Higgins)

ment of a blown-up bridge. They then found however that the infantry ahead of them had not succeeded in gaining the heights above the river. The fog cleared and, as German shelling descended upon the narrow bridge-head gained, it was realised that the cavalry was in a trap. The brigade was ordered to retire. The Scots Greys were to be the last regiment to run the gauntlet. They stood by their horses watching house after house around them collapse under the shelling which rained down on that most inviting of targets, units in plain view having to effect a river crossing – in this case two crossings. Wounded Scots Fusiliers filtering down from the hill were not the most encouraging sight as a lengthy wait had to be endured. Major Crabbe has written that when the order to make the fateful dash came, he was less than keen. He mounted and led his troop to the pontoon bridge, the area a shambles with dead and wounded horses on it and in the water alongside. Bandaged men were sheltering under a wall to the right and a dead Engineer captain (a man who was later to be awarded a posthumous VC for directing traffic onto the bridge) was at the left. The horse Crabbe was riding refused to face the music

and the Major shouted for the troop to go first and he followed. The pontoon crossing was made safely but then came the bridge just as shelling was accurately directed on them. 'The tendency was to make a mad rush to get across, but the Colonel was wandering about on that bridge despatching wounded horses and telling people not to get excited, so one just had to go peacefully across and hope for the best. One shell hit full pitch a horse with a hanging leg about a yard to my right, blowing it to bits, and incidentally probably saving my life.'[22]

The 29th Battery RFA had come into action in the grounds of a chateau beside this bridge and Gunner Guest was never to forget the grim sight of the return of the Scots Greys under shellfire. From their own position, clearly under direct fire, the battery remained in action for five days before it was ordered to make the crossings and then, under torrential rain, they had to get across and dig emplacements on the hill above Vailly. They were not to know that during the night the pontoon bridge would break, four horses, a wagon and its ammunition being lost in the fast swirling waters of the river.[23]

Facing vastly superior artillery, firing from more elevated positions, the BEF's advance came to a halt. In constant heavy rain, the hard chalky earth was made slimy, slippery and sticky but by no means soft to the entrenching tools which attacked it for cover. Somehow the first trenches dug for more than brief shelter were constructed, but there was as yet no wire for their protection nor many howitzers to discomfort the Germans in their entrenchments. Separate dugouts, caves and camouflaged wooden shelters supplemented the defence line being scooped out. Shrapnel, in short supply also, was ineffective as both sides dug in, leaving a no man's land between them; a zone which could be dominated by small arms and machine-gun fire, thus rendering, as the future would demonstrate, all attack costly in casualties and generally unproductive of military dividend. Of course the Northern Flank remained open, inviting attack and counterattack to circumvent the stalemate but, before looking at battle experience in those attacks, some reference must be paid to the abortive Antwerp expedition designed to prevent the fall of that city and hold German forces in what might be turned into a fruitless drain upon their Westward initiative.

At the end of August, Royal Marines had been landed at Ostend. The insecurity of this position necessitated early evacuation and with the development of a serious threat to Antwerp, the whole Allied position was in danger of being outflanked and the Belgian Army of being completely destroyed. As a result of this worsening situation, the two new Naval Brigades were sent to assist in the defence of Antwerp with two Regular Army divisions to be landed in support at Zeebrugge. The northward move of the BEF from the Aisne was designed in coordination with this as well as the new significance of the open flank towards the sea. In the event only the 'sailor soldiers' were to play a part in the débâcle of Antwerp's fall, with men lost to German captivity and to internment in Holland. Those who were able to withdraw through the outskirts of the city and by various means – bus, rail and foot – break contact with the Germans, fell back behind the screen of the covering Regular Army divisions dug in outside Ghent. As the troops made their way westwards, they were to enter a city famed for its unspoiled architectural beauty, the perfectly preserved gem of Flemish commercial, religious and domestic heritage, the city of Ypres.

The Antwerp enterprise had been too small, too late, too little trained and too ill-equipped for its task. The naval character of this affair required its inclusion in *The Sailor's War 1914–18*,[24] but the correspondence from internment of one of the young Royal Naval Volunteer Reservists called to serve as a soldier, may be taken as representative evidence of what fell little short of a disaster. 'We went into the trenches at Antwerp on the 5th – shelled all day and night – no enemy seen the whole time – retreated on Friday at 10 p.m. – had a march through Antwerp in flames, shelled all the while, marched 36 hours with only ten minute rests – no sleep – no food except what the villagers gave us such as apples etc. During the week we have had 2 biscuits and one slice of corned beef once a day – sometimes no biscuits, and sometimes no meat. Thousands of refugees. Surrounded so passed into Dutch territory and under their protection. Arms surrendered. The expedition seems to have been a huge crime from start to finish – men, most of whom couldn't shoot officered by men who proved themselves totally incapable – probably because they had no military training – and practically unsupported by artillery.[25] Properly to balance this verdict of contempt for the military quality of the personnel, it will of course be realized that it cannot have applied to the Royal Marines and in any case the brigades of the Royal Naval Division, when brought up to strength and having undergone further training, were to serve with distinction at Gallipoli in 1915 and on the Western Front from 1916 onwards. None the less, the Antwerp affair was a frustrating humbling business even for those who were able to avoid German capture or Dutch internment.

The loss of Antwerp made still more important the need to exploit the open flank, now that the Battle of the Aisne had ended in defeat for any hope of winning the war according to current doctrine. It was in the La Bassée–Armentières area where 'encounter battle' was to be joined. Here, coalmining villages met farmland on flattish canal-crossed and dyke-gridded ground, as unattractive for offensive military operation as it was scenically drab. The French took over the British positions on the Aisne and the BEF moved north. A tiny vignette of but one of the numerous actions occurring, is revealed in the diary of a private in the Dorset regiment. 'Givenchy, 13 October: Order received to advance at 2 p.m. met by murderous rifle and shellfire. Dorsets suffer heavily. Lt. Col. Bols splendid behaviour in trenches but unfortunately wounded in back by shrapnel.

Here a soldier displays before men of 'B' Company, Artists' Rifles (28th Battalion, London Regiment) his goatskin overcoat. On the reverse of the photograph he has been nicknamed 'Hitchikoo' after the song popular at this time. The scene is near Bailleul during the first winter of the war, when the BEF copied French Army practice and issued the goatskins. (Captain A. K. Totton)

15th Brigade compelled to retire but for a short distance. After renewed attack Battalion regained former position. Fighting slackened at 6.15 p.m. Casualties today very heavy. During the short retirement Lt. Col. Bols was captured but escaped when Battalion regained their former position. 454 NCO's and men, 16 officers being the number of killed, wounded and missing.' It should be noted that the battalion, after such a fearsome casualty rate, renewed its attack on the following day, dealt with a German counter-attack bayonet charge, attacked again on the next day when at 12.30 p.m.: 'enemy was reported to have retired, battalion was then relieved by 1st Devon's'.[26]

North again, to the Aubers Ridge and Le Maisnil, Bois Grenier and Armentières, the enemy was encountered, heavy casualties inflicted and suffered, but no strategic aim could be fulfilled – and further north still, chosen by geography and circumstance for a cruelly prolonged fate, lay Ypres.

The western approach to the city was intensively cultivated requiring a veritable network of draining channels criss-crossing the flat terrain to cope with the high water table. Viewed from the insignificant elevations, the farms, hamlets and villages were laid out in separated distinction. Had the pre-war traveller known that the gentle rises were to become known as ridges and hills, he would have regarded it as laughable.

On 11 October, before the Germans had concentrated their strength for an assault, the BEF began its attempt to overturn, by outflanking, the advantage the Germans had gained in the previous weeks of warfare. When the German broadfront assault was launched on 20 October, it needed the Belgians and French Marines on the Yser Front, north of Ypres, as well as the BEF to the south to hold firm in fighting which developed a character of concentrated intensity. In retrospect, this character is distinguished by an awareness that, after this month, the performance of individuals, of small groups of men, of platoons and companies or battalions will not again hold such significance. Artillery will from this time onwards, assume her role as Queen of the battlefield, protecting her material kingdom against mere footsoldier challenge, by spiked hedges of barbed wire.

The constancy of action is an impressive feature in the diary of Private Chant of the 5th Dragoon Guards at Messines from 21 October. Whether on oupost duty, moving from one location to another, sheltering in a church porch, in a billet, holding a trench, 'in touch with Germans at a barricade', in a wood with the horses, digging trenches, on horse-

holder duty, briefly at rest, fetching up tea from a house being used as a hospital, sheltering from German hand-bombing, he was almost always under shellfire up to 12 November when he wrote: 'Sunday morning. Just offered a morning prayer to God. Alone in a dugout, would to God I'll be spared for Mary's sake. Just looked at her photograph. Pray and hope for the best.'[27]

The street fighting to take the villages which were situated like the nails in a horseshoe with its base at Ypres, is strikingly illustrated in a cavalry officer's diary. Lieutenant T. L. Horn (16th Queen's Lancers) gave covering fire for an attack up a street to take the centre of Warneton by siting his machine-gun on a roof overlooking the street barricade behind which Germans barred further progress. A field gun was manhandled from a lane to blast the barricade at close range while a troop from 'C' Squadron of the Lancers was to lead a dash for the breach. The whole affair took place in the dark, three deafening shells brought glass out of every window in the three-storeyed houses and the small arms fire maintained the racket. Further barricades had to be dealt with in the side streets and suddenly every figure was caught by a dazzling Very light which revealed opposing machine-gun teams so that like angry cats they commenced spitting at each other not more than 25 yards apart, sparks flying whenever the bullets hit the cobbles or walls. In this fashion the village was fought for and the cavalryman wrote, one may presume with feeling: 'Hope we don't do any more street fighting in the dark, as it doesn't seem our job, not knowing when or where one may be attacked from next.'[28]

While the Allies fought infantry actions to hold the approaches to Ypres, the city itself was under shellfire. 'We were not allowed to enter Ypres until dark as it was being heavily shelled. Half of the town seemed to be on fire and the glare from the flames playing on the many towers and spires produced a most weird effect made more wonderful as we circled round the town on the far side of the moat and the above shades and shadows were reproduced in the water.' A guide, getting lost once, shepherded Royal Engineers' wagons round the outside walls until they reached the road leading from the Menin Gate. They proceeded up this road and: 'Turned into the grounds of a white Chateau and bivouacked there.' They were ordered to extinguish the acetylene lamps by which they were eating their evening meal, but which would in fact have drawn shellfire. Soon after 3 a.m. they were ordered up to a front line three miles ahead. The line was in a wood in which frequent sniper fire sounded and was most disconcerting. Little of the wiring which they had been called to carry out could be done as dawn lifted the damp fog from the sodden undergrowth and dripping trees. 2nd Lt Godsell, the diarist, was ordered to take his section, after its wholly useless exercise, back to a city the increasing destruction of which he was to record as well as such vivid details as the machine-gun bullets playing on the Menin Road as he was waiting to cross it one dark night. On such nights it was easy to get lost in the wood too. Shattered trees necessitated leaving the familiar paths to communication trenches and dugouts in course of construction. Already the sappers' big problem in the new Ypres Salient was drainage. All excavations rapidly filled with water and when, in one particular instance, the only means of getting up to the front line was by crawling: 'on your belly along a 10-foot tunnel under the parapet of a rear trench', the problems were serious.[29]

Rain, sleet and snow fell on the opposing positions of shared misery in late November. Deliberate flooding by the Belgians further north had assisted in the closing of the open flank, and though the BEF attempted further attacks in the Salient in the second half of December, the soldiering experience of a different war from that which had been expected was now becoming familiar. The supplies for the improvement of entrenched positions and the weapons for waging war were beginning to reach the BEF, new techniques of warfare were being learned, men were beginning to grow accustomed to a singularly unnatural way of life when suddenly their daily pattern of living and of expectations was shaken by the wholly remarkable circumstances of the unofficial Christmas 1914 Truce. The truce, over a wide sector of the British line, brought out Germans and British into no man's land and suspended hostilities for days varying in number on different parts of the Front.

'Most peculiar Christmas I've ever spent and ever likely to. One could hardly believe the happenings,' was how Sapper J. Davey described what had started for him with Christmas Eve in no man's land exchanging souvenirs with Germans.[30] Private William Mockett (Queen's Westminster Rifles) wrote home of the Germans shaking hands and saying: 'You no shoot, we no shoot.' Mockett recorded that one of the Saxons had told him that they were fed up with the war and were ready to go home.[31]

When the Germans walked out into no man's land, 2nd Lt R. D. Gillespie (2nd Bn, Gordon Highlanders) was puzzled at his Sergeant hurrying into a dugout to say: 'They're out sir.' Gillespie found his own men going out too and, in the absence of a more senior officer to confirm or cancel what was being done, he too clambered out of the trench. A young German soldier gave him a Berlin newspaper but the only group activity seen by Gillespie on this sector, was the burial of men killed in an attack earlier in the month and then, more high spiritedly, the chasing of a hare which escaped into the German trenches – or perhaps it may have escaped! A joint service for the men buried was led by a Scottish Padre, Dr. J. E. Adams with an interpreter and a German Divinity student. Gillespie himself was taken into the German lines and shown a board which had been put up to honour a British officer who in one attack had got right to the trench concerned before being killed.[32]

In the German lines on the outskirts of Armentières on Christmas Eve, the soldiers had put up lights and small Christmas trees on their parapet and had sung carols. In the morning, fraternization had followed and an impromptu football kickabout had taken place:[33] Some men recorded this as a match between English and German troops. An attractive anecdote is related of a Pickelhaube being exchanged for a tin of bully beef and on the following day the German donor had asked to borrow it back for an official unit inspection. 'The loan was made and the pact was kept, sealed with some extra bully beef.' In this sector, Frank and Maurice Wray insist that the truce lasted until the New Year and, as evidence of this, they relate Brigade HQ's refusal to accept an inebriated barbed-wire-entangled German soldier as a prisoner because important defensive work on the edge of a wood was not yet finished and a prolongation of the peace would allow this to be carried out.[34] It is also beguiling to note Harold Startin's memory of the Germans lending the 1st Leicesters the superior Teutonic tools for trench improvements![35]

On Christmas Eve near Ploegsteert, German-speaking Captain R. J. Armes (North Staffordshire Regiment) called from his trench to a German who had just treated his listeners to one song, for one of Schumann's – the response was, 'The Two Grenadiers' and it was well received. After discussions and fellowship in no man's land, 'Die Wacht am Rhein' answered by 'Christians Awake', closed the conviviality for that evening.[36]

Amid this relaxation of tension, many remained cautiously alert, some quite serious in their conversational contact with the enemy and sceptical about what they heard. Captain Sir Edward Hulse wrote home of exchanges over the inflammatory effect of English Press reports of atrocities: 'We had

Fleeting friends. Germans rendezvous in no man's land with men of the London Rifle Brigade on Christmas Day 1914. The German on the left appears to have a torch clipped to his tunic. (M. Wray)

Christmas Day 1914, Givenchy. Men of 'C' Company, 1st Battalion, Black Watch in a front line trench. Momentarily all is quiet but this trench will be lost and then recaptured within a month. (J. G. Scott)

a heated, and at the same time good-natured argument, and ended by hinting to each other that the other was lying.'[37] As the exchanging of souvenirs and songs developed and the atmosphere grew still more relaxed, the Captain noted in his letter that: 'Later in the day I fed about 50 sparrows outside my dugout, which shows how complete the silence and quiet was.' Sir Edward's kinship with nature did not however extend from feathers to fur as it was he who gave the hunting cry to pursue first one hare and then other hares, the two kills being appropriately shared by field grey and khaki. It was not just the officers, like this Scots Guards captain, who viewed the whole affair with a measure of caution. A very young rifleman of the Queen's Westminster Rifles, who had indeed had a 'jolly good time' and found it all 'exciting and never having seen a friendlier sight' seems to have been rather relieved in finding that 'They were not nearly as strong-looking as English fellows and some were much smaller even than I. I feel much more confident about a bayonet charge now.'[38] Such an opportunity was not to fall to that particular rifleman. Indeed the actual incidence of 'bayonet charges' certainly does not match the commonly held myth of their regular occurrence; but, as one contemplates those men enjoying the Truce, it is sobering to be aware that they were unknowingly on the threshold of what was to be a truly awful year.

2

Battle: 1915

Well might the Official Military Historian write of 1915 that it is 'often very sad reading'.[1] More recently the scholarship of John Terraine has convincingly demonstrated that Britain, as the junior military partner in a coalition war, was logically committed to supporting France in clearing the enemy from her invaded territory and thus rescue areas which however agriculturally and industrially important were quite simply 'French'. The resultant constant search for the offensive was to challenge inexorable facts about the current stage of military technological development. Artillery and small arms fire were dominant in the battle zone, a zone crucially enclosed by wider and wider belts of barbed wire. There was at the service of the attacking commander no means of exercising voice control of battle movements and no means of bringing mechanization to the aid of an attacker seeking to break through (as opposed to the defender using roads and even rail to bring support to any threatened sector). These factors combine to explain so much of what lies behind the record of almost unrelieved failure which attended the offensive operations of the BEF in 1915.

The first major attack undertaken by the British in the early spring of 1915 was that at Neuve Chapelle in March. It was designed to open the way for the taking of Aubers Ridge thus lifting the BEF out of flat, wet, observed ground into a position from which it could play an effective part in support of the French drive to cut the rail communications of the Noyon Salient. It was this salient which jutted so menacingly into the Allied line and betokened an ever-present threat to Paris. Let there be no mistake about it, Neuve Chapelle was no ill-prepared affair. There was a formidable concentration of heavy guns, aerial photography of the enemy positions, detailed information given to officers beforehand and special assault training for the troops to be involved.

Morale was high, a regimental Medical Officer describing the evening beforehand as if they were all 'hanging about waiting to go on the field for a big footer match'.[1A] The preliminary bombardment lasted for only thirty-five minutes. 2nd Lt Rory Macleod wrote of the batteries being one behind the other in rows, wherever they could fit in. 'There seemed to be an earthquake going on by the way the ground shook',[2] but the German counter-battery fire cut to ribbons the telephone lines laid so carefully before the battle and thus the means of informing the gunners how the infantry was progressing was left to aerial reconnaissance which was hampered by cloud cover and the smoke of the battle. Infantry officers synchronized their watches as the troops crouched as instructed in the bottom of the trench. 'There was something curiously exhilarating about it . . . the men seemed to become more and more elated'. The Cameronian officer, M. D. Kennedy, who wrote these recollections, felt that the only way he could explain this phenomenon was by likening it to the effect of listening to the bagpipes. 'Some of the men laughingly held out their hands for me to shake. This was in case either they or I got "blotted out". One realized then, as never before, what a wonderful bunch of fellows they were, and how damned lucky one was to have such men to command.' Kennedy wrote of Captain Ferrers being a particularly cheering inspiration and then the Adjutant, Gray-Buchanan, drew his attention shouting: 'There goes Ferrers!' 'Looking up I saw him, monocle carefully adjusted and sword in hand, in the act of scrambling over the parapet 20 to 30 yards to my right; so, calling to the men to follow, over I went too. For a moment everything seemed strangely silent as the barrage lifted, only to re-open a few seconds later on to the village to our right front. Simultaneously, with a sound as of a nest of giant hornets suddenly let loose, the air became filled with the whistle of hundreds of bullets as German machine-guns enfiladed us from our left, and the German infantry to our front opened rapid fire with their rifles.' There was no cover whatsoever for the attacking troops and the anticipated artillery destruction of the enemy's positions had simply not occurred. 'It probably did not take more than a minute or two to reach the German wire but I remember a fleeting glance at "A" Company on our left, with the men dropping as though some giant scythe were sweeping through their ranks.' How they got through the undestroyed wire Kennedy doesn't know, but he and a corporal dragged away a barbed wire obstacle only four or five yards from the parapet where a German fired at them but missed. Then from this spot the German bolted back down a communication trench and Kennedy from the parapet fired his revolver into the press of jostling backs. With difficulty the officer and corporal got through the wire and onto the parapet above the vacated German front-line trench. The Germans were either intent upon departure through an orchard behind the front line, or firing at what seemed to be the sole survivors of the company's attack – perhaps four men in all. Kennedy shouted to the corporal to jump into the trench with him when he was sent reeling backwards by being hit. Before he had regained his balance he was hit again and pitched back off the parapet and through the hedge of wire and to the ground. A German who had scrambled onto the parapet in the last seconds before Kennedy was hit was bayoneted by one of the Cameronians and in consequence he crashed down beside the wounded Cameronian. Kennedy refused to be carried back by the corporal and one of the surviving soldiers, Private MacHugh, but they left him with a young soldier who attempted with his own coat to keep Kennedy warm. The soldier took bandages from the dead all around, bandaged and bandaged again Kennedy's severe wounds from which blood continued to seep. He used the officer's hip flask to keep him plied with brandy to stop a lapse into unconsciousness. The cold was intense and with Kennedy unable to move his legs, they were to become frost-bitten before stretcher-bearers

arrived to take him to a field ambulance. Private McHugh was killed in carrying wounded and so was Kennedy's bugler, Forrester, armed with nothing more lethal than his bugle and some wire clippers – they were among some 200 men and thirteen officers of the battalion who were killed or died of wounds.

Kennedy was carried by the bearers to a line of huddled figures laid out on the ground. Another stretcher was brought to be aligned next to him. Its occupant was the burly Major Lloyd. His face was contorted with pain, though he never made a sound to show it, except to ask for morphia. He was given an injection and it seemed to bring him some relief, but he was too severely wounded to last long and died soon after.[3] The Colonel, the Adjutant, and three of the four company Commanders had been killed, the fourth, Major Ferrers, the first to reach the German wire, was wounded in the thigh and stomach, refused to be carried back and had calmly proceeded to light a cigar. The four officers, who were second in command of their companies, had all been killed and when the battalion, originally of over 900 men, was relieved a day or two later, the 143 survivors were led out of the line by a young sub-altern and a sergeant major. The desperately sad but enduringly inspiring story of the Cameronians at Neuve Chapelle is superbly told and convincingly explained in John Baynes' splendid book *Morale*.[4]

The Battle of Neuve Chapelle, March 1915. It must have been something of a surprise to the bandaged German prisoners to be attended by Indian Army stretcher-bearers, from the 41st Dogras. A French soldier stands in the centre of this group. (Lieutenant Colonel C. A. M. Dunlop)

Neuve Chapelle, the first day of the battle and the death of these gunners serving a 2.75in, 12½-pounder of the 5th Mountain Battery, Royal Garrison Artillery, 3rd Mountain Artillery Brigade, Indian Army. (G. W. Sissons)

It was the first battle experience for Captain Deane (RAMC) attached to the 2nd Leicesters. His stretcher-bearers went off to bring back casualties to Deane in the Aid Post he had established. 'The show began for me when I got the message Capt Morgan is hit and is bleeding badly. I ran along the trenches to him fearful of finding a shattered wreck. Doubling round traverses, jumping over pools of blood, severed limbs with no owners, shattered corpses and groaning wounded. A Gurkha with his right hand handed me his left arm torn off above the elbow and wailed, "Sahib Sahib" and as I ran on I heard a Jock say "Nice bloody doctor, wouldn't treat a wounded man." Morgan seemed shrunk to about half his usual size and was very blue. 5 wounds mainly in the lung.' To read Deane's account of what he called: 'a nightmare of bandaging and iodine and blood' working in the dugout all day with bent back and with occasional trips round the trenches, then of men hit by shrapnel or shell fragments in the trench where he worked, is to bring one perhaps just within reach of the prolonged drama he experienced.[4B]

Neuve Chapelle itself was captured and in the centre of what was almost a five mile front, an advance had been made, but not on the flanks and very quickly all attacking momentum was lost. The 4th Battalion the Suffolk Regiment was brought into the attack on the second day of the battle, 11 March. They moved through the British jumping-off trenches, littered with discarded packs and great-coats, and came upon some dead Gurkhas. Under

shellfire they got through to Neuve Chapelle where they rested before moving out into an open field. They came under machine-gun fire causing them to go to ground and attempt to dig themselves in. A Corporal Killick was shielded by two dead cows 'green and stinking'. In due course the German artillery ranged accurately upon the battalion with shrapnel and Killick, like Kennedy, was to receive a severe head wound.

The immediate aftermath of a battle may not be strictly relevant to this chapter on battle experience, but Killick's stark diary account demands inclusion. A shrapnel ball had blinded him in one eye. A man in his battalion had put Killick's field dressing on the wound and later in the day the wounded man had dumped his equipment, the privilege of the wounded man, and staggered back down the line before he was found by stretcher-bearers who carried him three miles to a depot for ambulances. All the while there was shelling on this trek. He was taken to an overcrowded church at Merville and then to a second such 'hospital', a school at Estaires. Mattresses on the floor afforded some alleviation of the pain worsened by so much movement, but a degree of paralysis had set in and he could not eat during the long day of waiting spent in that school. At 2 the next morning he was put aboard another ambulance which took him to an ambulance train for what proved to be a fourteen-hour journey to Boulogne. 'During this time we had neither food nor drink and it was agony.' At No. 2 Stationary Hospital, an

No more shells? Spring 1915. Production difficulties were bringing ludicrous limitations upon shell use by the quick-firing 18-pounders – down to ten rounds a day in February and three a day in April. This gun – from the 87th Battery, Royal Field Artillery – was soon to be put entirely out of action by German shelling. (Captain K. W. Brewster)

injection of morphia and a comfortable clean bed prepared him for the following day during which he was deliberately kept without food and then at night: 'was taken to the Theatre where I went under chloroform and had my eye taken out by Captain Payne, RAMC, a Harley Street man.'[5]

The attack at Neuve Chapelle, after its initial hour of promise, had run into delays which had enabled the enemy to reinforce the threatened breach in their line and as the British re-invested in attacks which were failing, casualties not progress were bought. An especially sad legacy from this carefully considered battle was the delusion that so much more could have been achieved if a sufficiency of shells, among other things, were to have been available. The shortages were certainly evident and making them good was possible, but transforming the very nature of land warfare was a matter for technological inspiration, invention, proving and mass production and this was not something to be looked for in a matter of months.

Before a further attempt could be made to take Aubers Ridge, the Germans were to attack at Ypres and they were to use for the first time an asphyxiating gas, chlorine, and not the lachrymatory ('tear') gas which they had already employed in shells and of which the French and British had some record of use or planned use in different types of grenades or rifle cartridges.[6]

In the Ypres Salient, senior command chose to lay no special stress on Belgian reports of German gas attack preparations. No clear evidence by aerial photography had reported the installation of tubes for the release of the gas and when the attack was launched on 22 April no precautions had been taken. French Colonial troops in the north of the Salient were first to face the greenish-yellow clouds of gas and then Canadians to their right were to suffer. The way in to Ypres was momentarily open as troops in the gas affected areas withdrew in some disorder, but the Germans paused before resuming the attack, and troops of the BEF were brought in to plug the alarming gap which had opened.

Whatever the niceties of the Hague Convention on the use of poison or poisoned weapons, how did the soldier on the line record its impact on his sector or on a sector adjacent to his position? One man has left this baleful description of the desperate situation: 'I was about four miles from the German lines when the gas came over. We saw coming towards us a rising fog by now ascending and beginning to turn very slowly into a greenish-yellow cloud covering the whole sky. We were as completely taken by surprise as the men in the line for we had been given no warning whatsoever. At first there was just a most peculiar smell quickly followed by a choking sensation which made breathing difficult. Then as the full impact was made felt there was a severe irritation of the nose and throat air passages with a burning feeling and an uncontrollable weeping of the eyes. There was a strong nausea and a tendency to be sick therefore. The sun looked a ghastly green, low in the

sky, and we just did not know what on earth to do. At some time or another, hours later, the idea came filtering through that the the best way to protect ourselves from the effects of the gas would be to urinate into our handkerchiefs and clap it over our mouth and nostrils. This was no doubt sound advice, but in the dark and with a generally prevailing misery I certainly dismally failed to carry out the first injunction of the message.' A long night was spent without sleep or talk, dispirited, unable to eat or drink because of nausea. 'We found out for ourselves that sitting or lying down was worse than standing up because the heavier than air chlorine gas was strongest at ground level. It was also better to keep as still as possible and not to move around more than absolutely necessary because movement intensified the effects by breathing more and more deeply and so filling our lungs.' In the morning, F. P. Roe, who has thus remembered his encounter with the gas, was sent with an interpreter into Bailleul to buy protective gauze for his battalion, the 6th Gloucesters. He was to see in the large square, serried ranks of stretchered casualties, great numbers disabled through gas. 'Many were still alive but a great many were dead no doubt having died during the night after being brought out. The more severely gassed soldiers had a quite appalling blueness/purpleness of the skin.' For cash, lengthy rolls of white cotton gauze and half-inch-wide tapes were

The Salient: British front line trenches, circa June 1915. An officer is using his privatelly purchased folding trench periscope to scan the enemy's positions in safety. It will be a leafless summer here, the trees beyond the sandbags defoliated as a result of the German gas attacks. (B. H. Church)

bought but there were no safety-pins. No information filtered down to this battalion of wetting the gauze with a solution of bicarbonate of soda kept ready in a bucket for this purpose.[7]

A graphic picture of life in Ypres under the German bombardment emerges from the pages of N. C. Harbutt's diary. An officer in the Royal Engineers, Harbutt was in Ypres on 8 April when the Germans dropped leaflets informing the townspeople that the city was to be shelled to bits and he derided such a possiblity. His own confidence came under attack on 19 April. He was in a building serving as his Company Office when the blast and fragments from enemy shelling directed at a nearby gun position, blew out all the windows, the doors, brought down ceilings, wrecked the staircase, destroyed his own kit and set up noise and dust of awesome proportions. People were killed in the street outside, including a little girl urged on ahead of her mother, running right into a shell explosion. 'April 20 Ypres: The big square a shambles. Seven stall-holders killed by one shell. The whole square littered with human remains, stones, timber, glass.'

Canadian troopers ahead of their horses. Men of the Lord Strathcona's Horse hold the line at Ploegsteert, a circumstance which became all too familiar for the cavalryman. (Captain F. C. Powell)

Harbutt was fully occupied finding new billets, organizing the repair of damaged trenches, checking the dugouts which had been constructed and then on 22 April, an intense bombardment and soaring signal rockets from the enemy positions gave some warning of impending attack. 'An artillery Major gives orders for us to stand to. We hear the Bosch have asphyxiated the French with their gas shells and many small parties have broken through. Canadians stand and hold them. The whole place is in an uproar. Hear Germans are in Wieltje. All our kits are packed for a moment's move. We're all rather worried. Ypres is in flames in many places. Shells keep on bursting behind us, and the bits and pieces fly around us. Just as I write a man has come in to say a horse has been hit outside by a bit of the last one over. The rifle fire is terrific and machine-guns make things worse.

The Turcos [French Colonial troops] come flying through the village in a panic. Terror in their faces with tales of awful gas shells – many are wounded. Villagers with their children and household goods make one long stream of wailing humanity. The gas from the shells made our eyes smart and run with water and we were at least 3 miles away. No bed for me and no sleep.'

April 23 – St. George's Day – was no day for this Englishman to celebrate. 'They start shelling our huts, billets and horse lines. The awful suspense as these awful tearing sounds come screaming through the air – nearer and nearer.. Everyone rushes to a steep bank for shelter and in it we start digging ourselves dugouts 6 feet across and about 9 feet in with 2 feet of earth on top supported by timber from wrecked houses. And all the time the shells continue to fall. We shrink into the places we dig and wait for the burst.' In a period when the shelling seems to have diminished, they came out and saw two large craters, six dead horses and two men of the Wessex Signal Company killed, but somehow even worse was the sight of poor little children, shrieking with terror, attempting to hurry away to safety carrying heavy bundles of possessions. Well might he write of wounded men seeking shelter under the same bank into which the new dugouts had been constructed. 'Poor fellows – physical wrecks let alone the wounds.'

For day after day Harbutt catalogued scenes which even for this experienced Boer War soldier must have long remained in his mind's eye – his shooting of wounded horses, dressing of casualties, burying the dead having emptied their pockets, then

Waterproof capes offer some protection to Artists' Rifles who may be having some difficulty keeping their pipes alight in this downpour behind Hill 60 in the Ypres Salient early in 1915. From left to right: Privates Drakeford, Fisher, Cooper, Green, Watson and Frazier. The Artists nurtured many future officers and of this group for example, Drakeford won an MC as a Captain in the King's Liverpool Regiment and Frazier became an officer (twice wounded) in the Lincolnshire Regiment. (Captain A. K. Totton)

FOR ISSUE TO ALL RANKS.
INSTRUCTIONS FOR USE OF RESPIRATOR AND SMOKE HELMETS

RESPIRATORS.

(1) These are already damped with chemical solution and **should not be wetted.**

(2) On the approach of poisonous gases, open the respirator and place the cotton waste pad over the mouth and nose grasping it with the teeth to keep it in position.

(3) Now tie off the ends of the veiling behind the head so that the cotton waste closely covers the nose and mouth and pull the free margin of veiling above the eyebrows to protect the eyes. **Breathe in and out through the mouth only.** After it has been in use for some time, move the respirator to one side or the other so as to breathe through new portions of the cotton waste.

(4) When the respirator no longer stops the entrance of the gas, apply a fresh one with the same precautions.

SMOKE HELMETS.

On the first suspicion of the approach of gas, remove the cap draw the helmet over the head and **tuck the lower edge of the helmet inside the neck of the frock or shirt** buttoning no latter. If the window becomes dim it may be cleaned by gently rubbing against the forehead. Do not damp the helmet.

N. B. — Where both a smoke helmet and a respirator have been issued, **the helmet should be used first** and the respirator kept in reserve.

The above instructions cancel all others previously issued on this subject.

G. H. Q.   TO BE FOLDED AND KEPT.
4th. June 1915.   IN THE PAY BOOK.

finding the identity disc, sewing the bodies up in blankets and actually recording in his diary pity for their relatives. A headless man lay on the Menin Bridge, his head in the bows of one of Harbutt's bridging pontoons. One can only guess at the purpose, literary or psychological of his recording among such detail, 'Have rhubarb for lunch.' It had been obtained in trench digging through a kitchen garden.[8]

The Germans carried out further attacks on the Salient to the end of April and into May. Costly attack was answered by equally costly counter-attack. Gas was used again, from shells on one occasion and the Germans won more than half the Salient but no more. Quite remarkable efforts, initially by Flemish and French women in response to an urgent appeal, quickly produced supplies of

elementary gas protection, taped gauze, the tape soon being elasticated which improved the positioned efficiency of the gauze. Nevertheless a contemporary account by Captain J. H. Young (1st Bn Argyll and Sutherland Highlanders) leaves one in little doubt that holding any of the Salient had been a near-run thing.[9] '11 May. At 5.30 the German began to bombard my trench. They were using whizz-bangs, high explosive, trench mortars and mine werfers [heavy mortars]. A hail of every kind of abomination landed round my trench and the Camerons' trench to my right. My trench being only dug the night before was in no way able to cope with this inferno. It was blown to bits and men trying to

It did not take the War Office long after the German use of gas in the Ypres Salient to ensure that some protection was in general issue. Different types of gas necessitated sophisticated development of 'the gas mask' and the accompanying instructions were to get more complex than this initial effort. (P.H.L. Archives)

24 May 1915. The 6th Battalion, Durham Light Infantry has suddenly been ordered to move up to the front line at Potijze as reinforcement against a surprise German gas attack. Company Quartermaster Sergeant Major Bennison marches at the head of the column as it passes through the ruins of Ypres on its way up the line. Private Perry, to the right of the next rank, will be killed in an hour and from the original caption of this photo it seems that Bennison may have shared his fate. (Captain P. H. B. Lyon)

escape in rear were caught by machine-guns.' Young ordered the evacuation of some of his men to the communication trench and the spreading out of others in the trench under shellfire. He sent back for reinforcements – they never came and, as the account accepts, they could not have come forward without annihilating casualties. 'At about 10 a.m. my sentry reported that the Germans were advancing along the trench into Lt Bolton's trench which meant that I would be cut off. A heavy rifle fire was now being poured into my parapet and the sentry could not watch – and then a cloud of gas came over the parapet. Unfortunately our respirators were not handy and as I knew reinforcements could not have had time to come up on my right and I was afraid of being cut off from behind, I gave the order to clear. Meanwhile the enemy had lengthened the range of his guns, and on leaving the communication trench we came under rifle and machine-gun fire, and eventually, more dead than alive, reached our supports. The shelling was very heavy and I can't make out how we escaped. The support trenches were at once converted into fire trenches.'

A Cameron officer in the positions adjacent to those described by Young wrote home of these days of fierce fighting and of one of the battalion's machine-gunners killing two Germans fleeing. 'We seem to have sickened the Huns of attacking Highlanders. They used gas fumes and trench mortars and innumerable guns but they could not break through.[10] Well might Cyril Falls refer to this 2nd Battle of Ypres as being: 'for its size one of the most murderous battles of the war'.[11]

As it happened, it was at the south-eastern head of the Ypres Salient at Hooge in July 1915 that the Germans introduced another weapon to the war, the flame-thrower. In the field message book of a subaltern of the 2/6 North Staffs the following notes are recorded: 'On 30 July the enemy attacked the 14th Division with fire squirts. The following particulars are extracted from the accounts of officers and men who were in the trenches. It was noticed that for some days before, the enemy was quiet and much more occupied with work, carrying timber about; also loopholes about 18in square and 10 feet apart were observed in the German parapets. At 3.30 a.m. liquid was squirted from nozzles in the direction of our trenches. Jets 30-40 yards long, about 20 altogether. Then the liquid was apparently lighted by throwing incendiary bombs. There was never a continuous wall of flame and the flames only lasted 4 minutes at most. No one was seriously burnt – very few burned at all. When flames went out there was dense smoke.' The notes, obviously from an

official source, are designed to be reassuring. 'There is nothing to fear from this device.'[12] It was not indeed a weapon which could make a major impact, but W. Hayes, a King's Royal Rifleman at Hooge when the flame-throwers were first used, has recalled that some who got out of the trench were in fact burned to death but not those who remained in the cover of the trench.[13]

While the German attack on the Ypres Salient was still in progress, the focus of Allied offensive intent was switched further south with a renewed struggle

Two 1st Battalion, Black Watch officers behind the lines at Le Touret, spring 1915. As he was six foot eleven and a half inches tall, Captain Hay would stand out in a crowd never mind in a pair – his companion is 2nd Lieutenant Jack Scott who on 9 May would lead his platoon into an attack on the German trenches at Richebourg and be posted as missing believed killed, as was in fact the case. (J. G. Scott)

for Aubers Ridge. As far as the British contribution was concerned, an insufficiency of heavy guns and high-explosive shells allowed the German positions to escape destruction and from them so terrible a fire was directed upon the advancing British troops that this battle on 9 May and its resumption further south at Festubert on 11 May were disasters without mitigation.

Second Lieutenant K. H. E. Moore (1/7 Bn Middlesex Regiment) referred in a letter to the 'terrible business of last Sunday'. Again planning had seemed to leave little to chance. Assembly trenches had been dug. Officers knew the infantry attack timetable and its relationship to the British bombardment. 'Sunday broke a glorious day with the corn and fields looking simply perfect. It was light at about three but it was not until five that the show was to start. The first line trenches in which we were and the assembly trenches were by this time simply packed with troops and of course it seemed an eternity waiting for our watches to point to five o'clock. However it came at last and to the very tick hundreds and hundreds of guns started pounding away on about a 2,000 yards front. The first 10 minutes were allotted for cutting the German wire by shrapnel and of course as we were only 50 yards from the German trenches we were in considerable danger from our own guns which like most other things are only human. The noise was terrific and the ground simply shook like a jelly. After 10 minutes on the wire the guns were turned on the parapets of the first and second line trenches and our heavy Lyddite and high-explosive shells simply blew them to hell. The German lines were a long sheet of flame and bursting shells. This went on for about ½ hour – we all waited anxiously for 5.40 at which time an enormous mine which ran under the first and second German lines opposite us and only 50 yards away was to be exploded. It was the largest mine ever made in the World and the charge of gun-cotton in it was prodigious. The engineers themselves didn't quite know what would happen and we weren't sure what would happen to us either. On the very stroke of 5.40 and in the middle of a frightful bombardment the button was pressed and up went their trenches. . . .' The writer saw the crater occupied by a charge from another battalion in the trenches with his unit and then, as the British shellfire lifted, the first and second assaulting lines in their attempt to advance across open ground were simply mown down by enfilading machine-gun fire. 'It was a terrible thing to watch line after line crumple up. Meanwhile the trenches were absolutely blocked with the dead, dying and wounded. If people at home really knew what a show like Sunday's was like. . . .' All the positions momentarily gained were retaken by German counter-attack though at considerable cost.[14]

On the very same day as Moore's letter, 2nd Lt B. U. S. Cripps (2nd Bn Welsh Regt) wrote of how easy it had all seemed in prior practice. What the Welsh Regiment subaltern had been told has for us today distressing similarities to the assurances officers and men would get a year later as final training was undertaken for the Somme. 'We were

5.50 a.m., Aubers Ridge, 9 May 1915. The British bombardment of the German trenches is under way. These men of 'C' Company, 1st Battalion, Cameronians are in support trenches behind Cellar Farm and with them is a Sapper about to depress the exploder to detonate a mine under the German positions about a hundred yards away. The officer who took this photograph, Robin Money, will be wounded and out of action by 7 a.m. in following up the assault troops. (Major General R. C. Money)

told that after the bombardment there would not be many people left in the German first and second line. We were all quite confident of the result and were very cheery. I got about 2 hours' sleep and then I had breakfast and plenty of rum and felt quite ready for any German. . . . My platoon was not to leave the trenches for two minutes after the first two platoons jumped up over the parapet ready to charge but they were met by a perfect hail of bullets and many men just fell back into the trenches riddled with bullets. A few survivors managed to get into one of the three water-filled ditches which ran through no man's land. Before the appointed time was up, the Company Commander told Cripps he had better see what his men could do. Two platoons went over their breastwork and of those not killed immediately a few got into the nearest ditch. No one got across the conspicuous white painted bridges put up by Engineers during the night. Cripps alone of his Company's officers survived unwounded. In the ditch from the banks of which grew willows, he had fifteen unwounded men and far too many wounded to carry through waist-deep water back into the British line. First they bound up the wounded and then, under shellfire and small arms fire from

Germans looking over their parapet, they dug a route back to the British line. 'It was absolutely past words, my best friends killed and we could not do anything.' The wretchedness Cripps felt as he wrote his letter was a compound of the shock at those losses, his having only 2 hour's sleep in forty hours, marching 20 miles to the breastwork system from which the assault was to be launched and then the physical effort and nervous stress of a day which had included what his letter had omitted, a dash over open ground to the British breastwork to tell of his intention of digging a way back and then his similarly chancy return to the ditch.[15]

It will not be assumed because we now move to the September/October Battle of Loos that the British line remained quiescent in the three central months of the year. Even though the Gallipoli campaign was commanding major resources which seemed at that time, as well as in historical debate, to have an ill-considered relationship to the spring and then autumn Allied offensive in France – there were quite simply neither the men nor the matériel for two major campaigns at the same time – the maintenance of an offensive spirit under the resented constraint of static warfare gave a special meaning to the mislead-

ingly passive-sounding 'holding the line'.

The Battle of Loos was planned to be the British element in a great French design to launch convergent attacks on the troublesome German-held Noyon Salient. Neither the location nor the timing of the offensive was welcome to the High Command of the BEF, but the reality of coalition war saw Britain dancing to a French tune. Of the tragic evolution of the planning of an unwanted battle much has been written: what was it like to face the music?[16]

In a coal-mining area where the slag heaps supplemented German observation from their generally higher positions on the two natural ridges overlooking pit villages and pit head gear, six British divisions would attack. It was hoped that German defence would be seriously incapacitated by chlorine gas emitted from over 5,000 cylinders secretly installed

This mounted sergeant was an unusual soldier; Francis Powell had served as an officer in the Welsh Regiment during the 2nd Boer War, was in Canada in 1914 and rejoined the colours as a private in the Lord Strathcona Horse. He was awarded the Distinguished Conduct Medal for his bravery as a dismounted corporal at Festubert in 1915 and by the end of the war he was Captain Powell, MC, DCM. (Captain F. C. Powell)

In action, 9 May 1915. The crew of No. '2' gun of the 5th Mountain Battery, 3rd Mountain Artillery Brigade, Indian Army, firing on the slight rise of Aubers Ridge, not quite the sort of terrain for which these 3-pounders were designed. (G. W. Sissons)

5th Battalion, South Staffs at Wolverghem in 1915. Peering out from the left is Sergeant Gorse who will be commissioned; next to him is Bill Mather who will be wounded on 13 October 1915 and will die from his wounds. After the man with the extreme Army haircut is a soldier who will be discharged as unfit and then, nearest the photographer, is Private Tonkinson (Tonky), much respected by his officer, 2nd Lieutenant Wilkinson, but who will 'disappear into the beyond' on 13 October of that year. (Captain F. Wilkinson)

for a maximum surprise effect. There were not enough heavy guns, there were insufficient high-explosive shells and for these factors the gas was designed to compensate. In fact there was insufficient gas, smoke was used as a supplement, and worse still, the meteorological conditions conspired to make the whole gas-orientated basis of the attack dubiously justifiable. The last entries in Captain E. C. Deane's diary for 24 September express a sense of foreboding. 'We are waiting to go up and do the charge. I imagine we will be a lot weaker coming home if we ever see billets again. I think this anticipation is almost worst for the men who have been through a show before. . . . I fear the wind is blowing the wrong way at present.' He was to be killed on the morrow.[17]

Over the front of the main assault from the La Bassée Canal, south to the village of Loos itself, and in the associated diversionary attacks, there were officers and men more sanguine than Deane. 'I have never seen the men more cheerful. They had all been told, days before, exactly what they were to do, and what was expected of them, but they sang and cheered as they marched as I would not have thought possible for troops who knew that in a few hours they would be the first over the parapet. . . .'[18]

In some units, officers as well as men in assaulting battalions seem to have been dreadfully overburdened. 'One is really like a small Christmas tree . . . one waterbottle, one haversack, maps and message books, one pair of wire cutters, one trench digger, one clasp knife, one pair of binoculars, one compass, one mess tin, one bandolier, one ammunition pouch, one revolver, one belt and slings, one great coat, one knapsack – oh also a periscope and I have a telescope and four bombs [grenades].'[19]

Almost seventy-five thousand troops were involved in the main attack. At 05.59 on 25 September the taps on the cylinders of chlorine gas were turned on but the atmospheric conditions were such that the gas did not surge swiftly from the nozzles of the pipes laid into no man's land. Instead of its moving towards the German trenches it seemed to linger and then drift across the front of the waiting British troops. Along the whole battlefront the effect was variable. On some sectors objectives were gained and legends made like that of the football kicked across no man's land by 1/18 London Regiment or of the inspiration derived from the bagpipes of Piper Laidlaw of the 7th Bn King's Own Scottish Borderers when fearful losses seemed to have destroyed all forward movement by that battalion, but nowhere were decisive gains achieved. All too frequently the experience of those who survived was one of confusion, bewilderment and worse. 'We soon realized that we did not know where we were going. The gas hung in a thick pall over everything, it was impossible to see more than ten yards. In vain I looked for my landmarks in the German line to guide me to the right spot but the smoke was impenetrable.'[20] This was from the officer whose unit had been so precisely told 'exactly what they were to do'.

In the south, the small mining village of Loos, its double slag heap and Hill 70 behind it were all taken but then, descending that hill, the British troops were faced with the undestroyed wire of the newly prepared German second line. No further progress could be made and despite the use of every imagin-

able improvised weapon for close fighting, by for example the 6th Camerons, German counterattacks wrested back the ground the Scots had gained. General Sir Philip Christison, then a lieutenant with the Camerons, has recorded axes, bill hooks, clubs and a 7-foot bomb-slinging catapult being used in hours of combat which cost in killed, wounded and missing all but two of the officers and 750 men.[21]

North of Loos, the Royal Sussex Regiment was one of the units facing the village of Hulluch. A soldier's diary records an attack which simply disintegrated. 'Over we got and advanced about 400 yards only to be met by clouds of gas and a murderous rifle fire from the Germans. Our men were falling fast, some gassed, some shot and some almost blown to pieces.'[22]

As if inevitability were not sufficiently cruel, further losses were incurred by the decision of the officer in command of the 1st Division to send reserves without artillery support to attack the Lone Tree Sector where all assaults had failed. Human capital was ruinously expended in this ill-directed gamble. Further north still, Hohenzollern Redoubt was captured. It was a 300-yard-long, convex-fronted strong point of wired entrenchments in front of tunnels, shelters, observation posts and machine-

Loos. The village, the 'Tower Bridge' pithead gear, a slag heap and midway between the roof tops and the horizon line, a chalk-edged German support trench. This photograph was taken from the British lines shortly before the battle. In a IV Corps Bulletin dated 3 September it is reported that: 'A new second line German trench is being made. . . . It is at present very shallow'. On 25 September what is seen in the foreground of this picture was captured, but the new German second line effectively shut the door on any further success. (H. E. Bridgen)

The 'Shiny Seventh' in the gloom of battle: Loos, 25 September 1915 and a rare photograph of the 1st/7th London Regiment advancing behind a gas cloud in front of Cité St-Elie two miles north of Loos itself. In this sector the gas and smoke did assist the British attack. (M. Wray)

Loos: the second day. This sketch of the 8th Lincolns attacking Hill 70 on 26 September 1915 was painted by the Officer in Command of 'D' Company, Captain L. McNaught Davis. This officer was wounded and captured in the action. In 1918 he was released into Dutch internment and there, in April, produced this sketch. (Captain L. McNaught Davis)

gun nests in a slag heap. There had been fearful losses particularly at a spot where enfilade machine-gun fire caught concentrations of men helpless before undestroyed wire. Wholesale failure attended all efforts on the most northerly flank. Here, two British mines were exploded, but they simply warned rather than inconvenienced the Germans. The attacking infantry had to move through their own gas, their exertions resulting in the misting over of the mica eye-pieces in their primitive helmets. Those who found their way between the mine craters and over other obstacles were only to win a greater certainty of wounding or death as they approached aimed fire behind undestroyed wire.

Tragedy compounded tragedy. High Command mishandled the question of the Reserves in several aspects. Two of the units concerned were New Army Divisions, the 21st and 24th. They were less than three weeks out of England and they had marched forty miles towards their point of concentration. They were then required to march for a third night on congested narrow roads totally inadequate for the troops and vehicle traffic they were bearing. Every

description of accident and misadventure ensued. Captain R. L. Bradley of the Queen's wrote home of the frustrations of the 24th Division's march. 'As soon as we got on the move we got stopped. This went on continuously, stoppages occurring about every 12 yards. Then we would move on 100 yards and then stop again for half an hour. Finally we arrived at a junction of roads where a distraught staff officer was trying to organize the thing. Our column you see got mixed up with a lot of motor transport lorries coming by the other road and in front there was a battalion of infantry and an ammunition column each bent on getting somewhere.'[23]

After these tribulations the divisions had still six miles to cover on the morning of 25 September before they reached their point of deployment East of Vermelles. Again there had been delays on over-crowded roads. In heavy rain the men formed up again that evening for a final cross-country march over the British trench system and then no man's land. Burning villages disfigured the landscape, everywhere there were sights and smells and the continuing sounds of battle. To the physical demand of the days of marching under difficult conditions was being added the emotional stress of the open evidence of what they were approaching. There could have been no helpful initiation for what would follow, but they had already been marked by mis-fortune.

During the rain and mist of the night, the New Army artillery got ahead of its appointed position and was exposed to the enemy batteries and could thus give no effective support when in broad daylight the two divisions attacked. Each had a 1,000-yard front and, in extended order, line after line approached re-wired, re-fortified German positions held by greatly reinforced numbers. The Battle of Loos had already been lost, but smoke, noise and destruction hid this from High Command: the début of the New Army in frontal assault on undestroyed wire and strongly held positions could not be arrested. A German regimental diary records what happened. 'Never had machine-gunners had such straightforward work to do, nor done it so effectively. They traversed to and fro along the enemy's ranks unceasingly. The men stood on the firesteps, some even on the parapets, and fired triumphantly into the mass of men advancing across the open grassland. As the entire field of fire was covered with the enemy's infantry, the effect was devastating and they could be seen falling in hundreds.'[24] To make matters still worse, the British artillery was under-ranging and shelling their own troops.

The barbed wire barrier was nearly nineteen feet wide and about four feet high. Long-spiked, thick wire, the unconquerable nature of which defies imagination limited by what one might encounter today keeping cattle in a field. Shellfire had cut no gaps in this wire, wirecutters were completely ineffectual. Some men, ignoring gashes being torn in their hands, arms and bodies, attempted by strength and athleticism to clamber on and over the wire by the stakes which fixed it so mercilessly immovable. Such efforts were foredoomed and the awful image of men hanging on the wire was further etched into

individual and so national consciousness.[25]

All accounts, personal and official, pay tribute to the bearing and conduct of men of the Guards Division marching up through chaos, not now to support a breakthrough but to stabilize a situation of great danger in the event of a major German counter-attack. It is not surprising that some Guardsmen recorded unflattering descriptions of what they had seen of the New Army performance. 'Most deplorable of all was seeing able-bodied Englishmen with nothing more wrong with them than mud on their clothes, coming the wrong way in straggling parties. The less said the better.'[26] The judgement was harsh, needs qualification and was not made in full knowledge of the circumstances, but no doubt, too much had been required of men who certainly paid a cruel price for their inexperience and, more significantly, for the nature of war in 1915.

The offensive was maintained until mid-October and on that date an entry in the diary of a Coldstream Guards officer nicely summarized the result of so much endeavour. 'We have effected very little.'[27] For those who experienced it and survived, Loos expunged the last of any lingering vestiges of innocence about the nature of battle experience in France. Only the introduction of vast numbers of men new to active service, uplifted by high morale and the evidence of seemingly phenomenal support in the form of artillery, could allow such naïvety to re-emerge – precisely such circumstances were to obtain in June of the following year in the relatively unscarred, fertile fields, sleepy villages and quiet woods of the valleys and sub-valleys of the Somme and the Ancre.

It does not look as if the men in authority who approved this design for their Christmas card envisaged a repetition twelve months later of the 1914 Christmas Truce. (L. Thomas)

A MERRY XMAS.

THE Bomber's Greeting
IX Corps 1915

Up to The Line, in The Line and out of The Line

'Early on Thursday morning we were woken up and told to be ready to march off in 2 hours. We had a snatch of breakfast and eventually our marching orders did not come till ten. Everything of course was packed up. We had a most glorious march through picturesque country, simply snow clad. It was ideal for marching. We did sixteen miles and stayed the night at [self censored]. By the time we arrived it was all we could do to stand in view of the sharp frost.' From a railhead, or a camp of Nissen huts or from rest billets, all troops marched up to the line and in this particular case the weather on the second day providing changed circumstances for the march. 'Before we had gone two miles we were in the worst snow storm I have ever seen. The roads were awful. We had to leave all our transport behind and we also left half our poor men straggling behind. It was simply too awful for words. We arrived 8 p.m. frozen up to our eyes in snow having taken 10 hours to do thirteen miles and walking knee deep the whole way.' Scavenging for food became necessary as the transport of this battalion, the 9th King's Royal Rifles, arrived more than a day late – nevertheless Captain de Courcy Ireland added in his letter of 27th February 1916: 'We shall probably go up to the trenches earlier than anticipated owing to the cold spell as men cannot stick it long at a time.'[1]

Under less severe weather conditions, the battalion's transport with the field cookers would have provided the men with a hot meal at the end of a day's march when billets had been reached and furthermore a billeting party would have gone ahead of the column to arrange with either military or civil authorities night accommodation for officers and

Tree-lined *pavé* without end. The 6th Battalion, South Staffs in their ten minutes each hour respite from marching on the awkward-shaped cobblestones which, with ill-fitting new boots, were responsible for so much footsoreness among the troops moving up to or away from the line. (Brigadier H. L. Graham)

men if a town or sizeable village were to have been their staging point. In an entirely rural area, billeting negotiations would have taken place with farmers or of course the advance party might well have found vacated half-ruined farm buildings near the support trenches. If a battalion were to have been accommodated on a farm, Captain de Courcy Ireland's accommodation would have been in the farm house itself at a rate of one franc, that of his men in a barn for five centimes a man, 20 centimes if straw bedding were provided. Subsequently the farmer would have presented to the military authorities in his area the signed certificate he had been given showing the payment to which he was entitled.

The system was liable to abuse and inevitably, soldier/civilian relations were brought too close to avoid fractious discord over the state of the 'billet', theft of farm produce, extortion for 'extras' which might include use of a water pump, or molesting of the women on a farm or in the potentially close juxtaposition of town billets.[2] Factories, schools and large public buildings in a town were earmarked by a British Town Major working with the local mayor to take the 800 or so men of a battalion, and a soldier could expect to have experienced a wide variety of billet accommodation in a year's service in France.

In May 1915, numbers of green-painted London buses took the 11th Bn King's Liverpool Regiment in convoy fashion towards the Ypres Salient to be billeted at Vlamertinghe in the grounds of a chateau. William Jaeger, a bugler, shared with another man a self-made bivouac of newly cut thick branches placed to support the men's oilskins tied together to make a roof. This open-air camp became a morass after heavy rain in June and the battalion was moved into Ypres; some men into a ruined cavalry barracks, some into the prison, others into a convent or an old magazine. So heavily was Ypres now being shelled that the men were pleased when they were instructed to build dugouts for themselves on the banks of the canal. Jaeger's Company ('D' Coy) constructed dugouts under the shelter of a row of houses using bricks and timber from the houses and soil from the excavation to provide fair protection against shelling. The interior was made as comfortable as possible with bedding and articles obtained from the houses. Civilian shirts and underwear were worn, the men not hesitating about wearing women's silk underclothing though soon such luxury would be sullied by lice. 'A common sight on a summer's afternoon was to see a row of men sitting on the tow path naked with their clothing turned inside out, every one busy with the slaughter of lice – some burning the seams with a lighted candle and others

The billet of Captain James Walker of the 4th Battalion, Duke of Wellington's Regiment in May 1915, was at Fleurbaix in the home of Belgians, seen here in their kitchen. For officers and men of this West Riding Territorial battalion raised in and around Cleckheaton, Fleurbaix would provide differences and similarities. Adjustments would be required as indeed they would for the Belgian townsfolk. (Lieutenant Colonel J. Walker)

making good use of their thumb nails and all the time passing jokes about the supposed size and colour of the vermin.'[3]

A more rural setting was enjoyed by the 21st Bn Royal Fusiliers early in the following year near St Omer. 'We were billeted in the farm buildings while the CO, the Adjutant and the Sgt Major were in the farmhouse. Actually we in the transport were all housed in a long shed, quite comfortable, plenty of fresh clean straw and three tables on which we have our meals. This is a large farm and in the centre of the buildings there is the usual pit of manure which is being lowered daily as carts take it away to the fields.'[4] In another rural location, tents in a field, the men were to be fleetingly more fortunate still. 'Our Sergeant went scouting round the vicinity on one of the horses and on his return told three of us that he had found a farm in the neightbourhood and fixed up for a consideration (cash, tins of bully beef, a pick axe and 2 shovels) for an outhouse on the farm. This was not too clean but we set about it and soon had it cleaned and smelling of disinfectant. The farm was run by a widow and her three daughters all good looking. The Sergeant slept in the farmhouse and after two days I found out that my two mates had

A Belgian farm at Lessines, recently the home of German officers, men and horses (see German Stencil) now becomes a billet for the 2/4 Royal West Surreys. Note the three gold bar wound stripes on the left arm of one of the soldiers in the front and the fact that the men on each side of him have four stripes at the base of their right sleeves indicating their years of service. At the top left is Captain R. B. Bannerman, MC. (S. W. Vinter)

fixed up with two of the daughters to sleep with them leaving the youngest one for me. I was indeed sorry when we were moved back to Beavrais.'[5] A more tragic liaison than the one above happily recalled by Tom Newsome, was that of an Army meteorologist whose farm billeting led to an idyllic love affair in a pastoral setting. All was shattered in an instant when the girl was blown to bits by the explosion of a shell, but this passionate joy and the searing sorrow were remembered by the survivor into his tenth decade.[6]

The 1915 letters of 2nd Lt D. Storrs Fox (6th Bn Sherwood Foresters) are unusually illustrative of many aspects of billeting circumstances. 'We detrained about 6 a.m. this morning and marched four or five miles to this village where we waited about some time for billets as the occupants had not cleared out. B Coy is billeted in four big barns at 3 farms near together. I got my platoon into their billet soon after 10, dug latrines and then made them wash and shave and clean their rifles. After a dinner of bully and military biscuit I held a rifle and face inspection.' Storrs Fox relates that he is in the farm, sleeping in the same room as the Sergeant Major, in fact giving the latter the only bed in the room as 'I had my valise and flea bag. The place seems quite clean and the farmer is very obliging, but there are rats as is shown by the hole gnawed in my bedroom ceiling. . . . I find talking French a great trial. The farmer is a most loquacious fellow. I can usually understand the drift when he has said it about three times. He understands me when I can think of the

words to say, but often I am at a loss for them.'

In another farm billet we learn from these letters that the officers take turns to sleep in the barn with the men and Storrs Fox found the straw-strewn floor of a barn more comfortable than his farmhouse bed which, accordingly, he forsook. It was not the only sleeping-place he would shun. In a mill town he slept on the floor of an estaminet until, on the following day, he saw the locals spitting on the floor. He then joined the men sleeping on bales of flax in a big mill.[7]

When actually moving into the line, the system of reserve, support and front line trenches would be reached by long winding communication trenches. The relief of units in the line would be effected at night to avoid the risk of German aerial observation. Fully equipped, the men would trudge along the duck-boards laid on the floor of the trenches giving some purchase to their feet. Halts allowed other burdened men to file past or hurrying, stumbling stretcher-bearers to proceed to a regimental aid post and then the rear. The journey for the incomers could seem interminable and, if they were new to the experience, fraught with apprehensive excitement at actually being under shellfire.

It is unwise to generalize about conditions in front-line trenches because so much would depend upon the local geography, the season, the weather, the degree of military activity. Some sectors required the throwing up of sandbagged breastworks because the high water table of the land precluded effective digging of cover. In others, trenches ran through and

April 1915. Support positions created out of the ruins of a small Belgian Village, Le Touquet on the River Lys. Basil Church, leaning against the wall sucking his pipe, is watching the construction of a catapult the use of which indicates the proximity of the enemy – in fact sixty yards away. This catapult was probably constructed from plans made available by the London store, Gammages. (B. H. Church)

utilized miner's ruined cottages or petered out in the morass of marshy river banks. Sections of interwoven wattle or timbered boarding shored up trench sides which were liable even without shellfire destruction to slip ruinously into the walkway, heavier baulks of timber or corrugated iron sheeting roofed dug-outs excavated into the inner face of the forward wall of the trench.

A firestep allowed both observation and firing from a parapet which might be loopholed by various steel-shuttered devices or from which, by periscope, no man's land could be surveyed. It was a sniper's duty to operate from and to fire against enemy use of such means of viewing a battle zone which in daylight was empty of all but barbed wire and the human and material debris of broken attacks or of unlucky night patrols and wiring parties revealed by flares and caught by traversing machine-gun fire.

Zigzags, or more properly, traverses in the trench made quick movement along the line difficult but were essential to avoid, in the event of the capture of a section of the line, enemy-installed machine-gun fire commanding the length of the trench. Shell blast shockwaves from a direct hit were also contained by the traverses. A parados raised above the rear of the trench offered some protection and further shuttered the soldier beneath his quite remarkably limited all-round horizon. With no refinements whatsoever, at intervals a trench would be sapped forward into no man's land to a small excavated listening and observing post where lonely duty would be served.

Natural needs would be answered by latrine tins or pits situated in offshoots to the rear of the main trench and permanently associated with the all-pervading odour of chloride of lime the spreading of which (together with the emptying of the biscuit tin buckets) was the unenviable duty of a Sanitary Squad or of men in the Pioneer Battalions.

On a cold wet day in May 1916, Louis Maude (10th KOYLI) wrote of life in his dugout and trench surroundings in a vein as one might to a male cousin – F. B. Chavasse, soon to be in France himself with the RAMC. 'It is a nasty wet chalky dugout full of rats and creeping things. Last week a "sausage" landed just outside it and removed a man. A bit of his water-bottle was found 100 yards away but otherwise he has not been seen since. The Hun is very active and sends over coveys of rifle grenades at most inconvenient places and hours. The trenches have been shockingly neglected and strafed and we have to work like hell to get them at all into shape. It is rather hard as the men have to stand to all night and have to work in their equipment and with their rifles. It is also very hard to get stakes, timber and other stores. There is one stretch here which was pretty well flattened out when we came in and I never go down it without wondering which way up I shall come out. We have been working at it for a week and now no crawling and not much stooping is necessary. I hate their furking rifle grenades. They are much more dangerous than shells and they have any number of them. Ours are not so good, they are often duds and are inclined when they do go off to burst in the rifle. . . . To crown our troubles the Acting Brigadier General, Col. of another KOYLI Bn came round the trenches and found 1) a smelly latrine 2) an officer who didn't salute him and 3) sentries who didn't stand up to attention as he passed. As though anyone ever paid [military] compliments in the trenches. He had us because an absurd Divisional Order months old which no one ever keeps about saluting and button polishing in the trenches was still uncancelled. So he stopped all leave for the Bn for a fortnight. . . . [The 10th Bn's CO complained and the leave was reinstated]. . . . Yesterday I was going down an old strafed communication trench and smelt the man I mentioned who left his water-bottle behind last week. The place was a long way from where the sausage landed. In the evening I had a look round on the top and there he was right enough which shows that German sausages have some pepper in them.'[8]

Under certain conditions, work and even movement in trenches could be difficult in the extreme even without the intervention of the enemy. 'The last four nights I have spent until the early hours of the morning laying out telephone lines and exploring places to put them in disused trenches behind the fire trench. It needs great physical exertion to get through trenches when they have fallen in. One bit may be water up to the thighs and in another you have to climb over a fallen-in part, yet another part is filled with the most awful mud imaginable. Your feet stick into it well above the knees with a sickening squelch and it holds you like glue when you try to pull your leg out. Water we can pump out, earth we can shovel out but the sticky mud is a terrible job (defeating pumps and shovels). The only way is to fill buckets by handfuls and empty them by scooping out with the hand. No really efficient means have been discovered of keeping the trenches drained [if there were no natural fall in the ground]. Large sump holes collect some of it but a day or two's rain and they are as bad as ever. It needs constant work to keep the trenches in order and large numbers of men.'[9]

Not 'Old Bill' but E. M. Dixon, a soldier in the Cheshire Regiment emerging from a front line dugout at Kemmel in the Ypres Salient in about March 1915. (Lieutenant Colonel A. H. Jolliffe)

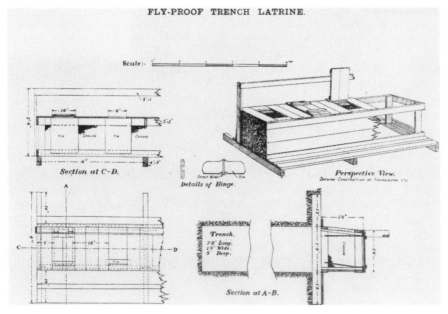

FLY-PROOF TRENCH LATRINE.

Scale:-

Section at C-D.

Details of Hinge.

Perspective View.
Showing Construction of Framework etc.

Trench.
7.6' Long,
1.6' Wide,
6' Deep.

Section at A-B.

Unrealizable ideal. In 'Fourth Army Standing Orders' printed in June 1917 this diagram illustrated in splendid detail the approved method of sanitation for the trenches. Few men in the line will have been seated so comfortably. (J. MacMurray)

Corporal Robert Iley with the Yeoman Rifles (21st KRRC) was introduced to the front line in the spring of 1915 at Ploegsteert. He found the trenches 'a model of neatness in a wood. Duck-boards led through the support lines where huts were built amongst the trees and after about half a mile there was a well built barricade of sandbags into the front line. More duck-boards led to Battalion HQ and to Company HQ and the front line. Everything was smart and quiet when we went in but we didn't kid the enemy. He put up a banner "Welcome to the 41st Division". . . . Next morning an officer, inexperienced like the rest of us, paraded his platoon for inspection. The Germans spotted us and we had our first casualties. We runners were sent all over the place and dead soldiers were sewn into blankets and one identity disc tied around each man's neck. My job was to go to the local Military Cemetery behind the wood and arrange for graves to be dug. I was horrified. Our joiners made lovely wooden crosses with KRRC badges but it was all horrible.'[10]

Two stretcher-bearers of the 24th Londons, G. W. Jarvis and H. E. Friend, wrote of their time in the breastwork front line near Festubert. With their stretcher adjacent, but carrying a medical haversack as well as rifle and infantry equipment, they 'stood to' from dawn until full light, alert against attack. After the order to 'Stand down', a small piece of bacon would be fried in a mess-tin lid, tea made on a small pile of wood chips. Water would in all probability have been in very short supply perhaps limited to a bottle a day for all purposes – washing, shaving and drinking. 'During the day we were, for the most part, kept busy as sentries or renewing small arms ammunition supplies and cleaning up the trenches, but it was not clever to show too much movement in the day-time as snipers were very active on this front for the slightest sign of movement above the parapet. . . . After the evening "stand to", men from each company were detailed for ration fatigues or working parties, the former meant going back some two or more miles to where the supplies were unloaded from the limbers and returning with them to Company HQ for issue.' The men in the working parties had to collect picks and shovels from Battalion HQ and then clamber out into no man's land for wiring repair work, the degree of danger of such work being dependent not simply on the width of no man's land in that sector, but also on the degree of hostile activity.[11]

As an illustration of this, a former sapper remembers that in one sector where the opposing trench systems were particularly close: 'We used to do our repairs at the same time as they did. When we finished we signalled Jerry and he used to signal us with one rifle shot and we then scrambled back to our trenches.'[12]

Breast-works in Ploegsteert wood, Ypres Salient. At this stage of the war early in 1915 the wood retains its branches and foliage. In the undergrowth, just off the picture to the right, is the grave of a Corporal of the Somerset Light Infantry killed at the end of 1914. The positions here are currently held by the 8th Battalion, the South Lancashire Regiment. (Captain J. E. Hibbert)

They were of course quiet sectors determined above all by High Command's lack of aggressive intent in that area and then beneath that level of authority by informally developed arrangements as suggested above. Live and let live accord, would never be officially sanctioned, but it could and did happen. Its prevalence should not be exaggerated and the action of three men on 12 December 1915 who 'walked out and met Germans half way and exchanged cigarettes for cigars' could only be expected to produce ructions and the issue of an order that 'all Germans are to be shot on sight'. The Medical Officer who recorded this in his diary and who described the fact that men from the battalion to which he was attached were not firing upon Germans standing outside their flooded trenches and no fire was directed upon his men similarly exposed in consequence of the elements, could not help but add, 'Surely we won't bring the war nearer an end this way?'[13]

What brought the war to an end for many, was the constant activity of snipers. Captain E. A. S. Oldham (7th Bn Seaforth Highlanders) regularly recorded in a personal diary the work of his precisely posted snipers and the entries read almost as a game bag: 'Sniper MacRae shot an old German, white haired with spectacles and a red band round a blue cap'[14] and Captain D. Storrs Fox (6th Bn Sherwood Foresters) with a background of country pursuits in Derbyshire, took readily to sniping and the posting of snipers. He wrote to his mother on 23 March 1915 'I was lent a regular little gem of a rifle with telescopic sights. I did what the best snipers do and went into hiding-places outside the trench – a ruined cottage or an old trench, grass grown and forgotten . . . Sometimes they signal a "miss" with a spade.

When one of my men (my best sniper) was sniping, one of the Germans in signalling a miss exposed his arm. My man had another shot ready and brought the signal to an abrupt end.'[15]

It should not be entirely surprising, on psychological grounds, that there is evidence that work in no man's land at night on patrol or wiring was considered by some to be an enjoyable and exciting experience, that is of course if one were to come out unscathed! John Fraser (7th Bn Gordon Highlanders) wrote in October 1917 of a ' "ticklish job" putting up wire in front of one of our posts' but he had had 'very good men out with me and we got the job done quite successfully. These jobs are very exciting to begin with but after doing one or two one gets quite accustomed to them. I think nothing about them now. I am feeling as fit as a fiddle and really am quite enjoying this spell.'[16] Very different was the case of R. N. Bell (Pte 15th West Yorks) who was in a wiring party caught either by the noise made by reeling-out barbed wire and twisting into the ground the corkscrew stakes to hold it, or observed in the light of a flare. 'Suddenly a machine-gun opened up accurately on us causing some casualties including the man lying next to me in the covering party who was hit in the shoulder. By the time we had struggled with our wounded through the wire and found the diagonally arranged gap in the breastwork to regain its protection, one of the party,

'What the sniper saw'. Here, in June 1915, the Belgian frontier village of Le Touquet contains opposing front line trenches. On the left the two British soldiers are merely posing for the camera, the third man is sniping through a loophole. On the right, through the loophole, is the sniper's view of the German positions twenty-five yards away. (B. C. Church)

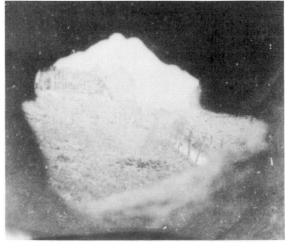

Sniping from No. 120 Breastwork trench, Ploegsteert Wood, 1915. Lieutenant Earl (South Lancs Regiment) is aiming the periscope-sight mounted rifle. (Captain J. E. Hibbert)

who had been hit in the leg, had lost so much blood that he died almost immediately.'[17]

A similarly tragic circumstance, but one brought about differently is recorded in Captain E. C. Deane's diary for 31 July 1915. This Medical Officer had: 'a tricky job the other night. The Germans are about 300 yards away and we have listening-posts out about 100 yards. A patrol went out beyond them at night to crawl out and try to bag a German. Coming in a young Tommy at the post got frightened and fired at about 10 yard's range and shot Copeman through the arm and a Cpl through the stomach and spine. He lay out yelling and I went out with two S.B.s and brought him in across the open.'[18]

The purposes of patrolling are nicely listed in the acutal instructions issued for such a patrol by the Colonel of the 11th Border Regiment. An officer, 2nd Lt McDonald, was to take L Cpl Skelton and Pte Evans and to find the position of an enemy post, the likely strength by which it was held, its nature whether it were for machine-gun use, listening or was an actual strong point. He had to report on whether the post were wired at both the front and the flank, the nature of the surrounding ground and the 'best way of attacking post by surprise'. McDonald was instructed not to attack the position but if an enemy patrol were to be encountered 'you should attack without hesitation'. This particular patrol was to be back within two hours and for its purpose the men were to blacken their bayonets and the officer alone was to carry bombs.[19]

When a patrol of six men and an NCO was led into no man's land by E. G. Bates in August 1916, his instructions were that on no account was the enemy to be engaged. They started off from a forward bombing sap then crawled 200 yards across open ground. In a destroyed wood, they cautiously explored an unrecorded trench and its dugouts. It proved to have been abandoned. On their return by a different route, they heard a German party making its way out towards the British lines. Concealed in a shell-hole, Bates's Northumberland Fusiliers waited until the enemy patrol was almost upon them, then opened fire. 'We put 40 rounds rapid into them and also hurled 20 bombs. They were completely taken by surprise and after the row had died away, we crept out. By the aid of star-shells and faint moonlight we counted ten of them – all dead. I went through all their pockets but didn't get much in the way of papers – they take care of that. The men collected trophies of course and filled their pockets and caps and trousers with things. Then we started back.'[20]

In moving from no man's land patrolling to trench raids, it must be understood that the latter operations could be on a large scale involving several thousand men with the necessary artillery support or it could be well below Company strength of 250 men. To secure prisoners on the night of 4/5 June 1917 2nd Lt Jones (2nd Bedfords) took twenty other ranks with him. The party was to be given Lewis gun and rifle covering fire on its flanks as it attempted briefly to seize a section of enemy front-line trench and its forward sap. As it happened, the small parties attempting to establish blocks to isolate the Germans got 'hung up on the wire' and the officer leading the raid, having got into the enemy trench which was 'merry hell' for a few minutes, managed to get a prisoner, send him back under escort and then blow the recall whistle. In addition to the prisoner taken, the officer estimated a high number of casualties

Morning reveals two Germans from an unsuccessful night raiding party at Givenchy. ('Realistic Travels', Photo Series/ P.H.L. Archives)

from the surprise bombing inflicted upon the Germans and additionally the destruction of an enemy machine-gun. The Bedfords lost five men killed and eight wounded but returned.[21]

Operations ordered for a two-battalion raid in September 1917 were planned to achieve far more than the capture of prisoners – the seizure and consolidation into the Allied system, of an enemy section of front line trench. The orders specify the roles of 'fighters, moppers and diggers' in this operation. There were wiring parties, men carrying stores, signallers establishing land lines, runners for the earliest communications, Lewis gunners and bombers, all, apart from the runners, heavily burdened with the 'tools of their trade'. Despite metallic encumbrance, 'every possible precaution is to be taken that there is no noise whilst the battalion is forming up. Men must be specially warned about this and steps taken to ensure that there is no loose equipment which might rattle. Mess tins are to be carried in the haversack.' In a nice afterthought under final operation orders: 'chewing gum is being issued as a prevention to coughing'.[22]

Official 'Trench Orders', issued at different levels of authority from Army down to Battalion, imposed a degree of disciplined routine for service in the line and these orders have much to tell us about everyday life. For the Third Army, concerning sentry duty by night: 'In places which have the reputation of being dangerous, i.e., where enemy are suspected of mining, advanced posts, etc., no man should ever be posted alone. There should either be a double sentry post or the next relief should rest within kicking distance of the sentry.' On the subject of rifles: 'In very cold weather sentries will occasionally work the bolt of the rifle to prevent the striker becoming frozen.' For the same reason in cold weather men were to sleep with their rifles close to the body . . . . 'On no account is the rifle to be used for the purpose of carrying camp kettles and other loads.'

'Stand to will take place one hour before daylight and one hour before dark. At this parade every available man will be present. Rifles, ammunition, equipment, clothing will be inspected. The firing position of every man will be tested.' It is interesting to note that except in emergencies, concealment requirements dictated that machine-guns would not be fired from their regular emplacements, but before dusk each gun would be laid on some particular spot to facilitate use in emergency.

Rum was only to be issued in the presence of an officer and usually in the early morning. 'Men undergoing punishment for drunkenness will receive no issue of rum for fourteen days after the offence, unless it is necessary for medical reasons,' the latter point being in line with concern for men in the front line during long cold nights for 'arrangements should be made to ensure that soup or some hot drink is available for the men between midnight and 4 a.m.'[23]

From early days in the war, men got protection from the cold by the issue of sheepskin coats, Balaclava helmets and cap comforters. Fires in proper braziers or hole-punched tins brought some comfort too though the danger of asphyxiation by the fumes of burning coke in unventilated dugouts was real as was the factor that smoke or glare at night might attract enemy shelling. On this point, salvage parties scavenging for fuel, in for example the Festubert area of runined buildings through which the trenches ran, could lead to shellfire because the men were observed or heard at their work.[24]

Of the problems affecting physical efficiency in the trenches like for example the amalgam of ailments generally known as trench fever, none approached the seriousness of the incidence of trench foot. This painful condition could develop from unrelieved duty in ill-drained trenches and the greatest efforts were made to prevent it by insisting upon individual responsibility to take the necessary precautions of washing thoroughly, drying and then whale-oiling the feet. The responsiblity had to be exercised in a supervisory sense at subaltern level too, but of course trench circumstances were so frequently against preventative measures that the problem remained till the Armistice as witnessed by the idealistic 1918 admonition that twice weekly feet inspections should be with the 'Battalion Chiropodist in attendance.'[25]

From feet to the inner man – the soldiers' bread came up from the rear in a sandbag plentifully accompanied by sand and grit in consequence. Bread might well be in short supply depending upon local circumstance and it would be supplemented by army biscuit. F. P. Roe has written of the standard 1915 procedure in his platoon being to fill a mess tin with the scarce drinking water available, bring it to the boil on a brazier and put in the iron hard biscuit. By pounding and stirring, a porridgy consistency would develop and into this would be emptied the contents of a stabbed-open tin of Tickler's Jam. The resultant mixture was called Pozzy – this and bully beef and later the popular meat and vegetable stew 'Machonachies' were standard fare supplemented on occasion by bacon to fry in a mess tin. Tea, ready mixed with sugar, would be further sweetened by condensed milk and was the universal drink.[26]

If, with the rations, there were to come up personal parcels, then, like mail in the trenches, such surprises were especially to be welcomed. Well away from canteens, estaminets, shops or stalls, a cake or chocolate would bring immediate cheer to rank and file, consumed with no less enjoyment that the range of Harrods' or privately-packed parcels which made an officer's meal in the Mess dugout by guttering candle that fraction nearer to what he may have been accustomed. R. B. Marshall, an officer with the 7th Bn East Surreys, was pleased to receive Port ordered from Harvey Bristol and though a cauliflower went bad and his tomatoes got squashed, chicken, ham, sardines, fruit and cream in August 1915 were to prove entirely successful additions to menus devotedly prepared by servants under conditions which may well have garnished the dishes with dusty earth before or during the repast.[27]

Accustomed as men became to the distinctive flavouring of food in the trenches, they had also to face the irrepressible louse or 'chat' as he was known. Brigadier Roe remembers lice as being particularly revolting in every possible way. Fawn coloured, they discernibly crawled but more obviously just remained, dumbly insolent in their favoured haunt, the shoulder seams of one's shirt. 'Extermination demanded knowledge, skill and patience. Mass killing was impossible, each louse had individually

Company Quartermaster Sergeant Maughan. As a QMS he would have responsibility under the Quartermaster for stores and perhaps the distribution of rations when they were brought up to a forward depot by the Army Service Corps and the battalion was in the line. Maughan served in the Durham Light Infantry throughout the war and here, in 1917, has indications of the worth of his service, the stripes and crown of a QMS, a Military Medal ribbon and a wound stripe. (W. Maughan)

A nocturnal long, long trail awinding. The artist, G. W. Madoc-Jones, served both in the ranks and as officer of the 3rd Battalion, Royal Welch Fusiliers. (G. W. Madoc-Jones)

'They also serve'. . . . Officers' Mess Orderlies of 'D' Company, 1st City of London Regiment, Royal Fusiliers, pose in France for an 'official' picture. (Captain E. L. Higgins)

to be killed.[28] Roasting them out with a match gave some personal satisfaction, crushing them between the forefinger and thumb nails (until a distinct cracking sound could be heard) would presumably account for still more when matches were in short supply or those using them were insufficiently adept.'

Loathsome and legendarily large, were the rats which infested trenches and dugouts. Hunting them could bring sport. 'We spent quite a lot ot time ratting in the trenches this last time as Fergusson brought back a ferret from leave with him and we adopted someone's terrier that was wandering about on its own and killed about 40 rats in the two days; at night the great amusement is to shoot them by the light of an electric torch with a revolver but the results are not quite so good.'[29]

Rats could well have spread disease quite disastrously as is indicated, if with some degree of amazement, by Douglas Branson in a letter home. 'The latest order the Staff gave us was that observation must be kept on the rats in the trenches and if they showed signs of illness it must be reported!!'[30] It seems that no such scare developed. The rats had a ready supply and a wide variety of nourishment but one rat's appetite for living tissue led to an alarming experience for the victim and the man charged with the responsibility of rescue. Second Lieutenant Roe's help was urgently requested by Sergeant Appleyard because a rat, having bitten into Corporal Arthur Major's nose while he slept, was fixed there swinging as the Corporal desperately tried to dislodge it. Roe used a bayonet on the rat and was rewarded by silence and then a sigh of admiration from the onlookers.[31]

Tom Harley (9th King's Own) found that 'rats frighten the life out of one generally. The Germans and their implements of war are nothing to the rats to my mind.'[32] Much later in the war, James Harford and officers of the 2nd Essex even tried smoking the rats out of their emplacement by lighting a bag of cordite inserted in a rat hole but more resigned than this was the recall of H. G. R. Williams: 'Rats and lice, like the poor, were always with us and we learned to take them for granted.'[33, 34]

Not all the men with specialist duties in the line can be adequately represented here, but some attention must be paid to signallers. A preserved pigeon message: 'Hostile raid repulsed. Situation normal' gives a flimsy indication of one useful means of communication, and certainly pigeons and lamp signalling at night had a good deal more application to the Western Front than had flag signalling or the heliograph upon which so many signallers were laboriously instructed.[35] The most basic way to keep in touch was by runner, but regular communication depended almost entirely upon land lines for buzzer, offering Morse communication, and field telephone for the voice, until wireless became more widely operable under front line conditions on the Western Front. 'Linesmen' had to trace the broken ends of lines no longer operating and repair them, a task beside which painting the Forth Bridge might be adjudged a short-term and a far less dangerous employment. Not infrequently the filching of wire from one line to repair another, cut off communication from a line still in operation so this as well as shelling or accidental snagging and breakage was added to a signaller's problems.

A serious disadvantage of the main means of landline link, the D3 telephone, which combined the possibility of both Morse buzzer and voice use, was that by induction it was possible for the Germans from quite some distance away to pick up its signals and it was not until the Fullerphone was developed that a continuous buzz could be emitted blocking the monitoring of its Morse signals.

By the end of the war, the operation of wireless

1915. Flour mill billet rat hunt: Meaulte on the Ancre near Albert. With the cooperation of the mill owner, men of the 7th Battalion, Royal West Kents organized a hunt against rodents which made their billeting conditions miserable. 97 rats were caught and buried. So noteworthy was the event that the Brigadier visited the mill on the following day. The rats were disinterred for inspection and the mill owner took the opportunity of photographing the collection and adding his children to the souvenir picture. (D. A. Hodge)

(PROVISIONAL) No. 205......

First Class Certificate of Signalling

(FOR N.C.O.'s & MEN) OBTAINED AT

NORTHERN COMMAND
AND RIPON TRAINING CENTRE SIGNALLING SCHOOL.

This is to Certify that:—

1937. Lance Corpl. Mc Intyre, D.G.
(Rank and Name).

3/1st Northern Cyclist Battn.
(Regiment).

Has qualified as a **FIRST CLASS SIGNALLER** at the above School.

RATES: Disc - 4 Words per Minute
         Lamp - 6 do.
         Buzzer - 8 do.
         Semaphore - 10 do.

Percentage of Accuracy. 98

Written Examination   *84* Per Cent.
Examination in Telephony (Oral and Practical)   *40* „
Knowledge of Map Reading   *G.* „

NORTHERN COMMAND SIGNALLING
AND GRENADE SCHOOLS
4 MAR 1916
No.
FARNLEY PARK, OTLEY

A.E.Burton
Major R.E.
Commandant.

Douglas McIntyre spent nearly four weeks at Farnley Park, Otley, qualifying for this certificate. (D. G. McIntyre)

Communications on the wing: 6th Battalion, South Staffs pigeon post, Hill 60, Ypres Salient, 1915. (Brigadier H. L. Graham)

transmission and reception from the front line was well developed. Sir Douglas Haig reported to the Secretary of State at the War Office on 28 April 1918 that 'during the recent operations the value of wireless sets has been proved over and over again and it is hardly an exaggeration to say that they are indispensable.[36] Corporal Rumsey had been at the heart of that particular wireless work and this NCO volunteered to repair wireless aerials which had been blown down by shellfire four times. The repairs were carried out under the same conditions.' It was in large measure due to him that wireless communication to the rear was kept up when all other means of communication had failed.'[37] This Military Medal citation may be used symbolically to pay deserved tribute to all front-line signallers throughout the war. Communications, those established by runners, telephonists, linesmen and wireless operators were of course of fundamental importance and the walkie-talkie lay well in the future!

Mining activity beneath the trenches was unsettling to troops in every sense. Captain Deane, in August 1915, wrote: 'Yesterday morning there was a sharp shock and the ground shook. I climbed up and looked over the parapet to see if there was any smoke about. As the Germans are mining under us it was not encouraging.'[38] On that occasion British countermining had exploded a counter-charge (a camouflet) to destroy the German gallery, but the degree of alarm which such work occasioned may be apocryphally illustrated by the sentry who is supposed to have looked puzzled on being instructed to blow his whistle if the trench were mined. It was reported that he revealed his puzzlement by enquiring whether he should blow his whistle as he was going up or coming down.[39]

Second Lieutenant A .S. C. Fox (2/6 North Staffs) spent uncomfortable nights in May 1915 crouching in a listening post because there was rumour of German mining activity. Digging was heard but adjudged to be on the surface. In a letter home he expanded on the subject. 'When you suspect mining the correct thing to do is to sink a bucket of water and put your head in and listen. I got an empty army biscuit tin and dug a hole for it in the dark and poured water in it but soon found that it leaked and I was kneeling in water the bucket nearly empty.'[40]

There were, in all possibility, British Sappers of the Tunnelling Companies digging away not far from Fox's bucket. With the pick end of an entrenching tool to break away soil clay or chalk, and the shovel end to clear away the spoil, sappers in eight-hour shifts would worm their way by precisely calculated plan to the excavation of a chamber

beneath an enemy strong point or section of trench. The objective would be approached by about ten feet each day with two men hacking away at the face breathing in gulps of dust-laden air just made useful in their lungs by the operation of bellows at the bottom of the shaft sending some fresh air towards the face. The spoil would be sandbagged and windlassed back to the shaft or drift entrance to the mine whence it would be dispersed with every effort at concealment of such glaring evidence of mining activity. Deception would not stop there because when the explosives packed into the chamber were ready for electric detonation and the chamber sealed to direct the explosion upwards, an attempt might be made clearly to show an intention to attack that particular sector thus drawing in the enemy to hold the position in strength. On 6 June 1915 a mine was exploded opposite the battalions of the South Midland Infantry Brigade and a watching Staff Officer, Lt Col T. H. Clayton Nunn, recorded: 'It was a great success. Blew anything from 30 to 40 yards of parapet away. Parts of machine-guns and plenty of equipment were seen and three dead Germans but many must have been buried. The explosion made two quite big young hills. As soon as the mine went off our men blazed [away]. Machine-

A Wireless Unit in training at Stoulton near Worcester in 1915. Two wireless operators are on duty with the apparatus built in to the trailer on the right and from the trailer on the left a wireless mast (scarcely visible) could be raised to a height of 80 feet. This particular detachment, under the command of a Lieutenant, had a Staff Sergeant, a Sergeant and 27 other ranks, transport being provided by two Leyland 6-ton motor lorries, two Daimler lorries and two motor cycles. The unit embarked for France in November 1915. (W. M. Rumsey)

Beneath Messines: one of the tunnels in preparation. The Sapper to the left is engaged in the preparation of a gallery towards German countermining. When this gallery had almost reached the German tunnel, a 'camouflet' would be exploded so that the main British work would progress undisturbed. ('Realistic Travels', Photo Series/P.H.L. Archives)

guns poured lead on the gaps and on roads and communication trenches in rear. Trench mortar bombs and rifle grenades were showered on the enemy.' Clayton Nunn does not tell us whether the further lip of the crater was to have been secured by assaulting troops and defences thrown up to link it to the British line, or whether death, destruction and demoralization were the purpose of that mine. He does, however, note that the shaft was 25 feet deep, the gallery 405 feet long and that, at fifteen feet short of its objective, the gallery had stopped because of enemy mining being heard, consequently a 70-foot second gallery was thrown out 333 feet from the shaft to make a double mine, each involving the explosion of 2,500lb of gunpowder.[41]

Anyone who has read the two fine books of P. J. Campbell and that of William Carr about service with the Gunners, would be slow to swallow an infantryman's sometimes slighting reference to men whose 'comfortable conditions' behind the trenches enabled them to deal out punishment to the Germans the retribution for which could fall on those in the trenches.[42] Quite apart from the exceptional 1918 circumstance of action and movement to the rear and then in attack, battery positions were seldom havens of ease and security. While artillery work, particularly planned shoots on pre-registered targets and with aerial observation for correction, may seem to have a sense of measured orderly unhurriedness about it, the gunner's life could be swiftly trans-

formed. Out of the line, interminable cleaning of leather and burnishing of metal, watering, feeding and grooming of the horses, parades, mounted and gun drill offered a full day made much the more demanding in action. The sheer physical labour, if the ground were muddy, of emplacing a battery and serving the guns with shells, is a factor to be considered. The Field Artillery's 18-pounders could be brought into action swiftly by a well-trained battery, but there is vivid photographic documentation of the difficulty which men, horses or mules could encounter on muddy ground getting up to the line and then into a battery position. With the heavier guns, battery movement under all circumstances would be slower, the transport more impressive – like the four caterpillar tractors each drawing a 9.2-inch howitzer and the thirty-three Thorneycroft lorries holding stores and ammunition, a Daimler Car, four Douglas motor cycles two with side cars. Shells for the 9.2 weighed 290lb. A shell could be lifted by two men

A reminder of the Army's dependence on the horse: Corporal L. B. Stanley, acting as farrier, with one of the horses of the 25th Divisional Artillery in France. (L. B. Stanley)

using twisted sandbags, twenty shells provided a lorry load, and in action one shell a minute would be fired thus avoiding overheating. For travelling, the gun was broken down into three parts, the gun on its travelling carriage, the carriage and the bedplate. In action, the three elements were assembled and erected on a heavy wooden baulk platform with a steel box filled with ten tons of earth mounted on its forward end to balance the force of the recoil.

A fourteen-man detachment commanded by a sergeant served one 9.2-inch howitzer, two guns in the four-gun battery, being commanded by a sub-altern. Sandbag ramps offered some security to the detachment in action, but there was no overhead protection from enemy shelling, just the camouflage netting as a screen against German aerial observation. Sir John Eldridge recalled that his men lived: 'at best in a dugout or pillbox, at worst in a shelter six feet wide and three feet high which slept three men on timber and wire netting beds. . . . For the observation post in a sandbagged, ruined house, a camouflaged, reinforced or dummy tree or a trench position we carried with us our rations for perhaps a week in sandbags, water in 2-gallon petrol cans and

cooked as best we could on a Primus. In the battery we built a proper field cookhouse. Officers lived on the same rations as men and usually from the Common Cookhouse. As for our work, we were employed mostly for bombardment of trenches, pillboxes and strong points, for wire cutting or for counter-battery work or by firing from the map on known enemy positions. In attack we were often used to deepen the moving barrage, firing 1,000 yards or more beyond the advancing infantry. In defence we responded to SOS Very lights and coloured rockets signals by our infantry to block the enemy advance.' Eldridge was Signals and Observation Post Officer and had twenty signallers, two or perhaps four accompanying him forward to the OP. 'I got to know my chaps well. Six of them were pre-war regular soldiers, all except one utterly dependable. Of the wartime soldiers one was a public school man (later commissioned) who was an expert on toasting ration cheese; one was a gardener from Kent absolutely without fear; one was a Plymouth Brother

A 9.2in Howitzer (Mark II) of 95 Siege Battery in firing position, summer 1918. (Major General R. B. Pargiter)

also fearless but apt in moments of stress to curse the enemy in Old Testament terms. Two were younger than I was at 19 – they had falsified their age – both first class. Though we had one or two weaker brethren, as a whole I have not met since a finer or more reliable lot. It was a strange ambivalent situation. I was 'Shop' trained [from Woolwich] and conscious of the gap between officer and other rank and of my duties to my people. On the other hand I lived for long periods cheek by jowl with them and in these circumstances a spirit of comradeship developed. I think they trusted and liked me. I know I did them.'[43]

Gunner W. Gates (RGA), from his 9.2-inch howitzer position at Zillebeke in November 1917, shows that to no inconsiderable degree the infantryman's misery was shared. 'It keeps on raining and the mud and slush is something awful. . . . We have scarcely any cover when in action, a more dreary desolate spot, I don't think there could be – its such hard work with the shells weighing 290lb and one slips and slides about in the mud. It's nothing but shelling here day and night. We keep on losing men. There has been about 20 men knocked out during the fortnight we have been here, that is up to November 7. I think Fritz must have the range of our battery for he shells every day.'[44]

An unusual contemporary account, that of Gunner F. H. Snoxell, records a battery in emergency action, but in this instance a Field Artillery battery of eighteen-pounders. 'I was awakened by a loud report just behind the dugout – Almost immediately an order rang out "Battery Action, Canal Retaliation H.E." Tumbling out in various stages of undress we found the gun pit knee-deep in water. Hastily we made ready to fire. "Ready No. 1 Gun, No. 2 Ready, 3 Ready – Battery Ready Sir." "Stand ready for salvo – Fire!" The wood was transformed into a blaze of flashes and the air is split with the noise as all the field batteries open fire. Orders are given to reduce the range and this causes some alarm – then an order comes "2950 [yds] H.E. 10 rounds gun fire, for Christ's sake get them off." ' One gun is reported out of action and the diarist records the Major shouting 'Get those rounds off Sergeant or I'll have you shot,' but the danger had passed and an attack had been broken as the next orders raised the range progressively.[45]

From trench mortars to the colossal rail-mounted guns, the variation in the nature of one gunner's experience from another's could be prodigious. Brigadier Shelford Bidwell in *Gunners at War* indicates how the development of the mathematical science of gunnery owed more to the RGA than to the RFA, concerned as the latter had always pre-eminently been with getting speedily into action under local circumstance which could not be predicted and firing onto targets which it might be expected would be under direct observation. In several areas, experience of the true science of gunnery might be indicated by personal experience as in for example the sighting corrections made according to meteorological reports or the calculations made at an RGA battery for corrections after the battery's firing had been observed from a forward area. Were it not for the fact that a good deal has been published on the subject, example might be given of work in a battery the fire of which was being controlled by wireless transmitted signals from observers in aircraft using a clock code to register the fall of the battery's shells on a pre-determined target.[46] What does deserve exemplification is the work of RE sappers in locating by flash or sound the position of enemy guns. The success of this work had enormous significance in the development of predicted shooting which did away with the need for ranging upon a target and for prolonged bombardments – the advertisement for an attack which in fact sold cheaply the priceless asset of surprise.[47]

Sapper B. W. Whayman was trained in Gunnery Observation at the School of Observation at Merlimont Plage. The Observation Post to which he was appointed in mid-December 1917 was near the top of a broken church tower and the equipment consisted of a Director of Fire instrument with three eye-pieces of different magnification, binoculars, a chronometer, a field telephone and a buzzer, and a magnetic compass. By field telephone the Laventie Post was linked to posts at Lacouture, Beuvry, and Annequin as well as Group HQ at Vieille Chapelle. A system of synchronization with the other posts allowed for the flashes and smoke puffs of enemy guns to be plotted on grid bearings. From the intersections – trisecting bearings taken by the other observation posts – data could be sent on to Group HQ locating particular German guns. 'We also assisted our RGA in the calibration of their guns and cooperated with their counter-battery office in aim correction on specific targets being shelled.' In another post, Whayman was actually near the top of the spire of a church which had been well shelled. 'Visibility inside the German lines was good from here (Lacouture) and Fromelles, Aubers and the top of its ridge were in clear view.'[48] Instrumentation a good deal more complex than Whayman used for flash spotting, was needed for the sound-rangers.

Frank Noddle could scarcely have had a more suitable scientific background to endorse his transfer to a Field Survey Company for sound-ranging after commissioned service in an infantry regiment. He had read Honours Physics at King's College, University of London, before the war. His recollections emphasize the confidentiality over the instrumentation and the anxiety lest it should fall into German hands in 1918. Together with this he wrote of the basic requirement of an accurate survey of a battery's own position before it could take advantage of the data provided on enemy battery positions by the Sound-Rangers and Flash Spotters. The wedlock of science and war at a personal level is well illustrated in Frank Noddle's notes. 'Accompanied by a Lance Corporal I set out to tackle No. 1 microphone position on a very clear day and without any trouble found a spot on the slope of a hillock with a view of four trig points away West. I started taking readings when a whistling shell burst about a hundred yards away. We hurriedly sought cover. Two more shells exploded further away. After a few minutes we resumed taking readings wondering if we had been the target. We found the coordinates of microphone No. 2 amongst light field batteries and the only possible position for our theodolite was on the top of an old railway embankment. Once more our readings were interrupted and we had to dive for cover. After a few minutes we climbed back and found the theodolite out of level. There was a half-buried dud shell about a yard away.' The work had temporarily to be abandoned and one must realize that microphones would have to be placed at perhaps six surveyed points in order that the difference in time recording on each microphone of the same German shell being fired, would produce data from which the gun could be precisely located on the map. On hearing a gun, the sound observers, positioned well to the fore of the microphones, pressed a button which set electrical machinery in motion at the recording station so that the microphone wires would be heated by the time the gun sound reached them and photographic apparatus would also be working to produce an image of the results being obtained. The results were being displayed on an instrument known as the 'Harp' which received on its electrified 'strings' the deflections occasioned by the sound recorded by the microphones. The Harp was fixed in position behind a narrow slit in an otherwise light-tight box and behind the slit there was a moving strip of photographic paper. The sense of both sophistication and yet simplicity is completed by the fact that the microphones were but oil drums across the mouth of which was stretched a wire kept heated by an electric current from the recording station.[49]

Before leaving such aspects of the soldier's application of science to his work, it might be mentioned that the Meteorological Section RE was to supply increasingly important atmospheric information which had direct relevance to artillery work and of course to the British or German use of gas. This information related to the direction and velocity of wind, what could be expected from an interpretation of cloud formation and assessment of conditions of visibility, air pressure, temperature, rainfall, upper air wind direction and velocity – assessed by calculations upon the observed movement of a free lift, hydrogen-filled rubber balloon. Pte J. H. R. Body was engaged in Meteorological work observing these balloons and: 'Very high altitudes were reached on clear days sometimes until the balloon burst and on occasions the balloons were shot down by aircraft (just for fun!).' The data gathered by men at the recording station was sent to Army HQ where a 'Met' Officer and his staff would prepare weather maps for forecasting.[50] There is simply no doubt that meteorological work in the field, as with the duties of flash spotters and sound-rangers, may be considered another example of the invaluable contribution made by the rank and file in the waging of the soldiers' war.

'Rest' for a soldier not in the line was not only a misnomer in that further training, physical fitness and the proper cleaning and presentation of himself and his equipment would be a part of such rest, it was also an integral part of the official means by which his military efficiency was to be sustained. 'Rest' was one element among so many which could play a part in maintaining good morale. Whether it were in marksmanship or football, rest activities started from a point of competition – individual or team; victory for one's battery or battalion was a worthwhile goal to pursue. Its pursuit brought with it wider ranging benefits than the trophy that might be earned. Soldiering was physically arduous, fitness for it was properly deemed essential for the efficient performance of a man's duty. There was every reason why this might be achieved most thoroughly through a sense of enjoyment and fun and so a battalion's sports day would include with the conventional races and tests of strength and skill and agility, sack races and three-legged races and a bolster fight over water.

However jokingly it may have been expressed, an officer in the Northumberland Fusiliers was making a valid point in writing home of the importance of football to his men. 'I am the only officer in the team which includes four ex-professionals. We are easily first in the Divisional league, are pretty certain to get

Ridgewood Rest Camp on April Fool's Day 1918. Australians in residence with their washing on the line. Charles Stephen, who served with the 3rd Battalion, Australian Imperial Force throughout the war took this photograph. (A. C. A. Stephen)

Seaforth spectators. The 15th Scottish Division organized a Horse Show on 13 May 1917 in the presence of the Commander-in-Chief, Sir Douglas Haig. The CO of the Seaforth Highlanders, Colonel Buchanan, is here checking his programme, a drummer reclines on the grass, drumsticks in hand and 2nd Lieutenant John Turing, seated on the wagon with his hand on the wheel, later wrote of the Seaforths' being: 'thoroughly relaxed and happy' at the event. (Sir John Turing)

A rest camp in France and a sergeant's private enterprise. Behind an imaginative Barber's Tent notice, soldiers await their turn for the Civilian luxury of a lather and cut-throat razor shave. (P.H.L. Archive)

the medals the General is giving. We had our hardest game against the Durham Light Infantry. I bet the canteen and estaminets are doing a roaring trade tonight. Nearly all the team are pitmen. But I always say if it wasn't for the footballing pitmen of Tyneside we might have lost the war by now.'[51]

Ironically one of the most detailed sports programmes produced, that for the two days of the 5th Divisional Artillery Mounted Sports in the summer of 1918, was cancelled because the Division was otherwise engaged at Le Hamel. The events were to have included, wrestling on horseback, a Mounted Balaclava Mêlée, an Alarm Race, a Field Artillery Land Boat Race, a jumping competition for Mules and of course a mounted obstacle race.[52]

Concert Parties were particularly popular entertainment when out at rest. Professional parties like those of Lena Ashwell or the National Theatre at the Front provided a better chance to see established artistes than would have been the case for many patrons. Soldiers were urged to come to hear Ellaline Terriss 'sing more sweetly and act more charmingly than ever for you'. Gladys Cooper would 'act and look more like her postcards than they do' and the Cinematograph would show 'thousands of feet of amusing films'.[53] Some of the Army concert parties were very good too, though few would aspire to the performance of Bernard Shaw's *Man and Superman* which the Artists' Rifles presented in November 1915. The 47th Division 'Follies' produced a revue 'Hell and Halifax' suggesting that the war would last until 1950 and the 4th Australian Infantry Brigade had a long-term party of entertainers, the Blue Dandies, a name to stand alongside The Chequers, the Casuals, the Duds and so many more. Not to be neglected for its emotional uplift among so much organized endeavour, were the more informal occasions one of which Captain Green described in a letter home in May 1917. 'A piano in one corner with two candles lit – then a large circle of men and officers with a big bonfire in the centre. Quite a nice scene all in the dusk.' The regiment concerned was to be in action within a day or so of this letter being written, Green himself being wounded and later to be awarded the Military Cross for his leadership.[54]

Out of the line there would be more opportunity to enjoy the humour in such unit magazines as *The Mudhook* (the Royal Naval Division) *The Dagger* (56th London Division), *The Cardiff Pals Commercial* (11th Welsh) or *The Buzzer* (49th Division Signals). The humour from the 5th Gloucester *Gazette* may be taken as a sample. The fourth of Ten Commandments for soldiers of the 5th Gloucesters was that 'Six days shalt thou labour and

do more than thou ought to do but the seventh day is the day of the CRE (Officer in Command, Royal Engineers) and in it thou shalt do all manner of work, thou, thine officers, thine NCOs, thy servants, thy sanitary men, thy signallers and the Kitchener's Army that is within thy trench for instruction.' The tenth commandment would also have been dear to the heart of soldiers at rest. 'Thou shalt not covet the ASC's (Army Service Corps) job, thou shalt not covet the ASC's pay, nor his billets, nor his motors, nor his mules nor any other cushy thing.' Another item which would have raised a smile was the General Knowledge Examination Paper with its question 5. 'A Munition worker works 5 hours a day, 5 days a week and draws £5 pay per week. Compare the scale of pay of those who make shells with those who deliver them.'[55]

Estaminets and YMCA canteens were the likely locations of relaxed cameraderie and the purchase of egg and chips, beer or vin rouge (in an estaminet), tea and cigarettes. Additionally the canteen or a Red Cross hut would sell notepaper, chocolate, boot polish and similar goods. Gambling except 'House' (Housey Housey) would not take place in a canteen but surreptitiously if on Army premises – Crown and Anchor being a special favourite.

Rest might well be in a properly designed camp or in town billets and under the latter circumstances the opportunity for sexual indulgence would be available and it would be easier to drink to excess. Of drink for his men, an officer wrote understandingly that: 'it is curious what a fetish is that magic word "beer". Give a soldier a pint of it, it matters not how frozen or weak it may be, he is happy and life has nothing further in store.'[56]

It would be easy to see in drunkenness a deliberate numbing of the senses against the awfulness of the immediate past and the similar prospect for the near future, but while this may well have been a factor, the normalcy of drunkenness as a feature of civilian life for many working-class soldiers (and this is not at all to admit that drinking to excess was restricted to them) suggests that one would be unwise to see in the Western Front a self-sufficient explanation of the phenomenon. Certainly it was, at all levels of authority, an anxiety. Padre Raven wrote in October 1917 that he spent his days 'in a ceaseless effort to restrain [his men] from over-indulgence in alcohol'.[57] The narrow balance between a shrewd awareness that drink would be regarded by the soldier as a proper reward for his service which had called for deprivation in that area and the danger of a breakdown in discipline, needed careful management. J. C. W. Francis may have got it right when he

An estaminet forms the background for a line of cyclists of unusual pedigree – they are signallers of an Indian Army Corps Cyclist unit and it is unlikely that men in so formal a pose (apart from the pipe!) had just been enjoying a refreshment break. Note the rifles strapped to the crossbars. (W. O. Ridley)

Estaminet contentment. Two New Zealanders and an English sergeant enjoy their beer in France. (A. Bayne)

got up a singsong for his men on a Saturday night, 'bought them two barrels of beer and cigars and cigarettes and everything went top-hole', but soldiering and drinking have timeless association and had there not been problems arising from inebriation among an unprecedentedly large British Expeditionary Force abroad it would have been wholly extraordinary.[58] Out of habit and from lack of any available or acceptable alternative, the soldier, from time immemorial, has drunk and to time eternal will drink. Talbot House, the source of religious and social solace at Poperinghe, was neither physically nor in spirit within reach of all when out at rest; canteens or estaminets were.

Without relying upon Freud or Lorenz to explain that sex is a vital element in sustaining a happy contented stable individual and that man has a strong aggressive compulsion towards sex, what can one say about the patronage of French or Belgian brothels? Certainly it was not simply an escape from

the terrible sterility of war and a need to demonstrate an individual's procreative capacity or just to enjoy what is enjoyable, surely it is again the universal soldier doing what he always has done and always will do. To explain why men crowded to visit seedy Red Light houses has been deeply analyzed by those who see an inter-relationship between the dominance, aggression, violence and death instinct of sex and war. Obviously prolonged deprivation and newly available opportunity would be an explanation understood more readily by most people. Sufficient was the need and sufficiently serious the danger of VD that Army registered and medically supervised brothels were authorized. Precautions were being properly taken rather than the doors being laid open to criticism that promiscuity was being encouraged.

From his camp, H. G. R. Williams with friends in his regiment (5th City of London) went out of curiosity and with no intention of sampling the wares to what he called 'No. 1 Red Lamp Establishment'

Bartering could lead to the development of closer Anglo-French relations. French women outside an army camp seeking an opportunity to sell the contents of their baskets of produce. (L. B. Stanley)

At The Con Camp

You're not supposed to sit and mope,
Or strain like gnats to find the scope
For grousing at and crabbing others.
Remember they're a band of brothers.
    At the Con Camp.

Should Someone any how have skill
Dont over whelm him with ill-will.
To get it he's gone through the mill,
Encourage him with right good will.
    At the Con Camp.

And if you don't like certain rules,
Dont dub a set of persons fools.
Be wary when you criticise
Silence is gifted to the wise
    At the Con Camp.

Times, rules, and men are often hard,
And other's may snatch your reward
For stemming tides against the odds,
While sneering with suggestive nods,
    At the Con Camp.

Smile thro' the hardship and the pain
You have endured and may again,
If here to-day and gone tomorrow
Conquer at least your erstwhile sorrow
    At the Con Camp.

And if you're thoughts and deeds are greater
For Empire, king, at some time later,
Think, in the strain and stress of strife
Of just that glimpse you had of life
    At the Con Camp.
                J. LUNN.

near his camp. It was a French Government-licensed brothel. The visit was paid in the afternoon and the soldiers were told that they could 'go upstairs' but not have drinks until 6 p.m. Madame was quite adamant on this point, ringing a bell to summon the scantily dressed girls to parade. 'I have never seen such an unattractive collection of females in my life. I would have thought it enough to put anyone off completely even if he had gone in with the usual intention. We hurriedly left to a torrent of abuse in both English and French.'[59]

A different and happier introduction to the ways of the world was that of a Field Artillery gunner intent upon visiting Amiens Cathedral but waylaid by the charm of a young girl standing in a doorway and then by the girl inviting the soldier into her house to meet the rest of the family and enjoy coffee and cognac. 'We had been there quite some time when the young woman took my hand and beckoned me upstairs. Off I went innocently to her bedroom

Infantry Base Depots and Convalescent Camps had various points of kinship, not least their being run by regulations considered irksome by those transiently within them. This poem, in a magazine of a convalescent camp at Rouen in July 1917, sought to encourage a positive attitude among those recovering to return to active duty and it must have met with the approval of the camp CO, Lieutenant Colonel H. L. W. Norrington, by whose express permission the magazine was published! (P.H.L. Archives) where she started to undress. I was of course a little discomforted but not too drunk to know what was expected of me. I enjoyed my first woman and lost my virginity. I will never understand why it happened but I shall never regret it.'[60]

Paris and a full wallet could provide more sophisticated entertainment for the officer able to get leave there and then ready to risk his health. Satisfaction might or might not result. A subaltern in the RE after failing to enjoy an experience with a girl near the *Folies Bergère* ('face like an angel and every vice that could be found in Alexandria') introduced himself – 'very brazenly I'm afraid – to the most charming little widow and we hit it off splendidly. I should have been convinced that she was *"une véritable femme du Monde"* if it hadn't been for a few mirrors too many in the flat and other aids to the enjoyment of life not usually associated with those recently bereaved. I left Paris feeling that after all the Front has its compensations.'[61]

In his splendid book, *Eye Deep in Hell*, John Ellis writes informatively on the serious incidence of VD and prophylactic measures to counter the danger: 'When the British did begin to favour such measures, they placed the bottles of potassium permanganate lotion and tubes of calomel cream in the latrines, where anyone needing treatment was forced to reveal it to his fellows.'[62] More humiliating still would be the unit inspection under the searching gaze and lifting swagger cane of the Medical Officer, but it is as well to remember the self-control which would in all likelihood be automatically exercised by the many men whose whole religious and moral upbringing would be likely to preclude their involvement in casual sexual relations. Furthermore

the tangible pressure of the Army pamphlets, horrifically describing the progressive development of the worst forms of venereal disease, would be felt by a fair proportion of those who might otherwise have been tempted.

It would seem appropriate at this stage to note that some form of thorough personal cleansing facility – perhaps huge barrels or vats in a brewery and also means to clean and fumigate clothes – were essential provisions for men out at rest. There is abundant evidence of the sheer joy of discarding filthy clothing, scrubbing away with hot soapy water accumulated dirt on the body and then dressing in a change of clothing.

At Reninghelst in August 1915, J. W. B. Russell took his men to baths which consisted of 'twenty or thirty big tubs with a hot shower bath above. Each man was allowed four minutes in the tub and was given a clean set of underclothing; his dirty ones were collected to be washed and used for future battalions. The khaki breeches and coats were sulphured and ironed and we could hear the crunching of the broken backs [the lice]. The officers had five tubs to themselves in a separate room.'[63]

Quite apart from the filling of time 'at rest' with training activities, intensive training at one of the base camps would almost certainly be a soldier's lot at some stage in his experience of active service. Gunner Snoxell thought the camp at Harfleur, 'tremendous, stretching for miles up the river valley'. He adjudged it to be 'very well fitted up' with canteens and cinemas but, 'what a hell hole this would be if it were not for the YMCA'. On huge training grounds where British and German trench systems were laid out, he saw infantry 'practise

In the 'Banker's Draft' for July 1916, the magazine of the 26th Battalion, Royal Fusiliers (Banker's Battalion), an artist takes a light-hearted look at the stress induced in a man brought up before his CO and the sense of relief if the evidence against him were to be dismissed. (L. H. Renshaw)

skirmishing, bombing and bayonet fighting and machine-gun work undertaken too'.[64]

In the training area at Rouen, adjacent to one of the colossal food depots, Pte L. W. Jacques had to go to gas chambers to test the efficiency of his helmet. 'We had to wait a long time as the number that passed through was thousands a day.'[65] The military scale of everything at the training areas and depots transcended the imagination of most men. At Calais and Le Havre there were huge camps too, and in 1915 the construction of what became probably the largest of all was commenced. This camp, at Etaples, seems to have established proprietorial claim to the name Bull Ring, though in fact the term was generic for a parade ground. At Etaples there were hospitals, a mortuary, a cemetery and a convalescent camp, supply installations, railway sidings, rest camps, infantry base depots, a detention area and vast training spaces. The demanding regime maintained by the instructors at this camp above all, earned a legendary reputation which has grown with the years. The instructors, nicknamed Canaries because of their yellow armlets, were not there to court popularity but, as recently as 1983, a 1917 victim of the instructors at Rouen, having described them as the most unpopular soldiers in the British Army, added sagely: 'It had obviously been a survival course to prepare us for what was to come and in our own interests.'[66] Men for whom Etaples was a transit area arrived there from England and then they were re-grouped according to the Brigade or Division in which their intended battalion was serving in the line. After further training designed to fit them for active service, they would be conducted up the line to their designated unit. In addition to this, the Bull Ring at Etaples provided demanding training for men now fit for active service after discharge from hospital or for men who were returning to the line after a period away from its rigour. Bayonet fighting, assault course, route marches up and down the sandy dunes of the area and physical training had to be undertaken under the strict discipline of Instructors and Military Police who, in general and perhaps accurate perception, had been no nearer the front line than this Channel-shore base. Thus resentment to be followed by inflammatory circumstance gave birth to a riot among some men at Etaples in September 1917.

What precise proportion of the several thousand men in the camp at the time, took part in the riot, is very difficult to establish. An interesting account, if from a somewhat prejudged viewpoint, is published in Dallas and Gill's *The Unknown Army*.[67] There is no doubt that military authority within the camp was

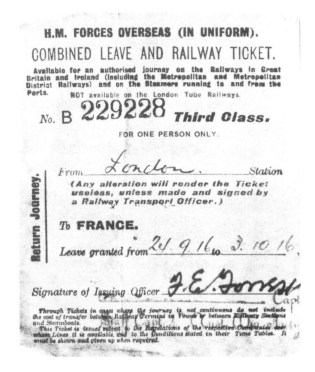

All good things. . . . The return half of a soldier's leave authorization and rail and steamer transport ticket. In this case, the soldier, Len Lovett, was a Tasmanian for whom London may have been second best to Hobart, but it still offered memorable opportunities for sightseeing and a 'fair dinkum' leave. (L. Lovett)

seriously challenged and that for some hours, whether in aggressive demonstration or passive observation, the men were virtually free from disciplinary restriction but lack of control of a riot is as much a problem for ringleaders as it is for the authority being challenged.

The troubles at Etaples erupted from long-held resentment and the unfortunate match to such stored gunpowder was the shooting of an Australian demonstrator protesting against the arrest of a New Zealander who had in fact provenly been released. The incident occurred at a bridge the Military barring of which closed access to the town and it was a Sunday when the men could have been expected to seek the freedom of the town and to shake the dust of the camp from their feet after six days of hard training.

The officer who had been sent with a small detachment of troops to bar the bridge, 2nd Lt James Davies (8th Bn Royal Fusiliers), was less than enchanted by his own experience at the Etaples Bull Ring. He was returning to duty after convalescence from his third wound and had endured the tedium of a Very pistol instruction session as well as physical training. He believes that falling out of one of the activities led to his being detailed for the problematic responsibility at the bridge. One look at the throng he was confronted by, even though he had his men properly stationed with fixed bayonets, convinced Davies that he would have difficulty getting his party to obey any orders to fire. The crowd far outnumbered them, there were threats shouted out to get a machine-gun up to clear the way and with no further ado Davies formed his men up and marched them off.

The crowd surged across the bridge into the town and of course while some simply 'had a day off', others, in the town and in the camp, found release for their excitement and desire for retribution on the Military Police in particular and Army restrictions in general with the stoning or rough handling of individuals and the wreaking of damage. Davies, who went with another officer into the town to see what could be done to get the men into camp, was thrown out of an estaminet but not actually struck. For the second time in the day his attempt to uphold authority had been brushed aside.[68]

For any ringleaders actually to direct their success towards the achievement of specified change in the way the camp was run, was difficult. The riot had no single focus, no acknowledged leader. Its immediate success lay in temporary chaos, it did not secure, in the flush of heady triumph, any acknowledgement of having forced irrevocable concessions. It could not have done this, given the small scale of the disturbance in relation to the figure of perhaps two million British troops in France, and given the basically sound nature of both the British Army and its administration, but for some days what happened at Etaples was a serious problem for the authorities concerned and this must have a relationship to the subsequent reforms instituted at the Base Camps. The authors of *The Unknown Army* accept that in comparison with what had already occurred in the French, Russian and Austro-Hungarian Armies, 'the troubles at Etaples were slight'. They might have stressed, but chose not to, that no such disturbance occurred in the line, not in the awful central years of the war and nor by the time the guns fell silent in November 1918.

The breakdown of discipline and the absence of good morale in a unit have of course a direct relationship. There are many factors which act upon the current state of morale in a battalion. Regimental pride, good officer-other rank relationships, a developed sense of comradeship with one's mates in a section, a feeling of 'necessarily doing one's bit'

which might be regarded as an evolutionary development of 1914 patriotic enthusiasm, are surely fundamental elements of positive influence. Assuredly basic too, would be a sufficiency of sleep, an adequacy of food and the requirement of not being exposed for too long a continuous period in the line. In support, in differing proportions for each individual, would be encouraging letters from home, parcels, some pay when out at rest, leave, spiritual conviction by upbringing with perhaps the influence of a good padre, well-run periods of rest with good billets and for some the prospect of promotion or decoration – official recognition of one's worth. It has to be noted beside such general points that the individuality of each man would ensure that some men coped less well than others in the circumstantial testing of a man's morale by extreme experience. As this is being written, the author has in mind, from countless examples, the badly wounded 16-year-old Frank Lindley, crawling down a trench to get to an Aid Post on 1 July 1916 and having to get past the body of a man newly cut in two by a large shell fragment. Lindley survived his wound and his experience – he returned to soldiering after the war – there were however men whose wounds were not immediately visible but whose effectiveness as soldiers was either flawed from the first or destroyed by the terrifying immediacy of war at its sharp end.[69]

Not all of the positive factors in sustaining morale can be illustrated in a book of this compass. A nice illustration of the sort of feelings about one's regiment which helps explain how the truly awful prospect of letting down both the regiment and one's pals overcame the instinct of self-preservation, is one from the 7th East Surreys in June 1916. They had been inspected by their 'Brigadier who was formerly in the Guards Division and we were told we were the cleanest and smartest battalion he had ever seen. On the strength of it the Sergeants gave a smoking concert last night in which the drink ran pretty freely and tonight we have a battalion concert so we have been celebrating consistently.' This battalion would soon need all its individual and collective pride in action on the Somme.[70]

Of all the misconceptions purveyed about the First World War, few so flagrantly deny the truth as the implication that across the socio-military gap between officer and man in the ranks there would be little kinship, no common identity in their wants, needs, fears, no understanding and sympathy based upon mutual respect. The letters and diaries of men on both sides of the divide between regimental leaders and led, conclusively refute such an interpretation. Representatively, a subaltern may have had his Fortnum & Mason parcel to share out in his officers' dugout, but he would in a literal sense lead his men over the top in any raid or battle in which his men were to take part. The evidence is there to be examined and if, on 1 July 1916, the 2nd Battalion Royal Berkshire Regiment were to have lost virtually all of its officers including its commanding officer who died of wounds, 27 officer casualties in all and 347 among its other ranks, is not an undeniable if terrible unity thus established.

Douglas Branson, throughout his service as a more senior regimental officer (4th Bn Yorks and Lancs) made regular requests home for all forms of support for his battalion. In May 1915 he asked his father for a couple of periscopes and a pair of field glasses for his Machine-Gun section and 27 respirators to the pattern as already sent by an aunt. Later in the month he thanked for 'hundreds of writing-tablets envelopes and pencils'. Clearly his parents must have been active in leadership of the Regimental Welfare Committee because they were asked to arrange for a visit to the family of a casualty, to send No. 1 Ever Ready batteries for his stretcher-bearers, torches, oilskins for the whole battalion and musical instruments. The CO's requests for Christmas presents for the men was passed on with the added urgency of the men being very tired in trenches so full of mud that they can only sleep on the firestep. Branson's father was told just before Christmas to cancel an order for pipes as few men smoke them and to substitute Woodbines and then in January 1916 he was asked to try to prevent the unfair eviction of a soldier's wife in Sheffield.[71]

Such general concern for the men can be particularized in that Tom Harley wrote home of his men coming to him with their home troubles. 'Most are complaints at their wives – some behaving badly and never writing and causing all sorts of doubts and anxieties, others again neglecting their children and allowing the home to go to "pot". A man has just been to me saying he can hear nothing of his wife and children living in Little Lever, near Bolton. I am going to write to try to find out but its awfully difficult dealing with these cases.'[71]

Of course the officers had their own anxieties and a subaltern in the Machine-Gun Corps expressed the universal officer concern over the concealment before his men of his own fears. 'There was a large stock of Mills bombs just in my part of the trench. They quite put the wind up me, especially when shells dropped very near. However I came through alright without my section knowing anything of my fears and funks.'[73]

We need not be cynical over the degree of self-interest in the cultivation of good officer–men relations. In a diary, G. S. Atkinson wrote of marching from the railhead to billets and arriving 'at 8.30 p.m. absolutely worn out. Like a damn fool I carried two of my fellows' packs – but it makes them love me.' This officer was just as shrewd as he may be adjudged humanly fallible.[74]

On leaving his men for promotion to command of a brigade, Harry Vernon, the CO of the 23rd Bn Royal Fusiliers, wrote to one of his subalterns: 'The Battalion gave me a most royal send-off and the band and everyone turned out. I was most awfully touched and went off in tears! I've been with the 23rd since Jan. 30th 1916 and during the whole of the time I've thought of nothing else except the battalion and how we could improve. There isn't a better battalion or one with a better tone and spirit amongst officers and men anywhere today.'[75]

Vernon was writing from one side of an equation well balanced by testimony from the men. Recovering in Seaham from a Gallipoli wound, a stretcher-bearer wrote to his Medical Officer who had enquired after him, 'I was sorry indeed to learn from another source that you had fell ill but I hope 'ere now you are yourself again and back among the boys as I know they would sadly miss you in A Section for we all believe our own officer to be the best.'[76]

From an Auxiliary Military Hospital in Rawten-stall, Private Sam Woodhead (9th Duke of Wellingtons), wounded at Mametz on 2 July, wrote as early as 16 July anxiously to enquire from the mother of his Lieutenant, J. W. B. Russell, if her son were to have come through the attack unscathed. 'As I was knocked out rather early on, a wound in the neck and thigh – you see I have been servant to him for a long time and have been in three fights and never a better lad or soldier ever stepped on a field and what I say every word true. Any lad in the Batt. would follow him and he was respected by all.'[77] Woodhead would have to learn that his officer had been killed.

Among documentation paying tribute to officer leadership, mention might be made of the letter of a Corporal Towler who unconsciously stressed the weight of responsiblity resting on the young, inexperienced officer as he sometimes struggled to fulfil it. In January 1918 Towler hesitated to request the special green envelope to hold an uncensored letter because 'our officers lack so much self-confidence that there is no telling what they might object to. At present they are nearly all men fresh out from Blighty and they are frightened to death of doing anything wrong or getting in a row for overlooking anything.'[78]

The 9th Devons at Gun Trench on 25 September 1915 in the Battle of Loos, in but a few minutes lost its Colonel, Second in Command, three of its four Company Commanders and seven other officers. One of these men who was wounded and evacuated, Jack Pocock, received a letter from Pte F. W. Hardy in his Company, written while Hardy was recovering from mild gassing. 'Well Sir, I think the Devons did as well as any troops could have done, don't you. It was a long way to double though and we were knocked up when we checked in front of the village. I was sorry to see you fall at our head, but very glad to find you are home and progressing. I don't suppose there is any prospect of your being fit for Active Service again, seeing you were hit so badly. It will feel strange with a new officer when I get back and I feel very sorry to have lost you as also the old members of the platoon.'[79]

With regard to 'Pay', it performed an entirely different and separate function in a soldier's morale. Relationships were an ever-present factor, pay was of use at rest and on leave. Few soldiers in their letters reveal any preoccupation with pay as long as an allotment was being received by a mother or a wife.

Mr and Mrs J. Morton of Kensington with their son Ronald at the end of his leave and about to take the train for France to rejoin his unit the London Rifle Brigade. Early in the war it was standard practice for soldiers to take their rifle and pack with them on leave – a unit might well have moved within the period of a soldier's leave. (Captain R. C. Morton)

Professional pride as much as financial interest could be shown by a man writing home of his receiving additional proficiency pay as for an example a marksman would have done.

In November 1914 on enlistment, a private in the infantry got 7s. a week, his pay being raised to 10s. 6d. a week in 1918. With some Arms, by definition, drawing proficiency, Engineer or Corps pay, there were differences for men enlisting in different branches of the Army. A Gunner in the Artillery received 8s. 5½d. in November 1914 on enlistment, a Sapper in the Engineers 11s. 8d. and a Private in the Army Service Corps, on satisfactory completion of his recruit training, received 9s. 11d. A Private in the RAMC, after training, received 10s. 6d. On top of this, there were small increments for years of service, additional payments for 'pro-

| For use in case the Rates of Pay given on p. 3 require to be amended— | Promotions, Appointments, Reductions, and any casualty affecting the net daily rate of pay. | | |

The paybook of Private B. P. Simpson (8th Battalion, East Surrey Regiment) records his award of the Military Medal and, in the following month, of a 6*d*. a day proficiency pay award. (B. P. Simpson)

ficiency' such as, for example, markmanship and then of course a rise in rate in accordance with promotion to an NCO grade.

From his pay, a soldier could make a voluntary deduction or allotment of money to be sent home, an allotment he might supplement by postal order if he wished, but he could also have penal reductions in pay as a result of some proven misdemeanour. Gunner George Trusty's paybook shows his receiving a daily rate of pay of 1*s*. 2½*d*. plus 6*d*. proficiency and from his total he made a voluntary allotment of 7*d*. On 31 December 1915 he is shown as getting no pay because he had been awarded Field Punishment No. 2 and thereafter his regular pay in the field was 10 francs a fortnight. Company Quartermaster Sergeant Robert Teasdale (7th Bn DLI) in 1917 had a daily rate of pay of 3*s*. 9*d*. proficiency pay of 6*d*., Pioneer Pay of 2*d*., War pay of 3*d*. and from his total pay he made a voluntary allotment of 1*s*. 2*d*. In the field he received a further allowance for performing on occasion the duty of Company Accountant so that there were occasions when his pay was above 60 francs for a two-week period.[80]

A 1916 *Whitaker's Almanac* shows that 9½*d*. was the equivalent to the French franc and from a general price list of Expeditionary Force Canteens for January 1918 a useful idea can be gained of the purchasing capacity of Trusty's 10 francs a fortnight.[81] A pint bottle of Bass Ale would have cost him 1 franc, a small packet of biscuits, 20 centimes, a bar of chocolate between 15 to 50 centimes according to make, two packets of Woodbine cigarettes (five to a packet) 15 centimes, a box of safety matches 60 centimes, a tin of Oxo cubes 75 centimes, an 8oz tin of sardines 1 franc 20, a bar of carbolic soap 20 centimes, a small writing pad 65 and in making all these purchases Trusty would still have half his pay left for more beer, egg and chips in an estaminet, an embroidered lace postcard and a packet of postcards

of Arras before and after the bombardment. A newly commissioned subaltern in 1916, receiving 7*s*. 6*d*. a day with a field allowance of 2*s*. 6*d*. the same allowance for lodgings and a 9*d*. mess allowance towards his mess bill, would be that much more comfortably off for his responsibility, but as it was likely that his normal expectations from life, his living standards, would be that much higher, he was not going to make his fortune while he risked his life. It may be added that he would have needed to supplement his basic allowance in kitting himself out as an officer and would have replaced uniform or items of kit at his own expense as such replacement became necessary,

Leave was a constant preoccupation for the soldier in France – waiting to learn if it were due and at the same time fearing that some unfortunate act of God, the Army or the enemy might preclude the realization of such anticipation. In the second half of the war, leave was organized for troops of the BEF more satisfactorily than had hitherto been the case. A man might receive one ten-day leave in a year, losing time at both ends of this period in his journeys. An officer could expect a better rate than this, perhaps as much as twice a year, and it was to this regularity for all, that the Army was aiming by the end of the war.

Some men had idyllic leaves, but the understandable turmoil of emotions within the soldier and within those receiving him, mother, father, wife, family and friends, and frequently the gulf of mutual incomprehension between them with regard to the soldier's new experience, would be deeply troublesome either heightening or dulling emotions. When understanding and tolerance wore thin, bitter frustration and hostility towards the symbols of what then seemed to the soldier an unthreatened, self-satisfied, alien Britain could unsettle him till he had returned to the 'real world' of France.

Whether it were workers on strike, former school friends still not in khaki, the excessively patriotic vicar, the evidently flourishing businessman, the bewildering rise in wages, even the questioning eyes and awkward efforts to please by a parental admixture of solicitous concern and some awareness of the danger of intrusion, all this could mean that leave did not live up to great expectations. However, it must be said that none of this in general terms could equal the universal frustration of delayed journeys as the sand in the hourglass of leave simply poured away. Similarly the joy of reunion and the keening sorrow of parting, even when the depressed soldier somehow sensed that the parting was far worse for those left behind, these factors remained constant in the soldier's leave. Pte Harry Innes (20th Middlesex) felt that he 'would rather go without [leave] than face the anguish of the inevitable return',[82] yet the diary of 2nd Lt Atkinson (RE) shows him as being in a 'blue funk caused by leave warrant arriving the night he is to go on patrol, as [he] fears being killed'.[83]

Rfn C. M. Woods, in his diary for October 1916, reveals no details of his nine-day leave but he is explicit about its commencement in France. 'Oct. 27 I received my pass to proceed on leave. I walked from Lestrem to La Gorgue. Oct. 28 Entrained at 1.30 a.m. at La Gorgue, detraining at Berguette half an hour late. Spent the rest of the night in YMCA hut. At 9.30 a.m. I entrained here once more for Boulogne, where the Leave Party marched to St Martin's Camp and were accommodated under canvas. Oct. 29 Marched down to the harbour, waited three hours, then told no more room on the boat, so returned to the camp disgusted.' In the event he arrived at Folkestone in the afternoon of October 30 and we are left to hope that when he finally reached home he would enjoy what he had surely earned.[84]

The return journey could be as haphazardly delayed. Gunner Robert Ford had not been amused when a band at Folkestone had struck up with *Take me back to dear old Blighty* nor uplifted by the crawling speed of the French train to the railhead and the five-hour wait there, but it had been the fading of the English coast which had affected him most. 'The terrible thought, and it seems terrible after ten days amongst decent people and civilization, that provided the war lasts, I should not see England again for another eighteen months came

over me and a most fearful depression with it. The boat, apart from the noise of the engine, was absolutely silent and when we landed once more on French soil, the boys found their tongues only sufficiently to curse everything from the Kaiser downwards. I have compared experiences with dozens of chaps and they all say the same.' Ford adds that the depression suddenly lifted and 'I now feel as before, just merely fed up, as we all are. . . . but please don't think that I regret having ever joined for I don't. It has been a fine experience if nothing else.'[85]

An officer on leave was no less subject to delays or homesickness on his return. In July 1918 Lt Col G. de Courcy Ireland's train to Calais was very late in arrival and the boat was further delayed. In London, however, he visited Cox's, his bank, stayed at an hotel before journeying to Kingswear, his home, the next day. His father and mother met him and after tea 'we went out for rabbits. We got 5. I got three.' On Sunday he read a lesson at Matins and then in the evening walked up to the cricket field with his mother. Monday saw him at the dentist and then sailing off the Dart and during the week he gardened, shopped in Exeter, visited family, took Miss Fenwick to lunch, then by train to Eggsford and walked up to Chawleight Old Hall. Walks, picking raspberries and a good Devonshire tea provide the evidence of a relaxing leave until the special interest of a hurriedly undertaken train journey to Aberdeen to see his Naval Officer brother and his ship, the *Pellew*, badly damaged in a torpedo attack. Before the end of his leave this officer dined at the Grill in Piccadilly, went to the Globe Theatre and saw *Nurse Benson* with Marie Lohr and Fred Keer being 'splendid' and to the Alhambra to see *The Bing Boys on Broadway* with George Robey and Violet Lorraine who were 'excellent'.[86]

In describing the fashion in which an officer without financial constraint might enjoy his break from France, we might remember that for officers and the men too there would be time off in France. One Sapper wrote of the CO giving his section a 'holiday' so he walked into Armentières and had a good look round. An officer might secure the chance of time in Paris for sight-seeing and the night-spots. Sgt Roland Richardson and a friend, Reg, in August 1917 had no doubt as to the way they wanted to spend the night out they had secured. 'Started quietly on beer and white wine, but fell in with the Goods [Concert Party Group] which led to our downfall. A merry muzzy night. Got home before one and just before Reg. who lost me.'[87] As it happened, Richardson's leave, which was due, was now postponed because of a planned 'stunt' in which he was to be wounded – still this 'game old cock' as his Captain called him, would no doubt soothe his Blighty convalescence with English ale.

There is abundant evidence of men who were content, even determined, not to seek a Commission when such a course was recommended to them and similarly, promotion within the ranks, was by no means necessarily courted. Nevertheless official recognition in the form of promotion or decoration could certainly be a sustaining factor in the maintenance of good morale. At the very least, self-respect has always been a sound beginning upon which to build efficiency in any activity and Sam Kelso of the 16th HLI possessed it. A particularly young NCO, he performed so well on the first day of the Somme that he was promoted in the field to the rank of Sergeant and was recommended for the award of the Military Medal. As his Company Commander wrote to Kelso's father: 'I am sure all ranks of the Company share the honour as it was well deserved as a symbol of work well done. By the express wish of the officer commanding he is getting leave in a couple of days which will probably be the most acceptable award of the lot.'[88]

There was indeed much talk of some awards, perhaps especially foreign decorations, as coming 'up with the rations' but men can speak in open disparagememt of that which they privately esteem. A further factor in what one has to accept was the subjective element of any award, was the inevitability of innumerable deeds deserving recognition but which for some reason, not just lack of an appropriately ranked witness, received no such reward. Fate might well challenge a man to show outstanding qualities or be found wanting; it would not necessarily crown his achievement when he matched the challenge.

Capt J. C. Armstrong (ASC) acknowledged a factor in the awarding of decorations in a letter announcing his own Military Cross award. 'Of course I am most awfully pleased and I feel sure you are, but I feel there must be dozens and hundreds of others who deserve it a thousand times more than I do.' Armstrong's diffidence related to the fact that his supply column work for the ASC, though it could bring him under fire, did not involve him in the sort of front-line infantry service for which the majority of young officers won this award. Still, his parents would be 'pleased that my efforts out here have not been considered a failure'.

A Buckingham Palace investiture, or an investiture in the field, was a memorable affair. On 9 July 1915, Captain Armstrong learned officially that 'the

Royal Reward. Sergeant C. L. Seely of the 1/4 Royal Berkshire Regiment receives his Military Medal from the hand of His Majesty King George V in May 1917 at an open air investiture and in the presence of Queen Mary. (Mrs Irene Seely)

King has been pleased to signify his gracious intention to decorate you with the Military Cross' and he was requested to attend at the Palace 'on Monday next, the 12th instant at 11 a.m.' On the day of the ceremony he arrived at the Palace by taxi a few minutes before 11 a.m. 'and was driven through the forecourt where the guard was being changed, to the main entrance in the Centre Court. Here I alighted and went up a stairway to a hall where my hat and gloves were removed and I was then shown into a large room overlooking the gardens. At the entrance a flunkey pinned a hook into my coat and my name was checked off on a list by an official in a frock coat and I found myself in a large gallery-like room full of officers waiting for the Military Cross.' As they waited, someone started smoking, the signal taken for all to light up, but the frock-coated official returned and put a stop to the smoking, the cigarettes, in the absence of ashtrays, having to be thrown out of the window. The officers formed up in lines and filed through several rooms each with a sort of cordoned-off pen, labelled Victoria Cross, KCMG, KCB, etc., each room emptied earlier of its award recipients. In a small hall in the centre of the West Front of the palace and with his back to the window, 'stood the King, dressed in khaki and looking bronzed and well'. Armstrong's name was called out and he walked up to the King and stood at attention. 'Simultaneously a gorgeous flunkey approached from the corner of the room, bearing a red cushion on which rested a Military Cross, a ring being attacked to the pin on the ribbon; the man bowed low and the King taking the Cross hooked the ring on to the hook in my coat and then shook me by the hand. I then bowed and moved off by another door into the hall where a flunkey put my cross into a leather case and handed it to me.'[89] It had been short and silent but impressive and unforgettable.

Among those subjectively selected elements which assisted in keeping up morale were two which are being left for consideration in the chapter on the soldiers' opinions and attitudes. Both a belief in a cause and a spiritual certitude could provide powerful props to a man under the battering of prolonged stress. Leaving that aside for the moment, a good example of an experienced unit still manifestly keen, is this letter from Private C. R. Coombs of the London Scottish, written just before the Battle of Loos. Coombs accepts that it had been 'murder' waiting in the trenches being shelled and doing nothing 'but now we are going for them, man to man with the bayonet and by Jingo we are keen. Its going to be a royal smash-up this time and no mistake.' Are these sentiments invalidated by reason of the failure at Loos, Coombs himself being killed?[90] The answer to this may lie in the fact that the tragic reality of the costliness of attack made the importance of high morale the greater. When the balance of military matériel shifted in favour of the Allies in the last six months of the war, the actual performance in battle of the units engaged would be vital in achieving victory. James Harford, newly commissioned, was to join the 2nd Essex at the end of April 1918. Early in May he wrote of himself and of his battalion. 'A sort of fresh interest has come my way – real esprit de corps and how it has bucked me up . . . it's extraordinary what a change I've experienced since I've come out here. . . . The great thing is that I've come to a magnificent battalion and an equally magnificent division. The battalion has been in all the big battles of the war and has done absolutely splendidly but its greatest shows and the ones that remain freshest in its memory are the two big fights it has had in this battle just a few weeks ago.' Of the men: 'it simply stirs your heart to hear these fellows talk about the regiment. There's a simply marvellous esprit de corps, which breathes through the description of everyone from the BHQ cook to the major. My only object [in relating all this] is to tell you how frightfully bucked up and keen I am, ready to die or anything as so many splendid men of this bunch have already. . . . The spirit of this magnificent regiment has bitten me and I long to go out and battle by their side.'[91]

It would not be easy to find evidence of personal experience so universally to portray the collapse of a unit's morale as Harford had praised that of the Essex. William Strang's diary certainly shows a company of the Worcesters under stress (see page 103) and a Sapper officer in 1918 indicated his fellow officers being worn down: 'Got back to billets find — had gone sick. More work for the rest of us and we are nearly tired out now. In the evening — crocked up and went sick too – pure undiluted funk on his part. Three officers left now to do the work of ten and the Major will go soon. He hasn't been to bed for a week and must have walked at least 25 miles every day . . . coming home about 4 a.m. I met the Major alone and although nearly finished I went back to help him lay out a new line. Poor old Major is nearly done but he will drop before he gives in. I hope we can last until some more officers come but my eyes are jumping and my head sings like a tornado – how few people know what it is like to be really exhausted in the body and yet to have a mind which drives you on. . . . We are all jumpy and are too far gone to talk.' Engaged in wiring, officers and men of this particular field company were then caught in a barrage of shelling. The diarist was blown several yards from where he was standing by the explosion of a shell, could not re-gather his bearings and, for company, had a man who had been struck blind by the same explosion. In a shell-hole 'I thought I would go mad – there were rats with us screaming with terror.' The shell-hole was immediately adjacent to a trench into which the unwounded officer pushed his fellow and then clambered after him. A ration party had also been caught in the shelling and the moaning from their wounded was additionally unnerving. 'Some of the kids in our trench began to cry and I felt like it myself.'[92]

It was of relatedly similar circumstances that Victor Sylvester (Argyll and Sutherland Highlanders) has recalled. Under the threat of imminent attack, one of his platoon had indicated that they must all run. After several times remonstrating with him, the platoon commander had shot him. In Sylvester's judgment, this had been necessary as the man was eroding Sylvester's will and, he presumes, the other men's will to remain at their post.[93]

The whole question of failure of morale, or an individual breakdown perhaps, a self-inflicted wound, desertion or of a 'cowardly' act and the tragic chain reaction this could have, leading to Court Martial, is one which cannot be developed here in the depth that a serious consideration of the moral and military issues involved would require.

Some thought-provoking example must suffice. F. P. Roe, at rest with his company of the 6th Bn Gloucesters, was informed of a man who had axed off the fingers of his right hand with a shout of 'Bugger this bloody war!' 'We got him evacuated on a stretcher at once but I knew he would be put under arrest and charged with a self-inflicted wound with the intent of avoiding active service. The charge was all the more serious because of the loss of his trigger finger. This was a very grave charge indeed and rightly so. He was sent down the line at once but I was officially told later that he had died. I was glad to hear this'[94]

It is impossible to know precisely what had reduced this poor man to his self-mutilating act: a less demonstrable case in the same battalion had as tragic an ending despite sympathetic handling. The man became more and more silent and morose. His Sergeant drew the man's condition to the attention of 2nd Lt Roe who in retrospect has written: 'It is undoubtedly true that there were a great many persistent and accomplished scroungers in France and quite understandably when none of us was properly oneself it was extremely difficult to send a soldier down the line unless he were wounded or diagnostically "sick". So — had to get much worse before we could set about getting him home and under proper care. He was eventually sent back and became quite deranged mentally.'[95] This particular soldier it seems had not suffered from near proximity to the waves of a shell explosion (militarily defined as 'commotional shell shock'), but his emotional capacity to cope with the demands of his duty was drained to insufficiency. This was something less easy to establish in terms which were other than condemnatory. Indeed an additional factor brought complications in any medical diagnosis or military/ legal deliberation, the question of the emotional stability of the individual in the first place, i.e., before he became a soldier. A pioneer psychiatrist, H. W. Hills, who became Fourth Army Neurologist

in 1918, has written that he found it hard to explain to a Court Martial board that a grown man could have the mind of a child, and childlike could not hold out'. The Court always gave prisoners the benefit of the doubt and many of them got off, 'not because of my arguments but because I was the "doubt". I am glad to say that in the seven months, until the end of the War there were no death sentences [from that Court]'.[96]

Field Punishment No. 1 was among the punishments which might have been awarded after a case had been proven in a Court Martial at a lower level that Field General Courts Martial (which dealt with the most serious and potentially capital charges). In general terms this meant the tying of a man to the wheel of a gun or a stake or to fencing and his remaining in that demeaning and uncomfortable position for two hours per day or a set number of days. There were other penalties too with FP No. 1, like losing one's position in the leave roster, but it was the open humiliation which, by some in France as well as in London, was thought to be so unhealthy an influence and so fundamentally degrading.[97]

It was the progressive erosion of personal self-control which led to a Northumberland Fusilier NCO failing in his duty and being stripped of his rank on a battalion parade in an ineffably humiliating experience. Again, two officers carried a burden of guilt over sixty years, not just because of the breakdown of their effectiveness as a platoon and a battery section commander respectively, but because understanding commanding officers had dealt sympathetically with them leaving each man with a nagging suspicion that they had been fortunate in their commissioned status.

The legal training of A. B. Ashby (Queen's Royal West Surreys) led him from increasingly valuable service at Courts Martial proceedings to work in the Army Judge Advocate's Department and being appointed VIII Corps' Court Martial Officer. In a letter home announcing his first Court Martial case, he wrote: 'I don't think any of them know it is my *métier* and I am rather relishing the prospect.' The result was an acquittal and Ashby annotated his letter, 'I think he would certainly have been convicted if I had not been there.' Captain Ashby's private and official papers present a picture different from the one held in current perception of the fairness of Court Martial proceedings. As Field General Court Martial Officer, Ashby's duty was to advise the Court on all points of law and procedure, to record the evidence or cause it to be recorded and no Field General Court Martial in VIII Corps sector, save under exceptional circumstances, could be held without his presence. The duties of a 'prisoner's friend' are incidentally laid out so fully in one of Ashby's official papers as clearly to demonstrate that every endeavour was made to open up possibilities of the best defence for a prisoner and to counsel against allowing the prisoner, through ignorance, to damage his own case. Nevertheless, in the event of 'an accused being sentenced to death the President [of the Court] will attach to the proceedings a certificate in the following terms: "I certify that A. F. W. 3996 has been handed to the accused under sealed cover in accordance with Army Council Instruction 570 of 1918" ' and the President would sign and date a certificate which informed the unfortunate man that he had been found guilty, had had sentence of death passed on him, with or without a recommendation for mercy and that the findings and sentence were "not valid until confirmed by the proper authority".[98]

A victim of F. P. No. 1, W. L. P. Dunn (Pte, 17th Bn King's Liverpool Regiment), has written of the tragic consequence on 20 March 1916 of the punishment being carried out on thirteen soldiers at Franvillers for their being deficient of two gas respirators each, at a snap kit inspection. The sentence was for but two hours on a single day. After a medical inspection to certify physical fitness for the punishment, the first part of it was the digging of a huge pit in which securely to bury food that could not be transported on the battalion's imminent move. Then the men were 'marched in double time for about ten minutes – being tied to the wheel of a limber in the village square (that is to say handcuffed) for a similar length of time. And so it went on for about a couple of hours. When we were released from the second tie up we were again marched in quick time and it was then that Private — collapsed on the side of the road shouting "I cannot go on." I fell out with him and he died in my arms. When we were paraded before the Doctor before starting the punishment Private — was standing next to me and Doctor Dakin pulled him out of the ranks and said "you are anything but well but quite able to be tied to a wheel".' An officer, on leave some time after, had called on the dead man's mother and given her details which were confirmed

by Dunn who was 'asked to go to see her' when he went on leave. This sad affair became a *cause célèbre* taken up by Horatio Bottomley in *John Bull* and then in Parliamentary Debate.[99]

Captain E. C. Deane (RAMC), attached to the 2nd Leicesters, had an even more melancholy duty than that exercised by Dunn; he was required to be attendant at an execution. '24.6.15. I had a rotten job today seeing a man in the Regiment who deserted shot by the APM. The thing was got over at 3 a.m. this morning. I doped him well with $2/3$ gns of morphia last night. The Padre, Irwin, walked out beside him to face the firing party, blindfold, the police tied him to a pipe. I pinned a target over his heart – the Assistant Provost Marshal signalled "the present". The Padre who had almost broken down said "Into thy hands" then [the order was given] "Fire" and we cut him down and I wrote a certificate that death was instantaneous. When the Padre walked out beside him praying and saw the troops drawn up on parade, the firing party, etc., his voice broke for a minute and it shook me more than anything I have ever seen out here yet. I must say I did admire Irwin and it will be counted to him for righteousness all right.'[100]

From so harrowing an account it may be appro-

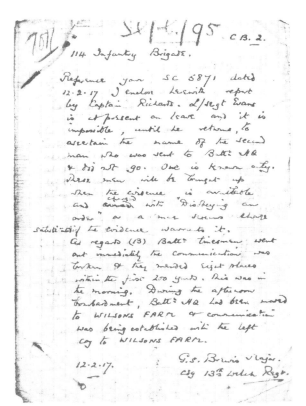

Refusal to obey orders or the possibility of a 'more serious charge'. A small party of men from the 13th Battalion, Welsh Regiment, in support trenches, has been cut off from all communication by an enemy 'pocket barrage'. Two runners, detailed to report the situation to Battalion HQ, have not set out on this dangerous duty. Investigations are being made to ascertain the name of the second man preparatory to charges being laid against both. (Major T. S. Richards)

priate to conclude this chapter with reference to the travails of men actually hit in action. Padre Evers's papers meticulously document the care with which, whenever possible, those men who died in the line were buried, a brief but moving service held, the grave marked on its spot and its site recorded on special forms. His papers illustrate too the melancholy task of writing to the next of kin, gathering together the man's personal effects and sending them off, adding tangible poignancy to sorrowing parents or widows.[101] The Colonel, the Adjutant, Company Commanders, indeed all the officers, as well as the Padre, would all fulfil the sad duty of writing letters of information and attempted consolation to next of kin. When one reads among the letters sent in reply to such communications, a father who had just lost a second son asking where his son was buried but 'if unfortunately you should have no pleasant news to give on this point, please do not give it as it would only upset his mother', the implication was of the father's grim awareness that his son might have been blown into unrecognizable fragments or simply have disappeared or be permanently entombed by the collapse and burial of a dugout in a shell or mine explosion.[102]

The father of Rfn Alan Liddle (16th KRRC) was informed in June 1917 that his son was missing but 'in the circumstances of the fighting in the field it is not possible for Commanding Officers always to know whether a man known to have been wounded has been picked up by our own stretcher-bearers'.[103] Liddle had, in fact, been taken prisoner and this potential aspect of a soldier's experience is to be dealt with in another book, but he might just possibly, like 2nd Lt Crerar (2nd Bn Royal Scots), have lain more than three days in no man's land, either inaccessible to stretcher-bearers or unknown to them. There cannot be many men who wrote what amounted to a diary in no man's land. 'About 2.8 on Thursday (?) I was hit on the leg somewhere round the thigh after advancing about 100 yards. Tumbled into a shell-hole where I lay till dark and attempted to dig myself in a little with my hands. After dusk someone appeared and I called. He approached and said he was taking a message from Mr. King, my Coy Commander and said he would tell him I was here and would come back. He never came. Two other persons I think approached and heard me whistling but seemed to take away someone else. No one else came though I waited all night and at 4.30 I thought of trying to crawl back but could hardly move and our men were sniping. This morning I tried to bandage

Notification of a military execution. In the context of the time we must see the publication of these tragic details as an essential element in all military discipline, that punishment would be visited upon anyone who 'misbehaved' in matters great or in matters small. 346 death sentences were carried out in 1914–18 and of this number 3 were officers. almost a third of the men shot were already under a suspended death sentence. (P.H.L. Archives)

GENERAL ROUTINE ORDERS
BY
FIELD-MARSHAL SIR DOUGLAS HAIG,
K.T., G.C.B., G.C.V.O., K.C.I.E.,
Commander-in-Chief, British Armies in France.

General Headquarters,
December 5th, 1917.

ADJUTANT GENERAL'S BRANCH.

2906—Court-Martial.— No. ▓▓▓▓ Private ▓▓▓▓ Cameron Highlanders, was tried by Field General Court-Martial on the following charge :—

"Misbehaving before the enemy in such a manner as to show cowardice."

The accused, having been warned to go over with his company on a bombing raid, remained behind in the trench, in circumstances which showed that his conduct was due to cowardice. The sentence of the Court was "To suffer death by being shot." The sentence was duly carried out at 6.50 a.m. on 23rd November, 1917.

2907—Promotion of Special Reserve Officers of Reserve Battalions.—1. The following are the ranks authorised for officers in the establishments for Special Reserve and Extra Special Reserve Battalions :—

	Lieut.-Colonel.	Majors.
Special Reserve Battalions	1	3
Extra Special Reserve Battalions	1	2

2. Lieutenants will be promoted under G.R.O. 2587 of 1917. There will thus be no fixed establishment of captains.

3. Second Lieutenants will be promoted under G.R.O. 2572 of 1917.
(Authority: Army Council Instruction 1691 of 17-11-17.)

2908—Multiplication of Routine Orders—Economy in Paper.—Attention is drawn to the fact that as all units receive copies of General Routine Orders the reproduction of a G.R.O. in Army or other Routine Orders should rarely be necessary.

my leg and it felt much better and I saw two more men in distance and whistled – they also went away. Spent a long dreary day. How I wish someone would come. They must come tonight otherwise I will try to crawl in again. My ideas as to the lines are rather hazy but I know which way safety lies. It is wretched to feel fairly well and no way to get to safety.'

Crerar decided to crawl in, but after every few yards he fell asleep because the effort so tired him. A German bombardment, covering him with showers of earth, stimulated his effort. In a letter from a Red Cross Hospital, he wrote that 'the rotten part was getting shot at by both sides but on the whole I wasn't a bad corpse and must have been mighty still.

I had got totally lost – fogged in my last shell-hole where I meant to stay the next day and had dug a little with a spade a ton weight when I decided it wasn't a safe enough hole and I made one more effort.' It was sufficient and he was soon to reach a British parapet, slither over it to helping hands, bread, butter and water. The trench he had reached was too narrow for stretcher-bearers and, 'I had a long walk embracing a stretcher-bearer round the neck while I toddled behind like a lamb. After a few hours I got to the first aid post and was labelled but not bandaged till later in daylight when I got down to the next station.' He still had trench journeying to make till a dressing station in the open was reached

'In the circumstances of the fighting. . . . it is not possible. . . . to know. . . .' Rifleman Alan Liddle (16th King's Royal Rifles) has been reported wounded and missing. On his father's anxious enquiring for further information, the War Office is still unable, five weeks after the soldier had failed to answer post-action roll call, to give any further details. In fact he had been captured. (A. Liddle)

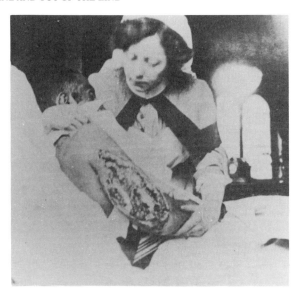

An uncaptioned photograph which grimly offers some idea of the suffering which could be brought by a wound. The photograph was taken in a base hospital in France or just possibly in a hospital in the United Kingdom, and it shows the effect of a shell fragment injury some three weeks, at least, after the wounding. There is evidence of considerable surface infection, but it appears improbable that amputation will be necessary. (L. W. Jacques)

The primitive surroundings of a Field Dressing Station where walking wounded have their injuries dressed by Medical orderlies. (Canadian Postcard)

Ambulance barge and RAMC staff at Abbeville near the mouth of the Somme. Space as well as smoothness of travel gave this form of casualty transportation obvious advantage – the absence of jolting, as in a railway carriage, reducing the risk of wound haemorrhage. (C. W. G. Gough)

where he had his first warm drink for six days. A horse ambulance took him further back by three more stages to a Casualty Clearing Station and then by Ambulance Train with a wounded Fusilier from his own regiment on the stretcher below him. 'We had a ragtime railway journey of 28 hours,' after which he was taken first to one hospital and then another, being operated on after an hour's rest from thirty-eight hours on a stretcher.[104]

Evacuation of wounded from the Casualty Clearing Stations behind the Somme battlefield was by hospital barge as well as by a hospital train of perhaps sixteen carriages. A barge of No. 4 Ambulance Flotilla based at St-Omer had thirty beds and was drawn by a tug, the smooth passage infinitely preferable to the awful jolting of road ambulances or the stopping, starting and shunting of the trains. From St-Omer, the French canal system allowed the barges to get quite close to the rear of the line and then return to Calais for the transference of their changes to hospital ships. In the recall of Sir Geoffrey Marshall, a former RAMC surgeon, most of the cases on his barge were head and chest wounds and the excellently equipped barges were perfectly smooth for travel and had two very good Queen Alexandra's Imperial Military Nurses, an RAMC sergeant and two corporals aboard. One of Marshall's nurses was particularly attractive and was principally responsible, it seemed, for the visits by French officers who had glimpsed her as she sat during quiet periods knitting on deck when the barge was moored.[105]

It is obviously not possible here for reasons of space to expand upon the subject of wounds and their treatment – the very word wound as with that of casualty loses its full meaning by repetition and an awareness of numbers beyond one's grasp. These two factors alone seem to preclude a true insight into

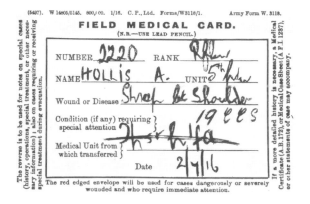

A Field Medical Card recording basic information on a casualty would be placed in a waxed windowed envelope and the envelope tied with string through a buttonhole of the man's uniform. The card provided a quick identifying reference for those concerned with the wounded man's transportation to hospital. Rifleman Hollis has been 'cleared' for such a journey by No. 19 Casualty Clearing Station. (A. Hollis)

The facts of life in every sense. Casualties meant paper work as well as surgery and bandages. Administration at No. 2 British Red Cross Hospital based in an ecclesiastical building in Rouen. The Royal Army Medical Corps personnel are from left to right: Sergeant Hine at his typewriter, Corporal Nicholson, Privates Carter, Benton and East and Sergeant Major Tozer. (Major C. H. Milburn)

an individual's bodily and mental hurt. The spirit may quail at being reminded of the men whose minds were permanently unhinged by mental wounding and who languished their lost lives in institutions. The senses may be affronted by pictured thought or actual sight of the severe facial wound or the painful fitting, discarding, refitting and getting awkwardly accustomed to the substitute wooden leg at Roehampton. That some men needed the regular cleansing and dressing of their wounds till their death sixty years later is a sobering consideration for anyone whose historical interest does not exclude sensitivity for an individual soldier in his bodily and emotional framework. To understand what being even slightly wounded meant to the victim is not easy for the man without related experience. Naturally we will be shocked by what lies behind the quavery writing of a British POW using his left hand: 'I have one little bit of bad news for you. The Doctors found that in order to save my life they had to amputate my right arm,'[106] but a less stark revelation of the reality of being wounded might be taken from the medical case sheet for Spr Hicking, 156 Fld Coy, RE.

Twenty-year-old Hicking was admitted to hospital for the third time on 19 June 1918 with a deep gunshot wound in his right shoulder received on 29 March. Portions of bone had been removed on the first two occasions. The wound was described in June as being a 'large cavity, deepest portion one inch'.

Hicking's problem was not wastage of the muscles or serious reduction in mobility in the joint but a persistent cough since being wounded and a feeling that his chest was 'full up'. The wound was opened up and treated with a 'salt sac' and such treatment continued for some months. On 16 May 1919 after more than a year of treament it was recorded that: 'Patient has been coughing at nights. Sputum examined and found to contain TB.' Hicking's left lung was found to be slightly affected but the 'patient should be fit with two or three month's treatment on sanatorium lines'. The 21-year-old's disability was moderate by comparison with many, but as a wounded soldier he may be taken as representative of two out of every five soldiers who landed in France whether or not they were to have served in the line.[107]

Duplicate with a difference. With and without the latest type of tube gas helmet, two Royal Scots Fusiliers officers, E. Hakewill Smith to the left, are commercially photographed not far behind the lines, 18 March 1916. (Major General Sir Edmund Hakewill Smith)

4

1916: The Somme

The sharp focus of words and pictures on the four and a half months of battle which together constitute the Battle of the Somme has been almost exclusively on the front-line infantry assault troops on the first day of the battle. The political and military context in which the battle was launched and maintained, the call upon troops of all arms, and that must include the officers and men of the Royal Flying Corps, the work of sappers and gunners (despite an obligatory reference to the bombardment) are seldom accorded their proper place. Tragedy is not diminished by being understood, and the historical context of the Somme is of fundamental significance. It can be stated quite simply: the relatively far smaller British military contribution to the Western Front war effort, against an enemy which chose to place her principal strength there, brought a quite proper degree of subservience to the military plans or needs of France, the nation bearing by far the brunt of the burden of the Western Front. The German invasion of France had enabled the seizure and maintenance of a strategic initiative. This placed upon the French the almost ruinous penalty of having to attack to clear the enemy from her frontiers when all advantage favoured the concealed defender. The position was critically re-emphasized in the German decision in late February 1916 to attack Verdun, forcing the French to drain their life blood of human and material resources to defend the city in order to avert what the French people as well as the German High Command would have adjudged a disastrous, irredeemable loss for the nation. With large numbers of newly trained British troops available, the time had clearly come for the BEF to redress the imbalance in military expenditure and for this to be done in an area, the Somme, where French and British could co-operate and not in an independent British operation further north which would have so much less relationship to pressing French needs.

There was much more; most notably in the Grand Strategy of concerting Russian, Italian and Franco-British offensives to exert a maximum impact upon the enemy. It has to be accepted that there was clear topographical advantage to the Germans in their lines north of the Somme overlooking the British positions. There also seems to be no indisputedly vital enemy objective to be taken in an Allied breakthrough on the Somme. The case against the Franco-British High Command may seem to be still more damning in their divergent thinking over the question of the length of the preliminary bombardment and the relationship of this to any attempt to secure surprise. As a further point in any indictment, it is retrospecively evident that the British Commander-in-Chief, with all chance of surprise gone, still hoped (at least initially) for a breakthrough while the Army Commander responsible for securing it, held to a more modest expectation of what was possible. With all this accepted to some degree, there are nevertheless strong arguments for attacking precisely when and where the attempt was made, as long as we accept that they are crowed conclusively if raucously by the French cockerel.

There are still matters to which reference must be made even if in an awareness that they will remain matters of debate. How reasonable was it to have such high confidence in the preliminary bombardment and such low confidence in the military capacity of New Army Divisions that this dictated the tactical formula by which the assaulting battalions were to cross no man's land in deliberately spaced successive waves of men in extended order, each man five yards apart, and held to a walking pace by instruction and by the sheer encumbrance of his equipment? We know that in the event, the German survivors of the British bombardment, protected as they were in their concrete dugouts, were not so disorientated that they could easily be mopped up by platoons in the later wave following upon the first lines of attackers whose duty was to press on to the next objective and maintain the momentum of the attack. Was there evidence at the time which invited a less sanguine anticipation of the effects of the bombardment and a greater awareness that the New Divisions had more than high morale to uplift them, but intelligence too, the exercise of which they were being denied? Should not more thought have been directed towards new, more flexible, infantry tactics? How well might New Army men have been expected to adapt to such revision? If there were some doubts about this, were there not Territorial and Regular Army Divisions whose active service soldiering offered reasonable ground for their successful employment of more flexible tactics? On these and other matters, such as the maintenance of the offensive to damage by degrees the very instrument by which the Germans made war, their Army, or the question of when, where and how the new weapon the tank might be employed, no categoric judgement will be offered here, but we shall look at the descriptive evidence of men training for the battle, serving the guns in the preliminary bombardment and at morale on the eve of the great day. We shall look too at those taking part on 1 July and in the desperate attack and counterattack of the first

Stokes Mortar ready for action. The simplicity of this private engineering firm design of a trench mortar led to its mass production and large-scale employment from 1916 until the mobile warfare of 1918 showed up its relatively heavy weight disadvantage. The Stokes 3-inch mortar range was about 400 yards. The officer on the right, holding one of the 'bombs' to be dropped down the barrel onto a striker pin which pierced the primer of a sporting cartridge set in its base, is James Hibbert (South Lancs) who was to win the Military Cross and two bars. (Captain J. E. Hibbert)

The eve of the Somme. Stretcher-bearers and orderlies of the 76th Field Ambulance, 7th Division, immediately before their work in front of Mametz on the first day of the battle. (Captain J. D. Todd)

weeks, at the September battles and in the ultimate demands of November before slimy, swallowing, winter mud rendered further attack patently futile.

Some attempt must be made by the reader to grasp the scale of the Battle of the Somme: more than one hundred and forty days of fighting on a British front of up to sixteen miles. One might usefully consider such a battle front extending from Central London almost to St Albans, or a distance approaching that which separates Salisbury from Southampton, Huddersfield from Oldham, Peebles from Galashiels or Merthyr Tydfil from Abergavenny. In a seven-day preliminary bombardment one and three quarter million shells were fired from two thousand British guns on the variegated pleasing pattern of green, brown and golden fields, dark green woods and pink-coloured farm hamlets and villages, a landscape as yet but slightly scarred by white entrenchments and grey belts of wire shielding four successive lines of fortified positions. Gommecourt, Serre, Beaumont Hamel, Beaucourt, Thiepval, Ovillers, La Boisselle, Longueval, Trônes Wood, Delville Wood and High Wood, Fricourt, Mametz, Montauban and Maricourt stood in the path of an obliterating tidal flood of exploding steel and shrapnel. A further twenty-six million shells would be expended before the offensive was closed four and a half months later. On 1 July in the minutes following the 7.30 a.m. zero hour, about 66,000 men in successive waves had clambered out of their forward trenches to attempt the crossing of no man's land. It was largely from these men that German artillery and then small arms fire took their terrible first day toll of 57,000 casualties of whom 19,000 had been killed. Such truly appalling losses were not to be repeated, but the battle had just begun, its nature progressively in less doubt as the German army and not the positions it held became the clear objective. John Terraine has identified 330 German attacks or counter-attacks upon the British or French, a chilling reminder of the two-fold character of the struggle being waged, producing a British total casualty list in excess of 400,000 killed, wounded and missing. Such statistics – and it would seem that the Germans suffered still more heavily than the combined British and French losses of 624,000 – numb clear thought, but if one were to look at the experience of individuals in battle, perhaps it is just possible to feel some identification with men dwarfed by the scale of the circumstance, but whose contemporary record does something to convey the unimaginable.

The pastoral peace of the sleepy Somme villages quite evidently stirred the troops whose arrival so transformed the region into one of concentrated military preparation. New roads, railways, gun positions, ammunition dumps, field hospitals, were constructed or emplaced under the RFC protective umbrella of offensive patrols and aerial observation of all enemy activity. Frequently the men in the build-up were bivouacked in the open: fine weather and the huge demand for billeting facilities combining to give unit after unit conditions almost akin to pre-1914 Scout or Territorial camping. An officer wrote, 'We have got a football and a cricket set and are amusing ourselves during the long evenings by playing both. I made 24 not out two evenings ago by the biggest lot of flukes one could possibly have. We only want some golf and tennis to make the place perfect.' In his next letter, the officer, Curtis Bain, made observations on the conditions of their wicket. 'Sometimes the ball would bounce right over your head and sometimes it would break over a yard. Just

For King and Country. Ernest Polack (on the right) sent this picture postcard of himself and his elder brother Benjamin, who had recently been killed in Mesopotamia, to a third brother Albert, serving at Gibraltar. Ernest wrote: 'The other side of this card is terrible to think of and has taken all the fighting spirit out of me.' The card was posted on 3 June 1916; Ernest himself had less than a month to live. (A. I. Polack)

Identification in battle. Designated insignia for units of the 4th Division and issued as cloth badges to be sewn on sacking covering the steel helmet. The sacking prevented the helmets from reflecting light and it also softened the sharp outline of the helmet. This secret order was issued by Major Stenhouse, a Staff Officer of the 31st Division. (Major S. B. L. Jacks)

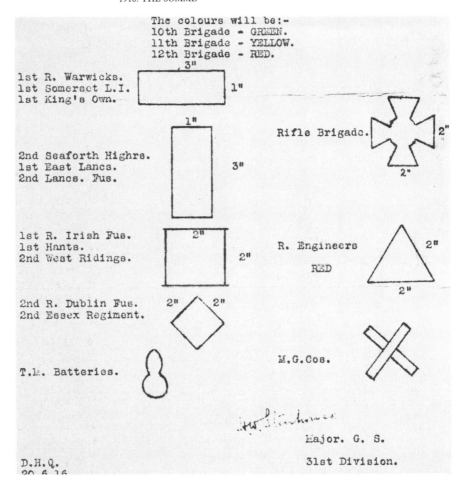

The colours will be:-
10th Brigade - GREEN.
11th Brigade - YELLOW.
12th Brigade - RED.

1st R. Warwicks.
1st Somerset L.I.
1st King's Own.

2nd Seaforth Highrs.
1st East Lancs.
2nd Lancs. Fus.

Rifle Brigade.

1st R. Irish Fus.
1st Hants.
2nd West Ridings.

R. Engineers
RED

2nd R. Dublin Fus.
2nd Essex Regiment.

M.G.Cos.

T.M. Batteries.

Major. G. S.
31st Division.

D.H.Q.
20.6.16

like those old games we used to play on the Stray.'[1] Officers and men bathed in rivers or canals, competed in battalion sports meetings while at night, cards and carousing completed a picture of troops in fine fettle and high morale. Hand-grenade fishing seems to have been one well-supported if unsporting pastime.

Officers of the 9th Duke of Wellington's Regiment lost no opportunity for fun. As late as 26 June: 'C. Coy. raided "B." Coy's mess at supper time and we went on ragging them until after 10 p.m. We had some boxing. I'm hoping that Hoole may have a black eye from a beautiful smashing round arm fling which landed full in his face. My style of boxing amused the spectators immensely. We ended up by blindfold boxing.' On 29 June: 'At 2 O'Clock we went out to a teashop and had coffee and cakes and champagne. We spent the rest of the evening doing nothing in particular, except a little mild ragging. Hoole hasn't got a black eye after all.' The ragging continued and the letter-writer, J. W. B. Russell, got

some: 'Nice clouts in on the Padre at Blindfold boxing.' The Battalion was not in action on July 1st, but Russell himself had but a week to live.[2]

Second Lieutenant F. B. Denham, with but a few days to live too, wrote to his schoolgirl sister of the idyllic setting of his billet, a: 'pukka old farm. There is a fine garden with plenty of rose bushes and some beaux lupins in one corner and bees in another. Milk, butter, cream and eggs are plentiful and last but not least the beer is quite palatable. What more could you ask after a really hard day,' a reference it may be presumed to the battle practice exercises he and his men were concerned with, though Denham himself called it: 'hard manoeuvres with Generals, nothing but brass and red tabs, all riding about and criticizing'.[3] According to Rifleman C. M. Woods, men of the Queen Victoria's Rifles were under 'strict training – small field days – lectures on the machine-gun for a full fortnight in May and then at night a new forward trench had to be dug by the men at the end of the month before he himself was sent on a three-week stretcher-bearing and first aid course.[4] On 21 June the battalion moved out of the line at Hebuterne for baths at Halloy, pay and to be 'allowed every possible privilege as this was to be our last rest before we attacked. Several rehearsals of the proposed method of attack were carried out!'

Naturally the tension mounted and found expression frequently in concern for those anxious at home. 'Don't worry about me Mother dear. I shall be all right whatever happens. I am getting in a stock of Field Service Post Cards so as to be able to send them off in case I couldn't send anything else. But I will write if I possibly can.'[5] To some parents, like those of Ernest Polack, more sombre letters were addressed. He was accurately to forecast his death: 'I consider it very unlikely that I shall get through it whole. Death has no terrors me me in itself, for (like Cleopatra) I have immortal longings in me. The prospect of pain naturally appals me somewhat, and I am taking morphia in with me to battle.' He gave instructions for the gift of his treasured books to members of his family and for money to a children's hospital and concluded: 'Our cause is a good one and I believe I am doing right in fighting. To you – Mother and Father – I owe all. The thought of you two and of my brothers will inspire me to the end.'[6]

Far more common than this stoic anticipation of death was a shared exhilaration of which H. G. R. Williams, in the ranks of the London Rifle Brigade, has written. 'Statistics showed that the number of men in all units reporting sick fell markedly once the date of the attack had been announced. No one wanted to miss it! We all wanted the LRB once again to distinguish itself, and to be there when it did so.' To this end they had trained near Halloy on ground where trenches had been laid out to represent their objective, the Gommecourt position, with name-boards showing the names given by Intelligence to the German trenches. The signallers had been told where their two parties (an NCO and two men) had to establish signal stations. 'One would roll out the wire and the other two between them would carry this man's rifle (as well as their own) and the buzzer instrument also a new visual signalling device, officially known as a "shutter" but usually called by us a "flapper". We actually ran out the cable just as we would do on the day. All the preparations for the attack struck us as being very thorough. Everyone knew exactly where to go and what to do.'[7]

Not all the preparations had gone smoothly, such could hardly be expected. An Ulster Riflemen with a working party was carrying his rifle, equipment ammunition and waterproof. Heavy rain had fallen on occasion in the last days before zero hour and he found the communication trenches densely crowded with other fully equipped working parties, the

New Zealand gunners on the Somme, well emplaced and with camouflage netting, in front of their 18-pounder. Gunner T. N. Sutherland on the extreme right. (T. N. Sutherland)

On the reverse of this picture postcard, Sergeant Stafford of the Northumberland Fusiliers has described himself as: 'Hair – Brown, Eyes – Blue, complexion – ruddy, Size of a 1/- Codling.' He was from Sunderland, a Marksman as his arm badge shows, and was killed on the first day of the Somme. A member of his Company wrote: 'We went over the top together. One minute he was there, the next he was gone.' (C. Cannon) resulting congestion and confusion making it more infuriating when his party discovered that its picks and shovels had been 'borrowed' so a further journey for replacements was necessary. Iron rations or a tin of Maconachies stew were not the stuff to re-invigorate jaded spirits in their short break and James MacRoberts has written of the best hours, when they were keen in the morning, being wasted by wearisome, sickening, wanderings and delays.[8] Detachedly it is all too easy but still perhaps fair to consider that, 'it was every thus'.

Not only by aircraft reconnaissance and by balloon, but by trench periscope or camouflaged vantage point, the opposition's lines had been constantly scrutinized. Aerial photographic mosaics provided photographic interpretation personnel with new details for revised mapping, while the artillery officers in Forward Observation Posts scanned the terrain for the smallest detail on their sector. '23 May 8.45 A German was observed at the crossroads in Mametz. White coat, light blue trousers and carried a water bottle in his right hand. 25 May Four Germans passed from Contalmaison Wood to Pozières.'[9] Then this officer, I. R. H. Probert, makes an observation of far wider significance. '27 May The new propellant NCT – nitro-cellulose tubular is very unsatisfactory as it not only shoots short but is also inconsistent. We have carried

out a very unsatisfactory experimental shoot this afternoon.' When so meticulous an artillery diarist is also in position to see the effect of the great bombardment when it commenced, our attention is commanded by what he wrote. On Saturday 24 June he records the 18-pounders having been: 'wire cutting steadily all day' and on 25 June he reports the wire as 'very effectively cut all along the line with 18 Pdrs. and 60 Pdrs. TMs,' but on 26 June, 'The 18 Pdrs had some prematures and several short'. For 27 June Probert wrote that an effective smoke barrage was fired using tins of red phosphorous with a 5-second fuse and on 29 June he reported that the centre of Mametz village was so completely flattened that on 30 June 'there was not much left to bombard'. He was, in a sense, correct for the wire in this sector had been quite well cut and defensive emplacements deluged with shells, but they had not been destroyed and from deep dugouts emerged men whose appearance Probert could not until later explain in his entry for 1 July for he called them, 'snipers', hundreds of them, 'left behind' by the Germans as 'our infantry took the front line and supports quite easily.'

No one should doubt the thoroughness of the artillery planning, but it was planning which failed to take account of the possibility of failure in its fundamental purpose, the complete destruction of the enemy's capacity to interfere with the progress of the British infantry. In secret instructions for the advance of the artillery on 'Z' Day it was stipulated that: 'During the afternoon Brigade and Battery Commanders each with an armed orderly and carrying loaded revolvers will meet the Brigade Commander at Brigade Headquarters. They will walk forward by the line of advance of batteries to reconnoitre and select positions for the guns.' Penultimate in ten instructions it was stated that: 'as many wire cutters as possible will be wanted'. Another set of orders detailed that practice bombardments would take place to: 'render everything foolproof as far as possible' but such practices could not make up for the insufficiency of heavy guns and of high-explosive shells, nor of the unanticipated number of dud shells – in any case it fundamentally underestimated what had to be destroyed to give the infantry a chance.[10]

Operation orders for the 23rd Battalion, Northumberland Fusiliers (4th Bn, Tyneside Scottish) listed the objectives of which the first included four successive lines of trenches at La Boiselle. The battalion was to follow the 20th Northumberland Fusiliers into the attack, every man carrying his rifle and equipment less pack, two extra bandoliers of small arms ammunition, 3 Mills grenades, one iron ration and rations for the day of assault, haversack and waterproof cape, four sandbags, two gas helmets and one pair of Spicer goggles, for all except bombers and signallers, either a pick or a shovel, a full water bottle and of course a mess tin. Attached to every man's back was the unit distinguishing mark of a yellow cloth equilateral triangle, base upwards. 'All ranks must be clearly warned that men are on no account whatsoever to assist wounded.' Additionally it was pointed out that hand-grenades were difficult to replenish and must not be thrown indiscriminately. There was, it may be remarked, encouragement amidst all that was burdensome or even, to some, an affront – the playing of the Pipes. As had been instructed, the Piper for each company was to play the men into no man's land and the official diary for the 23rd Bn recorded that the pipers had 'continued to play until either killed or wounded'.

At 9 a.m. on 2 July the remnants of this Battalion were formed up for roll call after the terrible withering of their attack. About 100 men answered with perhaps 20 turning up during the day. Two out of 21 officers were unscathed. There had been 629 casualties in all, out of an attacking force of about 750 men. It was not quite as overwhelming as the 710 of the 1st Newfoundland Regiment or that of the 10th West Yorks, but the figure cruelly mocks the care with which the attack had been planned and perhaps unfairly rivets attention upon the fact that: 'The Brigadier was delighted with the fine performance and bravery shown by the Battalion.' [11] Distanced from the Brigadier's need to praise and reassure and the circumstantial unseemliness of expressions of sympathy, I think we may safely assume he was dismayed too.

Officially expressed dismay there was. The Regimental War Diary of the 16th Northumberland Fusiliers for 1 July is not written with the detached language one would expect, the phrases are vibrant with a sort of outraged disbelief at what had to be recorded. 'The enemy stood upon their parapet and waved to our men to come on and picked them off with rifle fire. The enemy's fire was so intense that the advance was checked and the waves, or what was left of them, were forced to lie down.' Concerning subsequent waves: 'Getting over the parapet the first Platoon lost a great number of men and the remainder of the Coy was ordered to "stand fast" and hold the line. . . . The enemy's artillery continued firing on no man's land and our front line trench all day, which no doubt accounted for a large number of the casualties amongst the Coys that were lying out. [On orders to withdraw those lying out in no man's land]

"A" Coy of the 2nd Royal Irish Fusiliers commanded by Captain Williams rendered excellent work in carrying back the wounded men who were lying out. Our S. B. [stretcher-bearers] also did good work all day as did everyone who took part in the attack. The men of the attacking companies moved forward like one man until the murderous fire of the enemy's M. G. [machine-guns] forced them to halt. Not a man wavered and after nightfall we found in several places, straight lines of ten or twelve dead or badly wounded as if the Platoons had just been dressed for Parade.' [12]

The grief of the 16th's CO, Lieutenant Colonel W. H. Ritson, has been recalled by his bugler, Stanley Henderson, standing with his Colonel as they watched the advancing Fusiliers fall as if tied to the same steadily drawn string. The Colonel had forcibly to be restrained from clambering over the parapet, his cry of sheer desolation 'My men! My men!, My God my men' being imprinted ineffaceably upon the bugler's memory. [13]

Concerning the terrible experience of the Newfoundland Regiment, caught by small arms fire from 'Y' Ravine as they moved up towards the British front line at Beaumont Hamel, Frank Moakler simply put his head down to 'avoid' bullets and shell fragments and trusted that his steel helmet would see him through. When he reached the gap in the British wire he found it so choked with bodies that he had to look up for an alternative way forward. He had already been wounded, but did not know this until he felt his tunic wet with blood. He seemed to be alone and dropped down behind the wall of bodies at the gap just in front of the most forward trench. The distance being so short he was able to crawl back to the British trench and there found remnants of his battalion, attempting to use their field dressings to bandage themselves. He himself had emerged as one of the slightest casualties among 710. The battalion had taken three more than the normal number of officers used in an attack. Every single officer was hit and the battalion was recorded as having 14 officers killed, 219 other ranks killed and 91 missing. [14]

An individual's reactions, officer or man, are as individual as his finger prints and they were subject to change too. On 29 June, George Norrie wrote to his mother 'Very hot stuff here and I am enjoying myself. Talk about "Shell out" this show beats it – I think I was made for it,' and to his brother four days later: 'It is rather sickening that the only part of the line which is being held up is where I am . . . we are trying a new stunt tonight. The 6th Bn of my own regiment who are also in this division have suffered heavily early this morning and 3 of the fellows who were with me at Dover were killed. I am not in the show yet but waiting my turn. It is pretty hot stuff here. . . . Hell of a bombardment last night. There is nothing left of Clyde (Besch's) regiment, Colonel, Adjutant etc., all killed. . . . I feel perfectly confident that I will be alright when my turn comes but I am quite untrained as an officer still. We were told that we had come out to finish our training at Etaples as it is we have come out to be finished off.

3 p.m. Have just heard very bad news. An orderly has returned from the Adjutant to say the battalion went over this morning and came back 150 strong only – 4 officers left. As we are here to replace casualties we will be going up tonight. Apparently they were enfiladed by machine guns.' To his mother on 7 July 1916: 'I am in the trenches now but I would very much rather be in the Piccadilly Grill. . . . I have got a platoon and that is why I am up in the trenches. I was waiting for the the former Platoon Commander to be killed and sure enough he has been – how the men can be expected to follow me if we "go over" again God only knows – I have never seen them before – they have never seen me and I don't even belong to the regiment.'[15]

German troops, from the relative security of a deep dugout, await the British assault. (Photograph taken from a German soldier captured on the Somme). (C. G. T. Dean)

On the eve of the battle, some if opportunity allowed it, secured temporary oblivion in a drinking spree, others, not necessarily renowned for religious observance, turned to neglected Bibles, a source of comfort for many no matter how artificially precipitated the faith in its message. J. G. Barron was fervently to pray, but his fear of the thundering guns was to outmatch the protection he sought from prayer.[16] An intriguing contrast in mood is recorded in the memoirs of a 6th Cameron who noted the gleeful anticipation of a former 'graduate', not of Glasgow University as were many of this battalion but of Peterhead prison, whose stated intention was to come out of the battle with 'wrist-watches up to his elbows'.[17]

The fear of Private Henry Barber (5th Battalion, London Regiment) grew from both what he saw of the fate of the first three companies of his battalion attacking at Gommecourt ('men were falling like ninepins') and then what he heard from wounded crawling back from undestroyed wire where they had been held up, targets as pathetic as sitting ducks. The machine-gun fire was intense and Barber prayed that he would not have to go over the top. He was saved from this ordeal at the expense of another: a shrapnel ball striking him in the spine, opening up the flesh to cause extensive bleeding and necessary evacuation.[18]

A well sandbagged nest for this Vickers machine-gun of the Machine-Gun Corps. The officer to the right, Cecil Hibbert, was to command a Battalion of the MGC before the end of the war. (Captain J. E. Hibbert)

What left an abiding impression on George Ramshaw (Pte, 18th DLI) was the crowded trench conditions where he waited with an ammunition carrying party. Movement for the heavily laden men was made almost impossible as both lightly wounded and grievously wounded men clambered or fell back in the trenches from the front and in so doing added to the crush as support troops attempted to enter from the rear. The support troops were coming up through communication alleys and then had to filter to right or left ready to attempt a timed emergence of a new wave of the attack.[19]

W. J. Seneschall, a signaller with the Suffolks, remembered having heard it emphasized so strongly that there would be no opposition, that at first he found it impossible to credit that it was enemy small arms fire and shrapnel hurtling into and over his parapet. 'Then I began to feel panicky, I felt like bolting or something. I looked at the officer – a stranger – and he glanced at me. I don't know who looked the worse. However it steadied me and him too I think. We were afraid to be seen to be afraid.' Soon the sole survivor of his signalling party,

Seneschall was to crawl out of a shell-hole pushing the drum of vital wire ahead of him. He had to negotiate a route round corpses and great clods of earth, witnessing the shell tossing of a legless corpse high in the air. It fell near Seneschall who still remembers the vacant look on the face under the tin hat kept on by the chin strap throughout its ghastly flight. The trench ahead of the signaller still showed moving German helmets and all the Suffolk signaller could do was lie still throughout the day as the enemy speculatively shelled and machine-gunned no man's land. As the light faded and a German came over his parapet, Seneschall risked a stiff-legged stumbling run to the British lines, treading on wounded calling for water and attention and tearing his uniform on wire, but falling safely into a British trench after thirteen hours amidst the wreckage of his battalion's attack.[20]

An eve of battle church service was ordained for the 18th DLI as for other battalions. Sergeant Durrant surveyed the khaki throng. 'I don't think anyone was actually afraid. We simply wondered what was going to happen to us. The only thing we dreaded was being maimed for the rest of our lives. We sang "Away with hearts so gay, Away we go to fight the foe" but I'm sure there were no actually "gay" hearts.' Durrant was carefully to carry up two stone rum jars through the congestion of the communication ways to the trenches opposite

Beaumont Hamel. The rum was doled out and 'C' Company waited for news of 'A' and 'B' Companies' advance. Knowing that the village of Beaumont Hamel must have been shelled to smithereens, the waiting men were ready to believe that the first waves had seized their objectives. Durrant remembers that the 'battlefield itself was awesome. Dark clouds of smoke hung everywhere and our aeroplanes seemed to be doing low flying in all directions. Fountains of earth erupted from shell explosions and bursting shrapnel shells seemed to fill the lower sky. With the platoon officers I walked forward ignoring an appeal from a wounded Tommy to help him. We had hardly progressed ten yards, before the Officer was hit. As he fell he simply said "carry on Sergeant". I did but not for long. Suddenly I felt as if a whole mine had exploded beneath me, I was buzzed round like a top and fell to the ground.'[21]

Also opposite Beaumont Hamel was William Strang, a keenly observant if somewhat vulnerably introspective subaltern of the 4th Worcesters. Just before the attack, he recorded in his diary that: 'up by the wire, one foot in front of it is a brood of partridges. The male went off and made a disturbance leaving the hen still sitting within two feet of Bannister. Then she also rose and made a plaintive noise a few yards away. Pretty little things the chicks.' The partridges were not alone in disturbance and Strang felt concern for the French villagers being evacuated for their own good. 'The dear old things at our billet are leaving tomorrow. She is suffering severely but bears up: I had a long chat with her. For herself she would stay but she goes for the sake of her deaf and dumb daughter who would be left helpless if the older people were killed . . . if she had "Guillaume" she would tear his eyes out and cut him up into little bits.'

Strang's sensibility is clearly evident in his diary on the eve of the 'Push'. He writes of having to censor a lot of pathetic loving letters and, when he got a chance on July 16 to resume his diary, he provides an account of a searing collective experience, an account made the more significant because it turned out to be one of almost clinical observation of the individuals of a small unit under prolonged exposure to acutely stressful conditions. Strang was with what he called the 'wretched ten per cents' kept out of the assault on 1 July and when they joined his Company of 4th Worcesters he found the officers depressed, but evidently, of their number, Baird, had earned universal respect for his courage, energy, resource and cheerfulness. The Company was heavily shelled throughout the night and kept without rest. 'There were dead lying everywhere –

'Rhodes and the rooks'. A mixed bunch of soldiers waiting to be posted to units replacing losses on the Somme inspired this drawing by Allan Gwynne Jones who, after service in the ranks, was commissioned and posted to the 1st Battalion, Welsh Guards. In the picture, Rhodes, the officer, is depicted loading his pistol to shoot at some rooks, but Rhodes himself, and several of the men, were themselves to be casualties before long. (A. Gwynne Jones)

on the bottom of the trench, behind the trench, on top, in all sorts of attitudes, huddled up or extended, some badly blown about, some with hardly a mark. There were wounded everywhere whom it was impossible to move owing to the lack of stretchers. One poor fellow of the Royals lay behind one of my traverses for 20 hours till at last after repeated messages I manged to get the RF stretcher-bearers up. He was game though, cheerful to the end, despite a broken leg. There were others in worse case who filled the dark with groans. It was many hours before we could get them clear. One youngster of the KOSBs came hobbling along with a stick, with one leg disabled, the pluckiest little fellow I have seen for many a day. My men were splendid though there was a fair amount of shell shock. H., the late servant of Toose, the Staff Captain, lay flat in the trench shaking and groaning and moaning that he was afraid to die and half shrieking as each shell came back. He was at my feet most of the night. Also a report came in that Sgt. W. was in a fit. This proved to be incorrect though Corporal H. had become slightly unhinged for an hour or two. He did not go sick though but endured stolidly for many days after. . . .' The Company was ordered to prepare for an attack and just as it was to be launched, a cancellation order arrived. 'I was not sorry.' This particular unit held on to its position for several days. Casualties were suffered and Strang's supervisory duties led him to sleep at night in a variety of locations, one being an abandoned 'shanty' in a communication trench next to a huge crater. Here he was: 'comfortable but lonely and fearful of getting hit while alone. Nothing is more eerie than wandering alone at night through deserted trenches knee deep in water. Water is bad for several reasons – you splash in it and cannot hear shells coming and if you do hear them you can't run fast enough to take shelter behind traverses. . . . Dingley annoyed me at first – very typically Birmingham like Bruton only worse but later I saw his good qualities and repented. I was in a very bad state most of the time. Shells don't agree with me. I was ill-tempered, worried, querulous and absolutely lacking in energy or interest in the work. I managed to show a good face to the men but could not before my pals. If only Leland had been there I should have been different. I had no one to turn to.'

'Our tenure seemed interminable: day after day and no sign of relief. The eternal question to Ramsden – any news of relief. But no. The men broke down slowly, most of them. Some of my men stood firm – Smart and Cross, Helley and York, Dare and Hunt. Dare was buried and came back from Hospital next day. The platoon was cheered by the arrival of Court and Smith who took on Mess

Orderly and did it well. No game bringing dixies up 1st Avenue under shell fire. Sgt. W. stuck to the end but only just. He was nearly beaten two days from the end and burst into tears as he told me so – but most of the time he was nervy and loved deep-dugouts. It needed a great effort and much self conquest to allow [enable] him to perform his duties. He has not the confidence of his men, but he is a brave little soul all the same. I wonder what my men think of me. They looked a lot of wrecks, unwashed and unshaven. I had only one wash in 15 days and two shaves. In consequence possible I now have eczema. . . . We are for it shortly again – it may be any day. This weighs heavily on us all. We remember the Newfoundlanders on July 1st. It makes me feel eerie at night. I am not brave and I think about things too much. Much shell fire would drive me mad. I am disappointed with myself and am terribly afraid of giving way.'

On 20 July this officer recorded an unsuccessful British raid two days earlier. The three officers leading the raid were apparently not well supported by their men, one of whom was to be court martialled. The Battalion Commander, Cayley, addressed the 4th Worcesters and roundly scorned them, their Divisional Commander, de Lisle, (29 Div) 'threatens that if the spirit of the troops does not improve, if our men go on letting down their officers the Battalion will be sent roadmaking on the Lines of Communi-

14 July on the Somme in front of High Wood. The 20th Deccan Horse are assembled behind the 35th Battery, Royal Field Artillery whose four guns are in action (numbered on the photograph). At 7 p.m. a Squadron of the Deccan Horse would advance to give cover to attacking infantry and they would themselves be protected from a German machine-gun by a British aircraft locating and neutralizing the fire. As darkness fell the troopers dismounted (their horses being held behind a sheltering bank) and the men continued to give covering fire. (Lieutenant Colonel I. R. H. Probert)

cation. It cuts Cayley to the heart that his battalion should come to such a pass.'[22]

The 1st Border Regiment was also within the 29th Division and Sergeant A. T. Fraser had last-minute preparations to decide with his officers the precise position for a newly available step ladder to get out of their assault trench. He has remembered thinking that the officer would have to go up first and face whatever was coming and then, as Sergeant, he had to see the platoon up the ladder before going up himself. 'I think I prayed for him.' Fraser called his men from the protection of their deep dugout just before zero hour and when the mine exploded and the whistle blew, up everyone went, twenty-seven in all, seven being hit in their fleeting seconds at the top of the ladder. 'I just had to lay them on the firestep clearing the ladder for the next man to go up.' 'When I passed through the gap in our barbed wire into no man's land which was a shambles of bodies dead or wounded, tins, barbed wire, shell-holes, already a message was being shouted back telling me the officer was hit. I hurried to the head of the platoon to take command and although I hadn't paused to look for him I certainly didn't see him.'

Fraser was convinced that on his sector it was the machine-gun fire which cut them: 'criss-cross fire as thick as snow or hail blizzard'. He had seven men left when he heard an order to lie down and this they did for about a minute yet the second in command, Major Meiklejohn, 'Never lay down, he walked to and fro in front of us fretting at the delay and slapping his breeches with his cane.' When the order came to renew the advance, Fraser got to the enemy wire before he was hit, fell and has no memory of the seven hours he lay unconscious until he found himself on a stretcher before the Battalion Medical Officer, a 50-year-old, grey-haired Doctor, a pre-war Medical Missionary in China. 'His bare arms were covered in blood and needing his spectacles wiped by an orderly!'[23]

The work of a number of Regimental Medical Officers on 1 July was to be interrupted by their becoming casualties themselves. G. D. Fairley, attached to the 2nd Battalion Royal Scots Fusiliers, was a case in point. With his stretcher-bearers he brought up the rear of his battalion's crossing of no man's land towards Montauban in the second wave of the assault at 8.30 a.m. They had to cross a number of British trenches, occasionally lying down because of rifle fire from the left. Heavy high-explosive shelling delayed their advance up a communication trench and here he treated some wounded. By ladder he got into the open to cross to the next trench and found the ground everywhere cratered by high-explosive shelling. On the way up West Avenue, the trench leading to a jutting out position of the British front line, he recorded the walking cases of wounded. In no man's land: 'Heavy shell-fire was falling all round in close vicinity . . . a number of dead and wounded were lying around, some in the barbed wire entanglements. Up the slope the German fire trench lay less than 100 yards away. I decided to get in the wounded before further advance. While waiting in the open for the stretcher squad a shell burst 6 feet away and wounded me in the right arm as well as Private Alcock one of the stretcher-bearers who was near me.' Fairley got back to the British Front Line where his wound was dressed and without full use of his right arm he worked in the British lines attending to wounded before going to a collecting post to assist in the evacuation of casualties. At this post, three captured German Medical Officers were dressing the walking cases of German wounded, penned in a barbed wire compound. In the evening, Fairley and some of his stretcher-bearers crossed no man's land to link up with the Royal Scots. In German dugouts he recorded and treated wounded while the shell-damaged trenches were reconstructed by the new occupants. 'The German dugouts had a very narrow entrance and were very deep. They emitted a strange smell characteristic of the Germans.'

Quite apart from the craters and ruined trenches, Fairley, in his diary account, noticed large numbers of unexploded shells, witness to this serious feature of the British artillery programme. Nevertheless the trenches showed: 'Many score of German dead, killed probably by shell fire. Many had brain wounds. Occasionally I saw one living in a group of dead, indicated by a flicker of an eye.' Fairley worked the remainder of the day, only making his way to an Advanced Dressing Station to have treatment for himself, at midnight.[24]

It is perhaps excusable in a book devoted to First World War soldiering rather than to the Battle of the Somme itself, to concentrate upon 1 July, but it must be remembered that the prolonged battle made new or different demands upon the survivors of the first day and upon units making their way through summer, autumn and early winter to join a national effort on a transformed scale from that of the 1914 BEF. There were the changed tactics of pre-dawn, unobserved, concentration in no man's land on 14 July which brought significant success; there was the sense of isolation for small units engaged in savage formless attack and counter-attack in dank, destroyed woods when the only cover was hastily excavated foxholes, fallen smashed trees, sodden

Delville Wood. An Australian's photograph of a ruined
landscape, sacred to South Africans. (L. Lovett)

undergrowth and often a new grey rash of wiring,
further to slow progress through thorned clinging
vegetation.

In such circumstances an imperishable record of
endurance was carved by South African troops in
Delville Wood. Arthur Betteridge (Signaller S.A.
Scottish) as he entered the wood on 15 July took into

September 1916 and a funeral in the field. The burial of
Major Knight, Officer in Command of the Eaton Motor
Machine-Gun Battery, 1st Canadian MMG Brigade.
(Lieutenant Colonel George Scroggie)

action not merely his necessary, cumbersome equipment but; 'a small towel, hair brush and comb and
my diary. I was wearing an overcoat owing to the
rain'. Under continuous concentrated shelling, with
the wood a shambles of destruction; 'we had to clear
paths and small communication trenches of rubble
to bring up ammunition and what replacements we
could find for the casualties. It was not possible to
bring out the wounded for hours at a time and then a
lot of them were killed or wounded again on their
way back. In the wood itself, the few men still
surviving, repulsed numerous counter-attacks.'
Somehow tea was brewed, but in the main the troops
had to rely on emergency rations. Continuous action
denied them sleep and the intense shelling never

8th Battalion Norfolk Regiment before their ordeal on the first day of the Battle of the Somme. Although the Norfolks and other battalions of the 18th Division captured their Montauban Ridge objectives, it was at heavy cost – in the Norfolks' case, 11 officers and 292 men killed, wounded and missing. The subaltern on the right, Eric Miall-Smith, wrote to his parents on 4 July 1916 that the battle 'was perfect hell – it was a marvel how anyone could get over that alive'. He himself was wounded in Delville Wood on 20 July. On recovery he transferred to the Royal Flying Corps and was killed in aerial combat in September 1917. (G. E. Miall-Smith)

seemed to abate. On 17 July every available man, batmen, HQ sanitary men, cooks were sent forward to support the weakening hold over a section of the wood. On the evening of 18 July, such had been the casualties that 'there were no officers to give orders, the few NCOs still alive were carrying on half stupid from fatigue'. Not a single telephone line had been kept intact and all communication to the rear was by runner. Few runners reached their destination. Private Betteridge, who had reached Battalion HQ with one message, was returning to the wood in the evening of 18 July. Gas shells made the wearing of gas masks essential despite the problem for a sweating runner of peering into the gloom through the misting eye pieces but for some time to come the South African's problems were to be of a different nature as the nose cap of an exploding shell slammed into his thigh, breaking it, leaving him immobile and only rescued at the cost of further wounds to stretcher-bearers and original victim alike.[24]

In September, a renewed onslaught brought a new weapon of war, the tank, into the fray, but it is clear that even at the level of the individual soldier the character of the Somme was already understood – heady hopes of a breakthrough had been dispersed like morning mist by the sun, in its place was a more

firmly rooted realism. 'Some people at home seem to think we are only trying to gain ground and that because we haven't broken through we have failed. It is a wrong idea. We are simply killing Bosch and gaining ground in the effort.'[25]

Of the nature of fighting in Delville Wood, High Wood and Trônes Wood, something can be gathered from an original document in the economic wording of the late July diary of Sergeant G. Minton (17th Middlesex). '27 July. Still in same trench. Leaving at 1 p.m. take up position in Delville Wood (casualties heavy about 250) Delville Wood just captured. Counter attack easily repulsed. Terrible gun fire. 28 July. Still holding position in Delville Wood. Counter attack in morning repulsed. Digging in hard. Unable to get food or water up owing to curtain of fire. More rum than water. 29 July. Still in front of Delville Wood repulsing all German attacks hoping to be relieved during night. Heavy gun fire. Relieved about 10 p.m. by Essex Coy. Done up, glad to get out. Marched back about 3/4 mile to old German trench.'[26]

On 12 September, Private R. M. Liddle (1st Bn Coldstream Guards) wrote home thanking for a parcel which had been: 'a real treat. We have just time to finish it before we go up the line. We move

Mark I Tanks near Montauban September 1916: the first sight for New Zealanders and for many others. A New Zealander watches a Tank section trundling towards its assembly point. Note the short-lived wheel attachment at the rear to assist in steering. (A. Wilson)

this afternoon so don't expect any letters for a few days.'[27] He was to take part in, but not survive, the attack on 15 September renowned in the records of many regiments and not least the Coldstream Guards and having a place of premier distinction in the history of armoured vehicle warfare. On the geographical right of the British line on the Somme, battalions of the Brigade of Guards followed behind a creeping barrage in attacking from Ginchy towards Lesboeufs, but their penalty in approaching an objective more than two miles distant was in being enfiladed from uncaptured positions on their flanks. Sergeant Rumming (2nd Bn, Coldstream) who was to be wounded, simply noted the day in his diary as 'a day of blood'.[28]

Heavy rain had made the ground so slimy and boggy that even walking was difficult at Ginchy, and R. C. Bingham (3rd Bn Coldstream), confided in his diary for 14 September that he could not see how the Cavalry were even going to get up to Ginchy to follow up any attack if rain were to fall on the morrow. Everywhere was in a terrible mess, not even a recognizable brick in Ginchy itself, the sunken roads up to it an extended stinking charnel house. His orders held him to Company HQ, the staff of which was to follow immediately upon the assaulting troops, a moving location which he judged placed them potentially where the German counter-barrage would fall. That evening a: 'letter arrived from Irene hoping I have got a good billet. Trônes Wood [the

devastation of which he had just left] and with the prospect of popping over the parapet in 9 hours time. Ye Gods!!'

Four days later the diary was resumed. The late arrival of the tanks was noted, barrage and counter-barrage described and even the lighting of a cigarette to see if his hands and then lips could show steadiness. Crossing no man's land was made more acceptable by seeing German prisoners showing evident reluctance, despite bayonet prodding, to pass back through the German counter-barrage. Bingham was slightly wounded by a bullet which actually penetrated his steel helmet but he was not incapacitated. From his position, making a shell-hole in the German trench into a dugout, he could see the village of Flers on the left with British troops just beyond it and two tanks close by. Enigmatically he wrote of the tanks: 'It appears that those who meant to go went all right, but most of the others only poked their noses into Ginchy and then stopped.'

When survivors were drawn back to Trônes Wood, 'it was a tremendous relief to the nerves and I didn't know how done up I was until Whitaker told me that poor little "Four Buttons" had been killed. I confess I went away by myself and cried like a child for five minutes.'[29]

It is unusual to read in an original document, battle experience described with savage relish, but an example can be taken from the letters of an officer in the Northumberland Fusiliers, E. G. Bates. In a letter dated 25 September he describes a dawn affair in no man's land when opposing raiders encountered each other. 'I stuck 2 Huns with my bayonet and two more came for me. As I withdrew my rifle from No. 2 the bayonet handle stuck in his equipment. I slipped the bayonet off and got No. 3 over the side of the head with the rifle. No. 4's bayonet was now within a foot of my throat. I couldn't have got to him quick enough but I saw him throw up his hands and collapse gurgling. I looked round and saw my platoon sergeant with a satisfied grin on his face.' Bates's account goes on vividly to describe the capture of a section of German trench but the loss of all communication with British positions and the death of several runners until he was able to lead a party on the double journey for rations and water. He ends this letter with a tribute to a tall, wounded German corporal who had brought in casualties from no man's land. 'The whole show was packed full of interest and was I think the best I've been in yet and that's saying something.'[30]

Infantry reaction to the sight of tanks in action for the first time varied. A King's Royal Rifleman wrote: 'We had a wonderful new toy to go over with us. I don't know what it is really called officially. It is a kind of armoured car which spits forth machine-gun fire and 6pdrs. from it and goes over any obstacle.'[31]

Less enamoured was a Welsh Guardsman, W. A. F. L. Fox Pitt. He cautioned his father against believing what 'that ass Beach Thomas' the War Correspondent had reported. 'Two tanks did very well but on the whole they were a failure. They were much too slow and the infantry passed them in their first rush. Of course it is the first time they had been used and nobody really expected very much of them. They work along just behind our barrage which creeps or moves gradually forward and just in front of the infantry. The tanks are supposed to go 6 m.p.h. but they scarcely do 3 m.p.h. over this ground – it is one mass of mine craters and shell holes and smashed up villages. They look like great slugs creeping along and if they were a bit faster and not so liable to get engine trouble would fairly put the wind up Fritz.'[32]

Bob Tate drove one of the thirty-two tanks which did get up to the starting line on the morning of 15 September. Tate's tank performed well from the time a whistle sounded as a signal for starting up. A German shell wrecked the wheels at the rear designed to assist with steering but neither this damage nor the 'hailstones' of machine-gun bullets hitting the tank caused serious difficulty except for the breaking of the glass prisms in the viewing slots. Tate's recall is not of the problems of fumes, heat, noise, the overcrowding of eight men in a rolling bucking vehicle, the danger of a shell explosion igniting petrol in its containers, of hot moving machinery or fear of being incinerated, but instead one of elation and tremendous confidence in both the machine itself and in the team spirit of the crew.[33]

It is interesting to note that at least one young officer, Captain F. E. Hotblack, who was to distinguish himself later in the year, (on foot leading a tank into action as snow had obscured the direction tapes) had no illusions about the current limitations of the tank. Hotblack furthermore took the opportunity of telling Churchill to his surprise and a little displeasure that 'a man on foot could move faster and see much better than the crew inside a tank. Whether the man or the tank was knocked out depended entirely on what action the enemy took.'[34]

Conditions under which the final 1916 attack on the Somme was undertaken in November earned some succinct references in Guy Chapman's diary: 'Bloody cold and thick fog. Breakfast simply damnable. Mud everywhere, everyone peevish – Gas shells. Put on helmets: took them off again . . . lay in shell hole and hoped for the best . . . No. 1 Coy is badly knocked out. Lander and Young both badly wounded. C.S.M. Dell wounded Farrington killed. Sgt. Brown not expected to live. Sgt. Baker wounded. Westle poor fellow killed. Foley, the last of his family killed and a lot of other good men – too many to speak of. The Coy, apart from the Lewis Gunners, is 27 all told. It is impossible to describe the country. The impression is that some Volcanic blast has struck it. Vegetation scarcely anywhere . . . everywhere is desolate. By Beaucourt station lie the skeletons of five wagons and their teams, the grisly evidence of the tragedy of a Bosche ration convoy. There is a sickly stench, the mixed smell of exploded picric acid, gas, blood, putrifying corpses and broken bricks. Here and there still lie the bodies of the fallen – here an officer his back on the lip of the trench, his fingers stiff and clutching, down by the roadside is a Bosche, his helmet smashed at his side with a hole in his head showing how a piece of shell caught him as he turned to run back up the road . . . another, a fine man, proud and fierce with a moustache and Imperial. He died fighting. The burial parties work without ceasing. 800 Englishmen and forty Germans were buried yesterday – evidence of what price the assaulting parties must pay for some few yards of ground. Damn Germany!'[35]

Chapman was writing of an area where the Royal Naval Division had been heavily engaged. The war diaries of battalions of the RND provide evidence of the collective experience of many individuals in the final stages of the Somme. While in its Assembly Trenches, on 13 November, the Anson Battalion was caught by gas and high-explosive shells, its Colonel being among the killed. Hot cocoa was issued for all, great coats were dumped at 5.45 a.m. and the battalion followed the Howe Battalion by advancing in four waves into the mist, visibility being but a few yards. 'Considerable casualties were incurred in no man's land and near the 1st and 2nd German trenches on the right.' In those places where German positions were captured: 'the bottoms of the trenches were impassable owing to the deep soft mud in which a man could get completely stuck, the trenches were blown, in many places and outside the trenches the shell-torn land was nearly as bad and very difficult to cross . . . the remainder of the details of the Battn. were in German 3rd line where they were subjected to a barrage fire from our own guns for some minutes and had to retire to German 2nd line, reoccupying the 3rd line when the barrage had been stopped.'[36] The night of 13/14 November was very cold, men getting little sleep but rations were brought up under shell fire, the shelling continuing intermittently throughout the night.

In the following two days the subdivided battalion played its part in the capture of objectives up to and including Beaucourt, but this battalion and its sister battalion in the division had suffered losses fully explaining the two months they were to be accorded out of the line.[37]

No more convincing explanation of why the offensive on the Somme had to cease, but that the strain upon the British soldier had not broken him, could be offered than a letter written by a Northumberland Fusilier on 26 November. 'Walking down a disused trench one of our men stepped into a hole full of mud. He instantly started to kick and try to force his way out. In a moment he sank right up to the second button on his tunic (from the top) and there remained. . . . He could only be fed from the top of the parapet – which was under fire – bread and meat were passed to him on the end of a bayonet. He drank from a tin with a stick stuck through it. On top the mud was too soft to shovel and underneath too sticky to dig him out. On the second day he was hit in the shoulder by shrapnel. Finally we got him out, utterly exhausted and minus his boots puttees and trousers. I cannot describe what it is like anywhere near the lines – camps, road, villages, one sea of filthy mud. . . . In the lines it is much worse, trenches falling in and impossible to repair, men done up before they even get under fire and yet I saw my old company after ten days of the very worst of all this, with rain day and night and a biting wind all the time, and being covered in mud, carrying heavy loads, (having suffered heavy casualties) and yet whistling and singing as they marched down a road towards the rest billets.'[38] They had more reason to whistle than they knew, the 1916 battle of the Somme was over. They had survived.

Caught in the open: a burial detail sees to the animal remains from a field artillery battery shelled on its move up to the front. (Guy Chapman)

5

Battle: 1917

The sleet and snow which accompanied the final Allied attack on the Somme in November 1916 were the herald of an exceptionally cold winter. Climatically the extraordinary became an attenuated commonplace as thick overcoats froze even on the wearer and the entrenching tool day by day produced but a dissonant ineffectual ring on iron hard ground. Plans drawn up in mid-November to take advantage of the severe punishment it was known the Germans had received, would undoubtedly have tested British and French troops as seriously to the limit. In the event, all such plans were thrown out of kilter by the Germans who, abandoning their battered trench lines, retired to still stronger positions by the beginning of April 1917. Their new Siegfried – Stellung was to be lastingly named by their opponents, the Hindenburg Line.

When British troops were called upon to attack in the spring, it was in support of a huge French design on the Aisne. The Germans had been given added weeks to prepare, not merely by their calculated withdrawal but because of the time needed to mount so major a French blow. Neither at Loos nor on the Somme was the British supporting dance to the French strategic tune to be so filled with weighty consequence as in the fate of the Spring 1917 French offensive. The colossal scale of human and matériel resource committed to the French offensive, matched the degree of optimism of the new Commander-in-Chief, Robert Nivelle. When catastrophic defeat ensued, it so reduced the condition of the French armies that the burden of responsibility for attack to break the Germans on the Western Front fell upon the BEF. At British Headquarters level, this was to provide both problems and opportunity; for the soldier, quite simply it meant facing battle experience, something which for the survivor would be renewed and prolonged until the penultimate month of the year. On the Arras front in April and May, at Messines in June, in the whole of the Ypres Salient from the end of July to early November and then finally in that same month at Cambrai, assault experience for those who were called upon to undertake it, would be forgotten by none who were fortunate enough to survive.

Within the limitations of what success could have been achieved, the resounding names recorded above, even Ypres with its third battle, can be claimed as victories of a sort, but in few senses did the sun shine upon the soldiers who fought for such victories and the year was not one in which a man's inner lamp, dedicated to whatever cause of selfless or self-centred end, burned brightly.

It is a little surprising, since each of the great battles of 1917 merits study, that few of them have had detailed work focused upon them and in this chapter as well, only representational choice can be made. It seems right that as the battles show the role of artillery quite phenomenally expanded and refined, the gunner must be well represented. The tank crews, too, as they served under both awful and advantageous circumstances in that year, must be included but not to the exclusion of the foot soldier who, in the later weeks of the Third Battle of Ypres, had to attempt to 'assault' through the unimaginable mud of the Salient from so called 'jumping-off' points to his concrete pillbox objective.

On the morning of the opening of the atack at Arras on 9 April after a fifteen-day preliminary bombardment of more than two and a half million shells, thirteen hundred field guns and howitzers of the Royal Field Artillery commenced a creeping barrage to protect the infantry advance while the heavier armament of the Royal Garrison Artillery targeted upon the German artillery. In numbers of guns (especially heavy calibre), of ammunition expenditure and of Royal Flying Corps assistance to the artillery and infantry, the scale of the Somme was more than doubled.

As troops concentrated in Arras before the attack, an Artillery officer who thought the city much less 'crumped' than Ypres, found that the German shelling was to intensify as the day of the assault drew nearer. Cellars and caves offered shelter to troops and townsfolk alike, but accurate shell-fire disrupted the unloading of ammunition, one gas shell explosion releasing gas from British shells and causing eight of his battery to become casualties. Despite the snow: 'It was very interesting seeing all the preparations for the show. Stacks and stacks of

Early 1917 and a photographic break for a working party. As the men are wearing steel helmets their work must have been within range of German shelling. Note the sleeveless leather jerkins and the 'stray' Royal Flying Corps mechanics at the rear left. (P.H.L. Archives)

guns are up already and still they come.' He was impressed by the dumps of stores of all kinds 'for after the push'. The snow and rain affected ground conditions and on the eve of Z Day four tanks were seen to 'paddle up the road past our positions' and in the dark to take up their places. 'We fired about 1200 to 1500 (rounds) a day through the bombardment and from 9 p.m. on the 8th to 4 p.m. on the 9th we crumped off 4,899 (rounds) that is 816 rounds per gun in 19 hours.' Their firing only ceased when 'we couldn't reach any further'. The guns were worn already and B. G. Guy, the officer concerned, referred caustically to their unique distinction of being a battery of 4.6-inch howitzers rather than 4.5. Nevertheless, despite this reference to the likelihood of under-ranging, the work was all done scientifically. 'It was all on paper of course and the No. 1's watches all put to 12 O'clock at zero.' From the observation post, Guy heard one gun go off a few seconds early, then there was a slight pause and 'Hell was let loose: pandemonium for a few short seconds and we saw a dense cloud of smoke descend like a curtain where the Bosche front line should be. Marvellous shooting by the 18pdrs. every shell dropping as it seemed to a yard. From then on there was the devil of a row, accompanied at the other end by the most marvellous pyrotechnic display ever seen by mortal eye. The Bosche put up red green white orange golden rain all sorts of rockets most of which probably couldn't be seen by his gunners on account of the smoke barrage.' As recorded by Guy, for seven minutes no German shell was fired in

response and then their barrage struck well behind the British front line. In no man's land, darkness shrouded movement until first a tank could be seen crossing towards the German trenches from which prisoners were dashing across to the British lines. This diary continues with a noteworthy tribute to High Command: 'The whole thing was a brilliant success. The 9th Division Infantry are a great crowd and Tudor, their C. R. A. an admirable man. To him alone the credit is mainly due; he worked out every detail of the barrages himself including smoke and H.E. on graze.' With this private tribute paid, Guy described his looting of a German telephone, revolver, spur and 'harmonicas for the men'. His praise for the German dugouts is followed by what may be a reference to German emergency demolition as well as the result of British shelling: 'St. Laurent is beaucoup liberated.' The Cavalry, the pre-war social standing of which was not matched by its military usefulness, did not escape note. 'The Bow and Arrow Corps came trooping up and sat behind the Blue line competely blocking the road for 48 hours, during which no field batteries could get up any ammunition and very few could get forward. The Cavalry accomplished as ususal nothing at all and botched operations for the ensuing week completely.' Harsh words indeed and perhaps not altogether fair, but harsher still would be expressed in November in the inquest after Cambrai. If Cavalry were to be kept in being and ready for effective employment where should or could they be in relation to a modern battle frontage? Meantime where should they go in April 1917 but, as Guy scornfully wrote, 'Back to the seaside.'[1 & 2]

The Canadian role on 9 April was to take Vimy Ridge; this they did with great distinction. In *My Grandfather's War*, the author, W. D. Mathieson, has drawn together Canadian memories which on this battle form a picture deserving greater familiarity. 'Our plans worked beautifully. Everything had been carefully rehearsed. Each battalion had its own special work. Everything was mapped out. During the weeks before, we had studied the ground in front of our trenches as well as the Hun trenches from aeroplane photographs. It was very very serious training. Very serious. . . . Our artillery swept the Hun line and we walked out, following under our barrage. It was a wonderful sight I shall never forget. . . . Lines of Canadians with intervals between and on our right a Scottish division with kilts swinging and bayonets fixed. . . . Men dropped here and there but nothing could stop us. . . . It was a glorious day for Canada and the boys thoroughly enjoyed it. We paid for it but not too heavily.'[2A]

An interesting comment upon the infantry tactics used at Arras as at the Somme was that of 2nd Lt C. E. Pullinger (7th King's Royal Rifle Corps). Wounded in the battle, he wrote from hospital of his platoon being unable to move forward in support of the assault battalions. 'Advance was quite impossible on account of the fact that the men are only trained in the attack of positions under barrage fire that is to say extended lines following close behind one another in waves. The only possible mode of attack in that case would have been in the open warfare attack advancing in short rushes at the double. But the men in these days of trench to trench attack with artillery are taught to advance at walking pace and nothing on earth will make them do it faster without previously having had an opportunity to explain it to them.'[3]

As for the tank crews at Arras, there was little to reward their high morale. Fewer tanks got into action than at Flers Courcelette in the previous year. Even in the approach to attack, soft ground, rain and snow, bogged down the great ponderous monsters as their tracks gouged their graves rather than inched them forward. Slow-moving silhouettes against

snow in no man's land, nine were knocked out by direct hits at Bullecourt on 11 April and though there was the achievement of assisting in the capture of one fortified village, the lack of speed, armour protection and of offensive firepower, made the tank a very dangerous as well as a hot, deafeningly noisy, fume-ridden fighting station. The spirit of one Tank Commander, as evinced in his letter describing how he was wounded, is admirable, but the story does something to cure the misapprehension of those who still consider the 1917 tanks as a war-winning weapon. N. F. Humphrys wrote of the journey up to the starting point: '1st night: Broken main drive flexi coupling (fitted spare): Diff[erential] lock firmly jammed in on treacherous boggy ground – took off cover and waited for the dawn. 3rd night: finished off diff[erential] and started out 1½ hours late. Gaily chased two sections in front. Orders had been changed at last moment, section routes forked, our

Eve of the battle of Arras. Within a few hours of the taking of this photograph, the officer, 2nd Lieutenant Anthony Willis, will be trying without success to get some rest during the preliminary artillery bombardment as he waits in his Roclincourt Valley dugout ready to follow up the assault troops and organize the construction of strongpoints against German counter-attack. (A. A. Willis)

Vimy Ridge trenches and dugouts at a quieter time. The South Lancashire Regiment holding these positions in 1916 nevertheless suffered casualties from the explosion of German mines under the British positions. (Captain J. E. Hibbert)

Four Sergeants of the Liverpool Scottish, Armentières 6 June 1917. Left to right: R. G. Mackenzie, W. V. Dumbreck, L. Benedict and J. O. Johnson. Mackenzie and Benedict were to be taken prisoner on the 29th of this month. (T. Patterson)

tape carried away. Followed other until quite certain something wrong and then hunted around to find I'd over run by about 1½ miles. Did a cross country trek and joined up at starting point at the break of dewy dawn. It was some consolation to find that the place had been fairly respectably shelled all night. To our intense disquiet a number of "C" Bn rolled into our starting point and it was a damn sight intense we found out that the day before the blighters had laid a lovely white tape along the first 700 yards of our route in full view of the Bosch. Consequently when zero arrived at dawn we got hotted some by brother Bosch. Old Grayson was there – frightfully "well so long old boy, best of luck, shake hands again isn't it great". One Obus [shell] very nearly checked his career. I sheered off from that blessed line as soon as poss. and had a very jolly – tho' damn long run to our front line. They [the crew] were extraordinarily merry and bright.'

'I bundled over the first two Bosch trenches and got a topping target myself in the third – also a stoppage at the second round. The gearsman at the back heard me distinctly. Then over the top of a hill I obtained a temporary ditch when the others and the infantry passed me.

'We got out after a bit and I took a stroll to become aware of the "tactical situation". It was then a sniper did the dirty on me. Naturally I got into that comfy armour plated bus and darn well stayed there till I could get out in decent safety – which was some hours later. For which piece of conspicuous common sense I've been awarded the Military Cross.'

Captain Humphrys, in his Mark 1 tank, would have had with him a further seven men. He, with fixed mapboard and gun-mounting, sat next to his driver, each peering through a slit in the armour plating. A narrow passage fore and aft each side of the partially covered engine mounting which ran down the centre of the tank, allowed access to the side turrets for two men in each to service their front and rear gun mountings and then at the back to the gears operated by two men. The gearsmen regulated the caterpillar tracks to answer a required change of direction. All intercommunication was by gesture. There was no engine silencer and open exhaust pipes passing through the roof of the tank brought nausea to a crew already in danger of serious bruises and burning as the bucking vehicle threw them about. To all this may be added the real possibility of a hit sending the whole petrol- and fume-laden interior into flames. Humphrys' tank did in fact take a direct hit and did not catch fire, but his cheerful account should not detract from the evident particular perils of battle experience in what was still the 'Heavy Branch Machine Gun Corps'.[4]

Less than two months after Arras, the mines went up at Messines and attention is now be be drawn to the infantry assault which followed upon the cataclysmic explosion of those nineteen mines which left huge, smoking, foul-smelling pits where once

strong German positions on slightly elevated ground had dominated the southern sector of the Ypres Salient.

The Battle of Messines commencing on 7 June marked the opening of the British Flanders offensive which took place, as far as High Command was concerned, under the shadow of the shrouded secret of widespread unrest in the French Army. This unrest followed upon the awful casualties and ineffectuality of the Nivelle offensive. French support and a British capacity confidently to follow-up the anticipated success from so long projected and now thoroughly prepared a concept were important yet the new French factor undermined assurance on both these counts. In the short term, all was to go well, a resounding success being achieved, but the massive operations to follow lost weeks in the launching and in consequence more than time was lost.

Responsibility to blow two of the mines fell to an officer in the Canadian Engineers, B. C. Hall, and a

Prelude to Messines. An eye-witness's water-colour showing the shell bursts on Wytschaete Ridge, 2 June 1917, part of the preliminary bombardment. Mont Kemmel is on the far right. Ponsonby Hobday, an artillery officer, depicts the scene from the top of Mont Rouge. The Battle of Messines commenced early on 7 June and among the British troops who fell, was Victor Hobday, the artist's son. (Colonel E. A. P. Hobday)

Battle of Messines, June 1917. Mark IV tank in action lumbering over the cratered ground at the southern extremity of the Ypres Salient. (A. J. Collins)

Sergeant Beer. On 6 June, Hall had been given a watch, the zero hour timing of 3.10 plus 13 seconds, and ordered to blow the mine from the trench and not from the shaft bottom with its escape shaft already having been once blocked by a German shell. At the bottom of the 70-foot shaft, Hall and Beer prepared and spliced each of the twelve leads and then tacked them to the timber shaft. The leads had to be connected to a 120-volt battery issued to replace the 60-volt battery which was judged to be insufficient to overcome the resistance of the leads which were now to be so much longer. As a back-up against failure, a second pair of leads was connected to the 60-volt battery and the whole operation was completed with but 32 minutes to spare. At zero hour 'Down went my exploder plunger. Beer had a firm hold on his. We became airborne. On hitting the ground I noticed Beer shaking his exploder handle like a terrier with a rat: the leads were broken.' Over one and a third million pounds of ammonal had been used. 'It was like a tremendous quake down in the bowels of the earth: ten square miles heaved and shook. Huge red flames and columns of smoke belched more than 200 feet into the sky along the entire ten mile front, followed by thousands of tons of earth and massive concrete dugouts (with their German defenders). Last of all, the fine earth and clouds of dense dust settled back from where it had been heaved and all was quiet.'[5] The craters left by the explosion were up to 350 feet in diameter, 90 feet deep and with 20 feet lips round the rim from the outfall.

Lance Corporal E. C. Shepherd of the 9th Cheshires, waiting in their assembly trench, was to carry a bag of twelve Mills grenades and one of the same number of Hales grenades in addition to his rifle, 170 rounds of ammunition and entrenching tool. An unseen hand presented a tiny tin cup and he swallowed his offering of rum. 'A whisper came down the line "fix bayonets" and there was a sound of sliding steel and light clicks as the springs went home. . . . I had no great dread or even apprehension. I was merely calm and acquiescent.' In this contemporary account, Shepherd stressed that the sound of the explosions was drowned by the uproar of the artillery barrage, but scrambling out of the trench and groping through the dark to the rim of a dried water course, his surprise came when his platoon actually stopped and lit cigarettes. An order came to resume forward movement and, with slung rifles and glowing cigarettes, forward they went. Passing evidence of destroyed positions and reaching the crest of the ridge, Shepherd skirted a crater 'the red fuming earth of which sloped sharply to a pit of blue incandescence, writhing and seething in that horrid depth.' So strong were the fumes that many donned their gasmasks. What once had been a woodland next confronted them; it was now simply 'bare poles springing from a network of litter'. Their advance was slow and a German barrage on the wood halted them. 'I crouched as low as I could beneath a small bank that partly upstayed a massive elm, while Corporal Crawley with sweat running down his face from the black wisps of hair beneath his helmet, sprawled alongside. Propped up on the right was the long figure of Nobby Clark with his black eyes, black moustache and cigarette. The din was tremendous as detonation merged into detonation. Inky founts spirted from the battered ground, shrapnel rent the air overhead like the sound of tearing calico, and now and then the bare trunk of a tree wheeled over like a giant's club to smite the earth and send litter flying from the blow and again there descended upon our backs and helmets showers of clods, turf and small pebbles – the bright day being dimmed to gloom and the drifting smoke swirling in and out of the splintered poles.'

When the barrage lifted and they got out of the

wood into open ground they faced a shallow dip at the bottom of which was a copse fronted by a sand-bagged stronghold which had once been a farm. The copse was under intense and precise shelling. Down the slope towards the strong point they crossed a vacated German trench narrowly escaping the consequence of carelessness when a grenade tossed at the entrance to a dugout hit the lintel and bounced back at their feet. It did not explode. From their objective a stocky German was suddenly sighted speeding off towards the wood which lay up the far slope. Several of the men tried to shoot him, Sergeant Dempsey being successful. 'I liked it little for the man was unarmed and seeking safety . . . but he would have speedily been among his friends manning rifle or machine gun against us.' The enemy was more closely met in the copse, 'rising from the twisted network of branches and bursting forth from fresh green leaves – twenty or thirty faces grey with fear, and great staring eyes from which the light of reason seemed to have been driven. Some wore the great coal scuttle helmets, some soft field caps and they appeared before us with a forest of unthrown hands. Some cried out and gesticulated, some threw themselves and grovelled at our feet. It was a terrible unnerving sight.' No harm was done to the Germans who were swiftly escorted to the rear. It was noon, very hot and with the physical exertion

September 1917, Inverness Copse near Passchendaele. A shell bursts near positions held by the 11th Battalion, West Yorks. Note the rolled-up stretcher in the foreground. (Captain J. D. Todd)

Jones' nasty nightmare.
He won though!

Geraint Madoc-Jones portrays a nervous susceptibility to the currency of the Western Front. The drawing dates from August 1917 when he was a 2nd Lieutenant in the Royal Welch Fusiliers. (G. W. Madoc-Jones)

and emotional tension, Shepherd's small unit was exhausted. He wrote of this time that it was then that his will weakened. In inactivity he felt fear, fear of what he had been through, seen and smelled and not of what lay ahead. Never again, not even at Passchendaele ridge, was he to experience such a sense of hopelessness and helplessness and he attributed it to the 'terrible fire baptism of a sensitive mind'.[6]

Within a week all the objectives of the Messines attack had been secured. The only British success comparable to date had been that of the Canadians at

Vimy a few weeks earlier. Time was now of the essence and the delay in exploiting the new gains to the south of the Ypres Salient was to have tragic consequences. The delay is explicable, the explanation springing from wider matters than differences between GHQ design and local field commander appraisal. Not to be forgotten among the factors responsible for delay was the unsatisfactory relationship between high political command – David Lloyd George – and the Commander-in-Chief, BEF, Field Marshal Sir Douglas Haig. It will not be developed here nor will there be an evaluation of the reasoning behind the maintenance of the new great offensive North of Messines, the Third Battle of Ypres, when it became sunk into a slough of despond. The true nature of Haig's offensive (perhaps its dual nature of both striving for decisive gain and exerting such damaging pressure on the enemy that he would be permanently crippled), the real influence of Sir John Jellicoe's despair over the U-boat depredations unless the Belgian coast were freed, the actual degree to which the CinC, BEF was influenced by the condition of the French Army, these and other matters are thoroughly investigated elsewhere and must not detain us when our particular concern is to approach an understanding of what it was like for the soldier attacking in the Salient in the second half of 1917.[7]

The Third Battle of Ypres launched on 31 July and lasting until 10 November held within its grim parameters assault first of Pilckem Ridge, then on Gheluvelt and Langemarck in August and on Menin Road Ridge and Polygon Wood in late September. In early October, Broodseinde and Poelcappelle were the focus of renewed attack and then, from 12 October until the end of the battle, Passchendaele itself was to be contested. Even the Somme in November 1916 was not to match the scale of sheer physical disadvantage to the already unfortunate attacker in his prospect of assaulting an objective in the Ypres Salient. The disadvantage lay quite simply in making any forward progress whatsoever on feet and legs clutched, sucked and held by mud unconquerable. Earlier rain and heavier rain, on ground in normal times drained with difficulty and now with such drainage arrangements ruined by shelling, produced so unprecedented a brown porridge that today's imagination of its dangerous prison must fall far short of reality.

'On the deeds of each individual in the Division depends whether it shall be said that the 38th (Welsh Division) took Pilckem and Langemarck, and upheld gloriously the honour of Wales and the British Empire. The honour can be obtained by hard

That there were days to celebrate in the Ypres Salient battles in 1917 is shown by this Christmas card of that year, drawing attention to the 23rd Division's 20 September achievement in the Battle of the Menin Road Ridge and the capture of Dumbarton Wood and lakes, Inverness Copse and certain strong points. (Captain J. D. Todd)

fighting and self-sacrifice on the part of each one of us "Gwell Angau Na Chywilydd".' In such a fashion did the Divisional Commander, Major General C. G. Blackader, seek to inspire his men by ordering his exhortation to be read to the men beforehand.[8]

Further south than the assembly area for the 38th, was the 11th Bn, Queen's Royal West Surrey Regiment (41st Division) with a member of one of the Lewis gun teams, Private V. E. Fagence, preparing for zero hour and having tied empty sandbags on his legs to keep his putties clean. The sandbags were to snag on British barbed wire and the gun and ammunition drum had to be grounded while he used his jack knife to free himself. Fagence was further delayed by the somewhat unexpected appearance of

Following up the assault troops, 'moppers-up' use hand-grenades to neutralize the defences of a pillbox. Note in the foreground two of the defenders who have been caught outside the temporary protection of the concrete pillbox. ('Realistic Travels' Photo Series/P.H.L. Archives)

an unarmed German walking dazedly towards the pillbox objective of the British attack. Pleased at having secured a prisoner, there was still the problem of what to do with him and when Fagence attempted to hand him over, it looked as if the German might be shot there and then before persuasion was used to forestall this and then to encourage the German to walk in the other direction, hands held high to be taken by troops not involved in the assault. The next delay occurred from a sub-altern's orders to await the movement of a barrage from the pillbox positions to be attacked. There was no sign of life till Fagence's Company was within forty yards of the pillboxes, but on cratered, churned-up ground there was no hope of a rush achieving surprise. A machine-gun opened up on them from one of the apertures and then, as they fell to the ground, a stick grenade was thrown, landing close to Fagence but failing to injure him. 'I then rose to my feet, picked up the gun and ran off with it about fifty yards away to the right flank where I took cover in the remains of an old smashed-up shed. I

then aligned the gun on the aperture of the pillbox, pulled back the cocking handle and pressed the trigger.' The two spells on the ground had rendered the gun muddily defective and when Fagence sought to join other men in a nearby shell-hole he was hit in both hands and the stomach, the gun itself being riddled through the casing, radiator and grip. An escape was made from his exposed position by a series of dashes to shell-holes rearwards and then to a pillbox which held a number of Germans who fortunately were waiting to surrender. Fagence, alarmingly wounded and unarmed, found someone to whom he could hand over his twelve unwanted prisoners and continued his retirement to the Divisional Rest Station. In two more pillboxes he was to find shelter, but he was dismissed from one by the subsequent arrival of a party of signallers whose work, it was said, was being hampered by the presence of the wounded soldier.[9]

The German concrete pillbox defence earned its legendary reputation as a fearsome objective for attack and some fell to deeds of distinction like that of Sergeant E. Cooper of the 12th (S) Battalion, King's Royal Rifle Corps on 16 August. The machine-gun fire from one of the apertures of a triple pillbox solidified out of farm buildings was what had caused havoc to Cooper's section. 'I knew when I got to a certain position on the flank they couldn't fire on me but by that time I was the only one left.' From such a position Cooper made a rush to the door in the rear and shouted at the men inside, not remembering in retrospect what he's said except that it was to indicate that they were captured. He did the same to the two other doorways. Sergeant Cooper was carrying his officer's Webley pistol in his right hand, and in pointing it at the first man who came out, it went off, killing him and resulting in a scurrying back of those who were following him. The whole procedure of a shouted demand to surrender had to be repeated and, presumably fearing a tossed grenade in their midst, out came forty men whose capture, together with seven machine-guns found inside, represented a remarkable haul for the solitary Cooper. The citation for the Sergeant's subsequent VC award concluded that: 'By this magnificent act of courage he undoubtedly saved what might have been a serious check to the whole advance, at the same time saving a great number of lives.'[10]

As the wounded of the 30th Division filtered or were carried back to their dressing station, a Padre, M. L. Couchman, became involved in what he called 'The hardest day's work that I have ever experienced.' In his account he admits that at first he found that the casualties [arriving from 8 a.m.] a dreadful sight with all manner of wounds covered by temporary dressings. They were being received in a marquee. He and the orderlies helped to marshal them in and find seats for them, sort out the seriously wounded and get them through for attention. He then: 'wrote cards to send home for some and supplied tea bread and jam and cigarettes and then was generally useful! The heat and crush and stench in the marquee was dreadful.' The Padre managed to get a break at about 12.30 and then took a turn with the seriously wounded, but there were not very many in the marquee as the ambulances were coping with them expeditiously. He went back to the walking wounded and tried to speed up getting them through for attention, but it was not easy. This work

11th West Yorks officers' servant, Private Selkirk, and 'C' Company Officers' Mess cook, Lance-Corporal Oldfield, outside a captured pillbox in the Ypres Salient, September 1917. (Captain J. D. Todd)

continued until 8.30 p.m. In his diary he wrote: 'The cheerfulness, gratitude and patience of the men was truly amazing and their wounds just indescribable. No one can realize what a Hell on earth modern intensive war is that has not seen the wreckage of humanity that came back.' Couchman had been especially moved by a stretchered man naked but for his boots, black and seeming to be West Indian but in fact he had been burned in a tank and could not bear anything touching his body. 'When I saw him later he was swathed in cotton wood soaked in oil with just a gap for his eyes and mouth and nose.' The soldier had asked for a cigarette, smiled when told he looked like Father Christmas and when asked if he would like a letter written to his wife replied 'Yes but don't scare her, say I have been wounded and will write in a day or two.' Couchman buried him on the following day.[11]

Rain fell even on the opening day of the battle. All accounts attest the speed with which the shell-holes filled with water and the ground was transformed from being slippy to being a dreadful quagmire. On 8 August, Willoughby Norrie was writing to a friend of 'men drowned in shell-holes without even being hit, so you can imagine what a morass the whole place became'.[12]

By the end of August, heavier rain, the continued shelling and ruination of the drainage, made the ground wholly unsuitable for tanks as a contemporary account of a tank action from St-Jean on 22 August makes abundantly clear. 'It was so wet we found it hard to swing. The four of us got rather bunched and the Foam [name of a tank] received a couple of direct hits and Harris her Commander and two more of his crew were wounded. Harris was in great pain having his left arm nearly blown off from the elbow and also armour plate and rivets in his leg. . . . We got on a little further and got ditched so I got out with my two gearsmen and put on the unditching gear – we had to get out through the roof we were in so deep. Shells were bursting so near us that they covered us with mud and water. We got out . . . and proceeded on our way. We left Foam knocked out and Fiona with her unditching gear broken stuck in the mud.' Better ground and a drying sun helped, but the periscope was broken and the prisms were covered in mud so all sighting was being done through the flaps – navigation between the shell-holes now being particularly difficult. Then the tank stuck and so intense was the fire that to put on the unditching gear was obviously going to be impossible. As the crew was leaving the tank, Corporal Rear was killed outright and the weapons they had brought out with them were almost immediately rendered useless by mud. 'We got covered with mud and wet through as we had practically to swim through shell-holes.' The officer, G. H. Brooks, who wrote this account was hit and took shelter in a shell-hole up to his waist in water and here he remained from about 8 a.m. till dusk that evening thankful that the sun had kept the chill from the water.[13]

High summer was one thing, in the battles to break out of the Salient, late autumn and early winter another. For the attack on the 9 October (Battle of Poelcappelle) the 49th West Riding Division, after an exhausting march to their starting point, were confronted by a swollen stream 'the bed of which had become a morass 30 to 50 yards wide

waist deep in water in the centre.'[14] For those battalions whose approach denied them the use of a bridge, further advance along their designated line was impossible and for others fortunate to have bridges, heavy machine-gun fire met them on the far side of the morass. Protecting approach to the pillboxes whence came the fire, were belts of low wire-entanglement in places up to forty yards in depth and then the pillboxes themselves were shielded by apron fences of barbed wire. From shell-holes uncharted and difficult to locate, further machine-gun and rifle fire completed the neutralization of all attacking endeavour even though more troops from reserve were sent up sadly to share the circumstances, described with moderation in the letters of an exceptionally young Battalion Commander, Douglas Branson (4th Yorks and Lancs).[15] 'Sorry I have not written lately, as you may have guessed we have been fighting a battle and battles these days are no joke. It is no good my trying to describe it because you can see better accounts by reading the papers and I assure you they do not exaggerate the unpleasantness. I lost a number of good officers. . . . I want for the battalion a large number of "Tommy's Cookers" and refills and for myself a new set of oil skins. . . . My servant Mee was killed on the 9th with many another good man. Will you look after his widow if necessary at my expense until such time as his pension comes through. . . . We are busy re-organizing now trying to get the mud out of our clothes and selves and to find lost equipment and are slightly recovering from our weariness. 80 hours practically without sleep wet through nearly all the time and with the strain of a battle in the middle I find takes a lot of getting over. . . . There is little to tell you except that the weather is unpleasant, the shelling considerable and the mud indescribable . . . the men mostly live in shell-holes and a few lucky ones get old German pillboxes which if they were not so full of live animals and the smells of nameless horrors would be quite comfortable. . . . I can't give you more details [of the battle] but you may rest assured the Battalion did very well tho' it was unable to do quite all it set out to accomplish.'

Branson's concern for his men would of course be paralleled. From the same Division, Lieutenant Colonel J. Walker (1/5 Duke of Wellington's West Riding Regiment), wrote to his Brigade Commander (Brigadier General Lewis, 147 Bde) on 7 October 1917: 'Dear General, My battalion has had an extremely rough time this afternoon and the men are much exhausted with the very wet conditions and heavy shelling (casualties 4 officers, 60 O.R.). To do any justice to themselves they need a night's sleep. A lot of my equipment and two Lewis guns with many rifles were buried in the mud.'[16] Walker's report to Brigade after the attack on 9 October goes as far as it was possible towards stating that his men faced an impossible task. 'I found my leading waves actually in the firing line while the majority of the Battalion was in the crater swamp between Waterloo Farm and Fleet Cottage. . . . When I arrived at Fleet Cottage at 3 p.m. [there were] no definite orders for me and the situation was not clear. I was placed under the orders of Col. Kaye [in Command 1/5th Yorks and Lancs] and told to await developments. The situation seemed to me an extremely awkward one – as my formation rendered proper control impossible and I therefore strongly pressed to be allowed to go forward and take the crest in front in order to get out of the swamp and form up on the reverse side of the slope where "digging in" operations would be more possible. I pressed the matter very strongly but the orders I received were so definite that I took up a line in the valley and dug in – taking up my H.Q. in a shell-hole in the road. An SOS call went up and we were in the line of the German barrage for an hour, the men having to get where they could as their shelters were blown in – here we lost four Lewis guns and three Coy Commanders. After the bombardment my only men available were 80 strong and the rest were scattered in shell-holes. . . .' Walker carried out instructions to send support to his neighbouring unit under the command of the aforementioned Lt Col Branson and so the numbers of his troops were still further reduced. At dawn: 'all were exposed to sniping. We dug in and I communicated with Lt Col Kaye – my rifles were not usable owing to mud and five Lewis guns were knocked out. The stores had no ammunition so I did not take them

with me.' He was at last ordered to withdraw. 'This was done where possible at 11 a.m. in the daylight – the exposed companies getting out at dark. The men were greatly exhausted but still cheerful.'

Cheerfulness dashed all too quickly was to be the National response to the striking success achieved initially at Cambrai in the following month. This historic battle, growing out of its initial concept as a tank raid, gave the tank, in its Mark IV form, its first opportunity for use in large numbers, that is 378 fighting tanks and others in support, with guns and ammunition or with wire destroying, bridge construction and wireless equipment functions. The ground chosen was firm and surprise was assisted by the briefest but most intense of bombardments by predicted and not pre-registered fire. The Mark IV was not much improved on its predecessor, indeed in Major General F. E. Hotblack's unpublished memoirs he quotes an officer relating that the best thing about Cambrai was that it demonstrated that something better than the Mark IV was needed.[17] Inadequate in armour, armament, speed, handiness and battle conditions for its crew, it was but a staging-post en route towards a fighting vehicle which really could change the nature of warfare and, it may be added, such a revolution was certainly not achieved for service in 1918 either.

At Cambrai, launched on 20 November 1917 over a six-mile front, unprecedented gains were made – in some sectors up to four miles. Certainly the tanks had broken into the Hindenburg Line defence system, but by direct hit, mechanical breakdown or ditching, tank losses were severe. With further denuding of unit resources over the following days and the exhaustion of the men whose tanks were still functional, the Corps was in fact withdrawn from the

Passschendaele, October 1917, muddy graveyard for mules as well as men. This mule (note the telephone hand line reeled out over the animal's hoof) had been used to transport shells from the wagon lines up to the batteries, a short distance but one which could take up to sixteen hours and bring casualties to man and beast. At the end of August 1917, there were 81,731 mules with the BEF, the current wastage rate, that is from whatever cause, of mules and horses being 28 per cent. (Lieutenant Colonel J. Walker)

fray on 27 November. The potential of the initial success had not been exploited. The lack of available reserves of all arms, delays occasioned by one cause or another and perhaps, but more subjectively, the hesitation and then unwillingness of Cavalry Commanders to commit themselves to their out-flanking role against the weakened German defence, were factors involved. If truth were told however, the unfitness to achieve decisive gain by the very machine which had earned such credit, was at the root of the final balance which saw a German counter-attack regain the territory from which the enemy had been forced. In places the German infantry had not fought with their characteristic composure as the lumbering steel chariots loomed up to, or crossed or roared beside and above the German trenches firing into those occupants who remained. Elsewhere, most notably on the Flesquières ridge, tanks were successively knocked out, the fate of their crew being likely incineration if they were not quickly to get out through exits which proved under such circumstances to be tragically small and difficult for egress.

In this book, which focuses upon the regimental officers and men and not upon the Staff, it is worth re-emphasizing that the Tank Corps Commander, Brigadier General Hugh Elles, led his men into battle and so shared to the full the danger, discomfort and exhilaration of the first day as well as bearing his weight of command responsibility. It was the exercise of responsibility at a lower level to which a tribute was paid by the Commanding Officer of the 7th Duke of Cornwall's Light Infantry which was in co-operation with No. 7 Tank Section on 20 November. Captain Wilson exercised command of his three tanks: 'With the greatest gallantry and

judgement.'[18] A letter from another infantry source provides further indication of the footsoldier's appreciation of the Tank Corps. 'The show was a marvellous success and beat the 9th April to a frazzle even. The Bosche were completely surprised. The tanks did magnificently. We would never have gone on without them as we were often held up by snipers and MGs. The casualties were wonderfully slight and the men behaved superbly – better even than a "rehearsal" show! It is the best show the old div. ever did in all its time out here.'[19]

The tank crews certainly had had a 'rehearsal' for the Cambrai show. Bob Tate, a driver, remembers practice over ground designed to simulate the Hindenburg Line defence system at Cambrai and training in dropping the great bundle of chained brushwood into trenches so that the void could be filled and then crossed. On the morning of the attack as the tanks moved up, he saw their familiar shapes but now in great numbers silhouetted in the mist against a lightening sky. In action, glancing to his left, he saw a direct hit on his lumbering neighbour in which a friend, Harry Tiffen, was serving. In fact Tiffen and three others were killed in the disablement of this tank. Using his fascine, Tate drove over the first trench successfully but narrowly avoided what he said he had been warned about, pits which were by design tank traps. Shellfire as they approached Bourlon Wood hit and destroyed his left hand caterpillar track. German infantry 'swarmed out of the wood like bees' and vacating the tank and bringing out machine-guns, this particular tank crew was quickly to join the Scottish troops in infantry action.[20]

H. L. Birks had already suffered one direct hit on the tank which he commanded at St-Julien in

During the November 1917 Battle of Cambrai, more than a hundred German guns were captured. Here a German 5.9in Naval gun is towed away by a British tank from a wood near Ribecourt behind the Hindenburg Line. (P.H.L. Archives)

October. Five of the crew of 'Dashing Dragoon' had been wounded, one mortally: 'It had been very frightening,' though Birks himself was not hit. At Cambrai his tank came under concentrated machine-gun fire, the exhaust pipes riddled, flaps displaced, the unditching beam set on fire. Running out of petrol he had to bring his tank out of the action picking up wounded on the journey. He had the satisfaction of seeing the Germans run, but isolated individuals or groups stood their ground and sniped at the tank, Birks being wounded by a bullet through one of the apertures.[21]

J. K. Wilson's gallantry, to which reference has been made, arose out of circumstances less than reputable. It had been discovered on the eve of the battle that someone had been selling petrol and putting water in the two-gallon tins. With at least some water poured from such a tin, it was realized that trouble might lie ahead but it was too late for the drastic remedial measures necessary. Soon, enough water got into the carburetter and the tank stopped. It had been the leading tank and Wilson's dash to the second tank in order to continue action with it gave the appearance to the infantry of guidance and leadership being visibly in evidence. The fate of the second tank was however to be no more fortunate. It was hit and set aflame by a German field gun from the Flesquières ridge which first hit a track causing the tank to veer off course and present its side as a target. Wilson immediately ordered evacuation, but he and the driver were still inside when the second shell struck, killing the driver, wounding Wilson and leaving him with no recollection of how he got out.[22]

Cambrai casualty. Cyril Bertram (2/5 Battalion, Yorks and Lancs) sketched this accompaniment to his letter from No. 21 Casualty Clearing Station on 23 November 1917. It depicts his German-aided arrival at a dressing station suffering from a gunshot wound to the stomach. He was lucky to survive with such a wound and, as a staunch Catholic, attributed this to his parents' prayers. What is also remarkable is the cheerfulness of a letter written from a ward where 'the groaning never ceases' and six men had died since his arrival. (C. A. G. Bertram)

Post-Cambrai euphoria? A commercial postcard delighting in the Geman dachshund's surprise at an unfamiliar adversary. (C. A. Paul)

MEIN GOTT! A TANK!

Hilda, Elles's tank, was immediately ahead of a tank under the command of a Lt Hassall, and it was the latter's vehicle which seemed to have become ditched first as it slewed half off its fascine in crossing the first trench. The driver. a man named Callaghan, 'played' with the engine and clutch, repeatedly jerking the whole body of the tank until the track, which had lost anything solid from which to make forward traction, found purchase and escape was made. The only Germans now to be seen, were surrendering and Hassall took his tank through Ribecourt, turned right and then right again to flatten a huge belt of wire to facilitate the infantry's forward movement. One pigeon had by now been sent off to report successful progress and the tank turned to continue its advance, reached its final objective and a further pigeon message was sent off. In Hassall's memory there were no orders as to what to do next. The crew now got out to stretch their legs and have a smoke. They took pity on a big black retriever dog abandoned by its German master and took it aboard when further instructions were given from the Company Commander arriving with his tank. The two tanks lumbered off up a slope to the left but each was hit in turn, Hassall's right track being flung loose in the air as his driver tried to turn to get back down from what was obviously an exposed position (the Flesquières ridge). A second glancing blow struck the tank on the roof and a third in the rear. No one had been wounded but the tank was disabled. The crew made their way back to Ribecourt to spend the night in a cellar, but the tank commander's Cambrai adventures did not end there. In the morning he was assigned to take his crew first to find and then unditch Hilda, immobilized in the Hindenburg Line. This accomplished and the tank brought in to Ribecourt, he went back to his own tank, retrieved papers and mementoes, took the body of Lt Edwards from the other destroyed tank and gave his fellow tank commander a respectful if rough, Padre-less burial.[23]

The aftermath of Cambrai, especially at Bourlon Wood, became a desperate infantry battle and accordingly it may seem inappropriate to make honourable mention of that 'arm', the cavalry, which remained, in Major General Birks's phrase 'sitting on their arses', but such mention is deserved. Apart from the Canadian Fort Garry Horse, the cavalry, as has been implied, did not exploit the tank attack, but some units were to see sterling service in attempting to secure new positions to threaten the German counter-attack. Notable among such units was 'C' Squadron of the Inniskilling Dragoons, whose action on 1 December was officially reported thus: 'The

Aftermath of Cambrai. While German counter-attacks recovered ground they had conceded, battle was joined for possession of Bourbon Wood. This meant captured Germans had to assist in the evacuation of British wounded. ('Realistic Travels' Photo series/P.H.L. Archives)

Squadron advanced at a gallop on the left rear flank of the 2nd Lancers a distance of 3 kilometres – the last half of which was a fire-swept zone. The mounted advance terminated at the German wire at obstacle distance from a fire trench held by [German troops] who left hurriedly on their wire being crossed. Here the squadron dismounted for action, crossed the wire and gained the shelter of the trench just vacated by the enemy and already entered by the 2nd Lancers.' The trench was held against a bombing counter-attack. 'Reinforcement, communication and removal of casualties was rendered more difficult owing to the trench being filled with the horses (some wounded) of about 2 squadrons.' At night, a man to each horse, the cavalry units led their horses out in withdrawal while Very lights from a sap head and covering fire presumably deterred the enemy from a close attack.[24] And so there dissolved the final attacking opportunity of this grim year. Events far to the east in Russia were in fact to have passed opportunity and initiative back to the Germans. Cambrai may have heralded the dawn of mobile warfare, but in terms of battle plans on the Western Front, the immediate future lay with the enemy.

6

To distant shores to serve on far flung fields

An entirely appropriate introduction to a chapter devoted to the distinctively different experience of soldiering away from France and Flanders would be to give some consideration to what it was like to journey by troopship and also for those undertaking long train transportation, as for example those men bound for the Italian Front.

The longer troopship journeys, those from Australasia to Egypt, were those which by definition brought in largest measure the depression of boredom eroding the keen high spirit of troops splendidly bade farewell and God Speed from New Zealand and Australian ports and imbued with a high sense of adventurous mission. Overcrowded, cooped-up conditions, the heat and ever-throbbing engine vibration below deck, the lack of anything visually to stir the imagination apart from the surging away of the escorting HMAS *Sydney* on some clearly urgent business (in fact securing the destruction of the *Emden*), these and other trials such as grievances over food or petty restrictions do much to explain the frustrations riotously displayed when brief shore leave was granted at Colombo. Life aboard HMT *Medic* is briefly but graphically described by Private J. R. T. Keast, 11th Bn, AIF. On the second day of the voyage from Freemantle with the sea getting heavy: '50% sick. Beer is sold once a day. 12 noon at 4d per pint. I am on the water wagon. . . . There is a terrific noise at all meal times and a good deal of quarrelling goes on over the food. . . . There was quite a commotion last night. The lights went out on the Portside where we sleep and some of the chaps thought it was a good time to play tricks. Just as everybody was quiet, they started by tying a long rope to the hammocks and three or four getting hold of the end of it and pulling for their lives and giving everybody a rough time.' Quoits was played, and pay issued so that extras could be bought, something which many accounts suggest was a resented deception to manoeuvre men into paying for what was rightfully their issue. Innoculation and fire alarm boat-drill were felt to be worth recording to relieve the monotony. 'Nothing worth of note happened today.'

Even as deaths aboard *Medic* and other transports were noted, the Australian catalogues the boredom through having 'a lot of time on our hands'. Crown and anchor schools (on some boats washed away with a ship's hose) or housey housey were not the sort of activities to relieve the tedium for Keast as he was battling to understand the obscurities of the philisopher Emerson. It scarcely need be stated that Keast was no typical Australian private soldier: He wrote from another Mess table because he couldn't find a place at his; 'I have just counted 26 banker players. The table is only supposed to hold 16 and cramped at that. It is the usual custom to gamble your wages away.'

Concerts, sports, Crossing the Line ceremonies, boxing and greasy pole pillow-fighting were naturally the subject of many diary entries as was the heat when steaming through the Red Sea. 'Slept on deck last night and found it almost as oppressive as below.' Small wonder that an 18-gallon barrel of beer disappeared. As Alexandria was approached, the troops had a lecture: 'on Pox by Dr McWay. Told what a dreadful disease it was and how bad it is especially in Egypt. He warned all the men and gave them the best cures and preventatives that he knew. I reported sick on account of sore throat and constipation and was very soon fixed up.'[1]

Aboard HMT *Thermistocles* in a convoy a month later, Private W. M. Clark (10th Bn AIF) recorded a death almost immediately the ship left Albany and more deaths before Colombo and then Aden were reached.[2] Lance Corporal G. C. Grove (Australian Engineers) in HMT *Berrima* found that his unit was employed in a way which kept boredom at bay. Knot-tying, rifle cleaning, physical drill and semaphore, rifle exercises, tug-of-war practice, bedding inspection, sports, provided regular activities quite apart from clearing up after a heavy sea swept through open portholes, something which Keast had experienced in *Medic*. A treacle bun race commanded attention though it was less dramatic than the sight of shoals of flying-fish or of the problems *Berrima* had in towing the Australian submarine *AE2* towards her Dardanelles destiny.

Colombo provided colourful activity as *Berrima* coaled and watered and 'Coolies came aboard selling papers, postcards, beads, coins, cigarettes, and catamarans with bananas, pineapples and coconuts manoeuvred alongside for trade.' Despite the mounting of a special armed guard, 'Men broke leave and sneaked ashore down anchor chains and ropes into boats kept waiting by coolies. . . . Armed guard sent into Colombo to try to bring back absentees. Roll-call of all troops – about 60 missing. Guard had great deal of trouble with "drunken tourists from Cook's tours".' [These men were to find themselves serving two shifts as coal-trimmers].

A second innoculation for Sapper Grove led to his feeling rotten and unable to do more than detail that at an Australian Medical Corps Concert – an attraction had been 'A Salome dance by steward'. Though the only contact made with the shore at Aden was buying fruit from Arabs, the next day, 25 January, 'Eye disease caught by 200 men on board, certain parts of the ship in quarantine. About 50 men suddenly seized with ptomaine poisoning.'[3]

On some of the troopships with the great Australasian convoy, newsheets kept the men informed with items of war news and entertained them with sketches, poems, cartoons or jokes related to their current life. Troops aboard HMT *Afric* actually had to scrub the decks and sterilize blankets according to

Private Cobden Parkes whose diary also records a collision between two troopships causing two men to be thrown overboard, each being rescued.

The close confinement of troopship life could produce discipline problems when poor officer command and ringleaders of resentment were in combustible convention. Ivor Birtwistle, a Lance Corporal of the 22 Bn AIF, recorded just such a situation in a May/June 1915 voyage, aboard HMT *Ulysses* bound for the Middle East.

Indignation first stemmed from the prices of commodities at the Soldiers' Institute on board. 'Just forced to pay 1*s.* 6*d.* for a tin of ordinary fig jam.' Then at a special medical examination, 'utter lack of privacy irritated the greater number of fellows'. Following upon these petty but troublesome incidents, seemingly unnecessary restrictions on free movement through certain passages in the ship exasperated more men and a deputation demanded to see the Colonel. Colonel Crouch was told by a man called Ahearn that he [Ahearn] would only be able to take his guard party from one part of the ship to another if he were allowed through the

A game of 'House' – in modern parlance Bingo – a form of 'legal' gambling, here whiling away the hours for a draft of South Wales Borderers en route for Basra in March 1916. (Sir Joseph Napier)

closed door of the Sergeants' Mess or 'if he were able to transport them through the keyhole or waft them over the top of the ship'. Ahearn forced the issue and the Colonel into signing an authorization of passage through the intervening embargo, but obviously authority at two levels was diminished by the outcome.

At Colombo, when the men were forbidden to buy goods from the locals, but the canteen was replenished for further extortion, resentment returned, fuelled further by a route march through the town under a blazingly hot sun. 'Nearly every man was angry and grumbling for we were forbidden to buy any fruit from natives who haunted us.' A Corporal said to me: 'It only needs a spark to start a blaze.' Only officers and certain sergeants got leave in Colombo. Men who broke ship and took leave were brought before Colonel Crouch, dressed down, fined £5, given 10 days C.B. and no further leave till the completion of the voyage. The storm broke on the evening of 27 May. Two men, McIvor and Stevenson, drew up a petition requesting remission or modification of the punishments. A crowd gathered and there were menacing jeers directed at anyone in their vicinity wearing badges of rank. The Colonel's frequently uttered motto of "Wipe out the Bloody Germans" came in for bitter derision – its well-known initials WOTBG substituted by CTBOB – "Chuck the bastard overboard".

The Colonel appeared, ordered the men to disperse, but they stood their ground and amidst hooting and shouted demands he remained calm, pulled out a cigarette case, extracted a cigarette, lit it and smoked. The hubbub simply could not be contained even by such a display of sangfroid and Crouch had to withdraw to jeering singing of 'We'll never miss another Colonel like we'll miss you'. An attempt by the Adjutant to bring the men to order failed, but so did the men's attempt to prevent the closing of the canteen. All that was achieved was rough handling of officers and Military Police who secured the closure of the canteen. Later the men rushed the main source of their resentment, sweeping aside the picquet defending it and looting some of the contents quite oblivious to the Padre's diversion of playing hymns on the portable organ he had brought to the starboard side away from the tumult. The bolts on a punishment cell were filed through, defaulters released and the door thrown overboard.

The battalion's second in command, Major Smith, worked hard to reduce the tension, distributing tobacco from the smashed canteen and then the Brigadier came to speak to the men promising

March 1916. Private Fields, one of a draft of about 350 men from the Reserve Battalion, South Wales Borderers, aboard HMT *Royal George* en route from Devonport to join the 4th Battalion South Wales Borderers, below strength after its Gallipoli service and now to take part in the Mesopotamian campaign and the attempt to relieve Kut. The photograph was probably taken immediately after a boat drill and before Fields had divested himself of his life-jacket. (Sir Joseph Napier)

attention to their grievances. Things were quieter now. On the following day in considerable measure the grievances were redressed concerning both administration of the canteen and pricing of its goods and furthermore for those who chose it, they could be tried by Court Martial for ship breaking at Colombo. The serious disturbances were over but it may be wondered what contribution the troopship voyage had made to the development of the fighting efficiency of the 22nd Bn, AIF.[5]

It was to be expected that food and drink would be perennial sources of dispute aboard ship. F. L. Goldthorp has written of HMT *Berrima* in 1916, 'The cooks kept us short of food but made amends by selling it to us in the form of sandwiches after dusk and every evening when a normal man gets a bit

Shipboard equitation. Officers of the 10th Battalion, the Manchester Regiment enjoy the facilities of a troopship evidently still equipped, in some respects, as a pre-war passenger liner. The troopship is in the Mediterranean ultimately bound for Cape Helles where the officer's opportunity for riding will be distinctly limited. (Brigadier J. A. C. Taylor)

of a thirst, all the drinking taps were turned off. About half an hour later a man would stroll up out of the cook's galley with two buckets of weak lemonade, which he kindly disbursed at 2d. a glass. It was the sort of lemonade which left a dry taste in the throat and calls for another glass to wash it away. What a wonderful thing commerce is!'[6]

In several ways J. E. B. and L. W. Jardine, detraining at Southampton docks on 29 October 1914, were fortunate in their journey to the rigours of campaigning in Mesopotamia – they were officers (1st Queen's) and their battalion embarked aboard the new Cunard liner *Alaunia*, a vessel which had just brought Canadian troops to the UK. The two officers shared four-berth cabins so there was ample room to stow kit and their first meal was so splendid that one brother took the menu as a souvenir. However, it was 'a very unpleasant job to go down to

the lower deck and inspect sentries, as much vomiting is in process on the stairs' – indeed so rough was the Bay of Biscay that 'Church Parade is cancelled, as the troops have been decimated'.

The Mediterranean visually provided a great deal of interest with Gibraltar, the North African coast, Malta and the Greek Islands before Alexandria was reached, sights previously enjoyed by very few. Sunsets evoked the struggling literary artist within many. 'It was very impressive, scarlet and black in the West, while in the South there was an oyster effect, grey yellow and black silver point – the sea ghostly calm.' Less poetically, J. E. B. Jardine comments on the burial of a private who had died after an emergency operation. 'Our buglers played the Last Post very finely though one of them fainted. Altogether I thought it was a very good sort of burial – much jollier to be planted in the sea on a sunny morning than in a depressing cemetery.'[7]

A gentle attractive humour overlays Sapper Eric Wettern's letter descriptions of accommodation and life aboard HMT *Somali* taking his Field Company of RND Engineers to Egypt preparatory for service in the Dardanelles. 'Our quarters are not exactly first class, in fact to be quite precise we are in the hold and we are very scientifically packed in. We are on the second deck down and the place is fitted with rows of mess tables close together. At night we sling our hammocks from hooks in the ceiling just over our usual seats and as there is just sixteen inches between each row of hooks you can imagine that not much space is wasted. We have fairly early hours, Reveille is at 5.30 a.m. and all hammocks must be rolled up and stored in the bins downstairs by 6 a.m. Breakfast is at 6.30 and consists of porridge, bread and "butter". One of our principal pastimes in choppy weather is to watch the cook's mates carrying large dishes of thin porridge down a set of steep slippery ladders. One chap got a dishful over him and found is rather warm. He is now walking about in bandages. We have a parade on deck in the middle of the morning but it consists simply of a roll call and reading of notices, as there is no room for drill. Dinner is at 12 – soup, joint (or sometimes salt pork) and taters – occasionally "duff" as well. Tea at 5 – bread, butter and jam. At 6 hammocks are fetched out and at 6.30 our day's labours are rewarded – that is we have our rum served out to us. We spend the next two hours enjoying it, after which we go to bed – lights out at 9.'[8]

A major drawback to full enjoyment of the scenic and historic splendours of the Mediterranean was the danger of torpedo attack. There were many scares and adventures like those of the *Manitou*, the

15 April 1917 and 150 miles East of Malta. The last moments of the torpedoed troopship *Cameronia*. These photographs were taken from an escorting destroyer. Eleven lives were lost from the troopship. (J. Grimshaw)

Southland and *Mercian* and some tragedies like *Aragon*, *Cameronia* and *Royal Edward*.[9] The diary letter of Captain W. R. Matthews, written from the Union Castle line *Briton* in July/August 1917, made it quite clear that the submarine presence was felt. '*Briton* is painted in a very curious manner on her sides to make her less visible to submarines. Very uneasy going along but I did not get the wind up at all. No smoking on deck, no noise or singing or piano playing after 8 p.m. . . . . Started for Port Said from Crete on a 36-hour continuous voyage. Supposed to be the most dangerous part of the whole journey . . . glad to have got through the night safely. Steamed all day and looked out for submarines. . . . Arrived at Port Said. Everybody greatly relieved I think to find themselves safe.'[10]

Safety was not the word everyone would use with regard to Port Said. G. B. Harrison from *Alaunia* had been ashore a short while there as the liner carefully threaded its bulk through the Suez Canal, but had not been impressed. 'Port Said had lived up to its sordid reputation. Unpleasant men offering us smutty postcards, or to lead us to brothels or to pornographic shows. The whole place smelt and indeed was one vast latrine.'[11]

It was from Egypt that HMT *Leasowe Castle* departed for France only to be torpedoed a hundred or so miles from Alexandria on 26 May 1918. Lieutenant J. F. Alston, in pyjamas, supervised, as was his responsibility, the launching of two lifeboats and some rafts. Ships' crew rowed the boats to a Japanese destroyer but few returned to take off more

men. Alston climbed down a rope to the sea and swam to one boat standing off *Leasowe Castle*, was pulled aboard and then claimed seniority and ordered the boat to rescue more – forty-three in all. 'All on the ship could have been saved. The sea was calm. The men [the soldiers] were marvellous, no panic. The ship was still going away from us. We saw her turn on her side and the men still on her ran up her side. Then she slid into the sea. Some of the men were picked up. About 300 were lost.'[12]

When a torpedo struck *Cameronia* on 15 April 1915, Captain E. B. Hickson (RAMC) simply jumped out of his deck-chair, took off his British Warm, adjusted his lifebelt, inflated his Gieves waistcoat, answered a call to go to the lower deck to transfer to a destroyer and having dashed to his cabin en route to rescue his flute, stepped aboard the destroyer.[13] For Corporal Grimshaw, securing safety was much less easy. He 'tried to reach our parade deck but could not, so rushed up to the top deck of all and after assisting to lower a few life boats, got into one which, as it was being lowered, turned perpendicular and all the occupants were pitched into the sea. I fell on top of a number of fellows struggling in the water and grasped a rope hanging from the side of the ship. I clung to this rope for a short time which seemed like eternity. There were about eight of us and six fell exhausted into the water. Two of the destroyers came near to and a sailor threw a lifebelt to a man struggling in the water but he was unable to reach it. It floated to where I was clinging so I let go my hold and grasped the belt and then worked my way from the ship as I was afraid it might do down at any moment and the suction draw me under. . . . I saw a lifeboat with about fifty men in it and it was full of water. The boat was drawn under the propellers and smashed to atoms.' Grimshaw watched *Cameronia* go under, her siren still blaring. After a while he was picked up by a lifeboat which drifted all night to be found by HMS *Hydrangea* in the morning. The Corporal's contemporary account stipulates that 'None of the lifeboats had been allotted to the troops nor had we had a boat drill.' It had been a sad day; not only had 128 men and an officer been lost (and two naval officers, 9 ratings) but HMT *Arcadian* had been torpedoed too with not many short of 300 lives lost.[14]

More fortunate than these poor men, and quite extraordinarily so, was a private in the Middlesex Regiment, William Solden, who narrowly escaped drowning when HMT *Aragon* was torpedoed just outside Alexandria harbour on 30 December 1917. He had reached the steel netting of the rescuing destroyer alongside the doomed troopship when *Aragon* went down, dragging him from safety and sucking him under. He remembers being sorry for his parents who would learn of the death he was undergoing, but his life jacket brought him to the surface. He was pulled aboard the destroyer and was beginning to recover when the destroyer herself was torpedoed. He had lost his lifebelt which he had been using as a pillow but, stripped, saw a small boat within reach of his indifferent swimming capacity, jumped, swam and was saved a second time, this time as naked as the day he was born. His third escape was from the severe pneumonia brought on by his watery tribulations.[14A]

'I am afraid I have lost a good many comrades,' wrote Private John Parish to his parents a few days after having been rescued from one of the worst troopship disasters, the torpeding of HMT *Royal Edward* in the Aegean on Friday 13 August 1915, with the loss of over 850 lives. He had jumped over the side and swum well away from the ship and was in due course picked up by a lifeboat which was 'full of water and had only one oar and only one bucket to bail with'. Parish had used his boots as ladles for bailing, he and twenty-seven others being in a sort of floating bath for four hours before being picked up by a French minesweeper.[15]

No comparably tragic experience occurred for troop transport by rail except for the Royal Scot Gretna Green disaster in 1915, but in France every man in the ranks entraining at the Channel ports had to endure jolting hours in a cattle truck marked 'Hommes 40 Chevaux en longe 8.' The forty men in their uncompartmented seatless box en route to the railhead were fortunate that not many miles of slow, stopping, starting, shunting travel had to be endured. The same accommodation was likely to serve for the longer journey to the South of France and then east along the coast to Italy, but somehow it

seemed more acceptable because scenically the journey was so much more interesting. Such an experience really did widen a man's horizon perhaps even more than sea transportation because by rail he was constantly aware of a changing landscape and of differences in the everyday way of life.

The slow, hesitant movement and long delays in northern France were exchanged by those Italy-bound for a fair rate of speed. In November 1917 when just such a speed was kept up south of Troyes, a troop train stopped for ten minutes, and in restarting left a good number of people behind including 'Mr. Pinchbeck, Mr. Short and Mr. Maddock and one Platoon.' A subsequent train picked them up as the rest of the 2nd Queen's sped southwards with the Rhône on the left flowing 'alongside the railway for miles spanned by many fine bridges – on the right were hills and rocks with picturesque villages and châteaux on the sides'. After a cold night attempting to sleep, the men awoke to find the train in a large station, 'Some said Marseilles'. The next stage east, was far slower with many halts, but, 'by the sea shore nearly all the day'. Nice, Monaco and Monte Carlo were passed with the reflection of the moon in the sea attracting this diarist, Private T. H. W. Maxfield.

At the Italian frontier a band greeted them with the Marseillaise – 'all along people were cheering and flags flying'. They had good reason to, as the Queen's were with one of the British and French divisions hurrying to help hold the Italian line after the October defeat of Caporetto. The scenery was now a delight – 'through Italian seaside towns with numerous sky-scrapers many of which flew flags and the crowds cheered.' A series of tunnels then shut off the view until the train came out into a plain of cultivated countryside and scattered farms – this was the valley of the Po where they were to detrain.[16]

Half of the 9th Bn Devons travelled to Italy by a different route through Savoie and really spectacular scenery. For H. E. Baker, born and bred in Buckinghamshire, it was his first sight of mountains, 'Their grandeur and beauty left me speechless' but to balance such majesty was the less ethereal reality of the night-time 'darkness of our box wagon, lit only by candles perched precariously on the floor or stuck, until the jerking of the train shook them off', on the sides of the wagon. Ventilation at night was almost absent except where cracks had opened in the floor or between the planks at the wagon sides. From start to finish Baker's journey took from six to seven days. 'I can remember that it seemed endless.' The train stopped irregularly and travelled slowly, there were no times at which halts for meals or washing could be anticipated. What seems apochryphal about the anecdote of orderlies carrying heavy dixies of tea from the 'cookhouse' wagon back along the track to their thirsty fellows and suddenly being left standing as the train puffed itself away from them towards the next station and then for those same orderlies to be there waiting at that station conveyed by a kindly farmer in his horse-drawn cart, is given substance by first hand observation.[17]

The occupants of one train on the Riviera route, after it had crossed the Italian frontier at Ventimiglia were ordered out on to the platform to find great long tables with white covers upon which stood huge displays of fruit, wine and straw-covered Chianti. Senior Italian officers were there to welcome their allies. 'The wine was very good and morale rose accordingly. Some of the more obscene songs sung by the troops were clearly thought by the hosts to be musical gratitude. They beamed. We officers were relieved to entrain again with more or less straight faces.'[18]

In the First World War, British and Commonwealth troops served on at least fifteen different fronts and some of these fronts, such as East Africa, Macedonia and Italy, had markedly different conditions within their geographical boundaries. It is clearly going to be very difficult properly to highlight all the distinctive circumstances for each front where British troops were engaged and yet if the rich variety of such circumstances are to be indicated such an attempt must be made. To this end, only the most basic strategic context will be given in writing about any front and but the briefest indication, if this

be adjudged necessary, of how the campaign developed. It was in what surely must be the most distant location for troops from the United Kingdom to serve – China – that there is, ironically enough, particularly early indication of the nature of the land fighting which would be the characteristic of the war. 'We have all gone to ground like rabbits,' wrote Captain D. G. Johnson (2nd Bn, South Wales Borderers) of the military operations against the Germans defending Tsing Tau from the combined Anglo-Japanese force. From the time the force had landed in Laoshan Bay on 22 September 1914, Johnson had been pleased that in unloading stores 'our men are very much stronger than the Japs – [but] the Japs have helped us all they could in the off loading. . . . The Japs are very inquisitive and I think many of them have never seen English people before. . . . The difficulties of this country are immense as there are no roads and huge rocky mountains to be crossed somehow.' Significantly Johnson showed that he was surprised at how much forage was required for this single infantry battalion in co-operation with the Japanese. The needs of the mules for the General Service carts and the officers' horses quite dominated the stores to be taken the twenty-four miles to the outer defences of the German trading-post of Tsing Tau.

On 27 September, Johnson wrote that the battalion had undertaken three days' marching over 'the most awful roads imaginable made far worse for marching owing to a continuous stream of Japanese Howitzer Brigade guns and limbers with absolutely no idea of march discipline'. The Borderers were

Laoshan Bay on China's Yellow Sea coast, 22–24 September 1914. The 2nd Battalion, South Wales Borderers and sailors from HMSS *Triumph* and *Usk* disembark and unload stores preparatory to the march to join the Japanese Force besieging the strong German defences of Tsing Tao. Two Japanese officers stand at the left, and the sailor, centre right, may be carrying the canvas for a tent, but certainly not what its outline suggests, a 10-inch shell from the pre-Dreadnought battleship *Triumph*. (Major General D. G. Johnson, VC)

forced by the congestion on the road to march along ploughed fields. Johnson bought two bullocks to give his men a good feed and he found that the Chinese preferred dealing with the British who paid there and then, whereas the Japanese preferred 'war notes which the Chinamen of course distrust'. The interest the Chinese took in the British, even in their river ablutions, diminished as the column got 'nearer the square heads'.

It was on 30 September that this officer wrote by moonlight from his 'nice little hole in the earth which I have spent all day digging. . . . I expect we shall more or less live underground until the finish of this entertainment now.' Sad news of the death of his brother in Belgium stirred him deeply. 'The spirit of revenge was very strong in me.' He was to get no chance to express it as the Germans retired out of reach of the Borderers who, incidentally, seemed to the Japs so similar to the Germans that 'we have to wear a bit of white cloth in the top of our hats'.

Interestingly, the war in the air made an early début because not long after a German captive balloon broke away from its mooring, a German aeroplane dropped a coffee tin made into a bomb. 'It fell on my Company Cook's rabbit hutch – luckily it didn't go off.' The bomb was destroyed by a rifle bullet without impressive effect.

German shelling was directed upon the besieging positions to no great result, but very heavy prolonged rain caused drainage problems for the men's 'shelter-proof rabbit holes'. As they were at the bottom of a hill, the mud and flowing water got worse. Matting and straw had to be 'put up over the the fronts of their hutches' to keep the flood out and Johnson dug a ditch around his own bivouac. When the rain got heavier still, later in the day, his decision to evacuate the men to the nearby village was taken none too early as one dugout collapsed trapping its inmate who was only rescued with difficulty. Even the village looked as if it might be swept away by streams in flood and a further evacuation took place necessitating the dangerous fording of one torrent till shanties further up the hill were reached. These huts were filled to overcrowding by understandably unwelcoming Japanese soldiers and Chinese civilians. In a continuing downpour and in the dark, Johnson had still to find food from their earlier camp and see that it was cooked for the men to get something hot to eat.

The village had indeed been flooded out and in general, drying-out operations occupied one and all the following day with further rain preventing any possibility of military operations. 'One of those cold north winds driving the rain in bucketfuls – meantime I built a shelter of boards which would protect the cookhouse fire so that under all circumstances we should be able to feed. Rain and wind continued for sixteen hours and I was absolutely soaked through to the skin and frozen stiff.'

When the rain relented there was much to be done. 'I have three periods of digging each day totalling 12 hours, of course the men change but I remain. By day I dig trenches round the sides of the hill and at night crawl out to the front of the hill and dig there – that is most interesting as we have to continually drop flat when the searchlights look like

China – en route for Tsing Tao and drying-out after the deluge. Some degree of order seems to have returned to the HQ of the 2nd Battalion, South Wales Borderers after their prolonged drenching. Blankets and some clothing hang out, three officers on makeshift benches attend to administration or personal correspondence and one officer, while his tunic dries, gets warmth from the wintry sunshine. (Major General D. G. Johnson, VC)

being flashed on us. I stand in the middle and watch the lights and as soon as I see one working close I call "down" and when it has switched off us we carry on.'

In the midst of these siege preparations, the Shanghai Rugby Football Club sent 20,000 cigarettes for the men and a box of 100 for every officer. The gift was welcome as the digging, in continually gusting winds and rain, was wearisome. Suddenly it was all over, too quickly in fact for the Borderers fully to be involved except in their enduring heavy shelling. The Japanese troops captured a key redoubt. 'I saw the Japs were advancing and tried to get permission to advance but this took some time on the telephone and the thick of it was over by the time I got up and the white flags were going up – I was so angry at them giving in so quickly as I had some of my own to get back for the night before when I had 3 killed and 3 wounded.' Johnson's losses were incurred in an enterprising no man's land extension of the trench system, the capture of what he called a Martello tower and the bringing in of the casualties.[19]

Australasian troops too were fleetingly involved in Pacific adventure in the first weeks of the war, but in their case the South Pacific provided complete contrast in climate and the degree of opposition with that faced north of the Yellow Sea at Tsing Tau. German New Guinea was occupied by Australian and Samoa by New Zealand troops. In New Guinea some positions were contested, but four days sufficed to achieve German defeat. Australian casualties were six dead and four wounded in combat against native troops led by German NCOs and officers. For the occupying force the maintenance of health would now be a principal consideration with each Company having to appoint two permanent sanitary inspectors to ensure, among other things, that 'every man using latrines must use dry earth before leaving to prevent fly infection and odour'. Furthermore 'paw-paw is the best fruit, as it materially aids digestion. When ripe it is of a deep orange colour. Unripe paw-paw, when boiled, acts as an excellent substitute for vegetables. . . . Mosquito-nets must be placed in position ready for sleeping at 5.45 p.m. daily. O.C. units will see that the men of their command will take their daily quinine ration.'[20]

Less opposition still was faced by New Zealanders landing to occupy Samoa. An idyllic island paradise lay in the memory of L. P. Leary whose word-picture of soldiering in the Great War may be in every sense unparalleled. The troops were towed ashore in small boats to Apia, the capital. The scene was inviting and developed in interest as they

landed: a white beach, coconut palms bending seawards or scattered in clumps over a greensward with native huts, banana, breadfruit and paw paw, crystal streams and lakes and bathing maidens. Small wonder that Leary described the troops as being 'charmed'. There were no hostile forces whatsoever and apart from one incident the only danger was seasonal: 'It was unwise to sleep under a palm. The ripe nuts weighing with their husk many pounds, dropping from a considerable height, kill a Samoan or so every year and in a hurricane are terrifying.' The one incident, the arrival of Admiral von Spee's squadron, might have resulted in shelling, but such action was forestalled by a Senior German civil servant who made a hurried, unauthorized trip out to the German warships, *Scharnhorst* and *Gneisnau,* to assure the Admiral that Samoans and Germans as well as New Zealanders would be killed in the shelling and the New Zealanders had accidentally destroyed their own wireless by letting the governor of the engine jam, the flywheel as a result shooting through the roof to land in pieces. Danger passed and sadly to some extent so did

New Zealanders occupy Samoa. On 29 August 1914, a 1,400-strong force landed at Apia to dispossess the Germans of their hold over the western portion of the Pacific Island of Samoa. Beneath the palm trees in this photograph, men of the 3rd Auckland Regiment relax in camp at Vaimea. (W. M. Matheson)

paradise because Leary recorded that: 'as the heat increased, the regimental issue of salt pork, bacon, beef and potatoes was not suitable for the tropics. When it rained, the inside of the canvas tent was black with flies. Ants covered the sugar, the men got boils, mosquito bites became open sores, bathing produced ear infection, colic mounting to dysentery appeared, and swelling of legs and arms filled the hospitals with sepsis and the tents with sleepless men.' The troops in Samoa began to feel themselves sidetracked, not getting away to the war. Discontent grew and was answered by a tightening of discipline and the stopping of leave at Christmas (1914). Leave was taken, hotels and shops ransacked. For this, pay was stopped, the damage assessed by Court of Enquiry and paid and the force summoned away on short notice to be replaced by what Leary called 'middle-aged volunteers'.[21]

Far Eastern operations of a more dangerous nature involved the Mandalay Military Police in Burma where the Kachin tribesmen had been stimulated by German agents to strive to reassert their overlordship over the docile Shan tribe of farmers who in turn appealed to the Government of Burma for protection. The Second in Command of the force sent to deal with the Kachins was Herbert Todd who remembers that the militant tribesmen, who quickly withdrew from Shan territory to their jungle-clad hills, were difficult to punish. 'We had to push forward in single file with thick almost impenetrable jungle on each side.' The Kachins, of course accustomed to the terrain, sniped at the column from the flanks using old or even home-made muskets loaded with chunks of telegraph wire stolen from the telegraph lines alongside the railway. 'An Indian Surgeon whom we had with us was just in front of me when he received a chunk of metal in the stomach which almost disembowelled him.' It was obvious that the Kachins could not be brought to battle but were dangerous at night, necessitating camps being made within a thorn protected enclosure, a zariba. 'We concentrated on giving them as much trouble as we could by tracking down their villages, seizing all their goods and chattels and, in rare cases, capturing some of their women and children.' Driving out German spies and agitators certainly helped, as did paying Kachin tribal chiefs to endorse British policy. It was not too long before the young men themselves were being induced to become an official 'Scout detachment' of the Military Police; so the campaign had borne fruit, though the rebellion and counterinsurgency action involving troops and Military Police in the Chin Hills was to return as a problem in the winter of 1917–18.[22]

Burma 1918: Chin Hills Rebellion. A photograph taken just after the surrender of the Yokwa tribesmen. Gurkha and Indian Mountain Artillery officers including L. H. G. Conville, the broad figure in the centre. Standing next to Conville is a man called Faulkner of the Assam Military Police. (Lieutenant Colonel L. H. G. Conville)

Among the less well-known areas of campaigning in the early weeks of the war was that of the Cameroons. Doctor N. S. Deane, newly appointed to the West African Medical Service at Freetown, Sierra Leone, took up an invitation to be Medical Officer to the expeditionary force to leave by boat for Duala. He received guidance notes to make him mindful that a 'medical officer serves the force best by remaining unwounded and efficient. A battle ground can only be effectively cleared of wounded after the battle is over.' He was further to note that his equipment and support staffing would be on a scale of compromise between that required in France and what was considered necessary for bush warfare. Late in September the escorted troopships lay off the river which led to Duala.

On 26 September 1914, Deane and the regiment of native troops to which he was attached, the West African Regiment, attempted to land on the bank of the River Dibamba which offered a flank approach to Duala. Impenetrable mangrove swamps foiled the first endeavour, then, under cover of fire from two gunboats, a further attempt was made. Enemy fire made more awkward a difficult operation, the boat went aground and the landing was not developed. Meanwhile Duala, under naval bombardment, had been surrendered by the Germans. Deane was next required for service on another river expedition to take Jabassi. Field guns were manhandled through swampy grassland and the column came under fire and suffered casualties. When not attending the wounded or surveying the dead, Deane lay just behind the crest of the hill overlooking Jabassi, the

sun giving him a splitting headache and blistering his uncovered neck. He saw the body of a British officer, Captain Brand, being wrapped in ground sheets and brought down the hill suspended from a pole carried by some of his men. Another officer was shot through the back of the neck, the bullet coming out through his mouth; he, another officer and sixteen native wounded were taken back by camel under Deane's care to a troopship now serving as a hospital ship.

Deane was later to go on slightly more successful river expeditions but again casualties were incurred. Such were the movement problems away from the river that he could not fail to be impressed by successful drum signalling by a native pilot on one occasion. In his report on the casualties suffered, Deane drew attention to the fact that he had no native carriers so that if any men were hit when on reconnaissance ashore, he would have great difficulty in withdrawing them.

In a memoir, Deane noted that his rations, as a result of being attached to the West African Regiment and not the West African Frontier Force, were 'Imperial' consisting of weevil-accompanied ration biscuits, rum, tea, salt, sugar, bully beef, etc., much less suitable than the tinned food issued by the Colonial office to their Frontier Force.

When troop movement was required away from the rivers, a defensible camp had to be made, and it was quite elaborate – the bush cleared and burned, a *chevaux de frise* on the perimeter of the camp, then trenches dug, a block-house erected, of earthen walls within a corrugated iron framework, and then,

Cameroons, 26 September 1914 and the first action for a Medical Officer, Dr. N. S. Deane. Unsuccessful efforts to land on the mangrove swamp bank of the River Dibamba from the neatly named riverboats, 'Crocodile' and 'Alligator'. (Doctor N. S. Deane)

Cameroons, the advance on Jabassi, early October 1914. Two field guns being manhandled into the bush from the riverboats (top right). Dr. Deane, the Medical Officer with this party, had been ordered to: 'be careful to identify all cases of men killed whether of the British or of the enemy and keep a record'. (Doctor N. S. Deane)

behind the block-house, bush buildings as mess and living quarters. The *chevaux de frise* had machine-gun emplacements at intervals and a trench was dug to the river bank to secure rearward communication. Deane wrote that high winds, swampy ground and myriads of mosquitoes were a trial during his spell in such a camp. Snakes were quite common too and there were many alligators in the river and on its banks. Another unpleasant memory of this time was having to attend the flogging of a native soldier who had been caught sleeping at his post.

On one occasion, Deane was with a party in which swift officer and man action certainly saved heavy British casualties. Emerging from a bush path to the top of a hill, they were confronted by a German officer setting up his machine-gun. The British officer, a man called Minniken, seemed tragically unfortunate when one of the tripod legs of his gun broke, but his sergeant, an African, immediately knelt offering his knee as support while Minnekin fired, wounding the German who hurried off having thrown his gun into the bush. Minnekin's good work and that of the sergeant were rewarded and later there was more success when a German river launch was sighted and destroyed.

An interesting survival of these late 1914 military operations is Captain Deane's medical report on the condition at Dibombe of the troops whose health he had to investigate. Much of the report was routine, but when Deane added statistical details to show that one Company of West African Rifles had 21 cases of VD as against the next highest incidence of 6, and drew attention to the fact that opportunities for fresh

rather than previously acquired infection had occurred, he caused some offence to the Company Commander concerned. Dibombe was to be attacked by more than VD. Reconnaissance patrols were driven into the relative security of the little fortress there by aggressive German-officered raiders armed with spears as well as small arms. The laying of trip wires and mines and the setting up of barbed wire was to guard against further surprise and the 3-pounder gun which the fort boasted was a useful deterrent.

On his last extended patrol into dense, unin-habited forest, native guides led three companies of the West African Regiment, a hundred carriers with their 60lb loads and then a rearguard WAR Company with whom Deane and two stretcher-bearers travelled, walking in single file along the narrowest of tracks. The expedition was not well-handled – no ten-minute rests each hour which certainly the carriers needed and then, exhausted, finding themselves in a swamp in the dark at the end of the day, necessitating a continued journey to get to higher ground. In the dark it was impossible to find food from the stores, Deane, from his Medical Comforts box, making do with champagne and Bovril. Sentries were posted – fires lit to keep off wild animals, and sleep, on the ground where they had been standing, was attempted. Even the follow-ing day, the Officer in Command had to be per-suaded to stop for rice to be cooked for the men and did not allow sufficient time for this to be done properly. He followed this by ordering a continu-ation of the march in pitch darkness which led to continued collisions as exhausted carriers fell with their loads. The rearguard with the ammunition got completely separated from the vanguard with the machine-guns since the men in the rear, isolated and momentarily resting, were held in suspense by a herd of elephants moving across their path.

By this time, Deane's feet were giving him serious trouble. He joined a column en route for Duala rather than continue on the slow pursuit insisted upon by the thrusting Commander of their force. By foot and then boat, Deane and his small escort party – (he brought a very sick officer with him) – reached Duala. After hospital and convalescence, he was to return to his duty with the regiment. For all his adventures and tribulations, the Medical Officer soberly judged that his experience had been 'nothing compared with our troops in France and we have been particularly fortunate in the fact that the Germans appear to have no artillery at least in this part of the country'. It is a fair observation. His service, however, had certainly been distinctively different. His diary and that of his brother in France, also a Regimental Medical Officer at the time, make interesting comparison. We may note that the officer with West African Service survived, his brother did not.[23]

The vastly different terrain of southern Africa offered the opportunity for mounted action such as would not have been remotely possible in the Cameroons. General de Wet's anti-British rebellion in South Africa resulted in all men with good horses being called upon to join the forces against the rebels. Philip Fourie, whose father had been killed in the Second Boer War, was not keen on fighting and certainly 'disliked the idea of shooting against the great General de Wet'. Fourie's mounted detachment was stationed in the dry bed of the River Sand and had to assault a kopje with as little prospect of success as the British had enjoyed just over a decade earlier. Before the attack could take place it appeared that the detachment itself was under attack. Fourie and a still younger man, despite pressing fear shown by the youth through an audible prayer, volunteered to bring a wounded man out of the line of fire. This they did but the whole party was moving out of the river as it was clear they were being surrounded. Fourie's account does not explain what happened to the wounded man, but he himself mounted and raced off under heavy fire. He was hit in the leg and fell off his horse. A Captain Reitz came back and hoisted him on his own horse, but Fourie asked to be left when he realized that the double-burdened horse could not make sufficiently swift progress. As it happened Fourie was to be rescued, but his wound

was sufficient to prevent his being in the force which advanced into German South West Africa once de Wet's rebellion had been defeated.[24]

Hugh Leith has described his mounted volunteer unit as an old-style Boer Commando, but it was largely made up of townsfolk and was equipped with chaotic haste – everyone got new Bedford cord riding breeches with the Defence Force blue stripe down the seam, good army boots, leggings or puttees and khaki shirts, but there were insufficient felt hats so some got khaki police helmets. A sorry looking lot of horses was issued on a first come first served basis and then Portuguese rifles, bandoliers and ammunition were given out. 'Somehow or other we contrived, with much bellowing and bullying by our sorely tried permanent force instructors, to get a working idea of how to walk, trot, canter, knee to knee, avoid dropping our rifles and to know the various words of command. After a fortnight of such training, the Commando set off from Tempe for the 60-mile or so journey to Winburg. They had had a two-hour break near Brandfort and had ridden for about fifteen hours.

'As we reached Winburg, the Commando slowed down while scouts went ahead to find out whether that town was occupied by the rebels or not, in preparation for the pre-dawn encircling gallop which was to take the town by surprise. As the sun rose we were scampering crazily over the veld, cutting fences and spreading out so as to encircle the little dorf before the alarm could be given.' In fact there were no rebel forces and in the anti-climax of such a discovery the men had more opportunity to consider their discomforts in the form of raw patches on their buttocks and the inside of their knees and aching muscles from unfamiliarity with such prolonged riding.

For several weeks, fruitlessly, rebels were chased with only one action, dismounted, dislodging a few men defending a low flat-topped kopje. 'I hated that climb which meant dodging from stone to stone and hearing the vicious crack of Mauser bullets overhead. One red-headed man on my right was hit as we neared the crest of the hill while I was watching him. I was very nearly sick on the spot.'

While on this trek, the old Commando system was established with each section given some raw meat, dry mealie meal, salt, sugar, coffee and occasionally a loaf of bread. Cooking utensils were carried and apart from the listed supplies, the men lived off the land and fed themselves. 'I learned how to roast a whole leg of mutton to a turn. The only essentials were a stony stretch of ground, firewood, a match and the meat. The leg of mutton was stood up on its

The 130th Baluchis are joined at Serengeti camp by newly arrived South African troops in 1916. (G. A. Pim)

shank end in an empty cigarette tin and a cairn of small stones carefully built around it. When the cairn was complete, the meat could not be seen at all – then firewood was piled around and on top of the cairn and kept blazing for about 30 to 35 minutes, according to the size of the joint. On clearing away the ashes and removing the stones the joint could be extracted, done to a turn.'[25]

As unwilling as Fourie had been, F. N. Broome, with part-time military training experience when he had been at Oxford, realized what would be expected of him and before any question of compulsion arose, bought a horse and joined the Natal Carbineers, a unit to see service in German SW Africa. He has confessed to being terrified by the tiny, home-made bombs dropped by the single German aircraft in opposition when they advanced from the SW African coast inland to a waste of small, monotonous, light grey kopjes with stretches of yellowish sand between these little hills. 'The whole face of the country seemed old and tired and leprous.' The climate held no attractions and there was always a strong wind. Further inland sand dunes were constantly re-sculptured by the wind, prelude to the desert with its limitless horizon – 'A terrible country, profoundly hostile to life.' In the summer it was cruelly hot, 128°F being recorded when Broome was there.

There was no fresh water whatsoever, the town of Luderitz being dependent wholly on condensed sea water, but the condensation plant had been demolished and the town evacuated. The South African troops, in consequence of this, were entirely dependent on water shipped from Capetown until the plant was repaired. Campaigning consisted of making periodical trips inland from a base at Luderitz. These mounted expeditions were to find and occupy positions later consolidated by infantry. Broome did remember the excitement of a moonlit silent trek inland with the tread of the horses muffled by the sand and the only sound being the occasional jingle of a curb chain. 'Towards dawn the moon had set and the morning star rose in front of us, it seemed so bright as it came over the horizon that some of us thought it was the headlight of a car.' The objective of this night march was the capture of the lightly defended Chankaib. This was accomplished, but a daring German party blew up the railway line behind the South Africans' advance. Repair was soon effected but the raiders escaped the patrol sent after them. Hours in a sun so hot that perspiration was dried before it formed were not rewarded by any sight of the Germans. 'I myself was hallucinated, seeing quite a few things like little men that weren't there.'

When Broome first came under fire, his party approaching Garub on foot, the affair ended ingloriously in flight when dust clouds suggested that they were being cut off by a large body of men. Later the Germans retired from Garub, poisoning the wells nearby with carbolic. South African engineers pumped out one well but as it refilled the water was still strongly tainted. Some men successfully adopted the bushmen technique of scooping an arm's length hole in a dry river bed until water seeped in at the bottom. Using a tin mug to get water into a horses' nose-bag must clearly have been a laborious process.

What remained most vividly in Broome's memory was the period after rejoining his unit following the only real engagement they had been in – Gibeon. The column was somewhere near Rehoboth and it was mid-winter.'It was colder by far than anything I experienced later in France.' It was the contrast between the sunny warmth of the day and the near zero temperature at night which so affected the men who nevertheless had the valuable bonus of hot springs for washing.[26]

Teutonic ingenuity in the booby traps which became familiar in following-up through German vacated positions in France, found expression near Aus recalled W. Whittaker, a gunner in the Natal Field Artillery. 'On the trek from Garub to Aus we lost some men unnecessarily. The Germans had shot one of our scouts and buried him to the right of the road with a board giving his name and then set a land mine near his grave knowing some of us would go close to the grave and surely some did.'[27]

For infantry, the German South West African campaign required quite remarkable marching or trekking endurance. Arthur Harris, a bugler in the Rhodesian regiment which completed a march of such phenomenal length that the German Chief of Staff at his force's surrender denied that it was possible, was quite determined after this experience that he would never 'never walk around again if I could avoid it' and his subsequently distinguished RFC and RAF career supported the wisdom of his decision.[28]

South Africans and Rhodesians who had served in Southern Africa and who were, with British troops, to fight in the campaign in East Africa, were to find striking contrasts in waging war north of their homeland. The area over which the campaign was fought had the same seemingly limitless space but it was 'space' through which it could be infinitely more difficult to travel. Whether in coastal marches, river and track progress inland, warfare on or around the lakes or mountain trekking, the terrain waged a war of its own, climate and disease being its senior staff officers. Of course the Germans were in this sense to be under precisely the same disadvantage except that their predominantly African native force (under German officers and NCOs) was naturally better

attuned to the regional rigours and furthermore a properly limited German strategic purpose of avoiding battle and any chance of defeat was best fulfilled by a far smaller force than one being organized to neutralize it. The problems of campaigning in East Africa multiplied with the size of force engaged.

The Official Historian of the Campaign makes it plain that natural difficulties and obstacles were on a huge scale and of every variety, that the climate was enervating and unhealthy and that nature proved a 'more relentless enemy than any human adversary'. In short, the Historian concluded, the problems of command were 'unlike any elsewhere and often well-nigh insoluble'.[29] German East Africa in its 800-mile length was predominantly covered in bush with thick forests around the numerous river valleys and the lakes where swamps too, added to the danger, never mind the difficulties of making progress. A series of mountain ranges, characterized by steep, broken ridges densely overgrown with bush, raised barriers to intercommunication only evaded by passage of narrow valleys. In the rainy season, the network of rivers in the south took on the appearance of one vast lake. Mapping provision was sketchy in the extreme and in some parts so thick was the bush that small parties but fifty yards apart were completely out of communication. Co-ordination between separate columns designed to concert upon the same objective was frequently impossible, in one such case a five-mile separation representing a week's march.

Four inches of rain a day was recorded in one location and if the facts related above were to have had their influence first upon strategic planning, then an impact upon infantry endeavour at fulfilment, one may imagine the degree of difficulty for transport and supply support of a campaign which extended beyond German into Portuguese East Africa. Oxen, mules and horses succumbed to the bite of the tsetse fly and the overburdened survivors simply could not adequately maintain supplies on trails hacked through virgin bush, threaded across mountain sides and valleys or, when more fortunate, along baked or muddy dirt tracks.

When numbers of dead beasts could not be buried because of the nature of the ground and movement of the unit concerned was either not required or was difficult to undertake, the resultant conditions can well be imagined. The variety of disease was remarkable as well as the incidence of the predominant problems of malaria, dysentery and jigger flea, the insect which burrowed into a foot or an exposed part of the body and laid its eggs with inflammatory consequence to the sufferer. Enteric fever, typhus, cholera, blackwater fever, jaundice, smallpox, sleeping sickness, East African relapsing fever and meningitis awaited the unfortunate. Some of these diseases, like enteric, had a high mortality rate and others required a considerable period of convalescence. The Southern Nigerian Corps had an annual death rate of 394 per 1,000 troops, but native carriers are believed to have suffered even worse, the dreadful toll making their extraordinarily high rate of desertion seem understandable.

The sickness rate among the white troops was devastating. It seems that the acute shortage of clean water and in consequence drinking from impure sources was one serious factor, but certainly the myriad marshes and pools, paradise for mosquitoes, offered an awesome challenge to any preventative engineering and required medicine on such a universal and stringently supervised level that the medical authorities could not cope. In 1917 a staggering rate of 2880.9 men per 1,000 was sick from malaria, a figure which may be compared with that for the Macedonian front, generally accepted as being notorious, of 353.18. In under two years the 2nd Rhodesian Regiment from its total strength of 1,038 admitted 10,626 sickness cases to hospital. It is small wonder that the Director of Medical Services, East African Force, reported in August 1917 that 'the European infantry soldier cannot cope with this climate under present active service conditions. The strain of marching with heavy equipment, constant exposure to sun and wet, general hardship of active service, quickly enfeeble him and render him liable to rapid recurrent attacks of malaria, intestinal

disorders and other diseases incidental to this climate.'[30] The wholesale evacuation of European and indeed Indian troops, who had similarly found conditions insupportable, was begun in late 1917 and thereafter the true indispensable value of the native troops of the King's African Rifles and of the Gold Coast Regiment in bush fighting and in resistance to the privations of the climate, was fully evident. The Official Historian developed still further the pre-eminent suitablity of African troops for this campaign. 'The African is unaffected by the strain on the nerves which long periods in the bush, with its constant sinister suggestion of unseen dangers, tend to produce even in the best of troops of other races.'

In personal experience documentation for all British troops who served in East Africa, the region's problems loom large. Sometimes the evidence is quite stark as in Captain F. A. Archdale's account of lying wounded by a mine exploded on a bush track. 'Some 15 yards away were the remnants of the other occupants of the ambulance and sitting on the edge of the track were four huge hyenas waiting for us to die. Twice I heard lions on the prowl which put the hyenas to flight.'[31] T. N. Whitehead (ASC), whose letters indicated some apprehension from the lions which peered inquisitively at parked vehicles on the track, added that he considered 'there was not too much danger despite their awful noise because they get so many transport animals that they are well fed.' Whether it were to have been curiosity or hunger, one of the lions was to seek Whitehead's closer acquaintance by actually nosing round the bottom of his sleeping-bag and waking him up. It is certainly

The British inflict a measure of protection. In watching the 'agonies' of their fellows as they are dosed with castor oil, there is at least some enjoyment of the proceedings by native porters awaiting their preventive medicine. (Lieutenant Colonel F. A. Archdale)

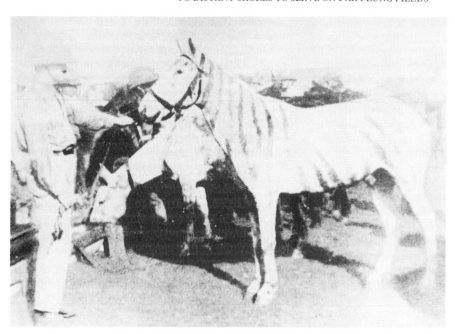

East Africa and equine camouflage: whether a German Askari scout would fail to detect that this was no zebra and hence the British were about, must be considered very doubtful. (G. A. Pim)

not for this author, given the circumstance, to disapprove of Whitehead's reaction; he shot the lion with his .27 calibre Mauser but surely he was very fortunate with such a weapon to escape further consequences! This Army Service Corps officer incidentally paid tribute to his vehicle, 'a miracle of engineering', the Ford car which carried him safely on dirt roads over 'mountain passes, through sandy desert with thorn bushes, up to axles in sand, through boggy areas and straight through jungle with men with axes making roads as they go'. In this remarkable tribute, which does sound almost too good to be true, he admitted that: 'my car and lorries have upset and run away backwards and forwards on the passes' but he would 'never laugh at a Ford car again, it is not only far and away the cheapest car on the market but it is easily the best and most capable car that there is for this sort of work. I have taken my Ford in places where no other car could have reached to save its life.'[32]

To return to East Africa's tribulations and perhaps their earliest sting – this came from the swarms of bees disturbed by machine-gun fire in the aftermath of the landing at Tanga. 'Suddenly, retreating men were seen to leap high in the air, caper about and perform grotesque contortions on the ground.' The bees were 'to European bees what a leopard is to a tabby cat; a single sting from one of them was the deep thrust of an acid-topped needle. . . . faces and arms swelled to twice their normal size . . . the entire force went almost literally insane trying to fight off

the angry swarms'.[33] This incident made its own special contribution to the panic which had spread among Indian troops retreating from failure to dislodge the small German force defending the coastal railhead at Tanga.

Hazard from African wildlife occasionally came in very large form. 'We were in very thick bush so thick that the advanced screen of men were only about 20 yards ahead of me. One of the flankers came across a water hole so I stopped the patrol and went to have a look for tracks human or otherwise. There was nothing but game marks but I noticed the water was very muddy and stirred-up looking. We started on again and had gone 50 yards, when as one of the advanced people came round a bush, a seeming large red ant-hill came to life and charged him. It was a huge rhino which had been rolling in the water hole and had then gone to sleep. The man flung himself to one side and its horn missed him but he was knocked over by its body. The rhino then charged a few yards towards us and then jinked round like a polo pony and went off into the bush.'[34]

Smaller game but fearful to behold and infuriatingly painful for those whom they attacked, were what Arthur Groves called the 'red, fighting or safari ants'. They used to traverse the country near his station at Boma Mzinga in a column which might be a foot wide and up to half a mile long. 'Nothing would stop them not even fire or water.' He was wakened one night by ants biting him and his account of the experience describes desperate attempts to pull the ants from their bite leaving them decapitated by the relentless incision of their pincer grip. Groves, a Sapper in the Engineers, had his own small victory in the East African campaign at Idete near Mahenge. He was walking in the evening not far from the camp when he encountered native carriers being escorted by six askari. One of the askari came up to him, saluted and handed him a note. To Groves's dismay it was written in German. He then used his commendable command of Swahili to order the column to follow him into the British camp. The British camp was clearly not the intended rendezvous for the column of over 200 porters but fortunately the camp sentry responded quickly to Groves's order, the Guard turned out and a useful haul had been very fortunately netted.[35]

When Captain Madge (RAMC) arrived at a camp in the neighbourhood of Kilwa at the beginning of November 1917, the Medical Officer's African boys soon had his bed put up in the banda allotted to him, a canvas washbasin set out and filled for a welcome clean-up and a satisfactory meal ready – sardines, bully beef and biscuits, raspberry jam and biscuits and good coffee. The tents, stretchers and drugs were en route so there was no medical work to be done that night and indeed his party was trekking further up-country. Madge's letters attractively illustrate the supportive value of a cheerful disposition under physical circumstances which most would have judged less than ideal. 'This kind of life suits me excellently and I feel better and happier already; if one can avoid mosquitoes and dysentery there is no real reason for getting ill. By being careful and looking after one's servants one can reduce the chances of dysentery and the mosquitoes are more a matter of luck than anything.' East Africa was to take its toll of such cheerfulness. A difficult motorcar journey and a field hospital staff not wanting to be relieved and making their replacement feel less than welcome, eroded morale until wounded were brought in and, by the light of a smoky lamp in a crowded banda, Captain Madge had twenty German wounded and two English officers to see to in a crowded hut. 'It was jolly good to have some work at last' but when there was less to do, neuralgia and toothache manifestly lowered his spirit.[36]

Malaria was to be the undoing of Gunner Tozer (RGA) who landed at Mombassa in late June 1916 and entrained 'packed in like sardines' for Maktau before being detached for service at Mbuyuni which offered inspiring views of snow-topped Mount Kilimanjaro. Tozer's diary records his first dose of malaria on 12 July, his recovery, a 'good job escorting lunatic to Nairobi', seeing lots of wild game and then being detached for howitzer duty travelling with his designated 14th Battery by ship from Tanga to Msassani Bay near Dar es Salaam. In this unhealthy spot, the draught bullocks died of 'coast fever' and many men went sick. The battery was shipped back to disembark near Kilwa again via Zanzibar but Kilwa was no improvement. 'Rotten place, lot of sickness, half of battery in Hospital in less than a week, parades nearly all day in blazing sun, went into hospital with dysentery 4th November.' On recovery he was detached for service with a Naval Brigade battery of one 12-pdr gun. The six mules required to pull it, all died and the gun had to be drawn from Kilwa by Swahili porters. It was the rainy season and the Column slept at night in soaking clothes and on wet ground. About six miles a day was managed but on the first day the gun overturned and the officer in command, having reconnoitred towards the firing line, had to accept that the road was too narrow and in too bad a condition to get the gun up.

Pioneers repaired the road but still the gun overturned. Kibata, the destination, was reached, the last miles being under shellfire on 23 December. 'Looking forward to a Happy Christmas and had one, I don't think. Nothing doing Christmas Day. Bully and biscuit rations. Officers gave us bottle of whisky.' The gun got into action on Boxing Day, a mini artillery duel developing.

Tozer had taken part in the Kibata Offensive and when he rejoined his howitzer battery he found almost all the men ill and his own malaria recurring. Good cheer arrived in the form of Christmas puddings from a benevolent newspaper fund, but the gunner bemoaned the fact that he was 'too sick to tackle it. Dead loss.' In the next weeks he went to hospital with malaria, was discharged and returned to hospital with rheumatism. Again he rejoined his battery and again he fell sick. Return to service and a route march resulted in his falling out 'owing to bad legs'. In all, before he was transported to South Africa and then the UK, Tozer's diary records six separate hospitalizations in a period between late February and the end of September.[37]

Malaria affected Sapper Whitty, an RE dispatch rider, but not with disabling permanence. His very arrival in East Africa, on the broad back of a native carrying him from a lighter through the surf to the shore near Kilwa, had been an experience to remember. The strength required to handle his $4\frac{1}{4}$ hp BSA motor cycle, in negotiating the stony or sandy bottoms of the dongas or erosion gullies which frequently cut across his route, was considerable. It was not much less difficult to hold steady on road or lorry ruts as a low gear crawl was made along narrow tracks, the engine in danger of overheating. Whitty shared the apprehension of other dispatch riders about his machine breaking down in isolated bush, his travelling encounters with a large python and two species of mamba doing nothing to ease his anxiety on this score.[38]

Problems of a different nature affected the work of a former lithographic artist, Tom Smith in No. 6 Topographical Section, RE, engaged upon cartography. Apart from the sticky heat affecting the chemical agent acting upon lithographic plates used in copying of maps, there was the fact that much of the country was uncharted and what was mapped was mapped inaccurately. The maps from which Smith copied had been originally copied from those drawn by explorers. In his recollections, Smith stressed that accuracy, to some extent, was an unrealizable aim as some regions changed each year in flooding, with new channels appearing and old ones disappearing.[39]

Among the papers of an officer in the King's African Rifles, C. G. Phillips, there are his own sketch maps of journeys he undertook for the re-cruiting of troops. The rivers and tracks are dotted with the names of the tiniest tribal settlements seemingly close but separated by hard trekking – Namuna, Puhu, Kuyu, Nampuita, Nahalia, Ngulun and then there are accounts of payments made. Chief Chapola was paid 11s. for eleven men, Chief Karango got a shilling for his single offering. A guide to Msingi river cost 6d. and three days food for 48 porters cost 12s.

The 'Army Book 152' for Phillips is a perfect illus-tration of both the universal features of soldiering like:

Punishments 17.12.14 634 Zebadia Pte Letting off his rifle in camp on guard dismounting. 3 extra guards C. G. Phillips

and those peculiar to where he was serving:

21.2.15 Msambu Camp Sgt Chibwana B Coy 1 K.A.R. Ndifuna ince Kubwera Pano Tsopano Pamodzi Anthu Onze Yako Pamodzi Patrol Wahindi C. G. Phillips O.C. B Coy

There is too, a disappointing note from Phillips who is clearly needing recruits but he cannot take thirteen men as he has had a long talk to one and they are 'all Nyamwanga and are not Yaos at all; they live to the north-east of Nyasaland, half in British terri-tory, half in German territory and are not as far as I know a fighting tribe. We have never enlisted them at all. Thus I must decline your kind permission to try and enlist them.' In another letter Phillips wrote

East Africa: discipline in the field for the King's African Rifles. A breach of military discipline has led to what the label on the original photograph calls: a 'kibokoing'. (F. O. Stansfield)

'please do not take any more Angoni and only take really good Nyungas'. In two months he had walked about five hundred miles, at the end of each day having then to bargain with the Chief of a village. Small wonder that he excused himself in a letter to his grandmother: 'I have really had no time for writing and I have written to nobody.'[40]

For all the absence of major battles in the East African campaigns, small engagements brought intense, close-order combat. A. L. Messum, a Sergeant in the British South Africa Police with Captain Murray's Rhodesian Column, took part in such an affair when the column, with King's African Rifles too, was invested at Mkapira. A square was formed and the troops dug in. Most of their ten days' rations was consumed and so a fixed bayonet attack to break through the enemy positions was ordered. It was specifically stated that the enemy's fire was not to be returned and at a deliberate trot an advance was made, the enemy forward pickets immediately retiring and then from their rifle pits the German askaris broke and ran too. The German officers and NCOs in machine-gun emplacements went on firing to the last minute and 'died at their posts' and Murray, who more usually harangued his men as skrimshankers, paraded and complimented them.[41]

The 25th Royal Fusiliers was also to be involved in a bayonet charge, in June 1916, following a German ambush on South African troops at the head of a column stretched out over many miles. Heavy firing was heard ahead and the Fusiliers were ordered to close, a very considerable distance according to Charles Shaw, who remembered the battalion still completing it in a day. There was a further march the following day in a move to outflank the enemy force, the Fusiliers being in the rear of South African and Indian troops. Through thick forest and with the only halts being for the clearance of obstacles, the small column toiled till midnight and was then given rest but without permission to cook or to smoke. It was not until early the following afternoon that contact was made with the enemy and the celebrated Lieutenant Colonel Driscoll of the Fusiliers was given the opportunity of ordering his sickness-reduced battalion past the weary-looking Indians and South Africans to go into the attack. Shaw has written that unit pride made them feel ten feet tall. In extended order and with a support line, the Fusiliers had to storm a steep, wooded hill which the former frontiersman cannot believe had been reconnoitred. 'The order was 5 rounds rapid – no stopping. Follow through with the bayonet. Move. Then all hell broke loose.' The noise itself must have been impressive, reverberating from the sounding-board of the slope facing them and those of the enemy who could, broke and fled.[42] Colonel von Lettow Vorbeck's German-officered askaris were infrequently to be caught in such a manner and the campaign assumed an interminability bearing kinship to the vastly different circumstances in France.

There seems to have been little for the soldier serving with the Aden Field Force to have led him to remember the experience as being other than intensely hot, loathsomely sandy and vilely boring though Colonel J. W. Watts has written intriguingly of 'visiting the mummified mermaids in a Parsee shop' and more prosaically, of the Union Jack Club at Steamer Point to indulge in gin-slings.[43]

An artillery officer, A. C. Smith, lamented that 'the whole place is covered in clouds of dust from 9 a.m. till 4 p.m. daily. Also there are occasional sandstorms when there is a tremendous wind and sand so thick that one cannot see 20 yds.'

There was an extended front to be defended by isolated posts and by a mobile column. On an occasion when a local village showed signs of sympathy with the Turks, who regularly exchanged desultory shelling with the Aden Field Force, Sappers were sent in to demolish the village. Though one letter-writer considered that 'everyone finds it too hot for fighting', there were numerous skirmishes providing action for infantry, gunners and cavalry.[44] After one such action, a composite force was congratulated by the Commander of the No. 5 Section Defences in September 1916 with the officer concerned, Colonel Campbell, assuring the men that 'it is only by fighting that we can learn to fight and maintain the offensive spirit which is the essence of victory'.[45]

Some idea of the small scale and the nature of such engagements can be gathered from the diary description of the 'hottest show the battery has so far been in'. A mixed unit British force of about 150 men was attacked by about 300 Turks. The Forward Artillery Observation Officer, A. C. Smith, was forced to retire upon his battery in the face of the enemy advance. The battery was firing lyddite at a range of only 1,200 yards but the men were themselves under small arms fire. The enemy got to within less than 100 yards of British machine-guns 'effectively operated by a unit of cavalry'. Enemy losses were not recorded, but British casualties in all amounted to 12 killed and wounded.[46]

Officers with the South Wales Borderers catalogued Aden's evils: 'If the men march by night they have got to rest by day and how are they to get any rest in the middle of the desert under the broiling sun. . . . I hear that the men arrived at their first camping place at about 7.30 and did not get their food till nearly 10 p.m. and started off on their next trek at about 3 a.m. This afternoon a telephone message came through that eight men with heat stroke were being sent back, and two, I am sorry to say of our fellows were dead. One I believe fell dead on the march and the other fell out to the side of the road feeling bad so they got a camel to bring him back when he died and here is a very curious thing, the camel fell down dead too.' What was perhaps as curious was that one of the men was a golf professional and the other a very good footballer! 'July 5 Three of our officers have been brought back collapsed. I hear terrible stories about our poor chaps and I am afraid the heat is killing a lot of them.' Then, after an engagement: 'All the kit was lost, even the General's as directly the Arabs who led the camels heard the firing, they bolted so that off went the camels with the kit, ammunition, water and everything else.'[47] Lieutenant, the Hon Lancelot

Bailey had written the above from base but the Colonel, the Lord Glanusk, had been with his men on the Column's march and battle and he wrote: 'It is difficult to describe the awful feeling for a Commanding Officer who sees men dying of heatstroke and thirst and has absolutely no means of doing anything for them.' The Colonel had ridden on to the camp to check the arrangements for water, food and rest. His weary, parched column were sitting by the roadside when firing was heard and the Arab Camel drivers departed taking with them 15 days' rations for 1,000 men.

Without its camels and stores, the column reached camp utterly exhausted, some wounded and some sick. The Turks followed up their surprise success and now prepared to attack the camp. The Colonel attempted to muster his men: 'Everyone was in an utter state of collapse and fatigue and, in spite of anything in the way of persuasion, I was only able to collect 7 men out of 100 and I think only about 50 or 60 more got in at all, all in much the same state and nearly all quite incapable of moving a finger even to save their own lives until they had rested and been watered copiously.'

The Colonel led his seven men to the top of the flat roof of a four-storeyed house. From here he could see where the firing was coming from, but dusk was falling and a field gun could not be got up in time to

range upon a large body of Turks. The Colonel now led his men 300 yards out of the town 'firing hard as we went to make the enemy think we were a strong force'. As soon as it was quite dark they returned to their camp which was in a walled garden about 100 yards by 200 yards. The senior officers in the beleagured force had a council of war which led to the decision not to attempt a breakout but to hold on till the morning and then review the situation. Meanwhile shrapnel showered down, scything through date palms, and bullets whistled across the garden.

The enemy made several rushes at a side street towards one entrance to the garden but each time was beaten back. An extraordinary incident occurred in the makeshift hospital. Men outside the hospital heard hammering and shouts from inside and believed the Turks had got into the garden. Then a figure with a white cloth around his head burst into the hospital, and was shot by the Doctor (Dr Townley) who immediately realized that the

The hostile terrain of the Aden hinterland. Indian Mountain Artillery establish a commanding position against enemy incursion. A rangefinder is being set up on the right. (Lieutenant Colonel L. H. G. Conville)

man he had slightly wounded was a man he had bandaged ten minutes before.

Before dawn and the anticipation of being shelled to destruction, the sick and then the fit men themselves were ordered to move out. The Colonel urged them to go hard for two miles and then take up a defensible position. They were not pursued but the march back to Aden, by men still weaker than before, was harrowing. More men fell out and the bodies of those who had fallen out the previous day were a pitiful and awful sight. After about seven miles 'we met the General who had been unable to get through the night before (for of course no-one had expected that we should find the Turks there on our arrival) and with him a most welcome supply of ice and water. From there on at intervals were motors (mostly broken down) and camels all with the life-giving liquid and more ice on board.' More men had died on this march and for the Colonel it had been 'without exception the worst experience of my life'.[48]

1916, India and a 2,300-mile railway journey from Bangalore to Burhan. The 25th Londons stretch their legs at a brief halt on their six days and seven nights of train travel. (C. J. Davis)

Sandwiched anonymously between the dramatic military campaigning of the British and Indian Armies on the North West Frontier of India in the 19th century and the renewal of such campaigns immediately after the end of the Great War, are the years of frontier duty, of exercising an urban military presence and the training undertaken in India by many units during the First World War. In his masterly book on the Indian Army, Philip Mason provides a graphically detailed picture of life in the Indian Army and a clear insight into the special character of an Indian Army unit. In a good British battalion, regimental pride was usually an all-pervading almost tangible entity and it was but rare for a man to shed it under whatever circumstance. Mason explains a distinctively different parallel – 'a personal relationship, implying service and devotion on one side, on the other the duty to feed and protect . . . . the recruit brought (this combination of loyalty and respect) and gave his allegiance to the regiment, to the army, perhaps especially to a single officer, perhaps to all the officers of the regiment; eventually, but in a remote and shadowy way, to the Sovereign. It was something officers and men both understood without words. It knit them into a close bond, from which the rest of the world was excluded.'[49] The point is not to be further developed here, but is a matter for remembrance in any refer-

ence to the service of Indian Army units on the Western Front, Gallipoli, Mesopotamia, the subcontinent or wherever they might have been engaged. India, with pre-war familiarity of course with the stationed presence of British Regular troops as well as those of the Indian Army, was in the war years to see and to be seen by British troops of a far wider background, one which never bound them into the social fabric of the sub continent in any sense comparable to that of the Sepoy and his officer and perhaps to some extent, to the regular and his officers too.

The security of the North West Frontier of India was of course a principal preoccupation of all Indian defence considerations. One might judge that this would be tackled by mobile patrols from established forts, blockhouses or defended camps but such a perception can hold the possibility of misapprehension. 'Being on the move along the hills and ravines searching the district is not at all what we in the Frontier Militia did. Our so-called patrols were in fact ambushes – lying motionless and hidden in a certain pass or ravine waiting for a possible "fly" to get caught in the spider's web on the principle that he who moves gets ambushed.' An ambush would consist of no more than twenty men under a native sergeant (a havildar) and if the party were bigger, a Pathan officer would be in command, the whole enterprise being based upon the value of recruiting from the tribes who did the raiding in order to have men with the local knowledge to catch such raiders.

At the headquarters of the Khyber Rifles at Landikotal, life would be much like that of any other unit within India, daily drill on a parade ground and daily musketry, an activity relished by the Pathan with free ammunition in large supply, a privilege he had not enjoyed in his native village. A British officer's supervision of these activities and then the completion of a mandatory ration of paper work would leave him free for some tennis perhaps until the evening parade. Colonel O. D. Bennett, with years of service in a Frontier Militia Force (Khyber Rifles), added to his recollections of the necessary regular inspection of the far-flung blockhouses, 'as the Pathan is by nature a lazy devil and has to be kept on his toes', some conclusions on relationships with his men. 'Talk his language well, be able to make him laugh but be as strict as you like on duty, outshoot him and he is then yours to handle firmly, cheerfully and fairly.'[50]

Interestingly Bennett recalled the counterpropaganda pep talks needed on numerous occasions when sweet tea loosened the tongues of the men on duty in an isolated blockhouse. After an inspection

August 1914 in the Khyber Hills. Captain Bennett of the Khyber Rifles rests with two of his men – and his dog – on North West Frontier duties which will continue to require the sort of soldiering one would scarcely associate with the conflict which had just broken out in Europe and will spread to the East. The circular marks on the picture are the result of the photograph's history as a postcard stamped by the Peshawar Post Office. (Lieutenant Colonel O. D. Bennett)

visit, there was relaxed informal conversation with the soldiers frequently citing pro-German and anti-British stories which somehow seeped along the frontier.

In the garrison towns there were differences: the military presence was far more concentrated but then so were the native peoples. The 4th Duke of Cornwall's Light Infantry arrived at Bareilly in November 1914, played into their barracks from the station by a native band. 'We found our barracks quite commodious. There are about eighteen large bungalows beside other buildings like the Sergeant's

Mess, the Orderly Room, the Guardroom, the Regimental Institutes, Cookhouses, etc. There is about an acre of ground around each bungalow, all in greensward and the bungalows themselves are roomy and lofty.' Sergeant Pearce then reported of his quarters that: 'they were partitioned off at the ends of the bungalows in which the men live. The men's beds are arranged down each side, similar to a ward in a hospital and in the centre of each bungalow is the dining hall.' The sergeants were soon besieged by natives seeking posts as bearers at 1s. 4d. a week, the privilege of the Sergeants' rank being further indicated by their Mess having two tennis courts adjacent and having within the Mess itself a bar, a reading and recreation room, a dining room, and a billiard room.[51]

In the garrison towns like Bareilly or Lucknow, once a week, a regiment would march through roads, lanes and gates offering by intent, evidence of its presence. An observant officer of the 4th Queen's Royal West Surreys, Olaf Caröe, remembered at Lucknow that the shopkeepers and hawkers on the whole received them reasonably well but he was learning what was then known as Hindustani (Urdu) and 'I began to hear some taunts mingled with laughter, as we marched along. I remember too that

the soldiers as they sweated along in the narrow lanes, smelled even worse than the crowds of shoppers round the stalls and I came to dislike these regimental progresses with the Deputy Commissioner at the head of the column.[52]

Apart from the 'tourist interests' of India which naturally drew even the most Philistine, garrison duty as recorded in diaries seems to have been filled by military repetition. For Private C. J. Davis (25th London Regiment) near Jullundur in April 1917, there were rifle inspections and roll calls, fatigues, flag drill, signalling lectures, patrolling the bungalows, church parades, Morse reading tests, semaphore and helio, a route march, miniature range practice, all of these activities being regularly repeated. At the same time he played in company football and hockey matches, saw the film of the Battle of the Somme, visited the Bazaar and played

21 April 1916. The 25th Battalion, London Regiment return to their barracks after their Parade Service at St. Mark's Church, Bangalore. The carrying of arms to a church service would perhaps be less incongruous in India than in the United Kingdom. (C. J. Davis)

Waziristan, Mahsud territory, June 1917. The British
column pauses before passing through the narrowing gorge of
the River Shakur. (F. G. Banks)

bridge. In June, drama transformed monotonous routine when the battalion was ordered to make a forced march to assist in dealing with a Mahsud rebellion. It was a long march with night halts requiring vigilant picket duty. '16 June D coy stayed in camp while Battalion straffed a village and burnt crops. C coy captured a lot of loot, mostly old guns.' Heights had to be picketed while a road was made but the work still drew sniper fire. Unfamiliar denial of creature comforts drew grumbling. 'I was in front line (of an advance guard) with screen under Mr. Batt. We had no grub between 4 a.m. and 8 p.m. and it caused much grousing, also the shortage of water.'

At Ispana Bagza, the battalion suffered casualties in day and night attacks on its camp. Further and further up a river the column was fighting its way into Mahsud territory. Though under sniper fire for much of the day, Davis still recorded the 'wonderful

scenery'. It seems quite extraordinary that in the midst of this fighting progress in remote territory, this soldier received two letters from home.[53]

As it happened peace talks were just leading to the conclusion of this frontier episode contemporaneously described by a Corporal in the same regiment. Among the worst features of the experience for Corporal Banks had been marching along a stony river bed, often wading through but with never a flat surface for safe foothold and then there was the loading and unloading of the mules and camels, as well as the heat and the dust storms. Stern Mahsud opposition was sometimes met when 'every hilltop

150

End of a rebellion, at least for some time, Waziristan 2 July 1917; a Jirgah or peace parley in progress. The Officer in Command of the British force, his staff officers and a Political Officer (all on the left) with a ring of Mahsud tribal leaders debate terms for the end of hostilities. (F. G. Banks)

along the sides of the river bed had to be fought for', and clever use of a searchlight lit up the ground from which tribesmen were sniping at a picket at dusk. Mountain battery guns shelled the illuminated ground but in that small engagement seven from the column were killed and fourteen wounded. A day or so after this, Banks watched through a telescope Indian troops in the column storm a hilltop position while the Mahsuds were rolling boulders and stones down upon them.

With their mission carried out, the column retired. It was to be particularly painful for wounded

men stretchered either side of camels for a jolting journey down the same rock-strewn track, the ascent of which had been so difficult.[54]

On leave, recreational activities like hunting, climbing or hill walking were available to officers who also would take opportunity for playing polo as a matter of course but, for officers and men, a shared enjoyment of concert party productions was an especially beneficial factor. In this area, India offered a kinship to fronts like Macedonia where unhealthy boredom was a real enemy or to the Western Front where the different circumstances of sufficient space behind a very active front and the need to boost morale for men 'at rest' from service there, encouraged concert parties to flourish. The 2/6 Sussex Regiment Concert Party, 'The Versatiles', returned in August 1918 to India after entertaining troops in Baghdad and the professional preoccup-

A billboard notice giving advance information of the Royal Sussex Regimental Concert Party's next show, soon after their entertainment of troops in Mesopotamia. (Captain R. C. Morton)

ation with which every aspect of their shows was conducted is clearly shown in the diaries of their impresario, producer, writer and occasional actor, Captain R. C. Morton.

'16 August Dalhousie. Did some writing necessary for our shows up here before walking down to the barracks. We are to give 3 shows in aid of Lady Beynon's local charities. I succeeded in getting them put back until 24 August and September 2–6 to give my fellows time to rehearse new items. Called at the Post Office and brought out a parcel of grease paints.' Morton spent the afternoon assisting in the improvement of a children's charity concert and then in the evening 'typed numerous official letters and thought out certain points for my shows'. Wisdom-tooth extraction limited his administrative concentration for the next day, but on 18 August the price of the seats was decided, and booking arrangements too. On the 19th, the programme was taken to the printers. A problem had to be solved over double booking of the hall with another Concert Party. On 20 August, Morton designed and produced the posters advertising the show. 'This took a long time for I drew it with the lettering shaded over black and white stripes representing our curtains.' He had a further problem in needing to persuade the Sergeants to cancel a dance they had arranged as this was a further double booking.

Morton was not finished with diplomatic delicacy as he had to deal with a deputation from his own men protesting over the wording on one poster which seemed to give the Sussex Regiment less than its due.

There was still so much to do – attempting to borrow gas lamps from another concert party, the Kents, but without success – and also having little success in getting decent chairs. 'Dalhousie audiences must be accustomed to sitting precariously on uncertain seats, in balancing themselves on three legs and in having dresses and suits torn on obtrusive nails.' He mended the curtains, arranged for food for the performers and the band, stewards and programme sellers and at last: 'The show itself passed off splendidly. I was congratulated by the General and Col. Johnson – the band played well. We put on our best programme which was a mistake because it left us with so little for Wednesday but "sufficient unto the day".'[55]

The existence on the Frontier of anti-British propaganda inspired by German agents may have been a current cause of anxiety for the British authorities, but more traditional worries arose over interpreting the paw prints of the the Russian bear. If Anglo-Russian entente and then wartime alliance were to have diminished such fear, Bolshevik revolution in Russia was sharply to change the whole picture. In 1918, British soldiers were to find themselves in North Russia, precursors of others later to serve in Siberia, the northern shores of the Black Sea, the Caucasus Mountains and elsewhere. A newcomer had been added to the list of 1914–18 opponents in combat – the Red or Bolshevik Russian.

Within the framework of this book, only the circumstances of 1918 service in North Russia can be examined and this in no real military sense but in the way men coped with unfamiliar surroundings and climatic conditions. Some reference will also be made to a further question, the factors which tended to erode belief in the worthwhile nature of their remaining in this far distant land under such harsh conditions at the tail end of a long, long war.

The 29th Bn. London Regiment arrived at Murmansk in late June 1918. Corporal Vincent Yearsley had a naturalist's eye and it was not just the intense heat and the mosquitoes that he recorded in his diary, but on 29 June, 'Heard the cuckoo. How strange – cuckoos in the Arctic Circle. They are the only birds I have heard yet – curiously silent is the little copse near our camp.' He thought the scenery to be 'like Staffordshire. I love it . . . were it not for the mosquitoes. They hamper everything, chiefly one's visits to the latrines.' Yearsley took the opportunity to walk into the hills, 'All rocks with a few birches growing in crevices, heather and bilberries. Some climb. Climbed over 1,000 feet and made snowballs in July in sweltering heat. Very wild – could imagine bears lurking behind every rock. Found a couple of antlers and disturbed two eagles.' He bathed in the harbour but then military matters begin to predominate – the town has to be searched for arms and then he is detailed for the party to land at Archangel. Bolsheviks are first encountered through their successive bridge demolitions in the land expedition which followed the seaborne journey. Bolsheviks in strength cause a retirement and then a march has to be undertaken 'through a mosquito-infested swamp to a village where food will be supplied'. The food was poor compensation for the march. Bugs and cockroaches inhibit sleep in a station waiting-room and then a new advance was rumoured – to Vologda.

'I wonder what the outcome of this business will be. Shall we get to Vologda? It is typically British to start on a 400-mile journey through unknown country with 350 men. What madness it seems. If we get through it will be glorious and if we fail, well the British public will be fooled with the old Dardanelles story, of a moral victory.' In the event, matters requiring attention in Archangel and then Murmansk preempted the dubious enterprise so recorded with apprehension by the London Regiment corporal.

News in October of German defeats brought rumours of the men being returned to the United Kingdom, but what came with the news was much colder weather and snow. Yearsley developed a cough: 'Everything goes to the chest and lungs out here. Everyone's got flu and pneumonia and the hospital is a scandal. Another Mesopotamia methinks. Far too many poor beggars are pegging out. No winter clothing for us yet. No fuel, no water supply and streams practically frozen up already and latrines out in the open. No extra blankets yet and 14° of frost.' There are rumours of leave and grumb-

The maintenance of railway communications between Murmansk and Archangel required military occupation of Soroka on the western shores of the White Sea, and in winter snow conditions demanded some quickly acquired ski proficiency. Two British officers make a start. (G. E. Coghlan)

ling declamations among the men that they won't come back to Russia at the end of the leave. 'Anyway, what should they want us back for? The war is practically over and at any rate there's no need to re-constitute the Eastern Front.'

The German Armistice brought high hopes of going home for demobilization, hopes to be dashed by being sent to Kandalaksha 'Oh what a bastard hole. Worse than Murmansk. Living in railway truck.' And that was where they remained to see the year out, guarding railway installations from strikers.[56]

During the final months of 1918, some men, like those of 252 Company MGC, were trained in the use of snow shoes and toboggans, then taught how to live in sub-zero temperatures, sleeping in tents heated by a small stove. This company was then dispatched

North Russia: Technological imagination assists 2nd Battalion Hampshires in this withdrawal down the River Pinega. Major Finnemore (Royal Engineers) adapted two barges to be powered by lorries for a shallow stretch of river. The back axle was connected up to paddle wheels and the rudder to the steering wheel. A speed of 10mph was achieved. The original photograph is labelled, 'Finnemore's Follies: Another triumph for Henry Ford.' (Brigadier A. R. Koe)

into the hinterland to hold timber block-houses set up in the seemingly limitless forest. Machine-gun field of fire zones had been created by felling avenues of trees. From the blockhouses, patrols were conducted – the enemy during these winter months being seldom encountered so harsh was the climate and deep the snow. According to one officer of 252 Company, G. C. Wheeler, their clothing was particularly good 'thick vests and pants of wool, flannel shirts and our ordinary uniform, four pairs of socks, 2 thick, 2 thinner ones, Shackleton boots with ½-inch leather sole, felt inside, white thick canvas uppers, with gusset in front, calf length and tied with heavy tapes round the ankle. Woollen gloves and mitts on the hands, white canvas hats with fur lined ear flaps and peaks.' Toboggans were towed by one man and pushed with a pole by another. All was well on smooth ground but fallen trees made the going arduous. 'Stepping over the tree, turning round, in snowshoes quite a job, lifting the nose of the toboggan, lurching into the harness and then waiting for the toboggan to strike the back of your legs when it came over the tree' required patience given to few. Exertion caused sweating and momentary rest encouraged the cold to bite into bone marrow but no-one seemed to catch cold. By contrast, the Vickers

guns, in a sense, did – water, despite being mixed 50/50 with glycerine, froze or escaped through the barrel packing and in so doing caused stoppages.

All food had to be thawed out, meat, bread, margarine, tins of bully or Machonochies, but it was plentiful and was not a factor in disturbing morale, this being occasioned, according to Wheeler, by letters from home and Bolshevik leaflet propaganda.[57] Colonel C. H. D. O. Springfield's account makes it quite clear that morale certainly was low in the 1918–19 winter. The perpetual night, the cold, the dull routine, the feeling of having been forgotten and the insidious effect of propaganda drained the men of their natural resilience.[58]

The tensions of being involved in a Civil War with its ideological commitment and its particularly harrowing nature, the swift shock this could bring and the slow grudge which grew from simply perceived political perspective, must have made their impact felt. Even in the apolitical diary of an RAMC private, the scene is set for dissociation and resentment. '11 December. This afternoon some Russians refused to go up the line to fight; their barracks were surrounded by British and Americans with rifles and machine-guns; we were not allowed out tonight. Issued with rifles and 30 rounds of ammunition. Stretchers and dressings prepared. 13 of the Russians were shot as ringleaders.' 12 December This morning 25 Russians and 30 others were shot by their own men. Had they not done so they would have been shot as they were covered by the D.L.I. The men who were shot had to dig their own graves, little thinking they were going into them. One soldier who knew pleaded to be sent up the line, but it was not allowed.[59]

There were occasional engagements like the one in which Lance Sergeant A. J. Goodes was wounded. An opposed crossing of a frozen river went seriously wrong when the ice broke throwing men into the river to be drowned. Goodes scrambled out and up the bank, his great coat rapidly freezing to the stiffness of a thick board, but he was soon hit badly in the leg. The casualties that night seemed to have been left to wolves, the unnerving howling of which got nearer and nearer. Goodes was unable to move and had a fearful fate to contemplate, but then lights were shone and Bolshevik troops appeared, picking up those men still living, putting them onto sledges and pulling them to the river for a journey which would end in Moscow and seven months of cabbage soup, dried raw fish and black bread.[60]

Finally, in a chapter which has necessarily been concerned with a wide range of geographical and climatic circumstance, it seems appropriate that this variation should be upheld within the campaigning conditions of one front, that of the Italian Front to which British divisions were sent following upon the almost terminal Italian disaster at Caporetto in October 1917. In time to be caught up in the headlong retirement were some British gunners of the single detachment remaining from the artillery support sent out from the United Kingdom to assist in yet further Italian offensives on the Isonzo in May and September of that year. Ashton Wade, faced with the emergency of how to render useless, eight hundred 100lb shells at his battery position, was far from satisfied with his limited answer of throwing the firing tubes into the fast-flowing River Vippacco, but time was short. He got his men into a lorry and

from his motor cycle piloted the lorry to the main road leading to a bridge over the Isonzo. There was a vast confusion of traffic – lorries, men, guns, horses and carts crowding the bridge and on the road ahead. 'When night fell, on all sides the country flickered with the light of innumerable fires as dumps, stores and depots were systematically destroyed. Yellow tongues of flame suddenly pierced the blackness of the night and as suddenly died down to glowing balls of red. Clouds of black smoke crept like shadowy monsters across the plain. The air was thick with the pungent smell of burning wood. Acid fumes smote the nostrils and brought tears to the eyes. The deep thunder of explosives and the sharp crack of musketry rent the air. Ever along the road plodded the army in retreat. A ghostly procession in the flickering light.'

After seventy-two hours of this under driving rain, Wade drifted off to sleep crashing his motor cycle, but bike, lorry and guns were reunited at Palmanova. There were more miles to cover under aerial bombing and machine-gun strafing. Unidentified cavalry suddenly appeared among the column of troops and refugees and a panic ensued of desperate men surging onto a narrow bridge with some men pushed or slipping to fall into the swift River Tagliamento. Not all the British guns had reached this point and Wade, going back to give assistance, found in one case three of the guns and a trench cart attached to one tractor, its engine straining and knocking and with steam whistling out of its radiator. As it happened a stand was not be made here but on the Piave, and the British gunners were directed elsewhere, not that this was to be of great consequence to Wade who had fallen victim to dysentery.[61]

The British troops swiftly entrained for Italy after Caporetto, had in the main left a more than adequate supply of mud and lice in Flanders and so were to find their new environment uplifting in many ways. 'We found ourselves in the sun and freshness of Italy. All this was a new experience and we revelled in it – the great thing was that the locals liked us – we felt we had never been welcomed before. We marched early in the morning when the sun was just rising over the Lombardy plain and we billeted outside lovely cities such as Castelfranco. At one of our billets our farmer host opened a bottle of his own best vintage – delicious, white Chianti. So new to us after the grim and mercenary Belgians.'[62]

To the welcome of speeches, flowers and wine were added individually proffered leaflets. 'To you who pass through our country to the front where the

Winter on the Asiago plateau. Snow affords its own concealment to a camouflaged British 60-pounder's position in the foreground. Note the dugouts terrassed into the hillside. (H. P. Sherwood)

safety of Italy and the freedom of the world is being fought out, the citizens of Mantova with steadfast spirit send their warmest greetings [and when you] return to us full of the glory of having hurled back beyond the Alps the arrogant Hun – and may that day come soon – then the people of Mantova will welcome you once more with gratitude and fraternal joy.'[63] Welcomed in such manner J. V. Faviell's RHA battery arrived at the Montello, a hill overlooking the River Piave where the Italian line was becoming stabilized. After Christmas 1917 when the frost seemed to become more intense, a night, closely confined in the battery's small observation post which scarcely allowed movement, was very uncomfortable. Awaiting dawn and warmth from a wintry sun was a prolonged ordeal but when the snows came, the battery fitter made luges for all the fun of sledging down the steep road from the battery position.[64]

Service on the Italian Front in winter offered the keen officer time and appropriate location for military contemplation before spring brought the prospect of serious action. Roderick Macleod (RFA), in his letters home, lectured his father on the strategic principles transgressed in the dispersal of military effort from France where he judged its application as the top priority. For the men of his battery he introduced prizes for the best harness and best gun park, stopping leave for those who performed badly. He instructed officers under his command to give lecturettes in the evening on wide-ranging subjects which required considerable application (for example life in South Africa as well as the more obvious topics like 'Field sketching') while he himself strove to advance his military education. 'Many thanks for the trouble you have taken to get me books on Napoleon's Italian Campaigns.'

Macleod, for himself and for his men, never lost opportunity for health-giving enjoyable physical exercise. In the months before battle was rejoined there was every opportunity for such recreation in Italy. 'Would you mind having sent out the following and I will pay you back:
1) 8 polo sticks 2) A rugby football with 2 bladders 3) A Badminton set with a dozen shuttlecocks 4) A set of boxing gloves 5) A pair of rubber soled shoes.'

There were busy weeks ahead for Major Macleod in undertaking liaison courses and keeping up the training of his battery. At battery inspection by General Plumer one day, the general adjured the men to increase the size of their families. One man, responding in the negative to the pointed question as to the number of his children, was cheerfully instructed, 'Have a good try next time you are on leave.' Macleod, with reason, presumed that the General was concerned with the loss to the nation of so many men on the Western Front. In letters which are a constant delight as well as enlightenment 'Rory Macleod' must be given the opportunity to re-utter from Italy what most will see as the perceptive judgement of a professional soldier on Lloyd George's own war with his Generals. 'A politician however cannot have the same mentality as a soldier but always seems to see the end without reckoning the means of attaining it. Whereas a soldier is trained according to the principle that in preparing a plan he must be prepared for any possible eventuality and have his plans for meeting each one.'

The Allied offensive planned appropriately for the anniversary of Waterloo, 18 June, was pre-empted by an Austrian attack three days earlier. Macleod's battery suffered casualties from the Austrian shelling but played its part in routing the attack – 'We had the time of our lives killing off thousands of them' – but in fact the gunners had had an awkward situation confronting them when Austrian troops appeared out of a wood indicating that they had overrun the British front line. An intervening ridge protected the Austrians from the flat trajectory of the British battery so the guns had to be man-handled back up the slope to a position enabling the crest to be cleared.[65]

The 18th DLI was one of the battalions attacked. Pte George Ramshaw was ordered to go forward from Battalion HQ to get situation reports. An early morning patrol from 'C' Company had been caught in no man's land by the Austrian barrage and Very light signalling and was delayed in its return. The Company Commander pencilled to his Adjutant, 'Sorry reports are late but had a fairly warm time round about here and towards the rear. Kept waiting for a lull in the shelling before sending a runner but had no luck. Everything alright but heavy shelling continues.' Bearing this report, Ramshaw moved

along the trench towards 'D' Company and risked a look over the parapet. 'Fifty yards away there were hundreds of the enemy advancing up the slope with only me on the firestep. I dashed into the dugout, told the OC and collected his reports and gave a yell along the trench.' The firestep was soon manned and, in the absence of a communication trench, Ramshaw crawled back to report to the Colonel. So agitated was he in reporting what he had seen that he forgot to hand in the reports.[66] On this sector the line was held, but in others it was temporarily over-run. The turn in fortune was remarkable and is reflected in the diary of H. P. Sherwood which records the 7th Warwicks and 4th Oxford and Buckinghamshire Light Infantry counter-attacking and restoring the line on the same day and then, on 16 June, further counter-attacks, taking prisoners, machine-guns and field guns, enabled sections of the Austrian front line to be occupied.[67]

Among operations more physically challenging than others for British soldiers in the war, was the attempt in October 1918 to capture a key Austrian defence position, Papadopoli Island in the River Piave. W. J. Bradley, then a Sergeant in the 2nd Bn. HAC, has recalled that the river was in spate following heavy rain and that reconnaissance from the river bank had not revealed much about the tree and scrub-obscured defences of the three-mile-long island. The HAC, assigned the task of storming the

Italy, Granezza on the Asiago plateau. The 11th Battalion, West Yorks, somewhat under strength as a result of influenza, parade for an investiture in May or June 1918. (Captain W. Barraclough)

British troops have boated, waded and fought their way across the River Piave. Due to their success they can look back past an Austrian searchlight, one of many positioned to illuminate any attempted crossing of the river with its sandbanks, separate channels, and islands, the main strongly defended one being Papadopoli. Soldiers can be seen here on the shingle or wading across to follow up the assault troops. (O. A. Dod)

a third channel of the fast-flowing river was fordable, thigh deep. The noise caused in dragging the boats across the shingle must, one presumes, have been drowned by that of the river itself. Bradley described well the eeriness of sitting silently in combat order beside the inky swirling water, whispered commands being passed as they waited for the returning boatmen. Suddenly an Austrian rocket soared up from the middle of the island and soon artillery opened up, machine-guns chattered and searchlights illuminated the flood bank behind them. A level of safety lay beneath the fire directed at the bank and the trenches behind it. The crossings were made and Bradley was ordered to take his platoon and two additional Lewis gun sections to secure the left flank of the landing. As the clouds cleared giving the dangerous benefit of moonlight, it became clear that the co-ordination of the advance of the three companies had not been maintained. A map was studied by torchlight, bearings taken and the Colonel led five platoons and the Lewis gun sections 'into the blue'. Bradley was finding telephone lines to cut and investigating sightings of men on their right when he heard shouts and rifle fire. 'We broke into a run to go to help and arrived in time for a free for all.' One of the Colonel's platoons had walked into the Austrian HQ position and the Austrians, faced with the new arrivals, surrendered but it was some while before all their officers were flushed out of their dugouts in an embankment. The remainder of the night was passed in attempting to intercept parties of Austrian reinforcements making their way to solidify defences of the island.

Soggy sacks of ruined rations scarcely sustained the endeavour to clear the island. There were still surprises as Bradley's men came under what amounted to ambush fire and had to plunge waist deep into a stream in order to take cover and on another occasion when from only ten yards they actually surprised a sentry getting out of his slit trench to stretch himself. It took sixty hours of continuous action completely to capture the island and then, to reach the mainland, required a tricky operation of men in groups of twelve linking arms and edging across against water chest deep and surging through them in alarming manner.

The days were now exhilarating as well as dangerous but suddenly the Armistice was upon them. 'I think we cheered but for myself I was smitten with the worst fit of depression that I have ever experienced.' Peace and civilian life were to be faced and the HAC Sergeant realized that he hadn't 'the slightest idea of what I wanted to do'. He was not alone![68]

island, sent out night patrols to explore the possibility of fording the channelled river from one shingle bank to the next. Whatever reports were brought back, it was Italian flat-bottomed boats which made the venture possible.

At night the men left their front-line trench and made their way up to and across the flood bank, then settled down on a shingle bank to await the boats. The whole operation was being conducted in silence and without covering artillery fire. The first crossings were made, seven men and the two boatmen to a boat. The men in the returning boats were able to report that the boats were necessary for two channels, 70 and 50 yards wide respectively, but

7

'Gainst Turk and Bulgar

GALLIPOLI

Briefly to provide a context within which to examine the essence of soldiering in the four major sideshow campaigns, all that really needs to be emphasized is that, in the case of Gallipoli and to some degree Macedonia, the men were there because it was adjudged that the whole war might thus be won more swiftly. In the case of Egypt and Mesopotamia, the men had been sent initially to protect vital Imperial interests, Suez and oil. Ill-prepared expansion beyond the securing of those interests had led to disaster or at best defeat and so a major rescue commitment was called for with at least the prospect of achieving morale-boosting victories.

An awareness of the ramshackle foundations upon which the Dardanelles campaign was built should not be allowed to cast too shroud-like a shadow over the evidence of the excitement, the hope, the special sense of historical mission which are manifest in the personal papers of many men proceeding towards the landings around Cape Helles or farther north, beyond the Gaba Tepe headland, on the Gallipoli Peninsula.[1] Such awareness by no means precluded a sober appraisal of the difficulty of winning a footing on a defended beach and had it done so for anyone in the 29th Division, his Commanding Officer somewhat lugubriously warned him on the eve of the adventure that: 'heavy losses, by bullets, by shells, by mines and by drowning' were to be expected.[2]

An officer with a sense of history who had recently expressed poetic thought on this the 'Last Crusade' was mindful of a much earlier expedition than those designed to liberate Jerusalem or contemplated for Constantinople – the gathering host of grey vessels in Mudros harbour, the island of Lemnos, he likened to the 'Greek fleet going to Troy [just across the narrow Dardanelles Straits on the Asiatic side], people collected from all over the known world; we have even got our wooden horse which I will explain later on'. The officer, Captain G. N. Walford, added that it had to be accepted that 'As far as the Intelligence reports tell us however, there seems to be no Helen of Troy.'[3]

The Wooden Horse to which Walford referred was the old collier, the *River Clyde*, run aground beneath a medieval castle at the very tip of the peninsula on the morning of 25 April 1915 when the beaches were stormed. In *River Clyde*, two thousand

25 April 1915, 7.30 a.m., Anzac. 14th Battalion, Australian Imperial Force, landing. The officer with the rolled cape over his left shoulder is Major F. D. Irvine of the 1st Infantry Brigade. Next to him stands Brigadier General H. N. MacLaurin. Sergeant Summerhayes, said to be the first man killed (according to the label on the original photograph), lies centre left at the water's edge. (Lady Craig)

Gallipoli. 'W' Beach, Cape Helles, where the Lancashire Fusiliers made their landing, was under shellfire throughout the campaign. It had continually to serve as an embarkation and disembarkation point and as a general base camp area. Here it is being shelled in August. (S. Parker Bird)

troops in three large holds had been cooped-up with their equipment and their inner tension till the moment to debouch from exits cut in the sides of the vessel. They would have to hurry along gangways which sloped down as ramps at the bows. From the ramps there would be a jump onto a steam hopper which had towed lighters in. The hopper and the lighters would somehow be secured and thus afford a bridge to the shelving shore. At this beach ('V' Beach) and four others at Cape Helles and at the location of the Australian and New Zealand landing, (miscalculated as it happened by the twin problems of current and the difficulty of headland identification in pre-dawn darkness) a tragically costly though imperishably heroic drama was enacted.

Captain G. W. Geddes, a Company Commander of the 1st Bn. Royal Munster Fusiliers, aboard *River Clyde*, recorded what happened to the men in the tows of boats approaching the shore to the left of the collier Trojan Horse. 'They were met with a terrific rifle and machine-gun fire. They were literally slaughtered like rats in a trap. The steamer hopper towing the lighters from the *Clyde* was either shot away or broke loose, anyway it beached alone. The lighters swung crossways across the bows of the *River Clyde*. In the meantime the Dublins were struggling to get ashore. Within five minutes of the *Clyde* beaching, 'Z' Company got away on the starboard side. The gangway on the port side jammed and delayed 'X' Company for a few seconds, and off we went cheering wildly and dashed ashore with 'Z' Company. We got it like anything, man after man behind me was shot down but they never wavered.

Lt Watts who was wounded in five places and lying on the gangway cheered the men on with cries of "Follow the Captain". Captain French of the Dublins told me afterwards that he counted the first 48 men to follow me, and they all fell. I think no finer episode could be found of the men's bravery and discipline than this – of leaving the safety of the *River Clyde* to go to what was practically certain death.'

'Leaving the Clyde I dashed down the gangway and already found the lighters holding the dead and wounded from the leading platoons of 'Z' Company. I stepped into the second lighter and looked round to find myself alone, and yelled to the men following out of the *Clyde* to come on, but it was difficult going across the lighters. I then jumped into the sea and had to swim some dozen strokes to get ashore. There is no doubt that men were drowned owing chiefly I think to the great weight they were carrying – a full pack, 250 rounds of ammunition and 3 days' rations. I know I felt it. All the officers were dressed and equipped like the men.'

'There was a small, rocky spit jutting out into the sea which was absolutely taped down by the Turks and few, if any, survived who attempted to land there. We all made, Dublins and all, for a sheltered ledge on the shore which gave us cover. Here we shook ourselves out and tried to appreciate the situation, rather a sorry one. I estimated that I had lost about 70% of my Company.'

'Seeing that Sed el Bahr and the beach to our right were unoccupied and fearing the Turks might come down I called for volunteers to make a dash for it,

Gallipoli: Stretcher-bearers on the shore. Men of the 87th Field Ambulance carry the wounded to a makeshift pier at Cape Helles. From here sailors will row them in a cutter to be picked up and towed by a picket boat to a hospital ship standing off shore. (W. A. Young)

and make good the right of the beach. The men responded gallantly. Picking Sergeant Ryan and 6 men we had a go for it. Three of the men were killed, one other and myself wounded. However we got across.' Picking up survivors of a party of men landing beyond the castle the walls of which came virtually to the beach, the little force tried and failed to get into the shell of the castle and had to settle for digging themselves some cover. The wounded Company Commander got a Semaphore signal to his Colonel aboard the *River Clyde* that he 'could do nothing, as I had no men left. He told me to go for my objective Fort No. 1 but it could not be done.'

Two hours later an officer and three men succeeded in crawling to join the beleaguered group and at 1100 hrs. 'Major Jarrett with half of 'Y' Company landed and met the same fate as the rest of us, after which no further landing was attempted.' At 20.30 the remnants of the earlier landings and two companies of the 2nd Hants joined with the Munsters and the officer who prepared the above report, recorded that, fearing the onset of gangrene into his wound received thirteen hours earlier, he had then returned to *River Clyde* for medical attention after which he and about 200 wounded were put aboard a trawler which was not, as it happened, to deliver its charges to the hospital ship *Alaunia* till the morning.[4]

This report, most unusually, was concluded by a note with regard to the officer's personal feelings: 'I felt we were for it. That the enterprise was unique and would demand all I was possible of giving, and more. That it was no picnic but a desperate venture.

I just longed to get on with it and be done with it. I felt I was no hero and that I had not the pluck of a louse. My nerves were tense and strung up, and yet, I never doubted that we would not win through, because I knew the splendid fellows at my back, highly trained, strictly disciplined, and they would follow me anywhere. Once started, everything went, one forgot and during that long day one had no fear or doubt, and it all seemed quite ordinary. Curiously one never felt the want of food or drink. Except for a cup of chocolate I had had nothing to eat or drink since lunch time the 24th till I got a cup of tea on the trawler the night of the 25th.'

The sort of desperate individual endeavour called for at the landings and on the following day when complete disaster could only be averted by a push inland against whatever circumstances, is sketchily revealed in an officer's field message book recommendation of a Corporal Cosgrove of the 1st Bn, Munster Fusiliers. Thick barbed wire barred any attempt to charge up the beach and under fire the troops waited while Private Bryant was doing his best, with the single pair of wire cutters available, to cut a passage through. 'Corporal Cosgrove seeing our difficulty jumped into the wire and hauled down the heavy wooden stakes to which the wire was attached to a distance of about 30 yards long in quite a short space of time. I personally consider he deserves the height of praise for such a courageous act and was much impressed to see him, though wounded in the back leading his section shortly before the enemy were driven from their trenches and the fort captured.'[5]

May 1915: the rear of Courtney's post overlooking Monash Valley. Behind these men a complex subterranean system of communications and defence was tunnelled out of the face of the steeply sloping ridge, the crest of which - just ten yards away - was held by the Turks. Mining, countermining, hand-bombing and the constant danger of an inrush of enemy troops from on top or from the tunnels made the occupation of such positions a fearful strain on the nerves and bodies of the Anzac troops concerned. (Lieutenant Colonel Gibson Bishop)

Gallantry and danger: there was no discrimination by rank at the Gallipoli landings. Corporal Cosgrove was wounded on the beach, his Brigade Commander, Brigadier General Napier, was killed trying to get ashore. On 25 April, three officers of the Munsters had been killed, nine had been wounded.

An attempt to set service in the Gallipoli Campaign distinctively apart from that of service on other fronts could rest its case on the initial landings because the storming of defended beaches is, Tanga apart, without 1914–18 parallel, but within this very context there is the further phenomenon of the extraordinary landscape which faced the Australasian troops where they came ashore in the little bay south of the Ari Burnu headland. Three successive irregular ridges, with sheer precipices having been formed out of some of the spurs which buttressed the main ridges, offered a challenging general picture the detail of which invited visual confusion and denied military coordination. From the soil-denuded stony summits on rounded slopes, suddenly the ground would drop into deep narrow gorges or merge into a confined bare plateau. Where erosion had not taken place, there were rough grasses, thistles and thick undergrowth of gorse-like bushes above which stunted oak trees emerged. It as terrain which bestowed salvation and tribulation even-handedly to invader and defender. Space was denied, a modicum of cover was offered. If Allied attack were topographically hamstrung, then no less were the Turks constrained in their attempts to throw their enemies into the sea.

A very particular consequence of the lack of space and the vulnerability to shelling of virtually every yard of the Peninsula was the bringing together in heightened degree of the problems of any siege campaign in a hot climate – latrines, unburied human and animal dead. Large loathsome flies flourished on the moist nutrients thus available and in adding tea, runny plum jam, sugar, tinned milk and sun-sweltered corned beef to their diet, they spread, at that end of their settling for nourishment, dysentery in its various forms.

In front of the Australian and New Zealand positions – the Anzac beachhead – so many Turks were killed on May 19 in an attempt to throw the invaders into the sea that, within a day or so, the smell and potential for disease united the foes in an armistice to bury the dead. It was described on the spot by an Australian sapper; 'The smell was something cruel most of the bodies being almost totally decomposed. The sight was most queer, men sitting round in bunches smoking and sharing their food with the enemy, amidst dead bodies, amputated arms, legs and heads and general horrible surroundings.'[6]

The penalties of dysentery were cruel. There was a 'diarrhoea rest camp' – not immune from shellfire of course – but with the 'Turkey Trot' problem being almost universal, it was accepted by the men as well as by their Medical Officers that they remain at their posts until near incapacitation. On this subject, Charles Mapp (Tpr, City of London Yeomanry) has written of ashen-faced, hollow-eyed men, too weak to walk to the latrine without assistance, still refusing to go sick. In Mapp's particular location, a new landing at Suvla Bay on a wide open flat area with but three or four pimples for hills (despite its proximity to Anzac), camouflaged Turkish snipers were a deadly danger to men dragging themselves back towards the latrines.[7]

After a July fortnight at Cape Helles, 2nd Lt J. R. Starley (9th Royal Warwicks) described conditions unguardedly in relation to the fact that his letter was to 'Dorothy'. 'Gallipoli is dusty, hot and waterless. There are about twenty flies per square inch and 1 corpse per yard. Between the two lines of trenches corpses of Turks lie every yard or so in various stages of decomposition and decay . . . some days we really knew what thirst was, and water was so scarce that you go without even the apology for a wash except on

On the Gallipoli Peninsula there were no 'rest areas' in the Western Front sense, but the relaxed crowds of men in this Anzac gulley show that some areas were more shielded from observation and direct fire than others. (Doctor N. E. Chadwick)

the rare occasions when you go down to the beach and bathe with shrapnel bursting overhead. . . . The first time I went into the trenches the indescribable smell of rotting flesh made me feel ill but in a day I got used to it, and then when I saw one of our men drop dead with a bullet through his head I felt absolutely nauseated, but have got used now to seeing a man have part of his head blown off and hear men murmur "another good feed for the flies". People who have been in the fighting in France and in Gallipoli say that the latter is a thousand times worse than France as here we have not the slightest comfort only the bare ground, unvaried heat and hard food. . . . The flies are the curse of the place and with an overdose of dust in the food no one feels in a good temper. We are tired of drinking tea or tepid water flavoured with disinfecting chemicals but must drink them or nothing.'[8]

There were frontal attacks at both Cape Helles and Anzac, attacks which left broken bodies and scarred memories among the survivors, but the nature of such conflict was not characteristically different from that experienced elsewhere in 1914–18. Even the log-covered trenches at Lone Pine which might be overrun in the assault but still had to be fought for by entry through the Turkish communication trenches, had their counterpart in the deep concrete dugouts crossed but not taken by the Irish troops on the Somme on 1 July 1916. What Gallipoli combat does illustrate to an unusual degree are examples of close-order fighting and in many sectors, quite astoundingly, the constant day by day immediate proximity of the enemy. It was not simply the fact of a no man's land, in certain places, narrowing to within seven yards, it was the sharing of the same trench or sap separated by a sandbagged barricade. Wire netting overhead offered some protection to the lobbed hand-bomb. Keen listening might forewarn of undermining designed to explode a charge immediately beneath the listener, killing all within close vicinity and creating a new crater on a crumbling cliff for swift storming and conversion for the purposes of the new occupants. Certainly neuralgia or neuritis may have seemed to have an identifiable cause like bad teeth (indeed a problem in itself given the Peninsula diet), but the strain on the nerves of every waking moment's awareness of the possibility of a sudden bayonet assault, an explosion from beneath or a bomb from above, must surely have eroded the wellbeing of all. It was at Anzac above all where such conditions prevailed and from Anzac exceptional physical endeavour would be required in fulfilling plans for a decisive offensive in August.

Anzac. A New Zealander photographed this soldier engaged upon the same casualty clearance work which earned a legendary reputation for an Australian ('The Man with the Donkey'). The donkeys were used to bring wounded men from forward positions back down 'Shrapnel Gully' to the beach. (Lieutenant Colonel Gibson Bishop)

Combined with a new landing at Suvla Bay, which was in fact badly handled at the level of Senior Command, frontal assaults at Helles and on the right of Anzac, Australian, New Zealand, Indian and British troops attempted night outflanking movements along the Anzac beachhead to the North. From the beach, the column split into three to change direction and climb unreconnoitred, thickly under-growthed gullies scooped out of the side of the heights which had to be stormed. The bold plan was bravely attempted, failing perhaps by a narrow margin and with tragedy to add to the narrowness of the divide between victory and defeat – Allied shells landing among New Zealand, British and Indian troops desperately endeavouring to hold the summits they had reached or were reaching. Bugler Bayne of the Wellington Regiment (NZEF), even if he were to have filled his diary on one of the days immediately following, as must seem certain, was to pencil a rare record of the drama. The Official Historian makes no effort to disguise the losses involved. 'Fighting grimly, the two Wellington Companies on top of the ridge (Chunuk Bair) maintained their exposed positions till nearly every man was killed. The few survivors were at last overwhelmed and soon after 9 o'clock (8 August) the enemy tried to close with the main line. Here,

however, thanks very largely to the magnificent leadership of Colonel Malone, the remainder of the Wellington and the remnants of the 7th Gloucestershire and 8th Welch continued to hold their own.'[9]

Bayne's diary for 8 August related that 'we are holding on desperately. Our warships and artillery are keeping up bombardment. We have neither food nor water. 2 p.m. Auckland Mounteds reinforce us. 8 p.m. Canterbury and Otago relieve us. Fierce fighting all night. All counter-attacks repulsed. Turks a few yards away bomb throwing.'[10]

Another New Zealander, Reg Davie, retrospectively wrote of the circumstances of his position on the shoulder of Hill 971 being overrun. The New Zealanders had been making for the summit when ordered back to a Turkish trench they had just captured. It was narrow and only waist deep. The ground ten yards further on towards the top of the hill in fact dropped, because of an intervening gully, and it was from this gully that Turks emerged. Though rapid fire on the Turks must have caused serious loss, most of the New Zealanders were killed or wounded. Davie believes he was the last unwounded defender until a bullet hammered into his elbow. A man called Surgenor ripped the sleeve out of his tunic and bound the wound up with his field dressing. 'Still the Turks didn't venture into our trench, but after a while threw in a few bombs. At last away down the trench on my right I saw a Turk gingerly get into our trench and make his way up towards me. He was soon followed by two of his mates. The first man killed either with his bayonet or the butt of his rifle every wounded man he came to. His two henchmen went through their pockets and kit bags. I was obliged to wait their coming, seeing and hearing them killing my cobbers on their way. When my turn came he made a jab at me with his bayonet which I grabbed with my left hand. Pulling it away quickly, he made several unsuccessful attempts, and then got home right through my left arm. This I thought was the end especially when I saw him slipping a cartridge into his rifle. He pointed it at me and (then) someone must have called him and ordered him to fire over towards our lines. Soon afterwards a Turk who was evidently an officer made a motion for Surgenor and myself to get out of the trenches' and formal captivity brought a measure of security.[11]

The month of August saw considerable endeavour at Suvla too, whatever may be said about the delay after the landing and the general conduct of operations there. Among the most celebrated events, was the crossing, under fire, of the huge dried-up white expanse of the Salt Lake. This was to reinforce the

Anzac, after the battle of Lone Pine in August. The Australian dead, wrapped in blankets, as was the practice, are here awaiting burial. (Brigadier J. G. D. McNeill)

Suvla, August 1915. The 3rd County of London Yeomanry establish themselves on the slopes of Lala Baba above a beachhead of ant-like activity and with a large number of naval vessels in support in Suvla Bay. (Captain J. N. Mankin)

Suvla: newly taken prisoners await interrogation. Note the tented bivouacs in the middle distance. (W. A. Young)

isolated positions ahead needing reinforcement for the full-scale advance which in fact was never to threaten the Turkish rim of the topographical ampitheatre in which the last high drama was played. Under shell and machine-gun fire, the low, tinder-dry vegetation caught alight, dense black smoke billowing up in clouds, hiding the tragedy of wounded men who had crawled for cover among the bushes and were later found by stretcher-bearers burned to death.

Apart from dysentery, the Gallipoli soldier and particularly those at Anzac and Suvla was to be exposed to one severe natural tribulation and then to the potential disaster of an evacuation from positions immediately overlooked by the Turks. Nature's challenge came in the form of late November rain, gales, floods, snow and intensely cold temperatures.

The suffering of Indian troops at Anzac drew concern from a Sikh officer, Reginald Savory. 'We have had three awful days: being flooded out of our trenches and dugouts and (then) with a blizzard blowing the whole time. The Gurkhas have had over 500 cases of frostbite: our men are standing it better. . . . The Turks apparently fared even worse than we did and were so cold that they got out of the trenches and walked about to keep warm, whereupon we shot as many as possible, poor devils.'[12]

At Suvla, a flood of tidal-wave proportions had surged through the gullies and trench system after a thunderstorm, high winds and deluging rain during the evening of 26 November. Bodies, equipment, crates, latrine tins, dixies, stores, revetment material were swept past drenched figures standing in the flow of the stream or on the firestep or even seated on the parapet anxious as much about the sides of the trench giving way as about the Turk whose military

Gallipoli, and a last letter home. The single surviving undated sheet of a letter written by Lance Corporal E. P. Fell (1st Battalion, Essex Regiment) just before he was killed. (E. P. Fell)

Exposure in every sense. The bleak landscape of Cape Helles, November 1915. Men in the open, beside Ayrshire Yeomanry-held positions. (Lord Sorn)

duty to fire upon newly visible targets might triumph over concern for his own security against the elements.

On the following evening, snow fell and blizzard conditions developed, the cold seeming the more intense as there had been no opportunity for drying out from the rain and flooding. A toll of 280 deaths and 1,600 cases of frostbite and exposure was imposed by the flood and then freezing conditions. The sheer misery for all can scarcely be imagined. Fortune favoured some, like Corporal A. G. Brown who had been able to grasp salvation floating past him, a box with whisky and brandy among other goods from Fortum & Mason, but for others, like his sergeant, it was too late. The blond moustached sergeant had been sniped through the head when he had got out of the trench to escape the flood. He had fallen back into the trench, his body became wedged and then, when the water froze, his face stared up at his men for several days from its icy tomb.[13]

There are occasions when collective misery is depicted so vividly from a general source that to look for evidence of the anguish of an individual is unnecessary. When the general source is official, designed to do no more than describe the daily activity of a military unit – in this case a Battalion in the 86th Infantry Brigade, 29th Division, we may assume that proper military understatement rather than exaggeration will determine the character of the report. The Brigade's War Diary for 27 November provides a sober statement of hardship in the extreme. 'By daylight the men who were capable of work had thrown up for themselves in most cases sufficient cover to protect them from shrapnel fire. The water had subsided in the trenches to an average of 4 feet. A few overcoats, rifles and a certain amount of ammunition was recovered. Great difficulty was experienced in bringing up rations for the men but eventually Bully Beef, a few biscuits and a little rum was issued. The conditions during the day were trying, men were huddled together in shallow trenches, dug behind the parados during the night with any implements they could lay their hands on. Any who walked about stood a great risk of being shot, in fact during the day casualties were fairly heavy from the snipers. A great deal of shrapnel was fired during the day, chiefly at parties of men who were given permission to leave the trenches, all in various states of exhaustion to go to the ambulances. Of these there is no doubt a great number who failed to reach the ambulances and died from exhaustion on the way. A cold N.E. wind blew all day, with a little rain and sleet at intervals and it is feared that a great number of men died from exposure. Towards evening, the weather got worse, developing into snow blizzard, with intense cold, and men were still struggling down to the Ambulances in large quantities.'[14]

Once High Command had decided upon evacuation of the Peninsula, an evacuation to take place in two stages with Anzac and Suvla to be cleared by the third week of December and Helles at the beginning of January, the most elaborate plans were conceived to deceive the Turks about the Allied intentions. For each sector these plans posed particular problems. The narrowness of the intervening distance between the enemies at Anzac and the way the cliffs and ridges commanded the evacuation beaches are obvious examples of the difficulty presented there by a gradual reduction of the numbers of troops while retaining both the semblance of an unimpaired defensive capacity as well as some real substance of strength till the very last men were leaving. Among the answers to this problem was the innovation of 'silent stunts' during which a purely passive holding of the line encouraged the Turks to believe that quietness was a new normality not to be confused with a physical absence of the defender. At Suvla the danger lay in the perfect daytime observation of all movement on the flat expanse of the open plain and at Helles in January the intent to evacuate had been all too obviously advertised by the December departures.

At night during December, defensive strength was thinned down, some guns were withdrawn, some dummy guns openly landed, technological ruses as well as tactical procedures were introduced. Rifles were fixed to fire by means of string attached from the trigger to empty cans which were slowly being filled by water dripping from another can above them. Existing and new tunnels were prepared for mine explosions, timed to deter curious Turks occupying empty trenches on the evacuation night. Stores were prepared for similarly timed destruction. At Suvla, warning had come to the 2/10th Middlesex in time for the carrying out of well-conceived preparations. Regimental officer mistrust of the plans would be confounded.

'December 9: I was right there was something doing last night, any amount of guns, etc., were shifted from "A" beach. I have just heard that the 53rd Div are off tomorrow night. . . . The XIII Div will cover the retreat (of the 2nd Mtd. Div) and then they themselves will fall back. It is hoped that all troops, mules and men will be off in ten days from yesterday. I suppose (we) will be the last to leave so we shall have a very cheery time indeed because the Turks will have discovered by then what is happening (if they don't know already) and they will give us hell with their guns. I can see that there will be some fun going on but I expect it will be a glorious muddle as organization is all that is required and so far as Suvla Bay is concerned no organization worthy of the name has been seen. I shouldn't be surprised if all their plans are changed in a day or so.' On the next few days, 2nd Lt Watson of the 2/10th Middlesex, recorded the departure of stores and of men. On 13 December it was so quiet that he was sure the Turks must be saving their ammunition for the last day. With many of his own men gone, he surveyed their deserted dugouts and accepted in his diary that: 'It does seem rotten after being here so long that not much good has been done and so many splendid lives lost.'

More ammunition was taken off the Peninsula and troops too on 15/16 December and confidence was clearly beginning to grow that the evacuation might, against all expectation, be completed without Turkish interference. Watson had daily duties at the South Pier and though the final orders he received had no reference to the precisely timed detail for troops in the forward positions to vacate them and file down through communicataion trenches and gullies to assembly points and then to the beach, there was the same precision at the pier. The lighters for ferrying the troops out were not to wait at the pier more than thirty-five minutes. Stragglers had to wait for the next departure but officers had to ensure that the lighters were loaded to their full capacity. 'Officers will therefore go below and see that their men close up. Men will not be allowed to sit down, until the lighter is under way.' Armed guards with fixed bayonets were to be stationed on the South Pier and at 'C' Beach, the other departure point, and then: 'The guards will embark on the last lighter of the Division.'

It was only at lunch on 19 December that the schedule was issued for the final evacuation that night. It showed that the first two lighters would be at the South pier at 7.30 p.m. and throughout the night these two and other lighters for men, guns and ammunition and sick cases, would ferry men out to the troopships, *Osmanieh*, *Rowan*, *Princess Ina* and *Scafell* until 4 a.m. when two lighters would take off the last men and a 'steamboat will be in for the Generals'.

'We had a nasty fright at 2.45 a.m. K44 [a lighter] suddenly started out sparks and flames, in consequence the whole of South pier was lit up and as there were three lighters in we were rather afraid it might wake up the dear old Turk. Up to this time not a shot had been fired.' The next alarm was the premature lighting of a store dump on 'C' beach as this lit up the whole scene but: 'there was not a sound. The last lighter left at 4 a.m. On this one I left and I was the last person to get in this lighter. Commander Mulock was most probably the last to leave South Pier and the beach party would follow on after him.' Watson watched the now blazing store dumps on shore. He considered that with not a single casualty 'we were damned lucky to get off like that', an understandable verbal sigh of relief but one which does scant justice to meticulously planned operations carried out with admirable discipline.[15]

With the evacuation of Anzac completed as successfully on the same night and that of Helles by 9 January, the Gallipoli experience was over, its distinctive features remaining clear in recall to survivors into their old age. The narrow confines of the Peninsula, the constant proximity of the sea, the geographically overlooking eye of the Turk, the naval support, the few but well-noticed aircraft and seaplanes, the multi-national force with French Senegalese, Algerian, Moroccan and Metropolitan troops, Indians, Maoris, Palestinians as well as Newfoundlanders, and the Australians, New Zealanders, Scots, Welsh, Irish and English – these factors together with dysentery, exposed latrines, the ever-present possibility of shelling, the close fighting and the use of hand-bombs and trench catapults, a certain relaxation of military formality, a sense of adventure in the approach to the Peninsula, the drama of the landings, the perceived nearness to success and the obstinate refusal to accept that they had been beaten; these were elements in experience never to be forgotten.

MACEDONIA

The sending of British troops to Northern Greece in the autumn of 1915 derived from circumstances not wholly different from those of Gallipoli in that an ally was in difficulty – this time it was Serbia and the peril was desperate – and also there had already been mooted within the War Council that in Macedonia there might lie the prospect of outflanking the Central Powers by a successful drive north into the Habsburg Empire.

As it happened the troops hastily transported in late September from Gallipoli were too late and in insufficient number to be more than witness to the Serbian retreat before the overpowering strength of their German, Austrian and Bulgarian foes. The single division of British troops (10th Irish) was to be reinforced, but the combined Allied strength in

Macedonia (for French, Italian, Serbian, Greek and Russian troops were in due course to see service there) faced a daunting task in fulfilling strategic conceptions made from the comfort of armchairs in London. The Bulgars chose not to thrust into northern Greece, merely to construct emplacements on the commanding mountain heights which overlooked virtually the full length of the Allied front. Where the British sector lay, there were not merely commanding heights overlooking them but a malarial infected plain and here patrols had to penetrate a wide no man's land of tall grasses and seemingly deserted villages which just might happen to be occupied by Bulgars bent on mischief facilitated by forward observation of British intention.

Assaulting strong points before the town of Doiran like Jumeaux Ravine or the high ground of Petit Couronné, Rip Ridge and the still more formidable height of Devil's Eye on the Grand Couronné, would incur costly loss for small hope of achieving success in the enterprise. While awaiting conditions deemed suitable for such an offensive, an enemy to be endured on the plain, infinitesimally small but far more numerous than the Bulgars, was the Anopheles mosquito, a carrier of malaria in virulent and recurrent form. By any comparison rate in the reduction of a battalion's military effectiveness, the mosquito was a more fearsome foe than the Bulgar who at least waited to be attacked. As if this were not sufficient, political uncertainties both with regard to Greece with its pro-German King and pro-Entente Prime Minister and in relation to the irregular swing of the Eastern/Western metronome in London and Paris, bedevilled Allied endeavour in Macedonia.[15a]

As early as 1 November 1915 Captain G. H. Gordon (RFA) in the 10th Irish Division was writing home: 'You'll probably ask why we don't get on (i.e., advance against the enemy) but there's a very good reason their strong position and our not enough men.' This artillery officer, still in drill uniform under gales and the drenching rains of early winter, did not exaggerate the discomforts experienced by men of his division. 'All our moves here have been done in inky blackness and usually under rain and on very ill-defined tracks in the hills. It's becoming a regular nightmare – this winter is going to be very uncomfy with none of the compensation they get in France which is anyhow nearer home and quick communications.' Gordon had been in Serbia the previous year on liaison work and campaigning in the Balkans offered no attraction to him. 'I wish I could get home to France, I'm sick of the discomforts here and the amount of paper one receives from people above who live in comfy huts and tents and expect us to be in 3 places and do 10 things at the same time.'[16] Worse was to follow for this Gunner, as

The Struma, November 1916: watering horses and mules. Note the headgear, though the photographer, Captain Young (1st Battalion, Argyll and Sutherland Highlanders) was writing at this time: 'The weather is awful. My dugout is pouring water just now, there is water everywhere. We are settling down for the winter now. I think it will be very miserable. I wish these Bulgars would go home.' (Lieutenant Colonel J. H. Young)

some guns had to be abandoned in the early December precipitate retirement before brief resumption of the Bulgarian advance.

Though the enemy offensive was not maintained, a decision was taken to wire and entrench a crescent-shaped fortified zone around the base area of Salonika and its hinterland, action which may have provided military security but offered a propaganda vulnerability which the Germans took up in claiming the establishment of their biggest 'internment camp'.

The Bulgarian attack had been anticipated. Officers of the 6th Battalion, Dublin Fusiliers had been told by their Commanding Officer on 2 December that: 'We should have to "*clear-out*" and we could only take what we could carry with us . . . we shall be the last battalion to leave here so we shall be in for a fine time. I wish we knew more than "*clear-out*". I wonder if Greece has come in or what.' On 4 December, this officer, R. C. McB. Broun, wrote his last entries in his diary. 'Big guns went off in the night. Breakfast 8.30 a.m. bacon fried biscuits and butter and jam. . . . Shells falling in this village trying to find our battery which is just on our right. . . . We hear we may have to stay here another 3 or 4 days. We understand that we have to "*clear-out*". We know nothing else. Lunch 1 p.m. Nice and sunny. Parade from 2 p.m. to 3 p.m. Yesterday I took a photograph of this house with some of D. Company officers. Tea at 4 p.m.' and that is the last entry in a very detailed diary, Broun being later reported missing believed killed.[17]

The 'Birdcage' defensive line was prepared with both civilian and soldier labour but always under taunts from sections of the British Press. A sub-altern in the Engineers, building a road, thought: 'it would be a good thing if some of the people who talk about Salonika slackers would come and take on the

Lake Doiran and to the left, the town of Doiran. Like the spokes of a wheel the hub of which is the town, two ridges radiate to the right above the lake; the first leads to the Grand Couronné at the point where the fold of the photograph is marked; behind this is Pip Ridge. Approach up ravine-scarred slopes towards the Bulgarian-held heights was from the British positions just off the photograph to the left. (Sir Alfred Norris)

Salonika in 1916. Nineteen-year-old Private Jack Webster (10th Devons) is at the 5th Canadian Hospital suffering from dysentery. Before long he will die of malaria. (J. A. Webster)

job,' guaranteeing them 'plenty of spare time in which to write objectionable articles to the papers'. In June, this officer, Drummond Inglis, condemned this: 'Godforsaken country – everyone hates it now. No one has enought to do to keep him from interfering with other people's jobs.'[18] He himself had been interfered with by mosquitoes because the advance in May brought his Field Company (28th Division) onto the Struma line to face the malarial season initially without quinine or any instructions in anti-malarial precautions. The impact of this was devastating with high casualties and about a 3 per cent death rate in 38 Field Company. Inglis and his section were fortunate in remaining at the base with responsibility for assisting in the forwarding of stores.

The 2nd Wessex Field Company, RE had the unenviable task in the high summer of 1916 of road building in the partly marshy, partly stony, Galiko Valley. From sunrise to sunset there was no escape from the broiling sun. The men sweltered and sweated without respite. Mosquitoes were everywhere. Sir John Boyd, at that time the unit's Medical Officer, has left a detailed scientifically objective account of conditions. 'Bacillary dysentery had started in May and was common throughout the summer. Malaria began to appear in mid-June and intensified as the year wore on, reaching a peak in September when the type occurring was mainly the malignant variety. Conditions for the spread of malaria were ideal – mosquitoes galore, an unseasoned population and the native reservoir of infection.' It was not known then that in siting this camp as high above the swamp as possible, the men

were left prey to a species of malaria-carrying mosquitoes which bred around the occasional mountain streams. Quinine prophylaxis was quite ineffective. 'One by one, rank and file and officers alike went down.' Ambulances evacuated the sick to Salonika at such a rate that the Company had to be withdrawn, unable to carry on its work.[19]

Soon after this Boyd was to become involved in army bacteriological research, but field application of the fruits of scientific consideration involved large numbers of ordinary soldiers wearing gloves, veils and anti-mosquito ointment, digging pits near the River Struma to trap stagnant water. After a day or so, 'the mosquito strafers' would test it to see if the mosquitoes were breeding and if they were, paraffin was poured on the surface to kill the larvae.[20]

Unquestionably malaria was the curse of the soldiers of the British Salonika force. Debilitating, recurrent, bringing insupportable headaches, uncontrollable shivering and a cold sweat, fevered temperatures, aching muscles and varied degrees of brain-addling misery. It is this which dominates recollections rather than the undoubted privations of heat and cold. For those who coped and continued in active service, leave was much less frequent than from France, but there were distractions, chief among them being the Concert Parties behind the front in Macedonia which reached a high degree of professional skill.

The 22nd, 26th and 28th Divisions all had fine Concert Parties, but smaller units had them too like the 1st Canadian Stationary Hospital (The Empties) and the 2/9 DLI (The Dixies). Sergeant Weston Drury wrote, produced and acted in many of the

Anti-malaria campaign, Macedonia, July 1916. A taste of the doctor's own medicine. Captain Boyd (RAMC) personally supervises a parade for the swallowing of the five-grain quinine draught. (P. G. Shute)

26th Division's shows such as 'Delightful'. 'Delightful' in 1918 had as special attractions, Miss Polly Pears, Miss Lily Lever, Miss Vi Nolia, Miss Kitty Carbolic, Miss Gertie Gibbs, each played with a sparkle by Privates Stuart, McLellan, Ward, Snow, Mackintosh and Bright. Pte Stuart demonstrated not least his versatility in doubling for Azizie a dancer and Miss Connie Colgate.

Robinson Crusoe was one of the most celebrated of the 26th's offerings and here, Drury, a Sergeant in the RAMC, J. Sackville Wiggins, a Corporal in the 9th Gloucesters and Sapper Sidney Clarkson (RE) worked towards all-round excellence in their productions making a striking contrast with their early days in Summerhill Camp where they were even without a piano. This Concert Party, (The 'Splints') was to perform at Gugunci in one marquee pitched against another which made a covered auditorium for up to 300 men. Weston Drury was later to write with justifiable pride of their enterprise growing into the Gaiety Theatre (Kalinova) Macedonia, under the noses of the Bulgar guns with electric signs, programme 'girls', a man in picture palace uniform shouting 'Early doors this way' and a musical director in full evening dress. Tom Barker had memories too of The Splints giving a performance in a ravine shared by an 18-pdr battery which opened up during the show. 'Our lighting was of acetylene gas and each time a round was fired, out went the gas lights and our stage drapings of Army blankets flapped backwards and forwards by the air displacement. Eventually we had someone standing by with a lighted candle, ready to dash along the footlights and headlights to relight the jets.'

It was no perfunctory acknowledgement that the Divisional Commander, Major General Kennedy, addressed in July 1916 to the Sergeant responsible for their entertainment. 'My dear Drury, I person-

Sergeant Weston Drury in 'Robinson Crusoe' poses with one of the 26th Divisional concert party's principal attractions. (Weston Drury)

Macedonian entertainment: The 'Dixies', the Concert Party and Orchestra of the 2/9th Durham Light Infantry. Of the Concert Party, left to right, seated: Freddy Turner, Max Rutt and Jack Pritchard, on the ground, Freddy White, Harry Cassidy, Teddy Staples and Jock Ross. (H. E. Cassidy)

ally enjoyed the performance last night and shall look forward to your next tour with great interest. Good luck go with you, you are doing a real good service to the Division for which I thank you.'[21]

Bill Mather in his book *Muckydonia 1917–19* eloquently provides further evidence of the professionalism of the 26th Division's Concert Party and of Weston Drury's outstanding achievement. Mather's 1918 diary documents his own assistance to the Business Manager, Captain Thompson. 'The jobs I get are of various character – taking the money after the show, painting a noticeboard, writing to DAAG or some other staff bloke, handing round drinks, looking after French NCOs and Lt. Michot if there is no officer who speaks French.' It is pleasant to read in this diary a compliment to the 28th Division's show, 'The Chocolate Soldier'. In *Muckydonia* Mather writes frankly of the homosexuality which he adjudged was an aspect of the wistful vision aroused by the female impersonations and he mentions in particular the exotic gifts brought for the 'girls' by French officers and indeed the jealousies roused by one temptress's come-hither looks from the stage.[22]

An officer in the 26th Middlesex named Simpson, wrote in his memoirs of the rivalry in the auditorium to occupy front seats to 'see a bit of bare leg and get the glad eye from some comely lad in the chorus. Officers would go to endless trouble to wash and shave and dress to attend these functions with the hopes of being the favoured one.' Care must be taken with the story he then relates of a flying officer whose handsomeness leaned towards feminity and of his being persuaded to occupy one of the box seats disguised as a nurse being accompanied by another RFC officer. Sure enough he attracted the attention of a very senior Army officer and a note was passed inviting the pair to Headquarters Mess for supper.

At the subsequent party, the nurse was monopolised by the officer – of no less than General's rank. All was going dangerously well towards goodness knows what dénouement when the General noticed an inch or so of khaki trousers peeping beneath a dress and an alternative eruption ensued involving the temporary arrest of all the flying officers concerned, their pinioned wings being released when, very fortunately, High Command took its embarrassment with better grace.[23]

The city of Salonika itself offered dubious attractions. All who were there remember the two great dramas of the shooting down of a German airship and of the great fire which destroyed so much of the city, but some specifically detail adventures in which they were more personally involved. Illtyd Davies provides more than a clue to the constraints upon his advancement from the lowly rank of Gunner in his account of a four day leave in the city. It was, it should be stated, his first leave in three years. With four new soldier acquaintances he settled upon the commercially named 'Mersey Cafe'. 'The owner dressed in a shabby swallow-tailed coat conducted us to a table and made many elaborate bows, hungry Tommies were big business. The dinner was bread, two fried eggs, bacon, chips a piece of fruit pie and a cup of tea.' Everyone ordered a double dinner and then a further double dinner, Davies contending that he and another continued in this fashion. 'The Greek proprietor was enraptured – never before had he had such customers.' Sadly the five soldiers on the loose had no intention of honouring the bill for their gargantuan meal and escaped via a skylight above the washroom toilet. 'The events of the remaining days of my leave are very hazy, being considerably under the weather. I do have vivid memories of a brawl in one pub where there were several Greek and Italian soldiers who gave us to understand that it was them

Army welfare work for the homeless after the great Salonika fire which broke out in the afternoon of 18 August 1917 – soup kitchen arrangements, complete with seats of a sort seem to be attracting fewer refugees than Army supervisors. (F. J. Ball)

A typical sandbagged position at the base of a ravine in the rocky hill country between Lake Doiran and the River Vardar overlooked by more elevated positions strongly held by the Bulgars. Anzac troops are among those photographed here. (Sir Alfred Norris)

Macedonia and an 'orthodox' pairing: A local Greek Priest poses with the Padre of a British military unit temporarily resident in his 'parish'. (Sir Thomas Harley)

not the British winning the war. It developed into a real shindig, tables were overturned, glasses, bottles and chairs flying through the air, mirrors were smashed and barmaids screamed – fists, boots, belts and buckles were all used.' Davies remembers no more of his leave, he became very ill on the train north to Karasuli and, reaching his Trench Mortar Battery HQ, he became unconscious. Macedonia seemed to have exerted fulsome retribution.[24]

Some letters in mid-1917 from Tom Harley (9th Bn. King's Own) illustrate not merely the work of his battalion but a subaltern's response to the war and to Macedonia. '5 June. We are in the line once more and so I am no end busy. It gets steadily hotter every day now. We were all very grieved indeed to hear the day before yesterday that Flemming [a wounded officer] had passed away – all the best people seem to be claimed and it is a noble thing to die for one's country. It is when one loses a great friend like this that one gets absolutely sick of the miserable war, it takes all the go out of you. . . . It was officially announced yesterday that leave to England was indefinitely postponed. I suppose on

account of wanting all the ships they can get for stores. It doesn't really make any difference to us though, for no one gets away on leave as it is. 11 June. One day is very much like the last isn't it, that is to say the war doesn't seem to shew any progress to a marked degree, I get very bored with it all nowadays. There are plenty of shells and things flying about and quite a lot doing all round but somehow one feels that it is quite time it was all over. . . . I would just as soon be in the line as out for there is no attraction out – nothing to see or do but work. One gets tired in the line of course, dog tired, but you feel it is in a good cause so that is some consolation to you. 30 June [in the line] Quentin has applied for a transfer to the gunners. He is absolutely sick of the infantry, and says he can't possibly stick another winter in the trenches. . . . I was feeling very poorly last night and so decided to rest as much as possible. This morning we got an awful shelling however for 2 hours – that just about did it. 23 July, I have been a bit seedy the last few days. I got a touch of sunstroke and felt thoroughly run down. However once more I have escaped hospital.'

'27 July. [Out of the line] We have some brigade sports on tonight and my Company machine-gun

A Mule's loyalty rewarded by a soldier's artistry. G. K. Reid depicts his 'ostreperous but faithful "Koolah" which took me every day in 1917 from Butkova Lake, Macedonia'. (G. K. Reid)

team is representing the King's Own in a competition so I am very keen to win and we are spending the day cleaning and polishing up. There is also to be boxing and other sports.'

Harley's raised spirits were overtaken by the lurking malaria which quite evidently had eroded his natural ebullience and his letters in August were written from the 49th General Hospital in Salonika and then from convalescence.[25]

Stagnation became so synonymous a term for Salonika that too easily forgotten, at the time and subsequently, were the infantry assaults of September 1916 at Bala, Zir and Barakli Juma on the Struma Front and at Machukovo on the Doiran Front. Then, in April 1917 and again in September 1918, bitter battles were fought for the heights dominating Doiran.

The 1st Bn. Argyll and Sutherland Highlanders was informed on 29 September 1916 that it would attack the two villages of Bala and Zir the following dawn. 'That evening we marched out to a place near the river where we halted for 4 hours. We dumped all our spare kit, and received 2 days' rations and steel hats. At 1 a.m. we marched to the river, crossed

by a bridge put up by the RE and formed up on the other bank in our attack formations, and waited for dawn. . . . At 5.30 the First Line moved off and the guns opened a quarter of an hour later. The first village was about 1½ miles from the river, and the country as flat as your hand for miles all around. . . . It was a fine sight to see line upon line of men advancing over the plain and the objectives being plastered with shells.' The village was entered but then the forward troops could make no further progress and Bulgar shelling fell among the men in the follow-up waves. When the time came for John Young, the officer who wrote this account, to order his men to provide covering fire on the sunken road from Zir leading into Bala, the problem lay in a Bulgarian machine-gun commanding the road. 'At this moment several officers were hit, and casualties were mounting and a machine-gun opened from the direction of Zir straight down the road, raking A Company.' Heavy casualties were suffered and the battalion had to withdraw to reorganize before any resumption of the attempt to take the village. In fact, during the night, it was Bulgar counter-attacks from the direction of Zir which preoccupied the Argylls. 'It was a most trying and anxious time. We had a little wire in front but it was soon cut by our own fire.'

At dawn, the enemy, though in large number, was seen retiring. 'We gave them a very hot send-off. The men were very delighted and kept up a grand fire. Just before this I received a report that the enemy were up to my wire on the right. I ordered No. 7 platoon to organize a bombing attack and clear them out. This was done with great success. Some 30 enemy dead were picked up within 20 yards of my right and many more were lying further out in the mealie fields. . . . At about 8 a.m. a party of 36 Bulgars put up their hands and surrendered. They had got to a sunken road about 100 yards in front and had had enough.'[26]

One officer, J. D. Milne (1st Royal Scots), had more than enough in a different sense. He had been greatly inconvenienced during that tense night because 'from 4 a.m. till about 7 felt and was violently sick, probably caused by a rum issue on an empty stomach.'[27]

Machukovo on the Doiran mountainous front was to be assaulted by a night attack, each soldier distinctively marked by a white patch on the back of his jacket and a white band round his right arm. Telegraphic messages among the papers of an Intelligence Officer, Lieutenant T. F. Higham, show what the attacking force was coping with as a Bulgarian searchlight illuminated them and soaring

Very lights brought their resultant retribution in the form of shelling to add to the problem of machine-gun and small arms fire. Ravine defences had to be stormed and wounded men, as might be expected, left behind. One man from the 9th Bn, East Lancs, hit in the shoulder, was brought in six days later. He had been living on blackberries and water. A sanguine report stated that he was 'Not much the worse for wear', but in fact he was to die in hospital.

The Intelligence Officer's account makes vividly clear the problem of the maintenance of field telephone communications, the lines being so frequently broken by shelling. Dawn exposed isolated bodies of men on the slopes and sub-ridges and an enemy aircraft directed Bulgarian shelling on these men. In the afternoon, this shelling intensified. 'About 200 of our men could be seen outside the trenches and H.E. was bursting among them on the splintering rocks.' The elevated positions reached could not be held and withdrawal was ordered.[28]

In April 1917, the heights beside Doiran, ten or so miles from Machukovo, were to be the focus of the British part in an Allied offensive. The 10th Devons

Doiran, September 1916. Two men of the 10th Devons photographed on patrol in no man's land, the great width of which, just over three miles in the Doiran sector, allowed for some impunity – nevertheless in the necessary security of two civilian-deserted villages, some encounters with the Bulgars were to be expected. The Devonshire Regimental history reports the Bulgars at this time as being: 'Unsatisfactory as opponents, because they rarely come out far beyond the wire or exposed themselves to punishment.' (Brigadier C. Greenslade)

were for a second time to make the acquaintance of the Jumeaux Ravine fronting Petit Couronné. As in February that year, they were to attack by night. Lectures and general distribution of maps seemed to suggest thorough preparations. Pte Frank Mullins had crammed his haversack full of Mills bombs. A day-long heavy bombardment of the enemy wire and front-line trenches gave the men grounds for optimism as they moved out in the dark to their assembly positions at the lower end of Jumeaux Ravine. In fact the Bulgarians had new searchlights in position to illuminate no man's land, knew the British were coming and the route they had to take. 'They seemed to know our every move. We got so far in the Ravine and then it was Hell let loose. Our lads were being knocked over like ninepins. We that were able to, got about half way. The noise of the explosions was terrible. Suddenly I found myself alone, nearly choked with cordite fumes but unhurt. I picked my way over bodies I could only see by the flash of the explosions.' Those unscathed, gathered in a depression – the 'pan' – at the bottom of Petit Couronné. 'We were under rifle and shellfire and were all mixed up and in the dark we couldn't find our NCOs. We had to move at a given time and when we made for their trenches how well I remember those searchlights. We took their trenches and got over the crest of Petit Couronné and into their reserve trenches. There we had to contend with them all night. They did make one mistake with the searchlights – they got their lights on their own men. They were bringing up reinforcements which made a good target for us but they soon switched off when they found their mistake.

Private Mullins, as the only bomber immediately available, was ordered to bomb an enemy-occupied dugout and this being done he was among three men ordered to go in to take prisoner anyone who had survived. 'We had to strike matches to find them. We got five men out who were able to walk.'

When the Bulgarian counter-attack was launched with much shouting and blowing of bugles, a hand-bomb pitched in among Mullins's Section wreaking havoc. The 10th Devon Private himself was very fortunate in that his own single remaining Mills bomb (he had not been able to move the pin) did not detonate. When he came to, his right leg seemed paralyzed. He had many fragmentation wounds, one had cut the sciatic nerve. A soldier injured in the hand helped him to his feet and together the two men assisted each other back over the crest through the débris of the battle and found a Regimental Aid Post where their wounds were dressed. 'I was put on a framework with two pairs of shafts, one pair in front and one behind, with a mule in the front shafts and a mule in the rear. I was in the middle with a mule's head looking down at me all the time. We had a Maltese driver and we travelled back for miles around the hills and got back to Janesh where we were put in wheeled transport and taken to a Canadian General Hospital.'[29]

The Official History of the Macedonian Operations summarized this spring offensive as: 'an appalling chapter of accidents'. Even when allowing for factors beyond Allied control, the men who had made the attack had deserved: 'better backing from home, better leadership, better organisation' and a better spirit of mutual confidence and co-operation between the leaders and Staffs of the Allied armies.[30]

A final opportunity for a 'glorious military victory' may have been within reach in September 1918. The glory eluded the British Salonika Force but the force can make substantial claim for a share in the victory over the Bulgar. The British preparations for their part in the September 1918 offensive were made under shortages of virtually all war matériel and with human resources depleted by influenza as well as malaria. Though the French and Serbs in their sector broke through, the British and Greeks only took more limited objectives in the Doiran area. Despite desperate efforts, Grand Couronné and Pip Ridge defied all assaults until suddenly disenchantment seized Bulgarian leadership and the positions held with such determination were vacated, enabling a general advance right along the Allied line, an advance which encouraged the enemy's surrender as early as 30 September, the first of Germany's allies to fall.

Captain Cumberland (RAMC) in the last days of the Macedonian War had his own particular struggle in weeding out influenza cases from the 9th King's Own to which he was attached as well as acting as Medical Officer to the new isolation camp to which the victims were moved. He made what provision he could for the isolation hospital, but went forward with his medical equipment and stretcher-bearers to be in support of his battalion's leading role in an attack following up one costly failure.

Cumberland was moved by the sight of the Battalion's Commanding Officer standing by a mule track as his men made their way up to their point of deployment to attack Pip Ridge. Passing through British gas had made Cumberland vomit a good deal and he felt apprehensive about his lack of instructions over arrangements for evacuation of the wounded. He walked with the CO and the Adjutant along the mule track at the head of HQ Company and then the first wounded were seen. 'A number of men passed us and it appeared as if they were panic-stricken. The Adj. and I stopped some and saw some were wounded and let them go but then I saw one of the Bn. malingerers and when he could not show me a wound, I cursed him and told him to rejoin his unit or I would inform on him and he would be court martialled and shot after the battle was over.' With this stern admonition having its effect and wounded men properly being instructed to make for a First Aid post at Pillar Hill, Cumberland hurried forward to catch up with the Colonel.

The Bulgarian shelling was heavy, one exploding nearby just as Cumberland was approaching the CO. Cumberland was slightly hit, covered by débris and

No. 5 Mountain Battery in action South of Dove Tepe, Macedonia 1917. These 2.75-inch guns were transported entirely by pack mules and were therefore eminently suitable for the hilly terrain of the Doiran sector. (G. W. Sissons)

through his own daze and the swirling smoke heard the screams of wounded all around him. The CO was badly hit about the hip and his thigh broken. As the Medical Officer dressed the Colonel's wounds, another shell exploded still nearer, killing some of the men just wounded. 'The machine-guns began to rattle and the bullets were striking the ground wounding or killing the remainder of HQ Coy.'

Lance Corporal Challoner (RAMC) and Cumberland carried the wounded thirty feet to shelter behind the brow of their hill and dressed fifteen cases, many being seriously injured. A half grain of morphine eased their suffering and then rifles and bayonets were used as splints, puttees from the dead as bandages. The Adjutant had been wounded in the abdomen by the second shell. Cumberland knew he would die so there was little point in using a splint to support the poor man's leg broken by the first shell. The CO was suffering terrible pain but he called for a runner to be sent forward and instruct Captain Whitehead to take over command of the battalion and then he asked after the Adjutant and several men of the rank and file by name.

The Medical Officer later got two walking wounded to retrieved a stretcher from between five dead stretcher-bearers and carry the CO down to the ambulance. 'I shall never forget the expression; pain gratitude and anxiety on his face as we said goodbye in the dim light of daybreak. Nor will I forget the sight of that spot strewn with débris and dead, and the pale anxious expressions of the wounded. The whole earth seemed to be rocking with the bursting shells and the air was filled with the sounds of shells, machine-guns rattling, guns roaring, shells screaming overhead and the cries, moans, prayers and curses of the wounded. The CO's servant had both legs, both thighs and both arms broken and was screaming with pain. I knew he would not live and gave him another grain of morphine to relieve his pain. Then he pleaded for his mother and gave a message to be sent to her – a widowed mother from her only son.'

When later in the day Captain Whitehead was encountered, he had 'laughed at the look of my face covered in blood and my arms covered to the elbows in blood too'. Whitehead had in fact been seriously wounded himself and was dreadfully pale but he refused the Medical Officer's advice to be stretchered away with a dismissive 'Not until every wounded man is evacuated first.'[31]

The whole sorry affair, with an aftermath of recriminations over the staff work involved, was a particularly peculiar prelude to victory and it may be left here to serve as a rightful challenge to anyone who may still be tempted to make patronising reference to an army shirking north of Salonika. Monotony there may have been but there were occasions when coping with boredom was far from being a principal preoccupation!

MESOPOTAMIA

There were deeply underlying as well as immediately circumstantial reasons for sending troops to Mesopotamia in the autumn of 1914, but in all this it may be properly presumed that the oil factor was fundamental. What is also fundamental is that out of a splendidly executed small combined operation which opened up this front there developed a campaign of such tragic mismanagement that its focus of failure, Kut, remains indelibly fixed (and with few rivals) as a symbol of 1914-18 defeat, brought about by errors and problems unsolved at the level of senior military and political command. Subse-quently, shame may have been visited upon some of those responsible; at the time, the penalty was paid in the field.

No contemporary campaign was so inextricably bound up with the natural element of water, none was fought in so flat and featureless a landscape and none was to the same degree so influenced by seasonal change. In short, for the first two years, troop movement for offensive operations was over-whelmingly dependent on river transport from the Persian Gulf up the Shatt al Arab to Kurna where this river bifurcated into the more westerly, Euphrates and to the east, the Tigris. These great rivers and the Karun and, at a later date, the Diyala, were the highways for all operations. The Euphrates and the Tigris, both with their narrow fertile borders bound to the many bends, wound their way through desert where the only elevations were the age-old attempts at flood bank containment. In the summer, throughout the day, the sun scorched without favour all who sought to follow any purpose, never mind military, in so hostile a terrain and at night the phenomenal drop in temperature chilled men to the marrow. At times of flood by reason of winter rains and then far more dramatically by springtime melting of the snows in the mountain sources of the two great rivers, the plain was flooded in truly remarkable transformation.

Essentially the first Mesopotamian Campaign grew out of the temptation to advance beyond what had been secured – the oil – and achieve the coup of capturing Baghdad. There may be a measure of unfairness in such a résumé as judgements differ on

6 November 1914 and two boatloads of troops of the 16th Infantry Brigade are towed by a launch to their landing point at Fao on the River Shatt el Arab. The photograph shows the Persian bank of the river. The landing took place under the covering guns of the sloop, HMS *Odin*. (Lieutenant Anderson, Indian Medical Service)

the extent to which oil security had been assured, but what is unquestionable is that at the highest political and military level, separate authorities overlapped, indeed perhaps competed and then, as the campaign developed, there evolved additional complexities. A detached Divisional Commander with the perspective of such a position, and a Force Commander in the rear, with rather different considerations to evaluate, were each committed to decision-making and its consequence. It was unlikely that the interrelationship of the War Office in Whitehall, The Government of India Military Department in Simla, The Intelligence Department of both of these authorities, the India Office in London with its own Military Department, the High Command of the Indian Government Expeditionary Force in Mesopotamia and then of the VI Indian Division far up the Tigris, could operate effectively. The task of defeating the Turk was from the start beset by these divisions of authority over responsibility for the campaign.[32] Certainly, however well they served, officers and men of the Indian Expeditionary Force 'D' were not well served themselves.

In the beginning all went well. A detachment of the VI Indian Division secured the island of Bahrein, took Fao, defeated Turkish counter-measures and occupied Basra. An engagement fought by the first troops landed, was watched by men waiting to disembark. More and more troops were landed on the muddy bank of the river and under a terrific downpour of rain: 'I saw one Indian regiment halt its advance to put on raincoats. How we envied them. We had none.' That evening a strong cold wind got up and Harry Rich, the subaltern of the 120th Rajputs who had watched the engagement, nicely captured that fusion of human apprehension yoked to regimental pride in writing that: 'before each battle I was terrified but I was still more terrified of missing one the Regiment was in'. Rich dug himself

into a bank around a garden of date palms. 'I scooped out a kind of grave in the bank but it was no protection against the cold. I unfolded all the maps I had and put them around me, but it was no good. Like everyone else I spent the night walking up and down to get the circulation going with intervals of lying down until I chilled off again.'

In the morning, Rich found that the boat containing their coats and blankets had been sunk in the storm. A few nights later, with a noise like thunder, horses from the artillery support stampeded through the camp. It was several days before they were retrieved from well into the desert and during this time the Rajput officer spent his days squelching in the muddied bank of the river supervising the unloading and then re-loading of stores because Basra had been vacated by the Turks and lay open to British occupation.

The appeal of Basra was distinctly limited, diminishing further on close acquaintance. Filthy beyond description, no sanitation or water supply, roads were mere slime tracks of muddy rubbish. 'We were on the Ashar Creek which runs through the centre of the town and acts as the main drain. We would watch the Arabs come down into the creek, wash, urinate, defecate and finally have a good drink.'

Advancing beyond Basra by river steamer, the Rajputs disembarked to take part in the storming of Kurna and here encountered the problems caused by mirage. 'Everything is elongated, a single stick can easily be mistaken for an Arab, a flock of ducks transformed into an infantry battalion, a flock of sheep actually being responsible for an alarm call to repel a cavalry attack.'

When Kurna, one of the reputed sites of the Garden of Eden, was taken, it belied so sanctified a reputation. Even in the cold December weather, the canvas inside the men's tents was black with flies and

12 April 1915: Gurkhas attempting to wade to Shaiba. (Major W. W. Phillips)

'the whole place stank like a midden'. The advanced brigade of which the Rajputs were one unit, moved upstream and pitched camp outside Kurna, sixteen men to a tent. In the case of the Rajputs, the ground level was wisely dug deeper and a mound of sand placed round the ouside as some protection against sniping by watching Arabs who in all but a literal sense were balanced on the fence between the Turk and the British Imperial Soldier, watching to see whom fortune would favour.[33]

In April, Arabs were in support of a strong Turkish force which attacked the British Camp west of Basra at Shaiba. Supplies from Basra to Shaiba had to cross the flooded desert by native river boats, bellums, while the reinforcements to the garrison at Shaiba took a circuitous and exhausting march through the flood where it was found to be fordable. Ironically a need for water, water fit for drinking, became a problem in the two day battle, an officer in the 48th Bombay Pioneers, Ilay Ferrier, actually ordering the filling of emptied ammunition boxes with drinking water for his troops and also sending it out by cart to wounded Turks.[34]

The charge of the 24th Punjabis at Shaiba is graphically described by the newly commissioned W. W. A. Phillips in a letter home. 'Forward we went in extended order towards a slight ridge. Only a few shots were fired until we topped the ridge when a heavy fire was opened upon us. We at once got down and returned the fire and then started advancing by rushes. Mother it was awful. There was absolutely no cover – it was open desert and men were falling all round. The enemy were entrenched and we continued to advance towards them until we were within 500 yards. There we were held up and lay for hours under a tremendous fire while our guns and machine-guns helped us to hammer away at them. The men behaved splendidly especially the Sikhs who were with me. Soon after 4 o'clock the Dorsets on our right made a forward movement which we

copied and then as the enemy seemed to be wavering, we charged. The enemy at once bolting and that was the end of the show.'[35]

During the battle, Harry Rich, serving as 'Galloper' to his Brigadier, was sent on an embarrassing duty to convey to artillery staff, who seemed to be having a field day lunch break, a peremptory written and verbal 'For God's sake do something.' The message was presented, the youthful Rich reeling his horse to race away precluding expostulation.[36]

Following Shaiba, consolidatory operations to the north-east and to the north-west were carried out and in the case of the latter the Royal West Kents were to distinguish themselves at Nasiriyeh on the Euphrates with a successful bayonet charge over several trench lines. In this battle, Corporal H. J. Coombs, in the absence by death or disablement of his platoon commander, sergeant and most of the platoon, had skilfully organized the capture of a low-walled, loop-holed defence enclosure by five men. A large number of prisoners filed out of the entrance after the men, standing between the loopholes, had fired blind but over the wall in among the defenders. Of this period, Coombs has memories of heatstroke victims being taken by stretcher for dunking in the Euphrates and then to be carried into what little shade was available and he has further recall of myriads of hornets nesting in the date palms being irresistibly drawn to a jam issue.[37]

During May 1915, the various authorities concerned seemed to give some encouragement and a degree of sanction for an advance up the Tigris but the force charged with this task, Major General C. V. F. Townshend's VI Indian Division, was already incurring exceedingly serious health problems under the hostile climate and related circumstances. 'Sunstroke and heatstroke were common, fever, dysentery and paratyphoid were rife, yet medical facilities were totally inadequate to deal with the heavy casualty list.'[38] Despite such unpropitious circumstances, the advance began well. Operations of a combined nature employing naval and native craft ('Townshend's Regatta') enabled the Division, by boat as well as foot, to capture several Turkish positions. The diary of a Medical Officer, Captain T. Osmond, brings together the twin factors of pleasing military progress and worsening medical problems.

'June 2nd. Naval boats chased on last night and caught Turks – heat bad, several cases. June 3rd. Most of fleet left behind. We moved on behind COMET and MINOR. River very shallow and winding. Got stuck many times. Passed several captured boats. Met by message to push on if poss. Finally had to stop 8 miles from Amara owing to dark. June 4th. Started 4.30. Reached Amara soon after 6 a.m. Found General Townshend and Naval Commander had captured whole place. 600 prisoners, arms and ammunition, ponies. June 5th. Many sick. June 6th. Sick off to Basra. June 7th. V. hot all day. Fixed awning for officer's latrine. June 8th. Col. Q.M. and self ptomaine poisoning. June 9th. Many sick. 3 heat cases. Hall's coat caught alight in the sun.'[39]

The men were now enduring the full punishment of the Mesopotamian sun, heat and dust. They had coped with mud, rain, floods, wind, cold (even snow was to be recorded in the desert near Nasiriyeh on 21 January 1916)[40] and there was seasonally the unwelcome company of mosquitoes, flies and fleas. Universally to confound teeth, palate and patience, there were the biscuits of the Delhi Biscuit Company – breakable only by determined wielding of an entrenching tool handle or bayonet hilt.

At the end of August came sanction to advance beyond Amara. A strong Turkish defensive position on both sides of the Tigris at Es Sinn provided Townshend and his division with an awkward challenge answered by a feint frontal attack on the right bank and a night outflanking march around the marshes which seemed impregnably to complete the Turkish defence on the left bank. Planning and execution must have been more problematic than it seemed in retrospect to former Private Vanstone of the Dorsets. 'Orders were given to dig and throw the sand in the air making clouds of dust and as darkness fell we retired a good way back, crossed a bridge over the river and after marching all night we were miles away and we the Dorsets attacked between two marshes while the others came right round the enemy's rear capturing many prisoners. A very successful operation.'[41] The operation secured what was then a little-known town, Kut, enclosed in a horseshoe bend of the Tigris and the defeat of the Turks, despite the lengthening line of British communications, seemed to the Expeditionary Force Commander, Sir John Nixon, to offer encouragement to press up the river to the great prize of Baghdad. In fact the enemy had constructed positions to counter such a move against their vulnerable historic city and these positions at Ctesiphon were occupied by the Turks who had retired from Kut.

Townshend, whose division had captured Kut, now made representation to Nixon against an attack upon such positions, strengthened, as there was reason to believe they would be, by considerable reinforcements. His protest was insufficiently firm to sway Nixon and accordingly the advance was resumed. Near the soaring-arched remnant of an ancient civilization at Ctesiphon, the Turks were waiting – they were in greater numbers than their foes and held the incomparable advantage in this period of warfare of needing merely to defend and to do so from entrenchments.

The stand which the Turks made at Ctesiphon in late November 1915 decisively defeated all hope of gain from the British victories achieved so far in the campaign. The Turks may have conceded trenches

Ctesiphon, early November 1915: 16th Indian Cavalry in front of the remnants of an ancient palace. Neither cavalry nor aerial reconnaissance had yet been able to establish accurately the strength and defensive dispositions of the Turks who were preparing to hold positions in the immediate vicinity. (H. L. Reilly)

On 1 December 1915 an 18-pounder gun team is retiring from Ctesiphon down river to Kut. (Major A. S. Cane)

and suffered casualties but the way to Baghdad was still barred. A tactically indecisive battle left the British unable to advance or to stand or to care for their heavy casualties. Their over-extended supply line and their denuded strength combined to compel withdrawal. The Turkish corpses in front of the 120th Rajputs did not disguise the reality of the British position from 2nd Lt Rich. He and his fellow officers had as yet not tasted defeat and they wondered what would happen next.[42]

What had happened to the British wounded in the battle tragically exposed the inadequacy of medical provisions for Townshend's force in the event of its becoming involved in a major battle. No contemporary letter could illustrate to the degree of the Mesopotamia Commission report just how appalling and prolonged were the sufferings of those wounded at Ctesiphon, but a letter from Major van Buren Laing (76th Punjabis) indicates the first stage in an ordeal which if it were to have been catalogued pictorially would run the risk of being thought to be from the exaggerated imagination of a fevered brain. Laing's letter refers to the whole plain being: 'covered with wandering Arabs looting the dead. We can only hope that none of the wounded fell into their hands.' Laing sent out parties to bring in wounded, one of whom told him that most of his fellows lying out untended had died during the night.

As the Punjabis retired to the positions they had captured earlier: 'It was impossible to get all our wounded away and the enemy was coming on.' At night, parties of volunteers were called to go out again and during the following day evacuation of the injured was carried out under enemy fire.[43] Three or even four men were wedged onto the mule-drawn springless carts to be taken back to a river base at Lajg and from there in large numbers on overcrowded river steamers, barges and the two hospital ships, for broiling days and intensely cold nights on the journey down-river four hunded miles to Basra.

On the steamers, aid for the disabled was as absent for basic natural functions as for the proper treatment of wounds. The small numbers of medical staff simply could not cope and in his book, appropriately titled, *The Neglected War*, A. J. Barker describes well the scandal and the tragedy piled upon tragedy of the downstream journey. Barker concludes his account with a memorable quotation of a Basra viewpoint offered in evidence to the Mesopotamian Commission. 'When the Mejidieh was about three hundred yards off, it looked as if she were festooned by ropes. The stench when she was quite close was definite, and I found that what I mistook for ropes were dried stalactites of human faeces.'[44]

Meanwhile the VI Indian Division retired first to Azzizieh and then, still pressed by the Turks, on to Kut. Here Townshend chose to make his stand. The retirement was not disorderly, but it was inevitably straggling. As units reached Kut, concentrated efforts had to be undertaken by the tired troops to put defence of the town in order and to prepare for a siege. Night and day the defenders dug and as Major Laing wrote at the time: 'It is not much fun digging in the open under shellfire.'

The Turks attacked in some strength in late December. They got into a mud-walled fort, a key point in the defensive line of trench-connected redoubts and the fort itself which secured the town and its defended area in the narrow neck of the horseshoe bend of the Tigris, but they were bombed and bayonetted out leaving large numbers of dead in the trenches they had temporarily taken. 'The stench was terrible but as there were wounded among them we could not spray the lot with oil and burn.'

Constant rain in January led to the trenches becoming filthy with mud and rubbish and the flooding was made far worse as the river rose in late January. The trenches of defender and besieger alike were flooded. Laing's letter, written as a diary, paints the misery. 'The rain continued all night and the temperature was just freezing. Only Milford, the Doctor and myself stuck it out. All the other British officers collapsed and had to be sent back. In the morning (22nd Jan) we found one man dead and had 60 more suffering from exposure. Many didn't speak for days and they all had their feet and hands badly swollen from the cold.'

Trenches had to be converted to a breastwork dam with Kut taking on more and more the aspect of an island, an island now being bombed even if in a desultory fashion as well as being shelled. Men who had expended a great deal of energy in trench-digging were now as exhaustingly employed in the building of defences against flooding. Food shortage and religious beliefs, which at first constrained Indians from taking sustenance alternative to their normal consumption, provided problems. 'The men very foolishly and from sheer pigheadedness have refused to eat horse which makes the ration question more difficult. They now only get 10 oz. of barley meal and ½ oz. of ghee. To keep off the scurvy we all eat boiled grass and all sorts of weeds.'

Among the ten thousand of so defenders of Kut, morale was periodically raised or lowered by the result of relief operations mounted by the British to break through the cordon of Turkish defence around their besieging positions. In the last days of a siege

Kut under siege. Dorsets in the trenches. Major Brown, Quartermaster of the 2nd Dorsets may well be wrestling with problems of rations and stores as he stands in front of fellow officers in Kut entrenchments, 1916. (Major W. H. Miles)

lasting almost five months, frustration and acceptance battled for supremacy. On 25 April, after the heroic failure of the store-laden steamer *Julnar* to break through, Laing wrote, 'We can see her quite distinctly and it is maddening to think of all the good things on board. Of course we can do nothing as the men are practically in a state of collapse. So we have to start our last ration. We have three more days all told, plus what aeroplanes can give us. Well anyhow this siege has got to end in a few days. We all still believe it will be all all right, but you can imagine we are not in the most cheerful spirit.' The following day news that he had been awarded the Military Cross in no way cheered him as surrender was palpably closer.[45]

More methodically than Townshend would have liked, the relief force had made its way up river from Basra. Townshend judged that it would not be wise to weaken further his beleaguered division by employing it in vigorous harassment of his besiegers and the relief force in consequence was unaided in its determined even if unsuccessful attempts to break the strong Turkish cordon. A particularly costly relief force failure was that of March 7–9 in front of the Dujailah Redoubt. Before this attack, the 27th Punjabis had marched off to their place of concentration with a 'great cheer and full of enthusiasm'. A night approach on regularly taken compass bearings and pace stick (or other forms of distance reading), was carried out successfully, but the very success in achieving surprise conflicted with the plan of an artillery bombardment as a prelude to the infantry attack. Time was wasted in establishing that the surprise gained was indeed to be sacrificed to the inflexibility of holding to the original plan and the delay consequent upon this resulted in the infantry move being launched in full daylight. A first and a second attack were pressed home, C. R. S. Pitman (27th Punjabis) watching one brigade, making for a redoubt, simply: 'walk steadily to death, never firing a shot, right up to the top of the redoubt, into the redoubt and then all was over . . . then the remnants slowly wended their way back and as they returned on the lower sandy slopes they were mown down by shrapnel'. Pitman's account is followed by description of a remarkable sequel. 'The Turks, sportsmen and gentlemen as they have ever shown themselves to be – collected all our wounded, tended them, placed them on a barge and then floated it down the river to our lines. You can't imagine the Hun doing that, can you?'[46]

It had not been merely in major engagements like that for the Dujailah Redoubt that sustained endeavour had been offered in attempting to break

Siege of Kut: a casualty being brought in. In the background to the left is Townshend's HQ with its laddered observation platform. (Major A. S. Cane)

Kut under siege: the sick parade outside the 4th Field Ambulance HQ. (Major A. S. Cane)

through to Kut. Captain Hodson (7th Gloucesters) with three officers and his Company (at that time reduced to 120 men), was ordered to attack an advanced Turkish picket. Of this he wrote: 'We were practically wiped out, 46 men being killed and the remainder wounded bar about 20, the high percentage of killed is partly due to the fact that the men gallantly charged the picquet which was very strongly held and were riddled with bullets, and part due to the fact that we were shot at all day.' The citation for Hodson's MC award, conferred after this affair, paid more attention to the officer's role than his letter home had revealed. 'He led his company gallantly against a strong Turkish redoubt, being twice wounded, once severely and refused to be brought in till all the wounded round him had been evacuated. This is the fourth occasion on which this officer has been wounded with his company.'[47]

In Kut, food expedients, according to Harry Rich, included sparrow pie and a loathsome mud fish occasionally caught. A sudden rainstorm produced additional flooding which, when drained, left flapping carp which tempted men out in the mudflat between the opposing lines where the 120th Rajputs assisted in the holding of the Woolpress extension of the Kut position across to the right bank of the Tigris. Ingenuity was of course not limited to food or there would have been no mortar made out of a cylinder from a Gnome aero engine, no anti-aircraft machine-gun mounted on a barrel which Heath Robinson would have applauded, and no illuminated rifle grenade which had one gloriously successful firing but so lit up the Woolpress rather then the

Turkish trenches that its use was not continued beyond its startling début. In the imminence of surrender, Rich and the other officers supervised the destruction of ammunition and most of the rifles and then threw their swords, revolvers and personal belongings into the Tigris. The little money in the Regimental Treasure Chest was divided up with the officers and sepoys all benefiting though they did not know how vital their portions would be avoiding starvation on the long journey to internment.

As this is a book on active service soldiering, nothing will be written here of the terrible experience undergone by the Other Ranks of Kut on their march to captivity (nor of the privations of the officers) – in any case nothing less than an attempt at a detailed account could possibly measure up to adequacy in retelling one of the most cruel stories of the war. Let it simply be mentioned here that even those who felt most deeply the personal humiliation of surrender and the enforced acceptance of arrogant alien authority as Turkish troops marched in to Kut in the late morning of 29 April 1916, can never have imagined the extremity of the ordeal which lay ahead. Bombardier F. S. Hudson, a long-serving Regular, was such a man and yet he was never to forget the Turks in Kut with fixed bayonets rooting through the British dugouts and forcing the handing over of wrist-watches and rings.[49]

Recovery from both the loss of Kut and the VI Indian Division and the heavy casualties incurred by the relief operations, took time. It was to be under the direction of a new Commander-in-Chief, General Sir Stanley Maude. Of all his qualities, his concern for thoroughness of preparations, facilitated as it was

In action and under fire, 7 January 1916, the Battle of Sheik Sa'ad, an attempt to break through the Turkish positions barring approach to Kut. Two 1st Battalion, Seaforth Highlanders, held up in their battalion attack, 'dig in for dear life' as the caption on the original photograph relates. (Lieutenant Colonel L. A. Lynden Bell)

No man's land exchange; British and Turkish officers arrange a truce at Sunnaiyat on the Tigris in mid 1916 to swap prisoners. (Major General H. F. E. MacMahon)

by considerable reinforcements in men and *matériel*, stands out as pre-eminently important in the transformation achieved by the turn of the year in the prospect of a successful resumption of the offensive. Base organization at Basra was improved, road and rail developments pressed forward, naval resources and river transport were increased, RFC supply likewise, military equipment arrived almost in abundance and artillery strength was vastly augmented.

The new offensive was launched in mid-December and on 1 February 1917, Cpl Jim Davey (RE) could: 'count the windows in the buildings of Kut' so closely established was his unit for an assault which would efface the shame of the April 1916 surrender. Davey's diary records respect for the Turks yet again proving themselves to be: 'the most capable fighters imaginable even against overwhelming superiority of artillery'. On 13 February, his tribute was repeated. 'We get in every conceivable position around Kut but we've not got it yet.' A few days later, streams of prisoners were brought in. It seemed clear to Davey that Kut must fall. Proudly he wrote 'Truly it has been a red-letter day for the Mesopotamian Expeditionary Force.' He was writing in advance of a coup of pyschological as well as strategic importance and was plainly thrilled by the resources being mounted for the attack – river gunboats, artillery, cavalry, columns of transport and infantry 'continuous for miles on end'.[50]

The defence of Kut provided against both direct and outflanking attack, but by deception it was hoped that the Turks would not deduce that they were to be outflanked by a crossing of the Tigris above Kut at the Shumran Bend. A particularly daring raid on the defences below Kut at Magasis on the night of 22/23 February played its part in focusing Turkish attention upon their positions here when ninety picked men of the 27th Punjabis led by Captain C. R. S. Pitman attempted to cross the Tigris in flood for this enterprise. Only five of the twelve boats made the crossing against the strong current, but Pitman reorganized his reduced force, accomplished his mission, capturing a trench mortar and machine-gun ammunition. The small party of forty men inflicted damage and casualties upon the enemy and suffered but few wounds themselves. In retrospect, another Punjabi officer, D. G. Rule, considered that: 'leading this raid would have daunted all except the very brave'.[51]

When the Shumran Bend crossing took place, it was carried out by Gurkhas and Norfolks. Artillery support here and elsewhere was considerable, but a major operation of this amphibious nature, mounted before dawn, was bound to be difficult to co-ordinate and the recent infantry check at Sannaiyat was a chilling warning against over-confidence.

Sergeant W. G. Gledhill (2nd Norfolks) was in one of the boats ferrying the men upon their dangerous mission. They were dressed in singlet, shorts, stockings, boots and topee, carrying emergency rations, rifle, bayonet, ammunition and a haversack of Mills bombs. Disembarking, they had as silently as possible to scramble up the steep bank to what

△ 1.   ▽ 2.   3. ▷

1. Mesopotamia in late 1916. After a cold night in the desert, officers and men of the 27th Punjabis are astir for breakfast. (Captain C. R. S. Pitman)

2. Hospital riverboats HP3 and HM3 moored in the Shatt el Arab, 1917. (J. Grimshaw)

3. Looking down upon Kut in 1918. Two British officers gaze from the top of a shell-damaged minaret upon the scene of the Indian Army ordeal two years earlier. (Captain R. C. Morton)

must have been an entrenched flood-bank ridge still higher. Complete surprise was achieved by the yell and short rush, the Norfolks taking their immediate objective.[52]

Despite all the careful preparation, which included an imaginative variety of deception ruses, not all went smoothly. Until river gun-boats wrought execution upon the thick column of Turkish troops retiring from Kut, it appeared as if the withdrawal were being carried out more effectively than High Command would have wished. A further matter of more continuing concern was that despite the improvements in facilities for the care of wounded and sick, Mesopotamian circumstances would not be denied. Attendant upon 'The Grim Reaper's' harvest from men being wounded in the new offensive was Pte A. N. Stevenson (RAMC). His

diary of work at the 23rd Stationary Hospital at Amara provides a melancholy catalogue scarcely softened by mechanical notation of weather conditions. '1.2.17 Very fine day. One death. We sew up the body of No. 15282 Pte Cooper T of the 7th North Staffs A Coy. Age 28 years. Died undergoing an operation of secondary haemorhage. Religion C. of E. Hut 11. 2.2.17 Very fine day. We sew up the body of Pte Paton of the A.S.C. Cause of death Secondary Haem. Religion Presbyterian Hut 10. 4.2.17 We sew up the body of Pte Crocker of the 9th Worcesters A Coy. C. of E. Ward A Hut 10. Cause of death Gangrene. Amputated leg as a last hope of saving his life.' Dead men in the mortuary, sewing up men in blankets – this and some boot repair work kept Stevenson busy throughout February to mid-November when he was transferred to hospital ship duties.[53]

The end of March, 1918, and a Light Armoured Motor Battery outside Ana on the Aleppo Road has overtaken Turks in retirement and forced their surrender. In front of the Rolls-Royce armoured car lies a dead Turk. (E. F. Bolton)

Pursuit of the Turks near Haditha in March c. 1918. 'Lewis-gun detachments' of some 150 men, their rifles and thirty Lewis guns transported in fifty Ford vans, assembled in a motorized column. The Turks are not far off; as this photograph was taken, the column was being subjected to shelling. (E. F. Bolton)

When Kut fell, the Turks fell back to such an extent that even with due caution to avoid a repetition of the earlier tragedy, Baghdad was soon threatened. A very difficult crossing of the River Diyala was effected following the magnificent bridgehead holding action of the Loyal North Lancs and then, on 11 March, Baghdad was entered.

'The populace turned out in its thousands to welcome us giving us oranges, dates, water, wine, cigarettes and fancy breads. Really it was a great reception.' Corporal Davey's diary described getting lost in the narrow alleyways when his unit of Engineers had to turn back to find its transport. 'The populace must have thought we were on exhibition for as we went back they simply swarmed over the few of us kissing our faces, hands and sleeves and crying out to us.'[54]

There was still hard campaigning to be undertaken. Pre-eminently the Turks had to be prevented from destroying the flood-water defences of the Euphrates and the Tigris, the conjunction of two Turkish forces had to be prevented and the important rail junction of Sammarah had to be taken. This was effected as a result of a number of engagements most particularly those of Istabulat and Band i Ardhaim in April, but the summer heat broiled away the possibility of more extensive operations – British troops suffering severely before Ramadi in July 1917, some men dying from heat exhaustion.

When the offensive was resumed in September, Ramadi was taken in an operation involving some infantry being transported into battle by van and lorry – truly a herald for the future in an ancient setting. The irreversible course of the campaign after the November battle of Tikrit and the removal of any further fear of major Turkish counter-attack were abundantly established by the British victory at Khan Baghdadi on 26 March 1918.

In a contemporary account, Lieutenant G. P. T. Dean (24th Punjabis) illustrates the way in which superiority in *matériel* for the attack determined the nature of battle experience for the British and Indian participants. 'We marched quickly with only short halts. The road was straight and the night not dark.' At 2.30 a.m. one company from each of the three regiments in the Brigade was sent ahead to storm the first trenches, the rest of the column waiting on the road, listening to the firing develop and then moving forward to take cover behind the reverse slope of hillocks as the Turkish shelling commenced. During a lengthy wait here, news arrived of two lines of trenches which had been secured but of no more success than this. The small scale of the attack deceived the Turks who mounted no counter-attack and in the morning the brigade got into artillery formation to attack across open ground. 'H.E. and shrapnel burst all around our "blobs" of infantry – however the whole regiment advanced perfectly steadily and only a few were knocked out. The Turks evidently got the wind up as soon as they saw us all in the open and started their retiring action. . . . The advance was taking place on the right bank of the Euphrates on a front of about one mile – the country was flat as usual, but very much cut up by the deep nullahs and steep hillocks. The Turks had by now been driven back to their strong position, along a steep rising range of hills. From 1 p.m. onwards my company was lying on the cliff at the river side and overlooking the Turks who were retiring along the road – we kept up fire with Lewis guns.'

At 4 p.m. the attack was renewed as the men prepared to advance again in artillery formation but this time 'under a splendid barrage of our guns and machine-guns – the Turk evidently kept his head down and I don't blame him – it was a continuous roar of shells and bullets over our heads and smashing against the Turks – one felt absolutely safe under this barrage. Then the barrage lifted and the infantry advanced rapidly with fixed bayonets. The Turks had given in and prisoners were secured in masses. . . . We did not come to a halt until dark . . . aeroplanes brought us news that the Turks had thrown their hand in – the infantry's job was over . . . [but] the show was not yet finished and the cavalry brigade, Light Armoured Motor Batteries and a company of infantry in Ford cars carried on the pursuit.'[55] When the Turkish GOC was captured and under escort by Captain L. W. Jardine, he spoke (in French) of his defeat being due to inferiority in motors to which Jardine added in his account that in fact: 'We have superiority in everything.'[56]

The final engagement of the Mesopotamian campaign was fought at Shargat on 26 October 1918 about 130 miles north of Baghdad. The strongly defended Fathah gorge position, barring further progress through the cleft in the mountains cut by the Tigris, was outflanked by a cavalry brigade movement and the Turks withdrew to make a stand at Shargat at the confluence of the Rivers Zab and Tigris. Lieutenant Kenneth O'Connor was in command of 'D' Company of the 14th Sikhs, faced with the unenviable task of advancing through the flat scrubland terrain between the river and the Turkish trenches dug in the low hills. The scrub (2 to 3 feet high) was too dense to see and fire through, and also too thick for an attack at the double so there was no alternative to a steady walk forward as they were being fired upon. In extended order, the lines of Sikhs did exactly that. 'Many bullets found their marks and our men began to fall. I heartily wished it were possible for sections to lie down and give covering fire to other sections running forward as we had been taught. A dry river bed was crossed at the double but this nullah was enfiladed by machine-gun fire. Our men began to fall thickly. I waved them on, running forward myself. We were more than halfway across when suddenly I felt a blow like a kick of a mule in the stomach. It knocked me over. Picking myself up I went forward again leading a sadly diminished line. It was then obvious that the attack would fail. I was hit again, more than once, notably in the left thigh. The lines of our men were simply melting away.' O'Connor's misfortune was not total. He was wearing a souvenired Turkish army belt as well as his own and the bullet which had struck him in the stomach had first hit his Sam Browne belt buckle, gone through it and the crossed-over leathers, then the Turkish buckle and through two layers of Turkish leather, shirt and singlet, simply to lodge in the skin of his stomach from which it could be thereupon extracted. His thigh wound was serious, right through the leg, leaving a large exit wound bleeding profusely. He strapped on his field dressing pad to the exit wound and tied the bandage as tightly as possible.

The Sikh officer had no water as a bullet hole had drained his water bottle. He had not the strength to open his iron rations, but he had the presence of mind to sham death to deter a rescue attempt by two Sikhs, an attempt which would almost certainly have resulted in pointless tragedy. 'I heard much later that it was first the absence of any movement by me and second the improbability of a British officer lying in the open with his breeches down and his bottom uncovered, unless he were dead, which had convinced them that I must indeed be dead.'

In the afternoon and in the absence of further enemy machine-gun fire, O'Connor slid down the salvation of the bank of the nullah and started to drag himself back across its stony bed. Somehow he made his way to an Aid Post after a three-hour ordeal. He lay outside the surgeon's hut awaiting his turn and was accosted by a jovial Irish RC priest who asked his name, and, perhaps encouraged by its Celtic ring, offered him tea, cocoa or soup. O'Connor answered that anything would be welcome then adding with remarkable concern for precision in spiritual terms: 'But I am not of your faith Father.' The priest went off and: 'I never saw tea, cocoa or soup.'[57]

A heavy price in casualties had been paid for this final retirement forced upon the Turks. An armistice was soon to halt the pursuit and for the Mesopotamian front there remains but a need to pay reference to a military mission which had been undertaken into Persia in 1916 and then to the more celebrated (or notorious) Dunsterforce venture and the associated extensions of an attempt to maintain a military presence in northern Persia – the Malleson Mission and Norperforce.

Clearly the whole Mesopotamian front was at risk if a serious threat were to emerge from Persia. Such a threat appeared through factors internal to Persia and Persian perceptions of alien influence in their country whether Russian, German, Turkish or British as well as from direct German diplomatic and agent machinations. Sir John Nixon had launched one punitive raid against Persian Tangistani tribesmen, but anti-British disturbances continued and in 1916 a mission to exert both diplomatic and military pressure was despatched under the Command of Brigadier General Sir Percy Sykes.

Sykes's force of British and Indian troops covered mile upon mile in Persia recruiting local men to its strength and attempting to establish the rule of law and punishing those who engaged in unlawful activity. Good discipline within the force served the purpose of diplomacy. A British officer, J. Le C. Fowle, recorded that Sir Percy: 'looks upon it as a great triumph of this march of ours that the people have all stayed in their villages and camps. When the Persian army passes they gather all their belongings together and fly to the hills, knowing that if they stay they will be forced to feed the soldiers free and will probably be looted of anything they possess.'

On one occasion in pursuit of a marauding band, a squadron of the force created by the Mission, the South Persian Rifles, covered 456 miles in sixteen days, for fourteen of those days living off the country. There were times when progress was far slower as when travelling through mountain gorges encouraging the rebellious donkeys and errant camels upon which the column depended for its supplies. There was often anxiety about flash flooding or sniping from the top of the cliff walls which enclosed them. Fowle's diary is eloquent upon the camels, 'the most hopeless set of untrained vicious "bud mashes" one could find anywhere',

Dispatch rider in Persia: Corporal G. R. Wilson Knight on his Douglas motorcycle at Kasvin, 1919. (Professor G. R. Wilson Knight)

getting excited, throwing their loads and charging off. Of course at times of unloading and loading, these particular camels fought, lay down or loped off to graze. Unfortunately for Fowle, commanding a rearguard on an occasion when the camels were especially recalcitrant, he had less than confidence in the co-operation of the two native camel drivers, one 'an old and decrepit idiot and the other a young and half witted maniac'. Journey's end sometimes brought its compensations like the ceremonial banquet at Kerman where the Persian Governor's hospitality was accompanied by Cognac, then the local wine was followed by whisky and soda and the proceedings were concluded with champagne.[58]

The work of the Sykes Mission and its offspring, the South Persian Rifles, continued and an officer with a battalion of Baluchis (3/124th) attached to the Mission in 1918 was involved in quelling the hostility of a confederation of Quashai tribesmen but also in the tragic consequence of mutiny by Persians in the ranks of the South Persian Rifles. The officer, John Teague, recalled that about twenty SPR men were sentenced to be shot for mutiny and killing their British officers. 'The firing party was purposely drawn from the culprits' own unit but because it was feared that the firing party itself might refuse to shoot or perhaps to fire low, the Indian garrison was ordered to surround the scene ready for action against the executioners if necessary. In the event Indian troops were not called upon to act but the distressing sight of several men being put to death in cold blood had a profound effect upon many and for myself a clear and sad memory to this day.'[59]

A bigger undertaking than the Sykes Mission was that of the Dunsterforce Expedition in 1918 bound for northern Persia and beyond with the lofty aspiration of assisting Armenians, Georgians and Azerbaijanis collaborate in the expulsion of the Turk, the creation of a 'bloc sanitaire' against Bolshevism and to build within this entity a military defence capacity against German, Turk, or Bolshevik aggression. In so doing, both the oil of Baku and the security of the North West Frontier of India would be ensured. Somehow the concept developed without a sufficient relationship to its geographical setting and for those in the Force, if there were to have been any sense of adventure and mission, it would diminish with a closer grasp of daily reality.

The 9th Warwicks was one of the units in Dunsterforce and its movement into northern Persia was completed by train to Ruz, by lorry to Hamadan and then on foot over three mountain ranges 152 miles to Kasvin. According to the diary of one officer, the halt and the lame completed their march on donkey back, earning their subsection the sobriquet, the Warwickshire Light Horse.[60] Ford vans then transported them forward until Enzeli was reached at the southern end of the Caspian. The final stage of their journey was by boat to Baku. The Turks threatened this city of Armenians and Russians, the latter being bewilderingly divided between those who did not support the Bolshevik revolution and those who supported it in differing and conflicting degrees. The Warwicks, with local units and two other British regiments, were to defend the city, the officers' bonus of local supplies of caviar being inadequate compensation for the difficulty of their task. Lieutenant Colonel John Haigh of the Warwicks has recalled that: 'at this time the Turkish Army was estimated to be some 30,000 and we never had more than 1,000 ranks of our Brigade and a quite unknown number of Armenian and Russian soldiers who were sandwiched between our units but we never knew if they were on the ground or not as they went into the town with their arms as they wished. On 1 September the Turks attacked our line at Digya our allies on both flanks fell back and just short of 100 ranks, including the M.O. and three other officers were captured.' A fortnight later the attack was renewed and a necessary but undignified withdrawal and shipboard evacuation of Baku were forced on the British Brigade. Haigh's diary makes no bones about the precipitate nature of the escape. '5 p.m. received orders that British would withdraw to town at dusk and evacuate town. 8.45 Bde with 18 pounder battery and several Dunster officers commenced to march into town prepared for street fighting, arriving docks about 9.30 p.m. Went almost straight onto three boats, Ford cars, armoured cars, aeroplanes, etc., were destroyed or thrown into the sea. Our boat commenced to leave about midnight with all Lewis guns mounted. Found all kits had been left behind.'[61] It was not just the Turks but also the Bolsheviks in the Soviet of Baku from whom they had escaped.

Dunsterforce as such was dead, but the Warwicks were to be transferred to what was geographically and militarily the nearest equivalent to such an ad hoc force, 'Malmiss', that is the Mission of General Malleson in north-east Persia and Transcaspia where localized hostility to the British was compounded by the danger of the Bolshevik bacillus spreading down the capillary branch of the Trans-Siberian Railway with its terminus on the eastern shores of the Caspian at Krasnovodsk. There were to be no Baku-type alarms, only the silent solitude of the Steppes – 'great undulated tracks of dull barren country just covered with dried camel thorn and nothing else' was the description left by Sir Ernest Goodale who passed the last days of the war after the Turkish surrender supervising the return of Armenian refugees to Baku.[62] In fact, other British units had been in action in this area and there had been an incident of serious political implications. Twenty-six Bolshevik Commissars, who had fled from Baku by boat, were handed over by the British military reception committee to the Mensheviks of the Krasnovodsk Soviet and the Mensheviks summarily executed their political foes. One of Malleson's staff officers has strongly denied British complicity in the execution, but whatever the facts of the matter, truth dies first on the threshold of a Civil War. A despatch from Malleson indicates the peculiar savagery with which such wars are conducted, British and Indians involved in engagements where idological commitment and not Geneva convention held sway. 'Our detachment received orders to make a large detour round the enemy forces with the object of destroying the enemy in Dushakh. . . . Enemy seeing his hopeless position blew up his ammunition dumps. At Dushakh Station seven trains were captured, the eighth retiring to Takir was stopped by our artillery fire and being surrounded by Turkomans the enemy in the train 300 in number, were killed. When Dushakh was taken the Bolsheviks left alive fled to the hills, but by our earlier dispositions they were met by Indian cavalry and every man was destroyed.'[63] A World War might be ending but a Civil War, on a grand and terrible scale, was well established.

Among the five dispatch riders serving communications at Kasvin for HQ Norperforce was Corporal G. Wilson-Knight. Kasvin was at about 4,000 feet above sea level, a cosmopolitan mixture of East and West, a natural staging-point between Tehran and the Caspian. The dispatch riders' roads were of loose stones and jagged flints, ruts, gulleys, and dust but the motor cycles were Triumphs in good condition, more strongly built than the Douglases, with greater horse-power, ideal for the Persian steppes. Local hazards were the scavenging pariah dogs, the crossing of water courses and of course breakdowns, running out of petrol and the all-too-frequent punctures. For all this, the Tehran run was still popular, a day in the city being allowed. Precise destination was the Telegraph Company whose employees led a civilized way of life which seemed irresistibly attractive to Wilson-Knight – swimming in the Legation's lake, luxurious meals in their bungalow, tea in cups and saucers, a trellised garden, superb wall-hung carpets. It has to be stated that this cultured dispatch rider who was completely captivated by Persia, finding a sensual as well as intellectual pleasure in its antiquity, was no typical soldier. Would any other dispatch rider as a 'profes-

sional traveller' have shown such understanding as to write after a perceptive generalized description of Persian towns or villages that the: 'Persian garden is a concentration of the Persian town, itself conceived as a rest place for the dust-caked traveller from the long roads.'

This particular dispatch rider was to be in the vanguard of those whose personal horizon was widened and enriched by surviving his 1914-18 service overseas; in varied degree behind him, stood every soldier who returned to British or Imperial shores. By no means was the unquestionable tragedy of war always the nadir of barrenness for the individual.'[64]

EGYPT AND PALESTINE

It scarcely need be stated that protection of the Suez Canal was the reason for there being a British garrison in Egypt at the outbreak of war. The garrison was hugely expanded and a campaign, indeed campaigns, developed from this and other reasons. First, Egypt was an obvious journey-breaking point for Australasian and Indian troops 'en route for the war'. Then, too, Egypt was to some extent geographically suitable as a spring-board for launching and maintaining the Gallipoli and Macedonian campaigns. Also, an enemy threat could be exerted directly upon the British position in Egypt. With regard to the Turkish element of that threat, that is attack on Suez from the east, the need to defeat the threat was obvious and a campaign developed out of this, but it also developed from a perceived need for victory here on grounds of both Grand Strategy and public morale and from the complex problematic germination of Imperial ambition in the area.

In the simplest of terms, soldiers for whom

Mechanized warfare in the Western Desert. Two mechanics and their responsibility from No. 2 Light Car Patrol, Western Frontier Force. Note the 'fore and aft' machine-gun mountings. (Major General G. W. Richards)

Alexandria or Port Said were destinations and not staging-posts, would be in Egypt to defend the Canal, maintain a military presence and train to fit themselves for war in the Middle East. Some would be required for service to the west against the hostile Senussi tribesmen, a tiny number would travel south, up the Nile to deal with the rebellious Sultan of Darfur and many would be committed to the advance across the Sinai Desert, the battles at Gaza and Beersheba to break through into Palestine and to the campaign there. Finally small numbers would find themselves in a supporting relationship to Arabs in revolt against their Turkish overlords.

For soldiers in Egypt, to set against the heat and the sand and the exhaustion from route marches or military exercises in the desert, there were compensations – sea bathing and sports, sight-seeing, from bazaars to the Sphinx, Anglicized, oriental and universal entertainment ranging from cinema shows, cafés, the zoo, bawdy shows and brothels. Australian trooper, Maurice Evans, clearly took Egypt in his stride. On arrival in Cairo in December 1914 after a cattle-truck journey from Alexandria and an eight-mile march to their camp at Ma'adi: 'We pitched the tents and unloaded stores and fodder and when bedtime came we were not sorry.' Leave was granted for the next day. Armed with an issue of pay, the deferment of some of which he accepted because he considered that many of his fellows: 'don't know how to behave themselves when they have money', he enjoyed the luxury of a hot bath in Cairo, his first since leaving Kyogle in Australia. He was not alone in finding it frustrating that he had to be back in camp by 10.30 and 'nothing starts here until 9.30' and he did not rush off to see the Pyramids from close quarters as: 'it is such an obvious thing to do that I don't care about it'. One Egyptian charm to which he did succumb was a dinner – a Christmas dinner in fact – in a café on the banks of the Nile. 'Large Palm trees on the opposite bank behind which the sun sets red, the Pyramids striking up a little to the right lower down the bank and a perfect stillness reigning over everything. One does not spend a bad existence here.'

Just before Christmas the Australians took part in a march-past in Cairo. From horseback: 'the Egyptians in their red fez caps make an awfully pretty sight like a gigantic flower garden'. Evans clearly enjoyed an AIF gymkhana and a symphony concert despite the fact that the music was Russian and he would have preferred German but I: 'don't believe they will play Wagner now because of the war – which I think is ridiculous for surely he can be regarded as international now'.

There was of course military activity too in the form of a 'four days' route march interspersed with field days' but by early March he was: 'getting very tired of Egypt from a Private's point of view. This part of the year it resolves itself into an endless round of sandstorms and what are known as "khamsins" which are periods usually of 3 days of extreme dry heat and hot winds which plus sand are distinctly unpleasant.'[65]

A New Zealand trooper, Ken Stephens, remembered in particular the Saturday popularity for soldiers of the Gezirah racecourse, but of losing so much money that he and his fellow trooper could not summon up the trainfare back to Zeitoun camp six miles away. His diary prosaically catalogues less memorable activities of church parades, exercising horses, marches, sham fights and drills.[66]

From Mena camp it was but a stroll to the Pyramids and on 10 January 1915 Private A. E. Joyce (9th Bn, AIF): 'went up to the Sphinx to get our photos but on account of the crowd we had to wait too long'. Not unnaturally it is difficult to find an original account from someone who availed himself of the pleasures of the red light district. Joyce was taken to the: 'dreadful spot known as the Wassar Bazaar which is beyond description. Hundreds of women of all nationalities on the globe dancing around one, or sat at the door of their hovels smoking eating or chanting to the horrid music of the Arabs who parade up and down the filthy alleys trying to sell sham antiques and anything imaginable. It is a sight one could never tolerate at home in a British city and I was jolly glad when we found ourselves out in the streets again.'[67]

On the day Private C. J. Walsh (1st Auckland Bn, NZEF) chose to sightsee, Good Friday, after attending Mass in the little Chapel at Zeitoun Camp, 'we heard there was a riot on in the Rue el Berka so we went down to see it'. He was actually to see the notorious 'Battle of the Wassar'. 'Some of the boys were busy throwing all sorts of gear out of the windows. Beds, sofas, chairs, washing stands, chests of drawers, petticoats and all the gear movable came bumping out of the fourth storey windows. Those below were also diligently engaged in collecting all this gear and piling it on the fires they had built. The fire brigade came and tried to put the fire out but they were powerless. Then the Red Caps came along and tried to chase the crowd away but they refused to go away. There was some unpleasantness and the Red Caps drew their revolvers and fired on the crowd killing two and wounding several. The crowd then chased them and afterwards they called out the Westminster Dragoons. They took things fairly

192

quietly after a while and all the crowd dispersed.'[68]

It had been an ugly scene as is the nature of a riot whatever its cause and an Australian Artillery Sergeant showed his awareness that: 'it will get us a bad name all over the world'.[69] Sergeant Clennett added quite reasonably that the men had been: 'bottled up here so long and were rather excited at the prospect of getting away – still that does not excuse them' and he was not the only Australian to find regrettable the conduct of some of his fellows. Sapper Grove listed in his diary: 'My impression of the behaviour of our Troops' and among his charges were that he had seen: 'Niggers beaten for oranges and chocolate because they would not bring prices down. In Mehemet Ali mosque there are lads who enter with their hats on, also break the glass and take it from the great lamp overhead. They have no idea of sacredness in regard to fine buildings. A lot of them are pigheaded with regard to fares on the trains.'[70] It might fairly be added here that for a short time British troops in Palestine were successful in passing off to Arabs, Chivers jam tin paper labels and those on condensed milk tins too, as £1 notes – the Chivers signature certainly seeming to help in the case of the jam!

When the British troops in Egypt were first brought into action it was in defence of the Suez Canal – a very slight engagement though the threat to the security of operating the canal was real and the achievement of the Turkish troops in crossing the Sinai Desert with their pontoons should certainly be acknowledged. In the first ten days of February 1915, the Canal between Tussum and Serapeum and then the Ismailia Ferry post came under threat. In one particular case Turkish surprise was lost by the noise of Arab Irregulars calling upon Allah and encouraging one and all of the attackers to die for the faith. Sergeant A. G. Jennings (1st Bn. Wellington Regt, NZEF) described in his diary going out with a composite force into the desert in front of the fortified posts defending the Canal. 'We marched 7 or 8 miles across to the hills where the enemy are and after about 6 miles march they opened fire on us. When the bullets came pinging over us not a man got in the least excited but went on as though we were doing manoeuvres in N.Z.' Then the artillery unit with the composite forces shelled the Turks and the infantry advanced again – halting at the last ridge from which they could: 'see the Turks plainly and after a while they retreated'.[71] Altogether it had not been an affair of any distinction though at other points attacks and actual pontoon boat crossings of the canal were attempted. Some Indian Army units inflicted casualties and suffered a small number, but

there is splendidly encouraging fantasy in the contemporary account of another New Zealander who wrote that following Turkish abuse of a white flag and the shooting of a Gurkha officer: 'the Gurkhas became incensed with rage and charged with their knives, beheading over five hundred of their enemy.'[72] As it happens the Gurkhas were not involved at all in that particular incident.

It was from the Western Desert that the next threat came. The Turks and Germans were trying to bring support to the warlike Senussi who were already engaged against Italian forces in North Africa and whose elusiveness raised a twin nightmare of a serious reverse in attempting to deal with them and secondly of inflaming into military reality rather than nominal declaration a Holy War against the infidel.

Despite British diplomatic efforts to forestall the need to campaign against the Senussi, the attacks of the latter upon Egyptian Western Desert defence posts and the fortified port of Sollum (the forced evacuation of which opened up the way for German shipborne supplies to the Senussi) were sufficient in themselves to frustrate hope of avoiding war. The danger to peace was compounded into disaster by the Commanders of German submarines handing over prisoners from two Merchant Navy sinkings into the not noteworthily tender care of the desert tribesmen.

In late November 1915, the Western Frontier Force was formed. Its detached columns progressively wore down the Senussi but without any decisive rout. In February, however, a celebrated cavalry charge by the Dorset Yeomanry cut off the tribesmen's retreat after being brought to battle at Agagiya. This secured the capture of the military commander of the enemy and the re-occupation of Sollum. One hundred and eighty of the Dorsets took part in the charge, five officers and twenty-six other ranks losing their lives and eighty-five horses being killed or recorded as missing. What Mark Ward remembers most clearly about the affair is the determination of his Colonel in a pep talk to officers and NCOs the previous day that the Dorset's reputation must be made as they had performed so far without honour. Ward himself admitted that he had played little part in refurbishing the regiment's record because his horse had not fully recovered from a December wound – this and its fear of machine-guns led to his being a straggler with the laurels of victory earned by those in the forefront.

Throughout the campaign there was the irony that seldom were the troops very far from the sea, but quite desperate on occasion was the shortage of water for drinking. In this connection the former Corporal

△ 1.

△ 1.

△ 2.   ▽ 3.

△ 2.   ▽ 3.

1. 1916, with the Western Frontier Force: A Westminster Dragoon shepherds in Senussi prisoners. (A. H. Bird)

2. The railway station at Mudawarra on the Damascus–Medina line was raided by the Hejaz Assault Column of the Imperial Camel Corps in August 1918 in order to disrupt Turkish communications. The raiders blew up the station buildings, including the pumping installation pictured here, and no further trains passed through. (L. Moore)

3. A Scot in the Sinai. Private Johnnie Houston has managed to construct a 'bivvy' for some shade from the sun. He is an experienced soldier (1/3rd, Lowland Field Ambulance) and he is only sixteen years old. At fifteen he had survived the torpedoing of HM Transport *Royal Edward* in the Mediterranean; he had then served in the Gallipoli campaign and is now getting accustomed to the sand and rock of the Sinai. (J. Houston)

1. The Sudan and the pursuit of the Sultan of Darfur. Model T. Fords are here being used as reconnaissance cars at El Fasher, July 1916. (Sir Angus Gillan)

2. Casualty in a camel-borne 'cacoulet', a paired stretcher framework harnessed in place each side of a camel to allow transportation of wounded – two cases lying or two seated. The natural gait of a camel was not conducive to comfort for men in a cacoulet, least of all for those with shattered bones, conscious and perhaps without morphia. (A. Weekes)

3. Dispensers of the famous No. 9 Pill: Corporal Lindsay and Private Jones of the RAMC rest in the marquee where they are accustomed to distributing the 'purgative pill of the day, the No. 9'. (H. O. Bigg)

Ward relates a memory which gives rise to an immediate reaction and then a second thought which points in a different direction, one perhaps with more understanding of the period. Ward was serving as a mounted messenger to the new Commander of the Western Frontier Force, Major General W. E. Peyton. 'One day we were parched with thirst having not had a drink that day, we stopped an hour or two in the middle of the day and the General and his staff decided to have their lunch. His batman produced a collapsible table complete with white cloth and laid the table with bottles of beer, a bottle of whisky and a siphon of soda. However he was a good general and we all liked him.'

Despite thirst and despite food being exceedingly limited in amount and kind (1 tin bully beef and 4 biscuits each day): 'We were very healthy on this front. I have since thought it was because of being on fresh ground every day. When stopping for the night a long rope was pegged to the ground and the horses unsaddled and tied to it. We slept in our clothes with boots and haversack as a pillow covered by our overcoats and one blanket. The nights were cold.' It was even more demanding on the horses although, as they failed, the men walked long distances to husband their strength. Corn and short bits of straw (tibben) were no substitute for the fodder to which English horses were accustomed and they collapsed first – Ward's having to be despatched in the desert, a long way from Dorchester where the poor beast had been requisitioned.[73]

Pursuit of the Senussi and rescuing the Merchant Navy captives were successfully undertaken by the Duke of Westminster's Armoured Cars while the light cars and the newly formed Imperial Camel Corps patrolled and secured the remainder of the desert – a brilliant light car raid on the enemy stronghold of Siwa effectively ending the campaign in February 1917.

G. W. Richards was with the six Model T Ford cars of the No. 2 Light Car Patrol. Four of the cars were armed with Lewis guns and two were for baggage. Carrying fuel, water, food and ammunition, the cars usually did about 80 to 100 miles a day on six-day patrols. There were no maps. Navigation was by compass and sundial, communications with base were by homing pigeons and between cars by flag signals and helio. Each patrol had its own tyre-tread enabling the tracking of a lost car and: 'the golden rule was to stop immediately one considered one was lost and wait, sometimes for days, before a relief patrol came from base'. The single native tracker employed by each patrol was not for the purpose of locating lost cars but for the interpretation of camel tracks.[74]

Far to the south of these operations a further threat had to be dealt with, that of the Sudanese rebellion of Ali Dinar, the Sultan of Darfur. The part played by the detached flight of the RFC in this operation is quite well known, but it was in support of a military column proceeding in May 1916 towards the focus of the rebellion, El Fasher, the Sultan's capital.

Ali Dinar's men attempted to entrench themselves on the reverse slope of sand dunes fronting the road along which the column would have to travel as it approached the village of Beringia en route for El Fasher. Imperial Camel Corps troops reconnoitering the route were fired on and withdrew whereupon the Sudanese rebels unwisely left their prepared positions and charged the somewhat hastily entrenched British square for which the Camel Corps had been but a skirmishing advanced guard. The native troops charged on foot with great bravery, inspired one presumes by their spiritual faith, and

Gullies in front of Gaza, 1917. A characteristic wadi could offer, as here for the 6th Battalion, Highland Light Infantry, a covered communication way and a safe assembly point, but when they ran across the direction of an attack, serious problems were posed. (Captain T. M. MacQuaker)

they were met by a hail of fire from mountain battery field guns, Maxim machine-guns and rifles – five hundred were killed and an unknown number wounded. The British, who had lost five men killed or mortally wounded, then advanced against the broken enemy and continued their progress to El Fasher. That night they camped in their defensive square, dealt with a further assault at dawn and entered the Sultan's capital without opposition later in the morning. Any real danger from the rebellion was now over and with Egypt and its borders secure from west and south, the question of removing all threat from the east, the Sinai Desert, could be tackled.[75]

The first advance into the Sinai had met with a serious reverse when the Turks had struck at the unsecured British forces at Oghratina and Qatiya, overrunning both posts in April 1916. Plainly there was still a threat to the Canal. The Sinai, desert avenue between Egypt and Palestine, would have to be contested. The trial of strength came at the battle of Romani, an oasis position held by the British and attacked by the Turks at the beginning of August. A British victory here would kill any further danger to Suez and allow for a prepared advance towards Palestine. As Turkish approach to the Romani position would be behind the shelter of sand dunes, it was judged that 3-inch Stokes mortars could form an important element in defence. P. G. Sneath was one of two officers and four NCOs running a Mortar school course at Zeitoun. In the emergency of the Turkish thrust, these men were ordered to bring four Stokes mortars and all available ammunition to 52nd Divisional HQ en route for Romani. 'How the guns were to be manned no one seemed to know but five men would be needed for each gun. It was work for trained men as such men could keep up a rate of twenty rounds per minute with the 10lb 11oz rounds.'

Sneath was sent up to Romani to command the mortars which were to be emplaced in four detached posts on the defensive perimeter. Getting the guns and ammunition by camel from the Romani rail head to the posts, was an exhausting business. 'It was very hot, 110° in the shade of which there was none and an almost unbearable stench from the camel transport.' When the rail unloading and camel loading was done, there was then a trudge behind the camels several miles in ankle-deep sand to the respective posts and in Sneath's case the difficult job of entrenching in the sand was only half completed. From a central command post, communication ways were dug to the oval perimeter and this was dug with traverses and fire step and then twenty yards beyond

there was continuous barbed wire entanglement from which an apron fence of barbed wire ran off to the left and right adjacent posts. A Vickers gun flanked the approach to the left, a Lewis gun to the right. All revetment was by matchboard sheeting nailed to three 2-inch x 2-inch timber uprights – anchoring of these hurdles was by wiring the protruding stakes at the top to the sandbags of parapet or parados. An attempt to prevent the sand seeping through the hessian mesh of the sandbags was made by spraying the sandbags with salt water from the nearest salt pan.

An unwilling horse, reluctant to come within scent of camel, gave moderate assistance to Sneath who supervised the Stokes emplacement at the four favoured posts and then in hurried days he organized training for those men who seemed most suitable from the nominal rolls he was given of the garrison of the posts. There was the problem of a missing clinometer (essential for calculating range through angle of fire) and there were also deficiencies in lamps, periscope sights and ammunition. Dummy round firing for training was sanctioned, fuzes were cut and prepared, a detonator crimped to the fuze and then fuze and detonator inserted in the bomb and the release mechanism screwed on. Sneath had arrived at Romani on 27 July and the Turks commenced the shelling of his post on 5 August. It must have appeared to the Trench Mortar Officer that he had had barely sufficient time.

In the battle, the conspicuous posts came in for Turkish shrapnel shelling which was accurate for range but burst too high to be effective. What caused a particular problem was dismounted Australian Light Horse taking up positions masking the fire of the posts' machine-guns. When they were asked to move by the officer in command of the post; 'he got a rude reply, and promptly ordered our Vickers gun to fire low over their heads. This had the desired effect. They got back through our wire under covering fire from both posts and as far as I could see suffered no casualties. Here they found what cover they could and lay out there all day in the sweltering sun. They had discarded all their equipment except cloth bandoliers of ammunition, had cut their riding breeches down to make abbreviated shorts and taken the sleeves out of their shirts and thrown away their puttees and leggings. They appeared to have no water-bottles or rations.'

The effectiveness of the enemy HE shelling seems to have been lost in the sand, and the shelling from monitors off the coast was catching the Turks hiding in the troughs of the sand dunes which obscured them from the British land-based defenders.

The band of the 6th Battalion, Highland Light Infantry plays the regimental march 'Scotland the Brave' as the Battalion toils through the desert scrub near Gaza, May 1917. The donor of this photograph annotated it 'Our Pipers never failed us.' (Captain T. M. MacQuaker)

On the morning of the 6th, an Australian Light Horse patrol approached the post shepherding a batch of prisoners. Closer scrutiny of the dunes revealed Turks throwing down their rifles, holding up their hands and waving white flags. They were being rounded up like sheep. The battle had been won and Sneath had to face the ironic fact that his mortar teams had indeed been under heavy shell-fire but, as he had to enumerate in his report, had suffered no damage to their guns, suffered no casualties, had no recommendations for mention in dispatches and had expended no ammunition. 'In no case had the enemy collected in numbers in the dead ground which it was our task to clear.'[76]

Even though the Turks were skilfully withdrawn from the battle, Romani had been a considerable victory. The enemy had been pursued off the field, had incurred losses approaching 6,000 in killed, wounded and missing and a great deal of war booty. Later in the year, after progress had been made in piping water, laying both a rail link and a wire road across the desert to facilitate attack, nibbling progress forced the Turks back to defend an obvious strategic objective, Gaza and the road linking it inland to Beersheba.

In their retirement, the Turks had a defensive position in the Wadi el Arish at Magdhaba in December 1916 and one of the mounted units which stormed that position was a company of the Imperial Camel Corps. Though it had antecedents, the Corps had been formed in that year and volunteers from the Australian Light Horse, New Zealand Mounted Rifles and British Yeomanry regiments had been trained at the Camel Corps School outside Cairo. The Regiment had served with credit in the Western Desert and was to match this with good work in the Sinai, particularly at Maghdaba, and with further distinction in Palestine. In the Hejaz, too, supporting the Arab revolt, a small ICC detachment acted as a real thorn in the Turkish flank. Liaison with Colonel T. E. Lawrence, as might be expected,

formed part of this work, and the surprise raid upon Mudawara in October 1918 was an exploit recalled with relish by those who took part. Well might the officer in command of the ICC unit co-operating with Lawrence write in his diary: 'I have covered nine hundred and twenty-five miles in forty-one days. I really believe that I have worried the Turk no end: I have been right on his lines of communication and he never knew where I was turning up next. It is a fine thing to have at last taught General Headquarters the right use of Camel Corps in this country.'[77]

One of the Cameliers, Chris Dawson, was the signaller attached to the officer leading the raid. Having left their camels, the first part of a stealthy night approach to the railway station was essayed following previously laid white tape and then by compass bearing on to the railway line itself. The billet for the garrison was surrounded, but the sleeping Turks had been warned by one of their number racing to join them from his slit trench sentry post. Fire was directed upon the billet and was returned, hand-grenades likewise, the good length of spluttering fuze on the Turkish pear-shaped bombs enabling some to be picked up and returned or thrown out of harm's way. The Turks surrendered and other buildings were taken by hand-grenade attack if surrender were not quickly to be forthcoming. A separate redoubt required short rushes before this final position was surrendered and the station buildings could then be systematically blown up.[78]

To return to the experience of men committed in the attempt to break through into Palestine, we must look first at the two defeats at Gaza in March and April 1917 because they were the first full-scale battles in which the Eastern Force was involved. In essence, the force commander had insufficient troops confidently to contemplate an approach across a deep wadi, up through hedges of cactus then an otherwise bare glacis-like slope to the ridges commanding the city of Gaza. It was a formidable objective now under reinforced defence.

What happened to one infantry battalion, the 2/10th Middlesex, may be taken as representative of both the physical endurance required from the infantry and then of the depression of enforced withdrawal after such endeavour. '26 March. We marched for what seemed miles as there was a bad mist and it was bitterly cold. (We crossed the Wadi and moved on in artillery formation.) We couldn't see more than 6 yards in front of us as the mist was still very bad. (We followed the Sussex who occupied the Sheluf heights without opposition) and here we had a long halt to enable the other brigades to complete their outflanking approach. Our objective was the Labyrinth, a maze of entrenched gardens which we had to approach from an angle and without knowing anything about this particular objective. As soon as we moved off we got very heavily shelled – the shells were bursting beautifully and nearly every shell seemed to find its mark. It was finer than any parade I have ever seen – our men extended as they went over the ridge and went straight on never halting for an instant. They were wonderful. We reached our objective about 1.30 – how we got there I don't know. The ground was terribly treacherous, deep chasms running parallel to our line of advance. As soon as our men came out of these they were shelled most terribly. (The Sussex were forced to retire and the Middlesex were left without support on either flank.)

3.30 – 4.30 p.m. We were growing weak through want of water or food. It was very hot. Urgent appeals were sent for water, ammunition and reinforcements. (Two companies of the Queen's reinforced the Middlesex, one on each flank). We knew night was coming on and that we had to hold on. Wounded were lying all round and we had no chance of getting them away. Any further advance was impossible and we were suffering from a machine-gun hidden in the cultivation on our left flank.'

No water arrived, no major reinforcement and the diarist, D. B. Watson, learned by ill-chance that his brother has been killed. 'I was feeling nearly done but God gave me strength to carry on.' Not long before midnight, orders were received to withdraw and the Middlesex retired, men being detailed to carry off the wounded, there being no stretchers for this purpose. Having moved back to a fresh position, Watson walked back another 2½ miles to the Wadi to see if there were any rations or camels carrying water. There were no such signs and this was depressing news to carry back to the men.

'11 a.m. We had to advance again and cover the withdrawal of the 2/4th Queen's. Then we went forward again, how I got forward I never knew, my feet were raw and I could just hobble along.' Twice more movements were called for before the men got rations and water and then the whole line retired to the original starting-points.[79]

Ironically the exhausted, parched infantry had been ordered to concede positions virtually won. The reasoning of the High Command was that the outflanking move of the cavalry was threatened by their fatigue and lack of water and the fact that the Turks were bringing up reinforcements. A narrow margin of defeat could not conceal a major reverse and more decisive still was the defeat when a less sophisticated plan was attempted from 17th April of assaulting Gaza frontally and with no attempt at envelopment.

British bombardment, which included the use of gas, before the infantry were called upon to attack Gaza for the second time, had not silenced the Turkish artillery or their machine-gun defence. A heavy penalty was paid for this and for the British shortage of artillery ammunition. The 2/10th Middlesex had got to take a redoubt on Samson's Ridge, consolidate it and push on further. The leading company took the redoubt but then: 'eight H.E. burst right in amongst them and laid them out in rows. It was an awful sight. Then I had to go up to the Redoubt which was filled with dead Turks and our poor fellows. Here we consolidated but some of our men had gone over down a steep razor back and it was impossible to get to them as M.G. and rifle fire was terrific. I tried to take a message but saw it was hopeless. . . . Our casualties were very heavy, also the Kent's. . . . Samson's Ridge we took, but what a place, if it had been shelled for a month it would have made no difference. The Turks had dugouts on the reverse slope at the foot of the razor back and nothing could touch them. Again the Battn did wonderfully and to see them go over the top was a sight for the Gods.'[80]

Circumstances on the right of the Middlesex were no better as is made clear in the diary of a signaller in the 54th Division, Corporal H. O. Bigg. 'At 7.30 Batt went over. We followed with the Colonel. Line broken by H.E. Sent Jones back to mend it. Got on within 200 yds of front line. Long and I alone. Lost Colonel. Unable to find anyone. Sent 2 Battn signallers on to find out where Batt was and 5 other people. None returned. About 30 men on right ran away. . . . 163 (Bde) on right running away. . . . Had to come back 1,000 yards in two goes. Several men sent out by Colonel. None came back.'[81]

Of many acts of gallantry performed along the whole frontage of the attack – more than twelve miles and nowhere with any prospect of success by the end of the day – that of another Signaller, Spr Sore compels admiration. With the task of destroying Turkish telegraphic communication between Gaza and Beersheba, in plain view of the enemy he had climbed a telegraph pole by the vital road link between the towns, had cut one wire and was brought to the ground wounded by small arms fire from under 300 yards. 'Undaunted, he climbed the pole again, cut a second strand and was in the act of cutting the third and last when he was blown to pieces by a shell fired from a mountain gun a few hundred yards away.'[82] Perhaps we can presume that the shell which killed Sore also completed his work.

Military principles are confounded when failure is reinforced, but failure can be profitably followed by consolidation to prepare a more effective springboard for a renewal of an offensive and that was precisely what happened under the new High Command of Sir Edmund Allenby. The two vital matters which had to be tackled if strong reinforcements were to secure the morale-boosting victory which Lloyd George wanted, were water supply and the development of road and rail communications. Much had already been done before Allenby's arrival and the laying of main railway track, light railway lines and road construction was vigorously pushed further forward. To this potential improvement of troop and heavy supply transport, may be added the worth of increased water supply by Camel transport, the extension eastward of water pipe-line provision and re-discovery and utilization of natural water

supply in the desert. A veritable transformation of the transport scene was achieved even if the best use were not always made of it. 'Last night I was out until half-past ten with a breakdown. Two locos moving in different directions towards the cross-roads are not going to take things quietly when the bump comes. I am beginning to see a little of the hidden meaning in Bairnfather's "Cross Roads". The damage was only slight and one loco was derailed but by means of packing and with the assistance of two more of the same type – we won.' Corporal G. D. Breffitt (RE), a 1912 apprentice to the London Tilbury and Southend Railway Company, was clearly playing a vocationally valuable part in facilitating the build-up of resources for the third strike at the Gaza Beersheba defence position.[83]

It is a commonplace to write of Allenby's commanding presence being felt throughout his force. His impressive physique, his reputation for ubiquity, his temper, his capacity to instil across ranks an imprint of his high requirement from every individual, his manifest thoroughness, professionalism and, for those whom it touched, the subtlety of his deception planning, all made their mark.

The impact the Commander-in-Chief made on his troops is illustrated in New Zealander, Hubert Hatrick's letter of 29 November 1917. The letter nicely links Allenby to the German General in Command of the Turks. 'Take it from me he is *some General*. Old Allenby has been out here a lot since we started to organize this line. He is a tiger to buzz from place to place. The German General Von Kress is said to be a "goer" too and even ducks about in

Wadi Nukibir near Gaza and the solution to a basic problem. Engineers have constructed and piped this new water point from which a lined trough has been prepared offering simultaneous drinking facility for large numbers of horses. (Brigadier G. R. Gilpin)

Camel-borne supplies cross a newly erected bridge at Yazur, Palestine in 1918. It appears as if construction were continuing and the Sapper officer who built it has labelled on his photograph that 'it could take a 60-pdr gun battery'. (Brigadier G. R. Gilpin)

Somebody's headache at Bala, Suez Canal: 2/10, Middlesex survey the first efforts by RE Sappers of the Railway Operating Department and men of the Egyptian Labour Corps in the railway crane hoisting of an errant locomotive back onto its right lines. (Lieutenant Colonel D. B. Watson)

aeroplanes. He must be a lighter weight than our fellow.'[84]

Of course, there were other factors which assisted the men of the Egyptian Expeditionary Force – Allenby's political mandate for the offensive and the very considerable reinforcements he was accorded. There was, however, a factor the importance of which should not be diminished, the learning of their trade by those troops, infantry, cavalry, artillery, engineers – who had gained experience as well as disappointment in the desert and some of whom had built on that experience by the policy of raids, patrolling and ambushes pursued by both sides in the summer of 1917.

Allenby's plan was to break the Turkish defensive cordon, to attack Beersheba on the opposite wing from Gaza, burst through and seize the wells at Sheria. This time Gaza and the coast would be but the diversion and to this end there was the famous incident of the British officer seemingly out on patrol allowing himself to be pursued and dropping maps and orders which clearly emphasized Gaza as the main focus of a planned offensive.

Australian Light Horse and New Zealand Mounted Rifle regiments were involved in mounted action to take Beersheba. In the case of at least two regiments, the 4th and 12th ALH, the men, 'having no swords, carried bayonets in their hands . . . as the charging squadrons swept down the gentle slope towards Beersheba, enveloped in a cloud of dust coming under machine-gun fire from the enemy trenches but [being] skilfully protected by the shelling of a battery of artillery which destroyed active defence from that position.'[85]

While the Desert Mounted Brigade was raising its cloud of dust at Beersheba, serried ranks of infantry were moving upon Gaza but there was infantry in attack at Beersheba too. The Kensingtons (15th County of London) had practised their attack daily on ground marked out to simulate that which they would have to cover. Broken country training had been undertaken too so that the formation for attacking across Wadis was fully learned. There had been a full dress rehearsal which had not been well carried out as a late revision of time meant that the men could have no breakfast. 'Everybody was in a bad temper, hungry and peevish – the men appeared sullen and doltish and I know I was in a raging temper.' The poor performance led to a damaging row developing between the regiment's Commanding Officer and the Brigadier who was to scorch the men and in particular two officers by name. A new Commanding Officer was appointed and very fortunately the officer was well-chosen.

Kenneth Wills, one of the officers criticized, was relieved to know that he was still to lead his company into the attack and in his memoirs he made mention of Allenby's insight into human nature in giving three days' leave to Cairo or Alexandria to Company Commanders soon to lead their men into attack. The leave was of course colloquially known as 'death leave' and for men who had for six solid weeks been finely tuned to the plan and their responsibilities within it, the move was shrewdly designed to prevent their becoming stale.

The men marched up at night on 30 October as silently as possible to their point of concentration but stray shots came in among them as the Lewis guns and their ammunition were being unloaded from the camels. The battalion's zero hour could not be fixed until an outflanking hill position had been captured by another unit, but Wills and Sgt Oldcorn viewed with misgivings the 600 yards or more of bare ground they would have to cover from the Wadi where they were concentrating. Accordingly the officer pushed forward two platoons to a wadi ahead of the exposed ground.

The sun rose and by ten, indirect Turkish machine-gun fire was searching for them as they waited for the signal to move off. Then, behind their position, a man running towards them was seen. The Turks fired on him and he fell. 'Without thinking what I was doing I dashed out of cover towards him.' Dust was thrown up all around the officer by bullets directed at him but he reached the man, Pte Barrell, and flung himself down beside him.

He ordered the private to follow him in a dash back to the safety Wills had left. It transpired that the message being carried through such danger was from the subaltern in command of No. 9 platoon to Wills, the Company Commander: 'When may my platoon drink their rum and tea ration?' Wills had given instructions that the rum and tea were to remain untouched until he gave orders accordingly and the junior officer had stuck to the letter of the instruction.

Soon after midday the Kensingtons were ordered to move, following behind an artillery barrage. One half-company of men halted and lay down to take cover allowing the Turks to concentrate their fire on the units still pressing on. 'I almost screamed with agony at this frightful mistake. I climbed up out of the wadi and shrieked across the two hundred yards of road to M . . . to get on. Nothing could have been more futile for in the fearful din that the barrage was making nobody could have been heard twenty yards away. I stood there for a few seconds absolutely stricken; it looked as if the whole attack was going to be messed up. In a wild moment of exhilaration I told Benke [another Company Commander] I was going to take the right half Company on – he tried to stop me for he said it was suicide to try to cross the road, but I was so worked up that I did not care what I did.' Wills dashed to them and the men were already getting up. He led them towards the enemy trenches taking a rifle from someone who had been hit. Fifty yards from their objective they went to ground as shells were still being directed upon it, then as the barrage lifted, in they went. 'I do not remember very clearly what happened when we got there; most of the Turks threw up their hands and I believe that some of them were bayonetted in cold blood.'

Wills then organized a bombing party to clear the trench towards a known machine-gun emplacement, his impatience to see that this was done leading him to get out of the trench and run ahead behind the parados until he came to face Turks whom he was in the act of charging when they were bombed. Very fortunately and by instinct or perhaps hearing a shouted warning, he threw himself down just in time.

His men were 'so mad with excitement' that it took some time for him to reorganize them to press on to a further objective. This was done and a Turkish camp behind their trenches was captured and looted of silk and brocade Turkish army winter issue waistcoats.[86]

Beersheba, Gaza, Sheria, all fell and at El Maghar a celebrated cavalry charge played its part in capturing an important railway junction. The Bucks Hussars' part in this charge was to cover 4,000 yards sloping up to a high ridge outflanking the village of El Maghar. Lieutenant C. H. Perkins, under an absolute hail of fire, had reconnoitred the ground and found a suitable location for machine-guns to give the Yeomanry regiment support on its lengthy approach to the ridge and then, in mid-afternoon, the Hussars scrambled out of the steep ravine from which their attack would be launched.

'As the enemy's fire hotted up, it became harder to hold the horses to the trot, so gradually the pace quickened while we still tried to keep the galloping squadron in line. As we neared the ridge swords were drawn and very soon we were breasting the rise with their gun blasts feeling like pillows hitting one's face. Then in seconds they were all around us some shooting, some scrambling out of slit trenches and

One of the eight tanks of the Palestine Tank Detachment. A Mark IV reinforcement to the older tanks which were already well worn in their use for training purposes in the United Kingdom before being employed at the Second Battle of Gaza. 'Revenge' is being informally inspected on the beach in September 1917, not long before taking part in the third battle where one tank is described in the Official History as flattening the Turkish wire: 'from Sea Post to Beach Post'. (Brigadier G. R. Gilpin)

Sergeant Johnstone (6th Battalion, Highland Light Infantry) poses beside his bag of three bedraggled Turkish soldiers – they look as if they may be Kurds – near Gaza, May 1917. (Captain T. M. MacQuaker)

The Damascus Gate in Jerusalem, a medieval entrance to much older sites of interest or pilgrimage for the modern Crusader. (H. O. Bigg)

some sensibly falling flat on their faces. Blown and galloping horses are hard to handle one-handed while you have a sword in the other – so hindered by the clutter of rifle butt and other equipment troopers found it nearly impossible to get at a low dodging Turk. One missed and missed again until the odd Turk wasn't quick enough. In just such a case the hours spent in arms drill paid off for one instinctively leaned well forward and remained so to offset the jerk as the sword comes out – in fact precisely as one had so often been told.' Only a small number of troopers had got to the sector where Perkins was still mounted and they were in the midst of a seething mob like policemen in a football crowd outside the ground. Shouting what they had been told were the Turkish words for 'Hands Up' proved no use whatsoever and the Turks were milling about and heading for the far side of the ridge so Perkins dismounted from his blown horse and got some cover in a trench. Most unusually the Turks had panicked, vacating a position they could have defended had they not been somewhat unnerved by the surprise and speed with which the troopers got among them.[87]

In the pursuit actions which followed, Captain Catford (RAMC) of the Yeomanry Mounted Division, wrote letters which incidentally started their journey home by camel-pack aboard the camels which had brought food up to the men.'We are in Ramleh after one of the most historic advances in history. Ramleh is a Christian village and we had a triumphant entry amidst the pealing of bells and the cheers of the populace – just like the picture-books.'

On 14 November, after a trek of eleven days, constantly in the saddle, eating on horseback, with perhaps just four hours or so good sleep at night, he had: 'loved it, though parts of it have been terrible. I am as fit as ever before in my life and hard as nails. It has been my ambition ever since the war to advance over enemy territory, and it has at last been realized.'

Heavy rain drenched the Mounted Division in the Judean Hills of southern Palestine. 'It was still raining; every stitch we had was soaked, and the whole Brigade settled down for the night in a circular cup of hills. We were unable to light fires even if we could have obtained dry wood because of the danger of disclosing our position, and to make things thoroughly cheery, rations did not arrive.' In the morning, sniper fire and then shelling inflicted casualties among the cold, unfed men but some men in positions further forward had been wounded. Bringing them in presented considerable difficulty. 'I had two stretcher bearers and took five hours to bring in two officers. My bearers were done – they had worked hard all day without food – it was impossible to go more than a few yards without resting and we lost our way meantime.' When they found the Brigade at 4 p.m., they dressed their patients and made them as comfortable as possible but this cannot have eased the men much as there were no blankets, no food and no drugs, even the stock of morphia having given out. Evacuation later for the wounded by cacoulets (camel-borne stretchers) would have been the next and prolonged ordeal for these poor casualties of the push towards Jerusalem.[88]

Concentrated Turkish counter-attacks failed to forestall the surrender of Jerusalem on 11 December. The occupation of the city with its fundamental importance to Moslem as well as to Jew and Christian, released a turmoil of emotions in those who had earned the privilege of marching through its hallowed streets. An Argyll and Sutherland Highlander, John Young, second in command of the London Scottish, wrote that his battalion of the 60th London Division had: 'had a stiff fight on the 8th which lasted all day and brought us to the outskirts of Jerusalem. It poured all the night before and was bitterly cold. We had no coats and were marching light. At dawn after traversing the most impossible country up and down precipitous mountains we attacked the Turks. They had fine trenches and put up a good fight lasting all day. The men spent another night in the cold and next day found the Turks had cleared. We marched into the town in the afternoon with pipes playing and were welcomed by the inhabitants. The Turks were just the other side on the Mount of Olives and we had to push them off. I have had the most interesting tour round the city. I visited the Mosque of Omar which now stands on the original site of Solomon's temple. It is the most beautiful thing I have ever seen. The mosaic work is really grand and the colouring superb without being vulgar. There was an air of sanctity about the place I have never yet experienced anywhere and I was greatly impressed. . . . Here according to Moslems, Abraham offered Isaac as a sacrifice and from this spot Mahomet ascended to Heaven. This is the most sacred place in the world alike to Christians, Moslems and Jews. It is now guarded by native troops and white men are not allowed in. However, I was lucky and entered before any restrictions came out.' The Scot, moved by his own spiritual convictions, then described the Church of the Holy Sepulchre. He did not like the gaudy adornment of the inner sanctum: 'lit by numerous little lamps and full of gold ornaments and paintings. Very vulgar to my mind. The place is run by Greeks. There is a Latin and Armenian and Russian portion also, all in the same church. It struck me as being just like the inside of an R.C. church and I was very disgusted and disappointed with the whole thing. It is of course only the traditional site of the tomb. . . . I also visited the Jews wailing place, which is just a stone courtyard outside the city walls. On Fridays in the afternoon, large collections of Jewish women come and weep there and pray that the Temple will be restored to them!' John Young may not have been attracted by display – (either emotional or in the form of over-glittering decoration) – but he still

bought 'two brass candlesticks which I think I got cheap,' and he hoped to 'pick up something else at Bethlehem'.[89] As it happened Turkish counterattacks would prevent his sightseeing or tourist shopping in Bethlehem!

Quite apart from the actual opposition put up by the Turks, and it had been fierce in the Judean Hills, the Holy Land was to provide particularly challenging campaign conditions. The geological trough of the Jordan Valley, so far below sea level, presented problems concerning which the Official Historian is quite explicit. After the awkward crossings of the swollen river were accomplished in late March and the summer months drew on, the intense heat and humidity gave rise to an: 'extraordinary lassitude and sense of helplessness'. Conditions were stagnantly airless. Dust raised by troop movements hung like a suffocating blanket occasionally disturbed into dust devils by sudden gusts of wind. This was the scene in which small actors played unpleasant parts. In dry area, scorpions, six-inch centipedes and great stinging spiders provided poor entertainment and in marshy regions mosquitoes were there in their myriads. Then there were the ever-present flies which swarmed repellently among horse lines and camps no matter how thorough the sanitary precautions.[90]

Men in small boats, on rafts and specially chosen swimmers led the way across the Jordan before an infantry footbridge, pontoon and barrel bridges facilitated the crossing of large numbers of men, horses and transport. Of the swimmers and those waiting to cross, Major Vivian Gilbert published a vivid account. 'These men, stripped to the skin, and with ropes tied round their waists, entered the flooded stream, and attempted to fight their way over. The Turks, either anticipating our plans, or becoming alarmed at the prolonged silence, lit huge fires of reeds and brushwood along the Eastern Bank, and commenced firing wildly with rifles and machine guns. I was concealed in the scrub by the banks of the Jordan with two sections of my company waiting for the first bridge to be thrown across. . . . Swarms of noxious insects, disturbed by the fires, rose from the rushes and settling on our bare legs, hands and faces, bit and stung us with utmost ferocity.'[91]

Following on from the successful crossings, Es Salt was taken but any thought of a relatively easy advance eastward to Amman decisively to cut the Turkish rail link to the Hejaz, was rudely dismissed in late March 1918. Those men who were to be involved in the two abortive Amman raids were to remember it as among their most demanding experiences of the whole campaign. Major Geoffrey Inchbald was with the Imperial Camel Corps and having crossed the Jordan where it entered the Dead Sea, the Camels had made slow going through a swamp and then, 'it began to rain, a pitiless downpour which was to last for forty-eight hours and turn the track through the Moabite Hills or rather mountains which we were now approaching into a morass.'

On and on the column had trekked through one day and then the night. 'As the track climbed up through the hills the sides grew steeper and steeper with sheer cliffs on one side and a precipice on the other. The camels struggled gamely but they were neither accustomed to such appalling conditions nor designed by nature to overcome them. . . . Many of

1918 and a long, long trail still a-winding. In this case it is the road to Jericho and the 2/4, Royal West Surrey Regiment marching in Indian file. (S. W. Vinter)

Aftermath of the Amman Raid: a detachment of the 2/16, London Regiment buries one of its dead below El Haud in the Jordan Valley after the second raid across the river. The officer in command of the Londons, John Hay Young, wrote after the raid that it was: 'the hardest marching and fighting I can remember'. (Lieutenant Colonel J. H. Young)

them did the splits with their legs splaying out in either direction, others slipped and went over the side of the ravine.' Those who did fall in that manner had to be put out of their misery if the fall had not killed them, and then their loads had to be lugged up again to the track and portioned out so that progress could continue. The delays had lost all prospect of surprise, the weather got still worse, men and animals still more exhausted. Through narrow defiles the troopers had to lead rather than ride their camels. 'This is the only time I have seen men fall asleep as they walked, even in mid-stride and there were so many delays that we did not reach our positions until some seventy-six hours after we had started out so hopefully.'

At dawn the following day a dismounted attack illustrated that the Turks were well prepared, were able to inflict heavy casualties and were bringing up further reinforcements. Enemy shelling and small arms fire neutralized attacking initiative. Bombing parties were sent out at night to bring a dawn rude awakening to Turkish snipers who were firing from caves upon the troopers in the shallow trenches they had won. A further advance was made, but at heavy cost and then came the difficult task of disengaging and retiring to where the camels had been left. The long miserable return journey was uplifted by no glimmer of achievement for their efforts and was spurred by the: 'expression on the faces of the villagers who spat in the dust as we passed and made signs indicative of their keen desire to cut our throats given the chance.'[92]

A German officer prisoner crosses the Jordan over 'Anzac' bridge; a pontoon bridge, seemingly under the supervision of its builders, who had constructed it under fire. A Turkish prisoner precedes the mounted officer and his escort. (Lieutenant Colonel J. H. Young)

The Turks were not yet beaten, but in the months before Allenby adjudged it right to resume the offensive, the balance in morale and *matériel* turned decisively in favour of the Egyptian Expeditionary Force. Troops lost to Palestine for the emergency on the Western Front were replaced and a daring plan augmented the significance of the British advantages by well carried out ruses utterly to deceive the Turks as to the real focus of the attack. A hole was to be punched by the infantry on the coastal front and through this gap would pour the Desert Mounted Corps racing Northwards in a move to outflank Turkish retirement. The Battle of Megiddo was launched on 19 September after weeks of careful endeavour to suggest by movements raising dust in the Jordan Valley and the setting up of dummy camps and horse lines that here in the Jordan the breakout would be attempted. To the west, troops were moved by night. In concealed camps men cooked smokelessly from solidified alcohol. Well-advertised plans for a race meeting and the release of 'helpful' rumours contributed towards the enemy's dismay when a far heavier artillery barrage than hitherto, heralded an advance by the infantry on the right flank of the Turks. This advance called for a high degree of fitness from those troops who had the longest distances to cover in a great wheel north-east to secure a corridor through which the mounted men could pass.

A measure of what was required from the 4th Cavalry Division and indeed what it had achieved may be taken from but one sentence in the official narrative of its operations. 'The Division had, on its arrival at Beisan at 1800 hrs on 20 inst. covered 85 miles in 34 hours, and with the exception of fords over the Jordan had closed all exits for the Turkish armies.' Despite an attempt to maintain good horse husbandry, twenty-six horses were lost in this phenomenal physical performance.[93]

Eric Catford's letter describing this vindication of the continued 20th-century usefulness of cavalry under certain circumstancs, first paid tribute to the secrecy of the move from the Jordan Valley to the coast. 'All through the staff work had been excellent and the suddenness with which such a gigantic stunt was pushed on speaks very highly for their work. . . . All day on the 18th we lay concealed in an orange grove, and in the afternoon I went to a conference at Headquarters and heard the news and plans.'

Catford was to be with a fast-moving RAMC unit dealing with freshly wounded casualties and then sending them back to the rear of the advancing column. With the infantry having broken through, the only resistance met was some guns, but the Turkish artillerymen were run down by Lancers. Very short halts were allowed for water and apart from this the cavalry moved north for the full day (19 September). After a three hour rest and watering of the horses, off they set by night through a long mountain pass opening out onto the Plain of Megiddo. After only a slight engagement, the next day was similarly spent, asking much from horses and men. So completely had the Turks been surprised that the RAMC was not so much dealing with wounded cavalrymen but sick, wounded and exhausted Turks and German prisoners.[94]

The consequences of Megiddo, together with the course of the war elsewhere, were conclusive. Operations to the east won Amman, the Turks were pursued through Syria, and Damascus was captured. Cities to the north like Beirut, Homs, Tripoli and Aleppo were taken, and the Turks formally surrendered on 30 October. However much one may emphasize the sideshow nature of such speedy triumph and its lack of impact upon the real heart of the war in France and Flanders, British soldiers in Palestine, for all their privations, had enjoyed for some weeks the elation of being in a victorious army. On all sides was the evidence of triumph and now it was for little expenditure. There may have been, for the discerning, evidence of highly charged antagonistic ethnic and religious passion prophesying trouble. There was indeed one regrettable incident before the end of the year which sullied the record of achievement and perhaps reflected truly the lack of accord felt by many troops for the Arab peoples through whose villages they passed. This was the infamous affair at Surafend when New Zealanders and Australians took vengeance for the murder of a New Zealander by people who, in soldier perception, had established a reputation for theft and untrustworthiness. The Arab males in Surafend were beaten or killed in thoroughly if informally planned operations which brought a serious cleavage between Allenby and the units concerned.[95] Nevertheless for all the shadows cast by this and by a general awareness of Arab/Jew tensions, Palestine perhaps more than on any other front, had provided the soldiers who served there with visible tangible victory to enjoy. The enjoyment lay long in the memory of those who lived to tell the tale.

The Khaki perspective: Opinions and Attitudes

More than in any other part of this book the author is aware of the subjective factors undermining the validity of generalizations about soldier opinions and attitudes. Furthermore in most chapters quotation had been offered reflecting an individual's patriotism, state of morale, regimental pride or feelings about his fellows all of which have a relationship to the questions raised in this chapter and so what will be attempted here, is to give what seem to be typical responses to some of the most obvious questions not already considered, but which arise from any consideration of the British Soldier in the First World War – what did he think of the seemingly endless war and of his involvement in it, of his enemy, of his principal ally the French soldier, and of the peasants and townsfolk he encountered? How highly did the soldier from the United Kingdom rate the Australian or American units, did he have views on staff officers and on the High Command and what about his reaction to the multi-faceted Home Front where parents and wives anxiously waited for news? Do diaries or letters reveal observations on munition workers or strikers, pacifists, conscientious objectors, politicians and politics? In conclusion, some example will be given of expression arising from the

interaction of soldiering and Christian conviction. There will be no new dissection of the obvious intellectual dilemma posed by soldiers in Field Grey singing with equal fervour their national equivalent of 'Fight the Good Fight' or 'Onward Christian Soldiers' as chanted by the khaki-clad church parade behind this side of the line – rather than this, evidence will be offered of the faith of a British soldier coming to his aid, fleeing from him, staying firmly beside him or trembling within him as that particular man was tested by war. In looking at such evidence, the influence of the Padre, with his duty to nurture that faith, will receive some examination.

In December 1916, a Coldstream Guards officer, Lt W. E. Baynes, sought to generalize for his mother on the attitude of the people with whom he had talked concerning the German peace moves. He considered that: 'everyone out here is ready for peace on reasonable terms' but those reasonable terms for Baynes included: 'freedom for Belgium, Alsace-Lorraine, Servia and Poland'.[1] These sentiments somehow symbolize what had changed in the nature of the soldier's attitude to war. A sincere but unenlightened early enthusiasm for the cause had been through the grinding machine of long months

A postcard artist depicts one side of the uncomfortable feelings induced in the more sensitive or more vulnerable soldier on leave. (P.H.L. Archives)

of military education in industrialized warfare, there was now no prospect of an end never mind of glorious victory and what had come out of the forge of war was a stoic, if perhaps grudged, acceptance that things had to be as they were – the Nation had to fight on, its manhood had to serve. Many more months still would have to be endured before the 'reasonable terms' envisaged by Baynes were brought within serious consideration by the Central Powers.

Even in mid-1918 when Captain G. S. King admitted to his father of getting despondent about: 'Whether the war will do anything to introduce clearer saner ideals as at one time I felt it should', he still considered that the war was: ' a fight against the very soullessness which Germany would enforce on the world and that others may never learn to loathe its crushing weight as I do – for that one can carry on'.[2] That so many men thought in terms of the war having to be 'seen through' and accordingly they simply had to cope with much that was at best alien, at worst awful, in no way should deny the voices of the men whose spirit became totally revolted by the nature of war, nor of those who confess to a degree of pleasure in their service experience. In January 1918, after a year in France, Captain F. C. Pritchard (RFA) considered that he had: 'never enjoyed a year more – so full of new interests and impressions – Though in many ways it's all rotten and beastly, as its here, I'm jolly glad not to have missed it.'[3] For some men, 'enjoying' the war, may have provided a sort of shield: 'If I were not able to see the humorous side of this war I could not enjoy it as I do. If once one begins to treat this war on its merits and believe that it is a really awful life, one is done and one suffers from acute depression everymore.'[4] This capacity of Lt Wilkinson (2nd Bn, Coldstream Guards) to focus attention away from that which was degrading and horrifying would be in varying degree exercised by most men consciously or unconsciously sustaining their ability to cope, but it would be a serious mistake to presume that all men possessed the hypersensitivity of some of the war poets. The idea that all men reacted with automatically triggered outrage at the indiscriminate, savage torture of war and that an almost universal disillusionment was bred during the war may be politically and socially 'attractive' to support certain theses, but it is patently untrue. There were those of course who came to question their earlier high ideals, there was an almost universal war-weariness and, after the war, there was the depression of awakening to the fact that a better world had not been built. This certainly spawned retrospectively a bitter resentment at

'Beginning to resemble butcher meat.' James Macgregor's wound to his hand was caused by a German shell explosion near a forward battery position on 11 July 1917. His letter, from a hospital run by Viscountess Harcourt, is cheerful and appreciative of all that is being done for him, not least by a 'plump and rosy VAD who is first rate'. (J. C. S. Macgregor).

the waste of war, but the dominant characteristic in any general assessment of how the British soldier viewed his presence overseas in 1917–18 would have to be his readiness to stick it out.

In contrast, an example is offered here of a man who, in sticking it out in the last months of the war, recorded a shatteringly convincing personal indictment of such experience. J. B. Herbert, a company commander of the 2/4th Royal West Surrey Regi-

The Kaiser's last moment. Colonel Hobday brings his long military experience into play as he thrusts at the target in Event No. 9, Officers: 'Kaiser's Head and Ring' in the 104th Brigade, Royal Field Artillery Sports Day at Westcliffe, Folkestone, 8 May 1915. One can sense that the target would provide Hobday with a professional challenge; for civilians, a day after the torpedoing of the liner *Lusitania*, the Colonel's success would mean something more symbolic and even more satisfying. (Colonel E. A. P. Hobday)

Lieutenant E. Merrett, in No. 2 Red Cross hospital at Rouen, humorously, but inaccurately, sketched in an autograph album this cartoon depicting a diminishing enemy capacity to sting. In fact the war had almost two years to run! (Major C. Milburn)

ment, wrote an account in October 1918 of the fierce fighting and physical exhaustion of August-September battles in which his battalion had been engaged. Lest his reflections, written in comfort behind the line, should be thought a testimony of his cowardice, he drew attention to the fact that he had been awarded the Military Cross for his work during the days which had brought him to his scathing verdict. 'I am firmly convinced that we are fighting because of old men's dead and rotting minds and by the folly of the mob. You see I'm a rank pacifist. I am *not* fighting voluntarily. I am a conscript, to nothing so vulgar as a Military Service Act, but to the good opinions of my neighbours.' Faith, honour, hope of victory had brought Herbert no inspiration. He considered that the deaths he had seen could not

conceivably have won honour. 'Its just waste, . . . if I am hit next week in our next "glorious push" I shall lie there a month hence, the skin shrivelled back from my teeth, grinning and mouthing and foul as it all [will be]. Can you think *I* shall have honour, or feel honoured or care a damn for you, or him or her or any one thing that makes death pitiful – now?'[5]

Towards the Germans it is often assumed that the British soldier felt little enmity, much respect and some envy of his equipment and even a degree of rough sympathy in shared miserable circumstances. Of respect for his soldierly qualities and his superior equipment there is abundant evidence, there are also letter and diary extracts which indicate kinship but it would certainly be ill-judged to discount the presence within some men of an implacable destestation for the German soldier. Such feelings might well be stimulated by matters concerning

September 1915. Officers of the Seaforth Highlanders outside their dugout, constructed within an abandoned brewery, near the 'Port Arthur' trench system. On the right is the Seaforths' interpreter, a French Army Officer named Bernheim. Of the three British officers, Maxwell on the left will be killed and Wilson and Anderson will be wounded within four months, all in the same battle but in Mesopotamia not here in France. (Lieutenant Colonel L. A. Lynden Bell)

which we, free from the frenzy and 'necessary distortions' of wartime, would feel uneasiness today as for example with the early reports of German atrocities and the execution of Edith Cavell or the torpedoing of *Lusitania*, and some men were aware at the time of the dilemma of equating automatically the individuals they opposed with a perceived iniquity of their nation. T. C. Gillespie, two days before he was killed on 18 October 1914, wrote of entrenched Germans two hundred yards away. 'There was a large brown barn door behind one man, a lookout I think. I and a corporal had several shots at him and later in the day I noticed through my glasses a white cross scratched across the door. It is a grim thought but you have to think of individual Germans as a type of German militarism even if they are not.'[6]

Close proximity and jocular verbal exchange early in 1916 did not diminish F. B. Denham's personal dislike for the enemy. He wrote of a shouted message from the opposite lines that the man concerned was in the trenches for sixty days as a punishment and wanted to buy English bread at a franc a loaf. 'He did not get any needless to say. I for one would not trust them a bit.'[7] A year later, William Foster had even less doubt. To make sure the Germans never again brought war to Europe: 'the enemy has to be extirpated nationally and individually'.[8]

Willoughby Norrie, in December 1917, recorded: 'thirty healthy looking Germans trying to slink away under cover of an enormous red cross, but we were not having any truck so gave it him in the neck. They are absolute swine and are up to the meanest trick.'[9] That doughty warrior, E. G. Bates of the Northum-

The inscription on the photograph pays tribute to the officer with his hand on hip, Lieutenant D. A. H. Hire of the 69th Siege Battery, Royal Garrison Artillery. Apparently, the battery, with its 9.2-inch howitzers, was working alongside a French Marine Heavy Artillery Unit in September 1918 and had earned the esteem of one of the French officers. (Brigadier D. A. H. Hire)

berland Fusiliers, wanted to know if the new tank photos in the Press early in 1917: 'actually show the swine being squashed to jelly under the animal. How I hate the Huns.' Such vehemence in Bates's letter is intriguingly paralleled by admiration; the outstanding bravery of a wounded German prisoner is detailed, and the Fusilier paid unreserved tribute in October and November 1918 to the wonderful show the Germans had put up, revealing themselves in: 'many ways a very much sounder nation than ourselves'.[10] In front of the British officer, a badly wounded Prussian prisoner was told of the surrender of Austria and Turkey. The German replied to his captor that his country would still fight on. Neither then nor a generation later would many British soldiers feel that the 1918 assessment of Martin Parr was wide of the mark 'Indeed the Hun is a wonderful soldier.'[11]

In some sense the man in khaki was better placed to judge the merit of his opponent that that of his ally. Only in certain locations at certain dates and then as it turned out in special circumstances did British and French units fight as it were 'side by side'. There certainly were liaison officers well placed to comment and some gunners saw periods of service on French sectors of the line, but in the main. observation upon the 'poilus' derived from taking over French trenches and not finding them kept according to standards required by British military authorities. Lieutenant Blackley (RAMC) was with a unit occupying barns just vacated by French troops at Mondicourt on 26 August 1915. His diary records that the: 'filth was indescribable and the stench awful'. The trenches near here, where Blackley's dugout Regimental Aid Post was established, were: 'fairly clean but sanitation bad. Some dead feet sticking out of parapet where they had built men in to assist in forming parapet.' Scornfully the Medical Officer wrote of the French having had: 'One killed in 5½ months. They did nothing. There apparently was a tacit understanding between them and the Germans that they exchanged no fire. We stirred the Huns up at once with artillery.' Naturally there was a price to be paid for what seemed to be recorded as evidence of the superior aggression of the British – two killed and twenty-one wounded by the counter-fire![12]

Entente Cordiale near Vermelles in 1915. Poilu and Tommy Atkins exchange uniforms but not posture. Sergeant Norman Janes (London Irish Rifles) on the left makes no effort to strike a Gallic pose and the Frenchman's stance certainly belies his British uniform. Janes, 'seemingly seconded' to the 17ième Régiment d'Infanterie, wears the Croix de Guerre as does the 'Irish Rifleman', whose award is pinned more erratically to his tunic. (N. Janes)

Les Brebis, June 1915 and an extension of the Entente Cordiale. A Belgian soldier drinks with a Poilu and two London Irish Sergeants, Halford on the left and Janes with his pipe. It is possible that the personalised foe overlooking them was the work of Norman Janes who was to become an artist of distinction. (N. Janes)

In a contemporary account, N. A. Turner Smith, charged with the responsiblity of finding habitable billets from accommodation newly vacated by French troops, hoped that: 'he would never have to deal with such dirty people as the French again. I have always found them a dirty crowd, but the condition in which the troops had left this village were simply revolting.'[13] Such evidence is too common not to have substance, but we should recall that at neither a national nor at a personal level was the *Entente Cordiale* deep-rooted. To reinforce the sense of balance needed in pondering over such striking British disdain we have only to remember that the war had lasted many months before, in French perception, their ally even began to share properly the onus of the struggle where it was really vital – the fighting in Flanders and France.

Not all the praise for Australian troops comes from Australian sources. A British staff officer, whose judgement on this matter would presumably not be queried by troops from the Antipodes, wrote in April 1918 of his brigade co-operating with New Zealanders and Australians who had got: 'their tails right up . . . they are splendid people to fight with.'[14] This officer, Willoughby Norrie, who again commended the Australians together with Canadians in August, would probably have been aware that among United Kingdom units there was a feeling that the Australians had been praised too exclusively for their Gallipoli endeavour. The Press, not least for shrewd propaganda reasons, had repeatedly featured their collective achievement and the deeds of individuals. Is it fair to consider that developing Australian national traits, further accentuated by such reportage, help to explain the comments of officers who encountered them in 1916? The Australians were attuned to a more informal discipline than was familiar to British units. Dismissive of restrictive regulation on dress or the compulsory carrying of passes, and in this instance of addressing their officer by his first name, it was not altogether surprising that an English Officer in Egypt, Ted Bowlby (6th Bn, East Yorks) thought them: 'an awful lot, calling themselves "The brave Anzacs".'[15] A Coldstream Guards officer too, on the arrival of the Australians in France, found them: 'making as much row here as everywhere else. They are reported to go about asking those they meet whether they have been fighting or whether they have merely been in France, but I dare say their manners will improve in a month of so.'[16] Here we are reflecting opinions and attitudes and not substantiating their basis in fact. The Australians had no doubt about their worth and to them shall be

American doctors made an invaluable contribution to medical provision for the BEF towards the end of the war. Among those seconded to British units was this officer, Captain J. W. Sherrick, posted as Medical Officer to the 5th Battalion, The Duke of Wellington's Regiment. Wounded while serving with them, he was awarded the Military Cross. (Lieutenant Colonel J. Walker)

left the last word: 'There are no better soldiers in the world than the Australians, and very few as good, certainly Fritz has nothing to equal them. This is not skite [swank] but history. . . . I would rather be an Australian than any other nationality in the world because the Australians for example have produced not only far more military endeavour than Canada . . . , and . . . What soldiers and fighters our men are . . . but the five Australian Divisions are the best Divisions in the British Army.'[17]

The self-confidence, high pay and late arrival of the Americans almost invited the jaundiced verdict expressed upon them by the experienced but drained British troops. Again we ought to be aware that the opinions laid out here on German, French and now on American troops are usually pictures taken of contemporary scenes viewed through the old but strongly acting filter of national prejudice. When did the unappealing British cocktail of envy, admiration and dismissive contempt for Americans originate? – certainly the First World War provides evidence of there being some taste for it at that time. Writing in retrospect of service in close proximity to Americans, in fact the 27th New York Division, a former officer of the 2/3 London Regiment found his allies: 'contemptible, inefficient and ill-disciplined and as ordinary human beings to associate with – terrible. The sacred flame of democracy burned high

Adrian Hill, serving in the ranks of the Honourable Artillery Company, registers his disappointment that rumours of 'belles of France' collecting for the Bastille Day flag appeal were unfounded. He wrote that he contributed from fear of being put under a curse 'if I had refused the gargoyle'. Hill's artistic talent led to his being seconded from the HAC in October 1917 and commissioned as an Official War Artist. (A. K. G. Hill)

in every breast and manifested itself in the grossest contempt of orders and the filthiest abuse in audible terms if one tried to enforce a neccessary military order. [There were some] officers who hunted out safe dugouts and sat in them all evening, leaving the men in the charge of NCOs and [there were] NCOs who curled themselves up and went to sleep, but what amazed me most was that this great nation of business experts failed in the simple essential of feeding their own men in the field.' In his account, this officer, W. G. Wallace, goes on to admit that a well-informed source had informed him that this division was exceptional and not to be compared with the other American units.[18]

Wallace's reference to inefficiency may seem strange, but the CO of the 9th KRRC who wrote that his men were getting on well with the Americans, added that: 'They are all hustle and nothing done. Their organization is awful.'[19] A strikingly different assessment in the same month came from Captain Martin Parr (5th Bn, HLI) who had an 'amazing' American officer attached to his battalion. He was: 'very cheering about the American army and seemed very keen. 800,000 men like that must be felt soon. I give it three months of the Hun as top dog and then I think he is for it.'[20]

It is proper to conclude British observations upon the martial qualities of their transatlantic cousins with Parr's shrewd and more generous judgement, but such generosity does not seem to have been a characteristic element in the interplay between the

British soldier and the Belgian or French civilian.

There was abundant sympathy for civilians seen as fleeing refugees, there was admiration for the stolid, determined courage of peasants or townsfolk refusing to flee from dangerous zones and continuing their business or agricultural enterprise, but inevitably, as has been mentioned, circumstances were all against fraternal coexistence. When Hélène Vilbert, Directrice du Pensionnat Jeanne d'Arc in Laventie, wrote on 14 January 1917 to the British Town Major complaining that soldiers of the 3rd London Regiment billetted upon her had stolen two rabbits, each one worth 4 francs, her claim was thoroughly investigated. On the skins being returned, she settled for 7 francs 50 centimes and this incident may be taken as representative of those from which two-way judgements were made.[21] The story of rent being charged for land for trenches may be uproariously apocryphal, but water pumps could well be chained up until payment was proffered. In this vein, men of the 1st Bn. Coldstream Guards were given an amusing interlude on their two-mile march to a rifle range in the Morninghem area on 7 June 1917. A farmer remonstrated with their officers for trespass. 2nd Lt Guy Salisbury Jones: 'gave him a piece of my mind to the effect that he would not be living comfortably on his farm, were it not for us'.[22] It is pleasing to note that on occasion tribute was paid to the kindness of French peasants, but frequently it was in passing discriminatory judgement on Belgians. Rfn W. A. R. Morrison (21st Bn, KRRC) on the Somme at the end of August 1916 remarked that the: 'French people still continue to show me that they are a much nicer set than the Belgians, for I can honestly say I have never received something for nothing from a Belgian, but on the other hand the French are full of kind impulses such as giving one a hot cup of tea.'[23]

In a certain sense the soldier's incapacity to view matters through the perspective of a civilian has a degree of similarity to his incapacity to comprehend staff work and the responsibility resting upon the staff. The remoteness of the staff officer was at one and the same time to render him beyond the horizon of the man in the ranks and merely a fleetingly encountered being to the regimental officer, an ideal target for verbal arrows fired with the venom of men whose currently dirty and dangerous surroundings stood in stark contrast to the visualized ideal world of the staff officers of Brigade, Divisional, Corps, Army or GHQ.[23a] Naturally enough censorship would explain why the man in the ranks in his letters does not vent his spleen against staff officers and the presence of Army authority might go some way to explaining why personal diaries are not a rich mine for serious research into the soldier's view of his senior commanders, but the plain fact is that the Staff was outside of the soldier's world. There are exceptions, a striking example being a soldiering sailor, Petty Officer Findlay (Hawke Bn, RND) whose Cape Helles Gallipoli diary apportions blame unequivocally for the campaign's misfortune. In June 1915 he wrote of the KOSB rushing the Vineyard and Essex and Worcesters being overwhelmed; 'two complete lines wiped out. Bad policy of the Generals. Same old tale. No reserves. Will they ever learn. Too few men.' Somehow he learned remarkably quickly what happened at the Suvla Bay affair, because on 9 August, the day after the landing, he wrote: 'awful series of blunders from beginning to end.'[24] Despite such a damning indictment, contemporary kindred material from the ranks is quite rare, indeed for the subaltern too, the expression of anti-Staff sentiment is by no means a preoccupation. When G. I. Larkins wrote in 1982 that the seldom-seen staff officer: 'might as well have been in the War Office in Whitehall' he added sensibly that he did not: 'mean to belittle them in any

way – staff work was after all their job and their responsibilities must have been heavy' but they were certainly not a consciously dominant factor in his service.[25] This reflective comment re-emphasized the gulf which existed, but shows understanding of it which would not be grasped from the sardonic Great War contemporary verses found in the papers of J. C. Urquhart:

> How nice to be a Brigadier
> removed from chance and change
> To prod my Colonels from the rear
> and say to them in tones severe
> "All details that are not quite clear
> Battalions must arrange".
>
> How nice to be a Brigadier
> when horses have the mange
> when rations fail and foes are near
> How nice to be a Brigadier!
> And say to my Staff Captain "Here
> Find me another Uhlan spear!"
> All details which are not quite clear
> Battalions must arrange."[26]

Examples are given in this book of regimental officers protesting about the impracticability of carrying out orders decreed from above, quite apart

A cartoon dated 22 November 1916 executed by 2nd Lieutenant J. Lough, Northumberland Fusiliers, to illustrate what the artist claims was a true incident. Perhaps it was true in general terms, apochryphal in detail. The caption reads: 'Scene No. 2 Red Cross Hospital, Rouen. Patients are being prepared for convoy to Blighty'. This patient (a lieutenant colonel who has got his ticket on account of senile decay) refuses to lie down, upon any such stretcher. (Long-suffering orderly calling along corridor): ''Arry! Fetch along one o' them 'ere silver-mounted stretchers!' (Major C. H. Milburn)

One form of disenchantment: it is not known whether Private Webster of the 10th Devons was dealing with this civilian worker because of news of strikes on the Home Front, or whether it was because the mufflered man is not in khaki. (J. A. Webster)

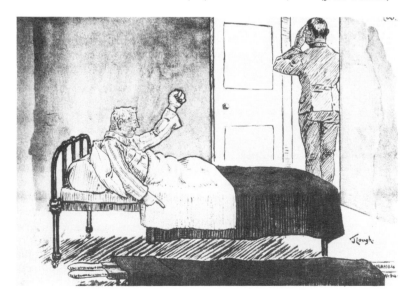

from the familiar syndrome of questionning the competence of anyone whose dictates governed one's work and indeed life when on active service. There must have been occasions without number when it seemed to those in command on the spot that the requirements of the staff were insufficiently based on knowledge of local circumstance. Each case in its wider context could be examined, but to whichever side of the military equation judgement today would incline, examples of regimental officer disdain for the Staff can easily be offered. In general terms the perception of the unfeeling attitude of the Staff appears in a 1918 diary of G. S. Atkinson, an RE officer. In considering his level of responsibility in the Army, he stated that he: 'was far too sentimental to be a staff officer – a man who unconsciously visualizes the widows and the orphans could never do it and to me it will always be something more than a game of chess. But perhaps that is only the natural attitude of the pawn.'[27] It is possible to see in such a comment an unintentional tribute to the awesome demand upon the Staff officer that he must necessarily detach himself emotionally from the human, individual consequences of the attempt by others to fulfil his plans, but of course it was within the vision of few in junior command in the field to see things in that way.

If the Commander-in-Chief and the successive layers of Staff Officer were, as has been suggested, so distant as to be neither a dominant factor of disgruntlement, nor, it has to be stated, a source of inspiration, did the geographical remoteness of the Home Front expunge or anaesthetize feelings towards those at home? In fact the ambivalence of the soldier's attitude towards the civilian is painted in highly coloured vivid detail. Love, care and concern shine in innumerable letters to parents, brothers, sisters, girlfriends, wives. There is in the main an endeavour to protect the family reader of a soldier's letter from too close an acquaintance with his world. Sometimes one senses that this is not simply protective but because the writer feels that the limits upon his power of expression and of the reader's imagination render the challenge of description not worth the effort, but the war correspondent, the man on strike or the able-bodied civilian reluctant to enlist are scorched countlessly in pencilled pages folded within the Army post-marked manila or green envelopes.

One of two brothers writing to their father in April 1917 remarked on how father was: 'always searching in our letters for any information that might lead you to conclude that we were not happy or were suffering discomforts. I would never think of letting you know

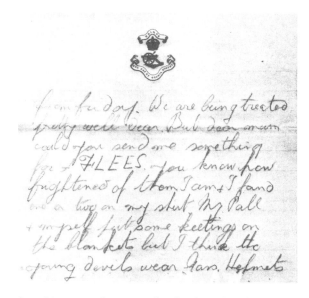

Something worse than rats or lice; in a letter full of concern to assure his family that he would be alright, Gunner Sweet admits that he is very frightened of 'flees' despite dusting his blankets well with the appropriate powder – 'Keatings'. (H. S. Sweet)

half the things that I have experienced in this war. When I do tell you anything it is all over and I tell you then so that you will not worry.' In the same letter Lt A. B. Waring admitted to his father that 'all my radical upbringing has come to naught. In future if I have any political learnings they will be on the Tory side, the reason is that I know the British working man – the best fellow in the world. I also know Ramsay MacDonald, Henderson, Bernard Shaw and others of that ilk.'[28]

Seventeen months earlier than Waring's letter, an officer writing from the Dardanelles simply could not: 'understand men striking at a time like this. Even if the employers are making a big thing, the Government should undertake definitely to limit profits and fix prices if necessary and then if the men go on strike, they should be dealt with same as soldiers mutinying – shot on the spot. The right to please oneself may be alright in peacetime but when the whole nation is at war the working man should obey orders just as much as those who wear khaki. And as the miner gets up to £6 and over a week in a safe job while the soldier gets 8s. or 10s. a week in the trenches he's not badly off after all.'[29] In the same vein many letter-writers, having shown concern for their own family in Zeppelin raids, show clear satisfaction that the raids help recruitment and convince those comfortably on the Home Front that there is a war on.

Resentment towards: 'the munition worker and others who benefit from the war'[30] is vehemently expressed in letters right across the ranks and from men themselves who had recently left the shop floor of industry. R. B. Marshall wrote thankfully in July 1915 that Home Front notables including the famous Union leader Ben Tillett had not sullied by their presence his sector on their tour in France as Tillett was: 'not too popular in these parts'. Marshall felt as strongly as Bumpus about strikers, advocating conscription to: 'put the fear of God into these strikers'.[31] While J. C. W. Francis, having scorned the Germans for their dastardly 'broadcast scattering' of bombs on the United Kingdom, wished that they would: 'bomb some of the Conscientious Objectors and the miners'.[32] 2nd Lt. Rowlerson (9th Bn, Lancashire Fusiliers) was quite convinced that 'if fellows get hold of some of the [Conscientious] Objectors they would soon cure them or kill 'em.'[33]

Though some admiration for Lloyd George finds a place in letters, particularly when it appears as if by personal wizardry he were to have solved the problem of the shortage of munitions, there was distrust of him too. Private Dutton (1/20 London Regt), it must be admitted, was fully satisfied. He adjured a relation of his: 'Never, now, say a bad word against Lloyd George to a soldier. The way he has managed this shell question is superb and no other man could have done it.'[34]

A good deal more frequent than this eulogy of a politician is suspicion in varied proportions amounting in some cases to derisive contempt. As we might expect, the ire of the professional soldier is drawn most cataclysmically by the open emergence of some of Lloyd George's clandestine outflanking strategic moves to defeat his own military High Command. The Prime Minister's success in evicting Sir William Robertson as CIGS so infuriated Willoughby Norrie that he wrote even to a girlfriend a barrage of missives airing the subject. At first it is merely: 'I hear Sir William Robertson has either resigned or been kicked out. I don't know which. Its a great pity as he is a wonderful man.' Then as more is gathered: 'The Robertson affair is causing great excitement out here and there is rather a current of unrest about. We are expecting all sorts of things to happen in Parliament. I wouldn't be surprised if in a few months time Robertson does not turn out a second Cromwell and deliver England from these miserable politicians.' Norrie's opinion may be judged, according to one's viewpoint, as unwarrantably flattering to Cromwell, or generously unjust to Robertson, but it certainly does fairly reflect a groundswell of officer rank disapproval of political subversion of military leadership.[35]

A generally jaundiced view of the whole political scene to include Germany as well as Britain is caught in a letter by Captain J. E. Mitchell (RAMC) written as early as August 1915. 'You are shouting yourselves hoarse about a knockout blow, you are making enormous piles of money, you are living in luxury as you never lived before. Millions are dying in a dull way ignorant or why they should die, whilst your blind unreasoning hate is kept at a white heat by the press, the politicians and the military and other effigies you have set up as rulers. Believe me this war will only be a prelude to another and greater one unless the people make a gigantic effort to rid themselves of their antiquated governors and sacrifice their traditions.'[36]

It will have been noted that most of the examples chosen here to illustrate opinions and attitudes derive from commissioned rank sources. Several factors account for this and among them would have to be educational differences, the capacity of fluent expression, the social habit of keeping or not keeping diaries and of writing letters at length, regularly and without inhibition. There would also be the not

A Sports Day in France offered an occasion for the designer of this Northumberland Hussars' programme to nag at the idea of those unwilling to play their part. (E. Joicey)

"A Conscientious Objector to Sports"

insignificant matter of the conventions or circum- stances which conserved or did not conserve such documentation down the generations for examin- ation today, but not to be neglected is what has already been implied, the preoccupations of the man in the ranks were not with the great issues of the day. Many illustrations have been given of what chiefly concerned the non-commissioned soldier and, bearing in mind that there are noteworthy exceptions to what may be considered a limited perspective, these concerns were with making a fraction less unpleasant that particular day's living conditions which were likely to be very unpleasant. Warmth, food, drink, security, the avoidance of disapproval at any level, keeping the esteem of one's pals, hanging on to the link with home – it is upon such matters that we may fairly imagine a man's thoughts concentrating. To a large extent all else, from the enemy over the top to the High Command behind, was faceless, not meriting the drawing of one's concentration away from the essentials.

To all this there is a significant exception; it is on the question of the impact of the war on a man's Christian belief. Whether personal questioning were on the higher plain of intellectual enquiry as to the existence of God or at the humbler ground level of the simple need to trust and feel the presence of God [or strongly to deny such presence] the man in the ranks did make his contribution to the laying down of evidence for use in the unending debate between the protagonists of a spiritual or an exclusively materialist world. This is all to be expected, scoff or yawn as some may. The 'common man' in the conventional sense of attendance at church or chapel and in the far less easily quantifiable sense of his weekday thoughts having some link to his Sunday observance, had a place for religion in his life. In general terms, war service tested that place. Faith for some proved a significant even decisive element in coping – there is no need for a psychiatrist to tell us that apprehension needs medication as much as an actual wound. For others it was either insufficiently rooted, too frequently challenged or too horrifically confronted to survive. What took the place of faith so summarily swept away would vary from indifference through puzzlement to convinced atheism but it also needs stating that for some what was shattered was not faith as such but the former acceptance of the church or chapel's view of its essential formal cosily unquestionable role in the ordering of a man's spiritual life. There were Padres who played a strongly influential part in sustaining personal faith and yet found themselves less deliberately eroding the conventional foundations of their particular

denomination. The church itself for many men came nowhere near explaining the answer to the questions which demanded answering: 'How could God allow this to happen, how can God exist among this?' but for some men, God, aided by faith, could. What the war had done was to drag the soldier into a critical examination of what had hitherto been socially immunized against enquiry. Faith was not the only edifice to be so challenged.

There was much in Coldstream Guardsman George Venables' (Coldstream Guards) spiritual background wholly opposed to military service but an ingrained sense of duty was there too. He could scarcely be considered representative, in that actually through prayerful thought he had enlisted and a letter from France after the closure of the Battle of Somme showed the impenetrably secure armour of his faith. 'We are bound to live from hour to hour not knowing what will come next. What a grand thing it is to know one is a Christian and therefore can say "His will is best." '[37] The bodily frame of such men was as vulnerable as any man's to the outrageous slings and arrows of the Western Front, but not his spiritual welfare.

An actual conversion in the imminence of action has been documented by Percival Brown in the ranks of the Royal Naval Division at Antwerp. 'During the forced march we were ambushed by a body of Uhlans and had to take cover in the roadside ditches to await their attack. I believe that at that moment I was in abject fear of death. I was convinced my time had come to die and I remember taking off my cap and praying "God save me" or words to that effect. I don't think I had the thought of salvation in my mind, because at that time I was ignorant there was such a thing as being saved – but I did want my life spared and God graciously spared my life.'[38] The redirection of Brown's life was permanent and one imagines that there will have been many such deliverances which did not receive so committed a response from the man whose prayers had seemingly been answered. In this area a striking contrast is made in J. B. Herbert's recall of his response in harrowing hours of stress. 'I judge that only an emotional religion of great intensity and authority could survive the chaos of danger. I certainly never saw or heard of any of my men or friends finding time or remembrance, even then, of God. Personally I held it my one form of true courage, that I never once called upon God for help.'[39]

With regard to religion in the Army and more particularly to Army church parades, a former private in the 15th London Regiment, has written with sage simplicity that they were unpopular with

I. MUD.

I do not like the mud of France;
I took a violent aversion
To it when first it met my glance—
I do not shrink from this assertion.
And since my loathing is so great
I think it best to vent upon it
The concentration of my hate
By writing of it in a sonnet
But no— upon a second thought
A sonnet would be far too short.

Hugh Tredennick, who was to become a distinguished classical scholar, did not have many weeks as an Artillery subaltern to experience conditions in France, but in the few days between his arrival there and the signing of the Armistice he wrote and dated (18 October 1918) a poem on Mud of which this is the first verse. (Professor G. H. P. P. Tredennick)

everyone for two reasons. 'With the non religious they were not wanted for they meant nothing to them. They were disliked by the religious because the irreligious by bad behaviour spoiled the atmosphere of them and because they were like mangled Mattins, not the proper thing at all.'[40]

Sapper Percy Room expressed a discriminating disappointment with an August 1917 church parade near Bailleul. 'The Chaplain was an Archdeacon. He had a fine delivery but his material was nothing exceptional. I should imagine he was a type of the older clergy. His message was not practical enough. Tommies want something that is interesting straight and to the point with good wholesome truths – that is without doctrine.' Eight months later things were no better. 'I felt disgusted with the church parade we were forced to attend this morning. We paraded at 11.15 a.m. were inspected by the C.O. and after about half hour's standing in the sun we were eventually formed up round a table where the Chaplain was officiating. Fellows were cursing about the parade and am convinced parades of this kind do more harm than good. The Army may force some things upon the men but am afraid their attempts with religion are doomed to failure. I did not enjoy the service in the least – on the contrary. I enjoyed the service in the evening which I attended voluntarily.'[41]

It might be said that the Army were not in the business of saving souls, but its Padres in effect were charged with the responsibility of providing support for those conscious of the danger of losing their soul as well as their lives and limbs. That some did this work with marked individual and even collective success is well attested; that many made inappropriate, inadequate, ineffective attempts is as indelibly recorded.

An awful occasion, a military execution, had not found wanting the Padre, to whom Captain E. C. Deane paid tribute, and it is difficult to imagine Padre Mervyn Evers to whom reference has been made in the same chapter (Chapter 3) having been anything but a very present help in the troubles of men who were in contact with him. Writing to his sister after the Battle of Messines he told her that in the hour and a half before he had gone over the top with his Brigade at 3.10 a.m. he had gone round chatting with the men. 'I told them to put their lives into God's keeping, then whatever happened would be for the best whether they were killed wounded or unscathed – in that way you can shelve all responsibility and go forward with a quiet mind in the knowledge that God is at the helm and that nothing can happen without His sanction. A jolly good faith to live and die under – at least I think so.'[42]

It is easy, but perhaps impertinent to take issue with Padre Evers' spiritual message – more to the point is to consider its helpfulness at the time, a helpfulness reinforced by the presence of the Padre going over the top with the men. What is reinforced by such evidence is an awareness that while the faith of a man like Venables would hold against almost every circumstance, that of many men could be dependent upon the example or teaching of others. Where a Padre consistently maintained his worthiness as a man as well as Minister or Priest, his message stood some chance of providing inspiration.

For some men in the ranks, the first step the Padre had to take to earn respect was the difficult one of standing convincingly outside the built-in disadvantage of his commissioned rank. The kinship of subaltern and members of his platoon surmounted the Commissioned rank barrier in establishing close relationships more easily than could be achieved by any significant number of men of the eight hundred or so of a battalion with their Padre. Artificial mateyness would not bridge the gap which by rank and cloth separated the Padre from his men. Natural gifts of communication, human understanding and a wholesome attitude of togetherness sometimes did. Brigadier F. P. Roe has written of some of the Padres whose work he knew to be outstanding in uplifting

1. Life-jacketed service for the 1st London Regiment bound for Gallipoli. The Padre is either eschewing physical protection from torpedo emergency or has special dispensation from wearing his life-jacket. (Lord Nathan)

2. A soldier of the Leeds Pals, more properly the 15th Battalion, The Prince of Wales's Own (West Yorkshire Regiment), was given this card after taking communion at a service near Doullens on 15 October 1916 while 'out at rest' from the Battle of the Somme. (R. N. Bell)

3. A soldier's Hymnal: More modern than ancient. (Captain J. Davey)

4. 11 November 1918, Padre at Peace. Father Roger Morrissey, the Catholic Padre attached to the Royal Munster Fusiliers, stands outside the battalion's Orderly Room at Wargnier le Petit, immediately after the Armistice. (Lieutenant Colonel H. B. Holt)

△1.   ▽2.   ▽3.   ▽4.

spiritual and personal morale: Harry Blackburn in 3rd Brigade and 1st Division, G. A. Studdart Kennedy (the celebrated 'Woodbine Willie' of the 46th and 24th Divisions) T. B. Hardy, VC of the 8th Lincolns, the beloved Neville Talbot and 'Tubby Clayton' who provided in Poperinghe a location, Talbot House (Toc H) within which informality existed, tranquillity rested and an equal brotherhood in Christ prevailed – these men and others kept aflame unknown numbers of the guttering candles of the faith of British soldiers at war. Roe also dealt with the early restrictions upon the presence of Padres in forward areas, orders with which Catholic Padres in particular had not felt themselves bound to comply, well before the restrictions were lifted. Roe refers not merely to the more evident presence of Catholic Padres in such areas, but also to a detail which is almost as depressing to read as it must have been frustratingly inexplicable to experience. On the eve of the Battle of the Somme, Roe, with some others, asked the Senior Chaplain of VIII Corps if he would administer the Sacrament to them. The

Chaplain showed firm reluctance to answer their call unless: 'every participant would declare himself a regular Communicant of the Anglican Church'. The Chaplain listened to Roe's remonstrance and conceded that: 'he would administer the Sacrament in addition, to those who would promise faithfully to become Anglican Communicants if they survived.'[43]

It would be wrong to draw the inference from such a sorry tale that those who administered religious succour to their flocks were in general hidebound by such narrowness and it would be quite wrong to conclude that churches, churchmen, doctrine and practice, all failed on every front in the searching test of war, but it does seem reasonable to think that during the war the diminishing number of men holding on firmly to religious faith provided a new form of 'casualty' arising from military service. When many a citizen soldier returned to civilian life he would either have left his faith behind him in France or it would have changed radically into something more personal and less dependent upon an institutional intermediary with God.

1918: Tested and Proved

Sometimes when imagination paints a fearful picture of an anticipated ordeal, the actual experience fortunately fails to match the nightmare – the German Spring Offensive of 1918 was not such an occasion for those British troops who were to face it. Dugout discussion was not of whether the attack would come but of when and where. In varying degree, officers, NCOs and men understood that with the collapse of Russia, German reinforcement of their Western Front was axiomatic and that the German High Command would seek to strike decisive blows before the American presence in France was sufficiently strong to recharge tired Allied endeavour. Evidence of this would reach the men through the obvious channels of newspapers, rumour and that part of military orders of which they were officially informed. Some would be thoughtfully aware of the extension of the amount of frontage held by the BEF, of the incompleteness of defensive digging, perhaps there were even some who were speculatively aware of the insufficiency of troops out in France and hence frustrated at such strength being retained in the UK.[1] Whatever may have been the case, there can have been few who in the nights of mid-March were not wondering whether the morrow would bring their ordeal of defensive battle.

Where there was optimism, it was ill-founded. Letters before and after the attack sometimes cruelly reflect impatient confidence having been swept away by shocked dismay. '15 March: We have got a garden at Divisional HQ and a thirty acre plot of potatoes at the Transport lines; the whole thing being looked after by a 2/Lt who was a market gardener before the war. The potato question is even surpassing the long awaited Hun offensive, as they say we shall get no more after July except what we grow ourselves. We are getting very fed up with waiting for the Boche to push; it almost seems as if he's not going to, which will be an awful disappointment after the welcome we've prepared!' This officer, Lt William Foster (7th Bn, Notts and Derby) wrote his next letter on 25 March from HQ, 178 Infantry Brigade. 'Just a line to let you know I

am safe out of the battle and miles behind the line. All the Brigade practically has gone west. . . . Poor Winkle is killed I am afraid.'[2]

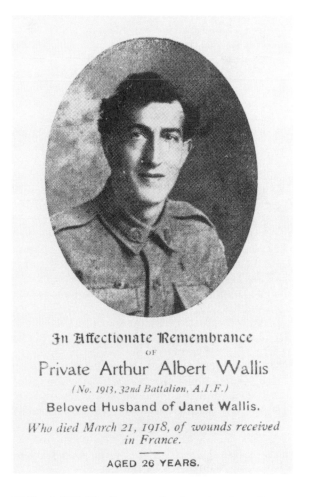

In Affectionate Remembrance
OF
Private Arthur Albert Wallis
(No. 1913, 32nd Battalion, A.I.F.)
Beloved Husband of Janet Wallis.
Who died March 21, 1918, of wounds received in France.

AGED 26 YEARS.

21 March 1918: The German onslaught and an Australian woman's loss. Memorial cards such as this one were common currency in response to expressions of sympathy to a bereaved family. Mrs Janet Wallis was no doubt representatively right, as well as sadly true, in her own case, when she used a phrase in a verse to face the photograph of 'sorrows so deep . . . that cannot be half-revealed'. (A. A. Wallis)

On 16 March, a visit by Lieutenant General Sir Charles Fergusson to Battalion HQ of the 7/8th King's Own Scottish Borderers (near Arras) was scarcely needed to confirm what was already anticipated. 'He was full of Intelligence of the coming German offensive. Indications show all along the line: new divisions from the east, new batteries, some advanced new trenches, prisoners' statements.' What would prove to be a fairly accurate lay-out of the German plans was then recorded without further comment in the diary of the Battalion Medical Officer, Captain G. D. Fairley. He seems to have made meticulous preparations, checking medical kit, parading his stretcher-bearers, giving further instruction in bandaging and dressing of wounds. He and his men would be as ready as was possible if shelling and battle circumstances were to give them any chance.[3]

A private in the 2/5th Notts and Derby Regiment, Frank Cunnington, both from a position named 'Railway Reserve' and from an observation post in no man's land in front of Noreuil (NE of Bapaume), saw regiment after regiment of German troops filing down the road from Dury to Hendecourt.[4] In the afternoon of 20 March he saw German troops entrenching in front of their wire between Riencourt and an enemy trench known to the British as Border Trench. A lugubrious Scot from the HLI, whom the Notts and Derby were relieving, had depressed Cunnington still further, addressing some of them as they passed: 'What sort of flowers would you like on your graves? You'll need them, 'He's coming over here any time now.' 'I remember we cowered in the dugout (in Railway Reserve) dozing and waking until suddenly a trembling of the ground and we were wide awake and went up into the open. All was dark but there was no mistaking the barrage on the front line. Just imagine millions of large saucepans all boiling at the same time, a weird effect.'

For several hours the bombardment continued and at daylight nothing but smoke and fog could be seen of the British front line from the railway embankment viewpoint. Suddenly the fog cleared but only momentarily to reveal storm troops, perhaps four hundred, then to the right on high ground, more appeared. 'I thought how much they looked like a flock of sheep. We fired at them and they seemed to sink into the ground.' This firing may have identified the British troops as a storm of shelling burst around them. 'It was impossible to stand with the blast and I was terror struck.' There was a lull and the seeming safety of the dugout was re-entered but the shelling resumed. After sheltering for an unremembered time, a shell-burst near the

entrance showered débris on the cowering men who emerged into the railway cutting to see storm troops ranged under the low bank of the far (West) side. More German troops dropped down from the bank onto the track. 'A huge fellow came over to us and we could just make out his shouting: 'Allez Tommy Allez, tout suite, Hendecourt.'' To Cunnington, years later, the details still stood out clear even to the narrow blue brassard on the German's sleeve bearing in gold lettering 'Gibraltar'.[5]

'On the bank a storm troop officer stood, his left forearm smashed by a bullet, two of his men had bound his arm and were holding him up to watch us go by with another wounded officer we had been ordered to carry over the bank of the cutting. The face of the big crop-haired officer standing to watch us was as white as chalk and he must have been in great pain. At his belt he carried a trench dagger with a black hilt, and he managed a smile.' There began a Bunyanesque journey for two miles along which Cunnington and another man bore their wounded burden. British shelling tore ghastly gaps in crowded Germans moving up the line and an aircraft strafed them. Two more prisoners came to help carry the German, now laid upon waterproof sheeting the corners held by the bearers, but the officer constantly moaned, calling for opium. A wounded German left on a stretcher beside their path seemed awakened by a nearby shell-burst, sat up and screamed horribly and the carrying party stopped beside another man shot through the chest and with a gaping exit wound in his back. His breath was wheezing through the wound, he was conscious but only just. ... There were thousands of men advancing and it seemed to the English private as if 'all Germany was on the march'. Apart from infantry, steel-helmeted cavalry, trench mortar gunners and also the new infantry assault guns (rather like British mountain battery guns), were identified before Riencourt was reached. Here grave-digging and burials were taking place and at the dressing station, wounded queued or simply lay on the bare ground awaiting attention from surgeons and staff in marquees while German field kitchens

German territorial gains in their spring offensive in 1918 brought Amiens under heavy shelling, the targets of particular attention being the railway station and the railway bridges over the Somme, west of the city. This nearly deserted city street, the destroyed building to the left and the rising turbulence of smoke from major conflagration are witness to an emergency which in fact was almost over because the German High Command recognised on 5 April that in this sector they could advance no further. (A. H. Gitsham) trundled their way past them towards the positions reached further forward. 'A crowd of prisoners was gathered and we joined them as a Uhlan appeared complete with Polish cap, lance and carbine, his horse with the shaggy coat, the saddle and harness in a dirty state. We were formed up and marched to Marquion on the Arras-Cambrai road and into the cage in an open field to spend a frosty night alternatively lying on the ground and walking about to try to keep our circulation going.' Cunnington's active service was over.

The 7th Queen's Royal West Surreys had been rushed up to man special positions prepared for the German assault and lost casualties in the event. When the remnants, not having been overrun, were ordered to retire, Private G. A. Fleet was assigned to guide out the last batch of men. At first there were no problems but when a solid mass of barbed wire obstructed their withdrawal: 'panic seized me and I forced everyone to crawl beneath the wire, the officer cursing me for an utter fool. Perhaps I was – but every moment counted and I feared for my own life as much as for theirs.' What Fleet had been told led him to expect that a German barrage would be on

them within minutes. Retirement was continued by regular stages. 'I had but one thought – to get away from the fighting – to leave behind the noise of shells and machine-guns.' His heart sank when he saw they were being remorselessly pursued by black, swarming, antlike figures in their rear, ever reducing the distance separating the hunters from their quarry. A wood with densely thick undergrowth barred further retreat and on its outskirts the British troops dug in for the night.

'How I feared to be left alone that night or sent on a journey but at long last dawn arrived only to display a heavy mist through which nothing could be observed.' They went forward and fired into the grey gloom. The fire was returned. The fog lifted and straight in front was an enemy machine-gun post. 'I am sure I was trembling from fright.' Firing recommenced and an attempt was made to find new cover. 'Bewilderment, anxious glances, lack of any kind of leadership or was it that we knew we were out-numbered.' One man turned and fled, others followed, Fleet joined them. Under cover of the wood there was a pause and an officer held them together as a unit attempting to defend its position

but as ammunition for the machine-gun was running out, the officer shouted 'every man for himself'. 'Nothing has ever put fear into me as that cry did. I ran through the wood not knowing in which direction I was heading, urged on by mere fright.' When open ground was reached, bullets churned up the turf they were crossing. They ran towards a road along which vehicles of all kinds were hurrying away helter-skelter. Crossing a stream they joined the motley throng the dominant feature of which was horse-drawn gun-carriages, the drivers lashing their horses in a frenzy to escape capture. The Germans were on their heels faster than they could withdraw. 'Sheer chaos reigned as tired men and their officers, and wounded too, jostled along with a sprinkling of refugees.'

Somehow as darkness fell, someone, or rather a number of men, brought a measure of control to a retirement near degraded to a rout. Men were sorted into battalions, blankets for rest issued and sleep officially sanctioned. Even though the men woke to a dawn chorus of machine-guns, order had been restored. Tiredness, thirst, blisters remained but perhaps all would now be well. Far from it: after further days of retirement all the men were formed up into a huge square. It seemed that the square, in open country, was to fight a last ditch 'stand or fall' struggle. The noise and further evidence of enemy fire led to the dissolution of the sandcastle square before the German tide – retreat recommenced. A senior officer failed to persuade the men to adopt a firing line behind the next village, but organization in another village provided shelter for the night. The men slept with their equipment on and it was just as well because the imminent appearance of the force which seemed to be hunting them impelled them up and off again into the night. At last the enemy pursuit was slower. The worst was over and 'with rest, food and drink we became normal human beings again'.[6]

German success was not uniform and it was not decisive, but for many of those over whose efforts or incapacity it was achieved, it brought fear, bewilderment and humiliation. It also brought to others and indeed perhaps in due course to most men, a call to show stoicism and determination that this was not the end. There was fortunately a positive response to that call.

In separated sectors, the defensive line of the BEF suffered successive strikes from the new German artillery barrage and storm trooper infiltration tactics. Early in April on the Lys front there commenced a battle the development of which posed serious potential threat to the Channel Ports and in

Sunset over Ypres: defending what is left of the City and the Salient. ('Realistic Travels', Photo Series/P.H.L. Archives)

May, four tired British divisions, moved south to a 'quiet sector', found themselves instead in the eye of the storm of a German onslaught in the Champagne – a new battle of the Aisne. The German attacks were not yet over and the experience of battle under the destabilized circumstance of precipitate withdrawal was shared by many British soldiers before the first signs of the turning of the tide could be discerned early in July.

On occasion, evidence survives of the contrasting elements of the overwhelming sudden strength of an attack and yet, at the same time, of sustained efforts to fight on in altogether impossible circumstances. 'April 9: called out at 4 a.m. to take up a position at Lacouture against Boche advance. Take up position in trenches and blockhouse we are let into. Germans came round on our flank. We are cut off and hold up attacks. April 10: Germans still advancing. We hold up portion of the attack. Casualties heavy. Germans bring up field gun and trench mortar and blow us out. We are taken prisoner, all that is left. Proceed under escort to cage behind Boche lines and then to cage at Lille where we join the other prisoners, very tired. No food or drink for 56 hours. Given black bread and cold coffee.'[7]

The deafened disorientation of men who survived the devastating German bombardment was the human parallel to the material destruction of all communication in order that co-ordinated defence should be impossible. B. W. Whayman, an RE signaller with a Field Survey Unit, was among men ejected from their billets by accurate shelling. The men had managed to burn their maps and Intelligence reports and destroy their instruments. Until the barrage lifted, they were cut off from retirement and, before withdrawal could be attempted, German infantry loomed out of the fog and smoke. As stormtroopers entered the graveyard of a church, from the church itself, their observation point, two sappers emerged to bolt towards their fellows. The whole group withdrew from their ruined billet retaining their rifles and ignoring a Portuguese officer's entreaty to fall in for surrender. In thick fog they found their way across country to a canal bridge and on crossing it faced interrogation from a Scottish officer whose troops were moving up in extended order. After satisfying the Scot of their identity (they had destroyed their badges), the instruction given was to convey two wounded men to a dressing station and then find their own unit in the rear. It was not unwelcome.[8]

The renewal of the German attack on the Somme in late April is particularly associated with the fighting in and around Villers Bretonneux in front of Amiens. Here in thick fog, thirteen German tanks and infantry including flame-throwing teams, broke through the British line and what was left of Villers Bretonneux was conceded. British tanks played an important part in stabilizing the position and the counter-attack which retook the vestiges of the little town was undertaken by two Australian and one British Brigade.

A hot meal did much to restore the well-being of the tired Australian troops moved up into position for this night battle. They had had a wearing day under high-explosive and gas shelling and some units had had a long march to their assembly positions. In the history of the 5th Australian Division it is fairly stated that large-scale night operations are so difficult, so liable to fatal complications and so often unsuccessful that they are rarely attempted.[9] All the current advantages to the emplaced defender were augmented with the single exception of the potential of surprise. The full moon, absence of heavy clouds and the light from burning buildings could have diminished the surprise factor but it aided the co-ordinated movement of the attackers. After some delay through the lateness of one unit, the assault went in with the fortunate benefit of dead ground protecting some of the advance towards the objective just over a mile ahead. This objective was taken without opposition, though units had become intermixed. The men were now approaching the top of the steadily rising ground where the Germans held commanding positions to assist in their retention of Villers Bretonneux.

When heavy enemy rifle fire was directed on the Australians, it spurred them into a charge upon that sector. 'Major Kuring, the senior officer on the spot, gave in loud tones the order for a general charge. A wild and terrible yell from hundreds of throats split the midnight air, and the whole line broke into a rapid run and surged irresistibly forwards, bayonets gleaming.' The Divisional History becomes almost luridly melodramatic in attempting to chronicle what must have been a savage scene of close fighting in which the bayonet proved a vital weapon as the troops advanced to take the successive posts from which fire was coming or emergency flares were racing up into the night sky. 'It had been purely and simply a soldier's battle, in which victory had been gained by the great dash and fighting superiority of the junior officers, the NCOs and men.'[10] Well might an Australian Sapper write home: 'It is something to be an Australian these days, something to be really proud of.'[11]

For an Englishman too, 24 April was 'a day that will forever remain in my memory' – a sentiment

Villers-Bretonneux 24 April 1918. The first tank against tank action. Newly introduced German A 7 Vs broke through in this section and three of them encountered three British Mark IVs, one 'male' and two 'female'. The huge German vehicles with a crew of eighteen and armed with a 57mm cannon and six machine-guns were engaged by the 6-pounders of the British 'male', the accurate fire of which caused one manoeuvring A 7 V to overturn, the crew of another to 'abandon ship' and the third to withdraw. In this photograph, an A 7 V in some disarray is to the right and a 'distressed' British tank to the left rear. ('Realistic Travels' Photo Series/P.H.L. Archives)

inscribed in a diary which records his 'personal reconnaissance since the enemy positions were unknown' and of being caught in a shell barrage which reduced his section to less than half its complement.[12] To Major W. Tysoe, then 2nd Lt in the 7th Bedfords, the day Villers Bretonneux was retaken was no less memorable. Two of the Bedfords' Company Commanders were to be killed and the other two wounded. Captain Browning, the Adjutant, borrowed sufficient white tape from Australians on his left to lay out stretches of tape on a dash and dot format to indicate the line of direction for the battalion's assault. In the dark, laying out the tape, the Adjutant actually bumped into a German who was persuaded to surrender though Browning was 'armed' with but a swagger stick. Astonishing as it may seem, Browning and his runner were to take more prisoners and the runner escorted them back leaving the officer to continue his work. When the attack went in, machine-gun fire took a heavy toll leaving only two officers, Tysoe and 2nd Lt E. J. Scott, in action. They decided to halve the battalion front, and managed to borrow a platoon of Australians to assist in consolidation on their right where there was a danger of being outflanked. A Private Hughes gallantly went forward to try to locate an overrun British ammunition dump, found it and came back for a party which then returned with five boxes, Hughes further distinguishing himself on that day by going out on several subsequent occasions to bring in wounded.

Danger of outflanking developed still more seriously on the right and in going for aid, Scott was wounded and taken prisoner, leaving Tysoe in command of a difficult situation. Tysoe's 'Staff' consisted of Company Sergeant Major O. K. Kirkby who acted as Second in Command and a number of NCOs who, on the death or disablement of officers, had taken command of small scattered groups of men. Two runners were sent to the rear to secure information on the situation in their sector. With neither coming back, Tysoe sent two more and one was to return without helmet or equipment. His companion had been killed when they were attacked by a German patrol. The Military Medal citation for this Private (A. G. Bailey) stated that he had shot three of the enemy and escaped in the resulting confusion.

The Bedfords were surrounded. At 8 a.m. on 25 April, two Germans were seen approaching their positions, one bearing a white flag. There was still sufficient confidence among the besieged remnants of the British to believe that the Germans were surrendering, but in fact one of the flag party could speak English and he brought a message inviting the British officer to surrender to avoid further bloodshed. Tysoe refused but circumspectly invited the Germans to accept being blindfolded and escorted to the British battalion's HQ to ask if the line were to be surrendered. The Germans agreed and even produced a handkerchief for this, but on their journey back the escorts were wounded and the Germans, maintaining their blindfold constraint, became lost until picked up and taken back for interrogation later.

Tysoe, himself refusing to receive a second flag-bearing party, then crept from shell-hole to shell-hole on his left until he made contact with Australian troops and confirmed to them that his men were holding on. One of his NCOs, Sergeant Walby, had managed to get to Battalion HQ for information and repeated his initial success on three further occasions. Heavy German shelling, as evening approached, seemed to presage an enemy attack and Tysoe organized a defensive flank of about 100 men to meet it. When the attack came, the Bedfords, many of them very young and newly out from England, repelled it with a bayonet counter-charge but it was not until early the following morning that the Lieutenant was able to take his men out of the action on their being relieved by French troops.[13]

The potential disaster of the German drives to the west had been averted though the attacks continued. It was not until 4 July that the first planned blow of the Allied counter-offensive struck, and the tide may be seen today to have turned even before the great battle of Amiens in the following month. Mention must be made of Le Hamel on 4 July, because soldiers at all levels were to experience a degree of inter-arm and inter-allied co-operation the efficiency of which bred a new confidence in superiority over the foe, a confidence which would be maintained through the succeeding months of victory despite the severity of the fighting.

Of Le Hamel, where American, British and Australian troops were involved, aircraft co-operated with tanks and dropped ammunition by parachute to advancing infantry; the artillery too played a notable part. In a contemporary account, a gunner, K. H. Cousland, considered that the battle had been 'the most clearly and perfectly carried out operation I have so far been in. The barrage appeared to be nearly perfect.'[14] Another officer saw the reverse side of the coin against which may be measured the raising of British morale. Having seen the German prisoners brought in, he was struck that they showed 'No sign of shame or spirit of resentment.' They all looked 'jolly glad to be there – very different from the grim-looking dazed but defiant crowds of Germans we used to see in the cage at Montauban on the Somme.'[15]

At 4.20 a.m. on 8 August in front of Amiens, on a frontage of approximately fourteen miles, Canadian, Australian and British troops and 324 Mark V fighting tanks went into action in a battle which branded upon the German High Command a conscious appreciation of the impending defeat of its forces. Two lines of skirmishing infantry, 30 yards apart, went out in a first wave to guide the tanks, the second, third, and fourth waves were composed of small section columns in single file, thirty to sixty yards apart with the machine-gun and trench mortar parties and brigade signallers in the fourth wave. Wave followed wave about 100 yards apart. Supporting battalions attacked in artillery formation that is in a 'diamond' or lozenge-shaped group. Cavalry and whippet tanks and of course supply tanks were available to exploit success and ahead of the infantry, screening them from observation, phosphorus bombs were dropped by the RAF.

A Tank Corps Staff Officer, whose job it was to find out precisely what the tanks had achieved, wrote graphically if indiscreetly of their success, in a letter to a girlfriend. 'The Huns were taken by such surprise that many were asleep with their clothes off and were brought in with just a greatcoat, in some cases not even that. The Australians and Canadians have been magnificent, nobody could have fought better than they did. Up to the present our casualties have been extraordinary light. Everyone frightfully pleased with the tanks. The whippets and our armoured cars have also done great work. I've enjoyed this battle more than any other. Its been most exciting at times.' The officer, Willoughby Norrie, a Cavalryman 'by origin', added, 'The Cavalry are still waiting for the 'H' of APERTURE but I'm afraid they won't get through it this time: the poor horses are unfortunately not bullet proof like tanks and have consequently been considerably knocked about.'[16]

According to the recollections of an Australian Lance Corporal, D. Wilson (24th Bn. AIF) the order at about midnight 7/8 August to retire from the front line to a rearward trench proved a journey to be made with care in the dark, not because of German shelling but from the danger of being run over in the intense activity of guns, gun limbers and tanks and with one's senses disconcerted by the low flying aircraft whose operations were to drown the tank engine noise. Still as Wilson accepts: 'The organization was wonderful.' His own battalion moved up to the front line at 8 a.m., Wilson noticed that his old 'possie' had been squashed by a tank and then, at 10 a.m. when the fog lifted, the evidence of great achievement lay before him. 'The country as far as the eye could see was in our hands. Pioneer battalions were preparing the roads for the passage of our guns and limbers. Prisoners were coming in by the hundred and we or many of our lads were getting souvenirs. The prisoners we met with all appeared to be happy and the war was over as far as they were concerned – before an hour had past the prisoners were coming in by the thousand – you would see one Australian leading a hundred prisoners. . . . The sight was wonderful for miles around. Every soldier on our side was in great glee and everything was on the move forward, guns tanks ambulances and everything that was used in an offensive, all moving to victory and the end of this horrible war . . . it was all new to us this open warfare – better than being hemmed in by trenches.'[17]

The nature of the war had changed for all arms, and frequent if irregular movement forward brought both exhilaration and unfamiliar problems to artillerymen. A gunner snatched time early in September to write in his diary that he simply had not been able to maintain daily entries. On 31 August they had only had an hour to move from the wagon lines near Albert, getting reconnaissance parties to go ahead and the batteries ready for action. 'We had to miss our dinner and go off practically unfed', this being resented as they had been doing nothing for four days prior to this pell-mell movement. 'We rode forward at a great pace with the

other battery parties through Montauban to Trônes Wood of evil memory. [Here] we got further orders and pushed on to Maricourt and Combles the latter had only just been captured by us and was full of most unpleasant looking corpses; all our own men, freshly killed lying about where least expected. After a few windy moments near Frize Farm, we pushed on again and were allotted gun positions behind the ruined village of Rancourt. I sent back my two orderlies to bring up the battery and I laid out the lines of fire for my guns as well as I could with a prismatic compass, with odd sticks and German helmets for aiming posts. After that I had a long wait alone for the Battery to come up. Though it was then quiet I had a presentiment that things would be lively enough before long. There were no dugouts on our position so I began to hollow out a huge shell crater behind our gun position to be used as our command post and officers' mess. The place was

At last, moving up to a moving line. Army Service Corps wagons pass large numbers of troops resting by the roadside. The absence of evidence of the destruction of war indicates that not every yard is having to be contested. (A. H. Kynaston)

Harassing the enemy retirement, Mazinghien, just south of Le Cateau, September 1918, Major Johns, No. 218 Siege Battery, Royal Garrison Artillery, plots a fresh target for his 6in howitzers. (J. H. Lawrence)

7 a.m., 29 September 1918. Softening up the Hindenburg Line. 6-inch Howitzers of 218 Siege Battery, Royal Garrison Artillery at Bellicourt laying a barrage on the German positions. The battery seems to be in an exposed position but has no problems with shell supply as a narrow-gauge rail track runs past their position only thirty yards to the rear. (J. H. Lawrence)

dotted with French graves of the 1916 battles, mostly rusty rifles stuck into the ground with black Alpine Chasseurs' berets stuck on them, all falling to pieces. . . . The Battery did not arrive until the evening and it was an awkward job getting the guns laid on their aiming posts in the dark and as I expected the Boche began to shell heavily all around us.' When they got orders to fire it was found that, in the haste, no map board had come up so the lid of the mess box was used. Being in the open and not dug in, made the gunners feel particularly exposed and liable to casualties and the officer in command had a difficult job working out the barrage calculations by the light of one guttering candle as the concussion of explosions 'seemed to jar and dislocate everything in my head. I must confess I felt pretty windy and the presence of one of the old stalwarts would have been very acceptable. As it happened the adjacent battery was less fortunate still. An 8-inch shell landed on the top of their old French dugout during the night and stove it in. All the signallers were buried and out of eleven men only four were dug out alive.'[18]

A great deal of heavy fighting had still to be undertaken. The victories of the 'Hundred Days' to the end of the war were hard earned. At Rum Corner near Béthune in August, an Adjutant, J. C. Urquhart, was handed a neatly German-stencilled message awaiting his unit. 'Dear Tommy, you are quite welcome to what we are leaving. When we stop we shall stop and stop you in a manner you won't appreciate. Fritz'.[19] Be that as it may, an average of 25 miles was retaken on the forty-mile attacking frontage between 8 August and 26 September and this despite the frontal nature of this advance and the absence of supporting attacks on the flank by either the French or the Americans. The advance had now brought the British and Commonwealth troops face to face with further major defence systems, the Hindenburg Line at the Canal du Nord and then at the St-Quentin Canal, the crossings of the Selle and of the Sambre and the taking of important contested urban objectives like Cambrai, Courtrai and Valenciennes.

The canals were formidable obstacles whether in water or dry. Photographs of the St-Quentin Canal with its steeply scarped sides to the narrow waterway at the bottom suggest that the task of planning and executing its assault, crossing and consolidation must have seemed awesomely difficult. Corporal George Scott (a Brigade Signaller with 46th Division) was one of nine signallers detailed to go with the 6th Bn. North Staffs in their attempt to cross the canal. In addition to his drum of a mile of D3 wire, ammunition, six Mills bombs, two Lucas signalling lamps and three pairs of semaphore flags and a rifle covered by an oilskin, he had a lifebelt! The signallers with all this equipment, the sappers, heavily burdened with barbed wire and explosives and the carrying parties with their stretchers and medical equipment made the assembly trenches where the North Staffs waited almost impossibly congested. Once over the top they found lanes cut in the British wire and progress could be made.

The German wire too had been so cut by British shelling that it was relatively easy to pick a way through. German dugouts seemed to contain only dead or troops eager to surrender. Behind the trench system was the canal itself and from binoculars Scott could see concrete pillboxes and a pillbox-defended road bridge across the canal. The pillbox at the bridge was not firing because the Germans had a rope ladder over the parapet of the bridge and at the

bottom of the ladder the men were evidently fixing explosives. The signaller spotted a British soldier creep up and shoot the Germans at the top and drop a Mills bomb on the men engaged in demolition work. The same soldier then dropped to the ground and started wriggling towards the pillbox from which a machine-gun was now firing. In the event this strong point was rendered defenceless by fire from a tank moving up to the canal. Scott and two other signallers descended the embankment to cross the canal with their precious communication wire. Wading soon had to give way to swimming, because of shell-holes in the bottom, but it was like swimming in mud. A wounded signaller had to be rescued from drowning, the canal had to be recrossed to repair a broken line and on Scott's return he noticed a

Canal du Nord near Havrincourt, the last days of September 1918. The canal had been unfinished and without water when incorporated into the German defence system. Some idea of its depth as a military obstacle can be gathered from this photograph of a lockgate section. A solitary sentry now stands guard while bridging problems receive consideration. (Lieutenant Colonel J. Walker)

'number of North Staffs just floating in the water supported by life jackets they wore'. As British troops got through the wire on the other side of the canal, the Germans were offering themselves as prisoners and more were found in the enemy trench system. Soaked and muddied from head to foot, Scott and another signaller learned that their division was to be relieved. Their journey to Brigade HQ brought home to them their state of exhaustion but there was little time to rest. A further advance led to Scott's physical collapse and he was to miss the opportunity of entering a nondescript little town just within Belgium, that of Mons.[20]

Where the 55th Field Company, RE was to cross the Canal du Nord, the canal was still under construction. The dry canal had steeply sloping brick walls which dropped about forty feet to a concrete bottom, itself about forty feet across. Number 4 section of the 55th Field Company had to make ramps down the sides for pack animals, walking wounded and stretcher-bearers to cross. Another Section, No. 1, had the responsibility of bridging the canal and this was more dangerously exposed to German shelling a fact which the section commander named Creed drew attention to when visiting his fellow sappers and shouting to them that they were 'skulking down in the safety of a nice deep canal'. Even when the canal was strafed by a black and red enemy aircraft, the sappers working on the sides were less the object of the attack than the troops closely packed, waiting in the canal bed for orders to move on.[21]

Where the 2/3rd London Field Ambulance (56th Division) crossed the Canal du Nord there was water in it and the crossing was by 'duckboards floating on bundles of virgin cork', according to Private Ellis's diary. His unit was able to cross by pontoon bridge and they saw Germans emerging to surrender from where they had been hidden in the rushy marshes of the far bank.[22]

In a letter to his wife describing one of the canal crossings, the Commanding Officer of the 2nd Bn, Royal Sussex wrote: 'We ran into terrible trouble as the lock houses were just the other side and full of Bosche and machine-guns in addition to which a hailstorm of shells greeted my people just as they reached a stream in front of the lock and fairly blew them out of it. As luck would have it I went up with the leading men and the [pontoon] bridges so was able to do a certain amount of bustling but I don't think I have ever experienced such anxious moments as no less than three times were my people blown back by shells, etc. and it really looked as if we would fail to get across. However I was determined that we

'I must have pressed the camera button in fright.' No. 218 Siege Battery, Royal Garrison Artillery is being shelled, 26 October 1918. 2nd Lieutenant J. H. Lawrence did not in fact realize he had taken this photograph, but in the shelling of his battery of 6-inch howitzers, positioned at Ribeauville, Gunners Fenton, Jamieson and Goodfellow were killed and Captain Henderson and Lieutenants Hoole and Randerson were wounded. (J. H. Lawrence)

should succeed and so we did. Some day I will tell you all about those twenty-five minutes which was in some ways the best and in some ways the worst I have ever experienced . . . remember what I have said is for your personal information only and I shall never forgive you if you repeat to anyone these details of my doings.' The personal courage and leadership qualities of this officer, D. G. Johnson, were to be demonstrated again in a later crossing, that of the Sambre on 4th November. For his work on this occasion he was awarded the Victoria Cross.[23]

Regimental War Diaries indicate even by their vocabulary that matters had changed, for example that of the 1st Bn. King's Royal Rifles records on 27 September that the battalion on the following day is to advance 'by bounds' to the east of the Canal du Nord. The same diary records the laying down of a barrage planned with well-founded optimism. 'At 4.45 a barrage was put down on Premy Trench remaining there 3 minutes and then lifting at the rate of 100 yards in 3 minutes until reaching the Grain-

A painting of a dressing station in the cellar of a farmhouse near Serain, at night, 8 October 1918. Through the showers of brick dust brought down by shelling, some light is provided by candles in bottles. Connaught Ranger and Manchester Regiment casualties are quietly seen to by the Medical Officer of the Manchesters. More vocally in charge, in the judgement of one of the casualties, A. Y. McPeake, a subaltern of the 5th Battalion, Connaught Rangers, was the gesticulating helmeted Manchester NCO behind the table. The officer seated in the left foreground, Lieutenant Waites, with McPeake and another Connaught Officer, left the cellar before dawn to rejoin their battalion which was soon to proceed in the direction of Le Cateau, but Waites was to be killed two days later. (A. Y. McPeake)

Victory parade, Tournai. The pipers and drummers of a Scottish regiment march to the music of the paraded band of the 7th Battalion, Durham Light Infantry. (F. Surtees)

11 November 1918. The 18th Battalion, Australian Imperial Force marches through Vignacourt. The sombre dress of many of the onlookers almost certainly indicates bereavement and adds poignancy to a scene of celebration. (J. H. McGregor)

court line, resting there 10 minutes and lifting again 100 yards every 4 minutes running from Mine Wood to Marcoing.' Such slight opposition was encountered that the leading companies were able to move beyond their planned objectives, but communication problems arose when the barrage of the 62nd Division cut off the supporting companies from Battalion HQ. A German gun team was captured and at Noyelles 'several prisoners were taken in pyjamas' but the canal bridge couldn't be crossed because of heavy machine-gun fire. The two KRRC platoons at the bridge were at least able to prevent its demolition 'driving off several attempts to blow it up'. For 97 prisoners taken, the battalion's casualties had been one officer and twelve other ranks wounded.

On 29 September, after a short barrage at 5 a.m., the leading KRRC Company crossed the canal bridge and before long the German positions of 'Marcoing support' and 'Flot farm' were taken. During the night, the battalion was relieved having lost in the action one officer and fourteen other ranks killed.[24] On their front the men had driven the enemy from over five miles of occupied France and, in considering the different character of battle now being experienced, one might be mindful of 10 March 1915 at Givenchy in an attack subsidiary to the Battle of Neuve Chapelle when the 1st Bn. KRRC lost four officers and 153 other ranks killed, the German wire being encountered intact and the advance across no man's land having thus been brought to a standstill.[25]

Open country and an enemy in retreat gave opportunity for troops to show their qualities. 'We went on at a tremendous pace – the men were perfectly splendid and showed amazing skill in the use of their Lewis guns and rifles. Thanks to that we had very little m.g. fire [in opposition]. Long before the Huns could do anything everyone was pouring lead in their direction. I have never seen greater skill in the use of weapons, nor a keener fighting spirit. Truly it was wonderful.' That the officer who paid this tribute, A. C. Wilkinson (2nd Bn. Coldstream Guards) was not swept away in enthusiasm by the exhilaration of the circumstance, is made clear by his immediate follow-up of criticism of his men for spending too much time searching prisoners for souvenirs as well as arms. In consequence of this they got out of formation even though it was 'amusing to see practically every man smoking a cigar after we had passed our first objective'. As Wilkinson himself was plainly delighted to purloin a 'long automatic pistol, a Zeiss glass and an Iron Cross first class' which he 'would not part with for anything', the problem of loss of formation does not

seem to have been one caused entirely by Other Ranks.[26]

The welcome of civilians in the villages or towns being liberated made a great impression upon troops pressing forward. 'We are moving day by day into villages where we are hailed with shouts of delight by the people and loaded up with cocoa, coffee, vegetables and everything they can give us. My goodness how they hate the Bosch here.' R. B. Marshall's next letter written on, 10 November, was of a triumphal advance, flags flying, people cheering, magnificent billets with the inhabitants absolutely unable to do too much for us. The place we came into today the table was all laid and a card placed 'Honneur aux Alliés Libérateurs'.[27]

Trees felled across roads and demolished bridges were not now seriously slowing the advance to victory. Two artillery officers went ahead of their battery by motor cycle and sidecar and thus saw some of the last fighting of the war. 'We got into Mons just at 11 a.m. at the moment the war finished. There was a most impressive review of troops in the square and great rejoicings generally. The place is full of civilians and we all came away minus most of our buttons and other decorations! Colin was able to sketch the review from the top of an ambulance.'[28]

As the war drew to a close there were opportunities to reflect upon the prolonged trial that was almost over. An unshaken faith in his God, a great sense of relief, a certainty of the justice of his Nation's cause and an untarnished faith in her achievement, these feelings and an awareness of the sombre shadow of the cost of the struggle, show clearly in Charles Arthur's letter written on Armistice eve. The news 'came in at dinner tonight at 8.15 and one bows in deep thankfulness to God. We drank the King's health very quietly and it was a moving moment. The glorious British Nation has broken the power of evil. . . . More than once the French tottered and wanted to give in, but England our England refused, tried to crush the Hun on the ridges of Ypres in '17, failed, withstood the bloodiest attack ever delivered from 21 March and in August turned and smote him hip and thigh culminating in breaking him to submission today – my God what a nation, surely a chosen people. . . . It is such a glorious victory but one is sad to think of the pals who have fallen to achieve it – Weathen (?) Ivo, Halliday, Thomas, Bill Thomas, Hilary to mention a few Calcutta men, then Wilfred, Willie Church, Robin Binning, Frank Scougal, Frank Carruthers, Alex Scougal, Allen Drew, Arthur Laird – a few of the old schoolboy friends, it is sad sad but there's has been a great death to give other's life.'[29]

Another Gunner on 11 November 1918 wrote to his mother: 'This is probably the best letter you have received for a long while! No more war! For the present at any rate. What a time it has been. I have been in the Army now for 4 years 3 months, and I think I have done my small bit in one way or another.' In both a general and in a personal way the letter writer showed prescience. 'The Bosch went away cheering. He does not know how stiff the terms are I suppose' – he continued: 'it would be worthwhile to have the car seen to. The front wheels are rickety (axles worn).' It is tempting here to see more than a concern to prepare for the resumption of civilian preoccupations. This officer, Captain George Eyston, would in due course achieve a world land speed record though presumably not in the car which had needed attention to its rickety axles.[30]

At some points in the last days of the advance, contact with the enemy had actually been lost. A platoon commander of the 3rd Bn, Yorks and Lancs received a message timed at 0850 on 10 November 1918 instructing him to 'send out a patrol forward along road and try to find the Hun'.[31] The end was very near. Units in the field, like the 6th King's Shropshire Light Infantry, received from their Brigade HQ just before 9 a.m. on 11 November 1918, the stark message 'Hostilities cease 11.00 Nov 11th a a a Troops will stand fast at that hour on line reached a a a Defensive precautions will be maintained a a a There will be no intercourse of any description with the enemy.' For the Artillery, matters were made still more specific. 'This means that Hostilities will cease from that hour. i.e. we do not shoot at the Enemy and the Enemy does not shoot at us.' Just in case there were any doubt as to who had won, Major E. H. Donnelly, Brigade Major, Heavy Artillery, XIII Corps added to his message that the enemy had agreed to suspend hostilities on the Allied terms; 'these terms imply that the enemy admits that he is defeated.'[32] There was still some uncertainty and the 11th Battalion Queen's Own Royal West Kent Regiment was informed by 46th Divisional Signals, HQ that hostilities would 'temporarily cease'.[33] Plaintively at 12.59, almost two hours after the end of a world war of unprecedented scale, a signal was received from the 'High Command, 2nd German Army' that 'a heavy English gun is still firing to South West of Binge. Please immediately cessation of fire.'[34]

The unknown British gunners who had violated those two peacetime hours had unknowingly postponed their sharing of the active service soldier's Armistice emotions, curiously and disappointingly flat and distinctively different from those which galvanized frenetic action riotously to celebrate on the Home Front.

The sense of anti-climax for the soldier is well caught in the recollections of a former stretcher-bearer, W. F. Browning. From his sleeping-quarters in Le Cateau he was walking to the school to which he and the other bearers had to report. He saw an unusual stream of noticeboard scrutineers at the YMCA hut on his route to the school. 'I joined the queue and went up to the board, in silence like the rest and read the stupendous words "An Armistice will be signed and fighting on the Western Front will cease today, November 11th 1918 at 11 a.m." Not a word was spoken, everyone went their several ways and I continued mine up to the school in the centre of the town.'[35] At last the war was over. Somehow it was difficult to grasp the fact; it was going to be much more difficult to adapt to it.

The first Christmas of Peace in five years. This captain wears the 1914–15 Star ribbon and has three wound stripes, indications of the length of his war service and that he has not come out unscathed. The child will be twenty-one years old in 1939 when there will be final proof that the officer's service had not been in a war which ended all wars. (H. A. Pearse)

End Notes

Introduction

1. Perhaps it ought to be stated that women in Army nursing organizations are being considered as outside the terms of reference of this book, i.e., distinctively different from women in the Army as such.
2. Major E. Humphries, Pte/Cpl 1st Bn Royal Scots and Cpl No. 32 Divisional Signal Coy Indian Army. Typescript recollections and official papers. P.H.L Archives.
3. H. Easton, Tpr 9th Lancers. Tape-recorded recollections. P.H.L Archives.
4. S. F. Waldron, Boy Trumpeter RFA. Tape-recorded recollections. P.H.L. Archives.
5. On this matter and for a well-researched and more sceptical assessment of the Territorials, see chapter 5 by Dr. I. Beckett in *A Nation in Arms*, edited by I. F. W. Beckett and K. Simpson, Manchester University Press, 1985.
6. H. G. R. Williams, Rfn 5th County of London Regiment. Typescript recollections. P.H.L. Archives.
7. Brigadier C. N. Barclay, Pte London Scottish. MSS recollections. P.H.L. Archives.
8. W. G. Bentley, Pte, 19th Bn University and Public Schools Bn Royal Fusiliers. MSS recollections. P.H.L. Archives.
9. D. J. Price, Pte 20th Bn Royal Fusiliers. MSS recollections. P.H.L. Archives.
10. Revd. A. L. Robins. Pte 15th London Regt. Typescript recollections. P.H.L. Archives.
11. F. O. Stansfield, Pte 3rd Bn Liverpool Pals Bde, 19th Bn Kings Liverpool Regiment. Typescript recollections. P.H.L Archives.
12. See note 5. Chapter 4 p. 106.
13. See note 11. Letter 23 October 1915.
14. See note 5.
15. A. Ball, Pte Somerset Light Infantry; letter 5 September 1914. Blathwayt Papers. Gloucestershire County Record Office.
16. G. Crew, Pte. Somerset Light Infantry; letter N.D. Blathwayt Papers. Gloucestershire County Record Office.
17. It is hoped that the case of the Conscientious Objector unwillingly in the Army will be the subject of a later book by the author of *The Soldier's War*.
17A. H. Innes, Pte 15th Bn Royal Fusiliers: Letters February 1916. P.H.L. Archives.
18. Daisy Philp (later married name Fillis), Asssistant Forewoman, WAAC. Official papers. P.H.L. Archives.
19. 'Employment of the Women's Army Auxiliary Corps with the British Armies in France. General Instruction No. 1 GHQ 1 June 1917' given in *Service with the Army* Dame Helen Gwynne-Vaughan. Hutchinson, London ND an absolutely invaluable account of the early days of the WAAC.
20. See note 19.
21. Letter from 'Gladys' No. 14694 WAAC Camp 26 Larkhill to Laura Chapman ND Mrs L. Sheppard in Chapman papers. P.H.L. Archives.
22. Dorothy Loveday, No. 13539 WAAC letters 1917–18. P.H.L. Archives.
23. Nora Steer, No. 2443 WAAC 1918 Diary. P.H.L. Archives.
24. E. G. Bates, Captain 3rd Bn attached 9th Bn Northumberland Fusiliers: letter 21 February 1918. P.H.L. Archives.
25. Captain A. E. Green 2/5 West Yorks. letter 5 December 1917. P.H.L. Archives.

Chapter 1

1. *L'Avenir* de Guise at du Nord de L'Aisne 18 August 1914. P.H.L. Archives.
2. Colonel R. Macleod, 2nd Lt. 80 Bty 45 Bde RFA: Account written September 1914. P.H.L. Archives.
3. N. Whitehead, Lt 635 MT Coy ASC: Letter 22 August 1914. P.H.L. Archives.
4. W. A. Wilson, LCpl, 1st Bn South Wales Borderers. Diary entries for August 1914. P.H.L. Archives.
5. A leaflet 'to be considered by each soldier as confidential' and to be inserted into a soldier's pay book. The leaflet's conclusion was 'Do your duty bravely. Fear God, Honour the King.' Kitchener, Field Marshal. P.H.L. Archives.
6. W. A. Wilson cited above, note 4.
7. W. G. Pelling, Pte, 2nd Bn Royal Sussex Regiment. Diary August 1914. P.H.L. Archives.
8. Sir Roger Chance, 2nd Lt, 4th Dragoon Guards. Typescript of original August 1914 diary. There is an annotation by the diarist that the demoralization was only at the apparently severe losses, losses which in fact proved to be much lower. P.H.L. Archives.
9. Lieutenant Colonel K. B. Godsell; 2nd Lt RE. Typescript recollections. P.H.L. Archives.
10. K. B. Godsell in a letter dated 4 August 1914 when clearly the month must have been September, wrote: 'I had five bridges to blow up and I think they were all successfully demolished.' P.H.L. Archives.
11. H. A. Taylor, Pte, 1st Bn Cameronians. MSS recollections. P.H.L. Archives.
12. Major General R. C. Money, Lt 1st Bn Cameronians. August 1914 Diary. P.H.L. Archives.
13. Audrain, E. Pte 1st Bn Dorset Regt. Diary August 1914. P.H.L. Archives.
14. Lieutenant General A. N. Acland, Capt 1st DCLI. Typescript of September 1914 letter. P.H.L. Archives.
15. This account is available for consultation in P.H.L. Archives. The Official History account is in vol 1. p 187, 188.
16. Colonel R. Macleod, 2nd Lt 80th Bty, 45th Bde RFA.

17. F. Luke, Dvr 37th Battery RFA. MSS and tape-recorded recollections. P.H.L. Archives.
18. From 'Experiences of a Platoon Commander', by General Sir Charles Lloyd. Reprint of articles prepared for Guards Brigade Magazine. P.H.L. Archives.
19. W. A. Wilson, cited above, note 4.
20. Sir John Crabbe, Maj 2nd Dragoons (Royal Scots Greys). Typescript account. P.H.L. Archives.
21. W. Lilburn. Lt 2nd Bn HLI. September 1914 Diary. P.H.L. Archives.
22. Major J. Crabbe. See note 18.
23. A. E. Guest, Gnr 29th Battery RFAA. Account written in 1917. P.H.L. Archives.
24. See *The Sailor's War 1914–18*. P. H. Liddle, Blandford Press, 1985, pp 42–4.
25. E. H. Carew, AB, RNVR. Card and letter from Holland 11 October 1914. P.H.L. Archives.
26. E. Audrain, Pte, 1st Dorset Regiment. Diary October 1914. P.H.L. Archives.
27. R. Chant, Pte, 5th Dragoon Guards. Diary October/November 1914 and recollections. P.H.L. Archives.
28. T. L. Horn, Lt, 16th The Queen's Lancers. Typescript of 1914 diary. P.H.L. Archives.
29. K. B. Godsell, 2nd Lt, RE. Diary from 7 November 1914. P.H.L. Archives.
30. J. Davey, Spr, RE. Diary 24/25 December 1914. P.H.L. Archives.
31. W. Mockett, Pte, Queen's Westminster Rifles. Letter 28 December 1914. P.H.L. Archives.
32. R. D. Gillespie, 2nd Lt, 2nd Bn Gordon Highlanders. Tape-recorded recollections. P.H.L. Archives.
33. Professor H. A. Gardner, Pte, Queen's Westminster Rifles. MSS Recollections. P.H.L. Archives.
34. F. R. and M. Wray, Ptes, 1st London Rifle Brigade. Typescript recollections. P.H.L. Archives.
35. H. L. Startin, Pte, 1st Bn Leicester Regt. Typescript recollections. P.H.L. Archives.
36. Captain R. J. Armes, North Staffordshire Regt. Typescript of Christmas 1914 letter. P.H.L. Archives.
37. Captain Sir Edward H. W. Hulse, Scots Guards. Typescript of letter 28 December 1914 published in *The Five Hundred Best English Letters* selected and edited by the 1st Earl of Birkenhead. Published Cassell and Co., London 1931.
38. M. L. Walkinton, Rfn, Queen's Westminster Rifles. Letter 26 December 1914. P.H.L. Archives.

Chapter 2
1. Official History of the War: Military Operations France and Belgium 1914 vol 1. Brigadier General J. E. Edmonds and Captain G. C. Wynne. Macmillan, London 1927, p VI.
1A Captain E. C. Deane, RAMC attached to 2nd Leicesters. Contemporary account. P.H.L. Archives.
2. Second Lieutenant R. Macleod, RFA. Letter 11 March 1915. P.H.L. Archives.
3. Captain M. D. Kennedy, 2nd Bn Cameronians: Typescript recollections. P.H.L. Archives.
4. *Morale:* A Study of Men and Courage, John Baynes, Cassell, London 1967.
4B Captain E. C. Deane, see note 1A.
5. Corporal E. W. J. Killick, 4th Bn Suffolk Regiment. Diary March 1915. P.H.L. Archives.
6. See L. F. Haber, *The Poisonous Cloud: Chemical Warfare in the First World War*, Clarendon Press,

Oxford 1986, p. 23.
7. Brigadier F. P. Roe, 2nd Lt, 6th Bn Gloucesters. Typescript recollections. P.H.L. Archives.
8. Captain N. C. Harbutt, Lt (Acting Capt), RE. Diary April 1915. P.H.L. Archives.
9. Lieutenant Colonel J. H. Young, Capt, 1st Bn Argyll and Sutherland Highlanders. Contemporary Field Message Book account. P.H.L. Archives.
10. J. D. Macleod, 2nd Lt, 2nd Bn Cameron Highlanders, letter 13 May 1915. P.H.L. Archives.
11. Cyril Falls, *The First World War*, Longmans, London 1960, p. 93.
12. A. S. Fox, 2nd Lt, 2/6 North Staffordshire. Contemporary Notes. P.H.L. Archives.
13. W. Hayes, Rfn, KRRC. MSS recollections. P.H.L. Archives.
14. Second Lieutenant K. H. E. Moore (1/7 Middlesex Regt), letter 17 May 1915. P.H.L. Archives.'
15. Brigadier B. U. S. Cripps, 2nd Lt, 2nd Bn Welsh Regiment, letter 17 May 1915. P.H.L. Archives.
16. See for example the Army Quarterly and *Defence Journal*, vol. III No. 2, April 1983. The Tragedies of Loos, P. H. Liddle, p. 176–86.
17. Captain E. C. Deane. See note 1A. Diary 24 September 1915.
18. W. Grossmith, 2nd Lt, 1st Bn Leicester Regt. Letter 27 September 1915. P.H.L. Archives.
19. Captain C. R. S. Pitman, 2nd Lt, 27th Punjabis. Letter 27 September 1915. P.H.L. Archives.
20. Ibid, note 18.
21. General Sir Philip Christison, Lt, 6th Bn Camerons. MSS recollections. P.H.L. Archives.
22. F. A. Colvin, Pte, 2nd Bn Royal Sussex Regt. Diary September 1915. P.H. Archives.
23. Captain R. L. Bradley, Capt, The Queen's, letter 26 September 1915. P.H.L. Archives.
24. Diary of the 15th Reserve Regiment quoted in A. Clark *The Donkeys* Hutchinson, London, 1961 (Golden Arrow Edition 1963, p. 171).
25. Even seventy years later there are impressive vestiges of the awful belts of wire in French woods or indeed on preserved battlefields like Le Linge near Colmar or Hartmannswillerkopf near Thann, both in Alsace.
26. Lieutenant Colonel R. C. Bingham, Lt, 3rd Bn Coldstream Guards, Diary 28 September 1915. P.H.L. Archives.
27. William Baynes, Ensign, 2nd Bn Coldstream Guards, Diary 16 October 1915. P.H.L. Archives.

Chapter 3
1. Lieutenant Colonel G. de Courcy Ireland, Capt, 9th Bn KRRC. Letter 27 February 1916. P.H.L. Archives.
2. There is a good chapter by Peter Simpkins on Soldiers and Civilians: billeting in Britain and France in *A Nation in Arms* edited by I. F. W. Becket and K. Simpson. Manchester University Press, 1985.
3. W. E. Jaeger, Pte, 11th Bn King's Liverpool Regt. MSS recollections. P.H.L. Archives.
4. T. Newsome, Pte, 21st Bn Royal Fusiliers. Letter extract March 1916. P.H.L. Archives.
5. Ibid. MSS Recollections. P.H.L. Archives.
6. Doctor H. C., 2nd Lt, RE. 'Meteor' Typescript recollections. P.H.L. Archives.
7. D. Storrs-Fox, 2nd Lt, 6th Bn Sherwood Foresters. Letter February/March 1915. P.H.L. Archives.
8. L. Maude, 2nd Lt, 10th Bn KOYLI. Letter 8 May

1916. P.H.L. Archives.

9. G. F. Potts, 2nd Lt, 17th Manchesters. Letter 25 January 1916. P.H.L. Archives.

10. R. W. Iley, Cpl, 21st Bn KRRC. MSS recollections. P.H.L. Archives.

11. G. W. Jarvis and H. E. Friend, Ptes, 24th London Regiment. Typescript recollections. P.H.L. Archives.

12. F. Keeley, Spr, RE. MSS recollections in letter to the author N.D., P.H.L. Archives.

13. Doctor F. J. Blackley, Capt, RAMC. Diary December 1915. P.H.L. Archives.

14. Captain E. A. S. Oldham, Capt, 7th Bn Seaforth Highlanders. Letter 23 April 1916. P.H.L. Archives.

15. D. Storrs-Fox, 2nd Lt, 6th Bn Sherwood Foresters, letter 23 March 1915. P.H.L. Archives.

16. Reverend Dr. J. A. Fraser, 2nd Lt, 7th Bn Gordon Highlanders, letter 8 October 1917.

17. R. N. Bell, Pte, 15th Bn West Yorks, Typescript recollections. P.H.L. Archives.

18. Captain E. C. Deane, Capt, RAMC. Diary 31 July 1915. P.H.L. Archives.

19. Doctor W. S. MacDonald, 2nd Lt, 11th Border Regt. Official Papers. P.H.L. Archives.

20. E. G. Bates, 2nd Lt, 9th Bn Northumberland Fusiliers, letter 28 August 1916. P.H.L. Archives.

21. Lieutenant Colonel K. C. Johnston Jones, 2nd Lt, 2nd Bedfords. Operation Order 3 June 1917 and later annotations. P.H.L. Archives.

22. H. H. Davies, 2nd Lt, 21st Bn, Northumberland Fusiliers. Operation Orders, 5 and 7 September 1917. P.H.L. Archives.

23. Trench Orders, Third Army 1916. P.H.L. Archives.

24. See note 11.

25. Official paper on Trench Foot: Army Printing and Stationery Service. Press A. 10/18. P.H.L. Archives.

26. Brigadier F. P. Roe, 2nd Lt, 6th Bn Gloucestershire Regt. Typescript recollections. P.H.L. Archives.

27. R. B. Marshall, Lt, 7th Bn East Surreys. Letters, August 1915. P.H.L. Archives.

28. Brigadier F. P. Roe, see note 26.

29. William Baynes, Lt, 2nd Bn Coldstream Guards. Letter 8 December 1916. P.H.L. Archives.

30. Sir Douglas Branson, Lt Col, 4th Yorks and Lancs. Letter 29 February 1916. P.H.L. Archives.

31. Brigadier F. P. Roe, see note 26. It should be stated that this incident took place in a barn.

32. Sir Thomas Harley, 2nd Lt, 9th Bn King's Own. Letter 25 September 1915. P.H.L. Archives.

33. Sir James Harford, 2nd Lt, Essex Regt. Typescript recollections. P.H.L. Archives.

34. H. G. R. Williams, Pte, 5th City of London Regt. Typescript recollections. P.H.L. Archives.

35. Major T. Martin, 2nd Lt, RFA. Surviving Pigeon Message. P.H.L. Archives.

36. Field Marshal Sir Douglas Haig to the Secretary, War Office, 28 April 1918 in papers of W. O. Ridley, Lt, RE Sigs. P.H.L. Archives.

37. W. M. Rumsey, Cpl, 4th Division Signal Coy RE. Military Medal Citation 10 April 1918. P.H.L. Archives.
NB: A really superbly detailed recollected account of Wireless work in the field as early as the 1915 Gallipoli Campaign is held in the papers of H. D. Billings, Spr, 1st Signal Troop, 1st Australian Engineers. P.H.L. Archives.

38. Captain E. C. Deane, Capt, RAMC (attached 2nd Bn

39. Leicesters) diary 4 August 1915. P.H.L. Archives.

39. Reverend Canon M. S. Evers, Padre, 74th Bde. Typescript memoirs. P.H.L. Archives.

40. A. S. C. Fox, 2nd Lt, 2/6 Bn North Staffs. Letter, 26 May 1915. P.H.L. Archives.

41. Lieutenant Colonel T. H. Clayton Nunn (Royal West Kents attached to South Midland Infantry Brigade as a Staff Officer). Diary 6 June 1915. P.H.L. Archives.

42. P. J. Campbell, *The Ebb and Flow of Battle*, Hamish Hamilton, London 1977; *In the Cannon's Mouth*, Hamish Hamilton, London 1979
William Carr, *A Time to Leave the Ploughshares*, Robert Hale, London 1985.

43. Lieutenant General Sir John Eldridge, 2nd Lt, 90th Siege Batt, RGA. Typescript and MSS recollections. P.H.L. Archives.

44. W. Gates, Gnr, 10th Siege Batt, RGA. Diary, November 1917. P.H.L. Archives.

45. F. H. Snoxell, Gnr, RFA. Late 1915 diary notebook. P.H.L. Archives.

46. See Brigadier Shelford Bidwell, *Gunners at War*, Arms & Armour Press, London 1970, p. 32.
Peter Mead, *The Eye in the Sky*, HMSO, London 1983.
P. H. Liddle, *The Airman's War 1914–18*, Blandford Press, 1987

47. *Flash Spotters and Sound-Rangers*, J. R. Innes, George Allen & Unwin, London 1935.

48. B. W. Whayman, Spr, Field Survey Coy, RE. MSS recollections. P.H.L. Archives.

49. F. Noddle, 2nd Lt, RE, Field Survey Coy. MSS recollections. P.H.L. Archives.

50. J. H. R. Body, Pte, Meteorological Section, RE. MSS recollections. P.H.L. Archives.

51. E. G. Bates, 2nd Lt, 3rd Bn Northumberland Fusiliers, attached to 9th Bn – letter 2 February 1916. P.H.L. Archives.

52. Sir Bruce Ross, Gnr, 13th Field Artillery Bde, A.I.F. Sports Programme. P.H.L. Archives.

53. Programmes for The National Theatre at the Front. P.H.L. Archives.

54. A. E. Green, Capt, 2/5 Bn West Yorkshire Regt. Letter 2 May 1917. P.H.L. Archives.

55. The Fifth Gloucester Gazette for April and for July 1916. P.H.L. Archives.

56. Sir Geoffrey King, 2nd Lt, MGC. Letter Christmas 1917. P.H.L. Archives.

57. Professor C. E. Raven, Pdre, 22nd Bn Royal Fusiliers. Letter 29 October 1917. P.H.L. Archives.

58. J. C. W. Francis, Lt, 19th Royal Hussars. Letter 27 March 1916. P.H.L. Archives.

59. H. G. R. Williams, Pte, 5th City of London Regt. Typescript recollections. P.H.L. Archives.

60. W. J. M., Gnr, RFA. MSS recollections. P.H.L. Archives.

61. G. C., 2nd Lt, RE. Letter 15 October 1916. P.H.L. Archives.

62. John Ellis, *Eye Deep in Hell*, Croom Helm, London 1976; Fontana, 1977 pp. 153–5.

63. J. W. B. Russell, 2nd Lt, 9th Bn Duke of Wellington's Regt. Letter 14 August 1915. P.H.L. Archives.

64. G. F. H. Snoxell, Gnr, RFA. Diary, October 1915. P.H.L. Archives.

65. L. W. Jacques, Pte, RAMC. Diary, September 1917. P.H.L. Archives.

66. W. H. Lord, 'Sixty-Five Years Ago' in *Stand To! The Journal of the Western Front Association*, spring 1987,

No. 19, p. 22.

67. G. Dallas and D. Gill, *The Unknown Army*. Verso, London 1985, Chapter 6. The nature but not the achievement of this book may be gathered from what appears on its back cover. 'A wealth of information on the brutal discipline and class differences that worsened the situation of the common soldier in France, the Middle East and England.'

68. J. Davies, 2nd Lt, 8th Bn Royal Fusiliers. Tape-recorded recollections. P.H.L. Archives.

69. F. Lindley, Pte, 14th Bn Yorks and Lancs. Tape-recorded recollections. P.H.L. Archives.

70. R. B. Marshall, Lt, 7th Bn East Surreys. Letter 14 June 1916. P.H.L. Archives.

71. Sir Douglas Branson, Major, 4th Bn Yorks and Lancs. Letters, 1915. P.H.L. Archives.

72. Sir Thomas Harley, 2nd Lt, 9th Bn King's Own. Letter, 7 September 1917. P.H.L. Archives.

73. Major M. L. Walkinton, 2nd Lt, MGC. Letter, 16 November 1916. P.H.L. Archives.

74. G. S. Atkinson, 2nd Lt, RE. Diary, 3 June 1918. P.H.L. Archives.

75. Lieutenant Colonel H. Vernon, I/C 23rd Bn Royal Fusiliers. Letter, 20 May 1917 to M. G. Milson, 2nd Lt, 23rd Bn Royal Fusiliers. M. G. Milson papers. P.H.L. Archives.

76. W. Reay, AB. RND Medical Section. Letter, 8 November 1915 to Surgeon C. Mayne in Dr C. Mayne's papers, P.H.L. Archives (it could of course be narrowly maintained that quotation from RND papers in a book on the Soldier's War is inappropriate).

77. Pte S. Woodhead, 9th Bn Duke of Wellingtons. Letter, 16 July 1916 in J. W. B. Russell's papers. P.H.L. Archives.

78. R. Towler, Cpl, RFA. Letter, 14 January 1918. P.H.L. Archives.

79. F. W. Hardy, Pte, 9th Devons. Letter, 22 November 1915 in papers of F. Pocock, Lt, 9th Bn Devons. P.H.L. Archives.

80. G. Trusty, Gnr, RFA. Paybook; R. Teasdale, CQMS, 7th Bn DLI. Paybook. P.H.L. Archives.

81. General Price List for Expeditionary Force Canteens, 1 January 1918. P.H.L. Archives.

82. H. Innes, Pte, 20th Bn Middlesex Regt. Letter, 10 June 1917. P.H.L. Archives.

83. G. S. Atkinson, 2nd Lt, 237 Fld Coy RE. Diary, 31 October 1918.

84. C. M. Woods, Rfn, 1st Bn London Regt. Diary, October 1916. P.H.L. Archives.

85. R. Ford, Gnr, RFA. Letter, 22 July 1917. P.H.L. Archives.

86. Lieutenant Colonel G. de Courcy Ireland, I/C 9th Bn King's Royal Rifles. Diary, July 1918. P.H.L. Archives.

87. R. Richardson, Sgt, MGC. Diary, 23 August 1917. P.H.L. Archives.

88. Captain W. Robertson, OC 'C' Coy, 16th Bn HLI. Letter to father of Sgt Sam Kelso. P.H.L. Archives.

89. Brigadier J. C. Armstrong, Capt, ASC. Letters, War Office. MC award notification, July 1915. P.H.L. Archives.

90. C. R. Coombs, Pte, London Scottish. Letter, September 1915. P.H.L. Archives.

91. Sir James Harford, 2nd Lt, 2nd Bn Essex Regt. Letter, 3 May 1918. P.H.L. Archives.

92. G. S. Atkinson, 2nd Lt, RE. Diary, July 1918. P.H.L.

93. V. M. Sylvester, Pte, Argyll and Sutherland Highlanders. Tape-recorded recollections. P.H.L. Archives.

94. Brigadier F. P. Roe, 2nd Lt, 6th Bn Gloucesters. Typescript recollections. P.H.L. Archives.

95. Ibid, note 94.

96. Taken from typescript provided by Clare Hills of an article by H. W. Hills, MD, MRCP, DPM. 'A Footnote of Medical History' published in the Cotswold Field Naturalist Association Journal, N.D.

97. Several aspects of this contentious subject are aired by the editorial adversaries of *Stand To!*, Peter Scott and *Gunfire*, A. J. Peacock, see *Stand To!* winter 1985 and spring 1986 and *Gunfire* No. 2.

98. Captain A. B. Ashby, Lt, 5th Bn Queen's Royal West Surreys – Capt, Judge Advocate's Department, Court Martial Office VIII Corps, letter and official papers. P.H.L. Archives.

99. W. L. P. Dunn, Pte, 17th Bn King's Liverpool Regt. Typescript recollections. P.H.L. Archives.

100. Captain E. C. Deane, Capt, RAMC attached 2nd Bn Leicesters. Diary, 24 June 1915. P.H.L. Archives.

101. Canon M. Evers, Padre, 74th Bde Fourth Army. Private and official papers. P.H.L. Archives.

102. Letter from Mr E. Green to Colonel Halkith in Canon Evers's papers. P.H.L. Archives.

103. A. Liddle, Rfn, 16th KRRC, War Office letter to his father, 2 June 1917. P.H.L. Archives.

104. A. H. Crerar, 2nd Lt, 2nd Bn Royal Scots Fusiliers. 'Diary' and letter, 24 October 1916. P.H.L. Archives.

105. Sir Geoffrey Marshall, Capt, RAMC. Typescript of an interview with him by Barbara Evans printed in the *British Medical Journal*, vol. 285, pp 18–25, December 1982.

106. Major J. B. Longmuir, 2nd Lt, 400th Fld Coy RE. Letter, 7 April 1918. P.H.L. Archives.

107. F. S. Hicking, Spr, 156 Field Coy, RE. 1918–19 Medical Case Sheet. P.H.L. Archives.

Chapter 4

1. Doctor C. Bain, 2nd Lt, Machine Gun Company Officer 147 Bde. Letters, June 1916. P.H.L. Archives.

2. Lieutenant J. W. B. Russell, 9th Bn, Duke of Wellington's Regiment. Letters, June 1916. P.H.L. Archives.

3. Lieutenant F. B. Denham, 1st Bn Worcester Regiment. Letters, 22 June 1916. P.H.L. Archives.

4. Rifleman C. M. Woods, Queen's Westminster Rifles. Contemporary account. P.H.L. Archives.

5. Ibid, note 1.

6. E. Polack, 2nd Lt, 4th Gloucesters. Letter, 30 June 1916. P.H.L. Archives.

7. H. G. R. Williams, Cpl, 5th City of London Regt. Typescript recollections. P.H.L. Archives.

8. J. MacRoberts, Rfn, 14th Royal Irish Rifles. Diary and memoirs. P.H.L. Archives.

9. Lieutenant Colonel I. R. H. Probert, 2nd Lt, RFA. Field Message Book Diary. P.H.L. Archives.

10. Taken from official papers with the private papers of Major A. A. Laporte Paine, Lt, RFA, 175 Brigade, 34th Division. P.H.L. Archives.

11. Regimental Diary of the 23rd Northumberland Fusiliers. Operation order of Lt Col W. Lyle. PRO WO/95 2498 X/K 1098.

12. Regimental Diary of the 16th Northumberland

Fusiliers. 1 July 1916. PRO WO/95 2398 X/K 1098.

13. Stanley Henderson, Pte, 16th Northumberland Fusiliers. MSS recollections. P.H.L. Archives.

14. Frank Moakler, Pte, Newfoundland Regiment. Typescript recollections. P.H.L. Archives.

15. George Norrie, 2nd Lt, 6th Buffs attached to 6th Queen's Royal West Surrey Regiment. Letters, July 1916. P.H.L. Archives. This officer was to be killed leading a platoon of the 6th Buffs into action on 12 October 1916.

16. J. G. Barron, Pte, 2nd Bn Tyneside Scottish. Tape-recorded recollections. P.H.L. Archives.

17. I. G. Andrew, Pte, 6th Bn Camerons. MSS recollections. P.H.L. Archives.

18. Henry Barber, Pte, 5th Bn London Regiment. Typescript recollections. P.H.L. Archives.

19. G. Ramshaw, Pte, 18th Bn Durham Light Infantry. Tape-recorded recollections. P.H.L. Archives.

20. W. J. Seneschall, Signaller, Suffolk Regiment. Typescript recollections. P.H.L. Archives.

21. A. S. Durrant, Sgt, 18th Bn Durham Light Infantry. MSS recollections. P.H.L. Archives.

22. Baron Strang as William Strang, 2nd Lt, 4th Bn Worcestershire Regiment. Diary, June/July 1916. P.H.L. Archives.

23. A. T. Fraser, Sgt, 1st Border Regiment. MSS recollections. P.H.L. Archives.

24. Doctor G. D. Fairley, Capt, RAMC attached to 2nd Bn Royal Scots Fusiliers, diary 1 July 1916. P.H.L. Archives.

24A A. Betteridge, Pte, South African Scottish. Typescript recollections per E. F. Slatter. P.H.L. Archives. See also Ian Uys's fine book *Delville Wood*. S. Africa Uys's Publishers Johannesburg 1983.

25. Doctor C. Bain, Source cited, see note 1.

26. Sergeant G. Minton, 17th Bn Middlesex Regiment. Diary July 1916. P.H.L. Archives.

27. Private R. M. Liddle, 1st Bn Coldstream Guards. Letter, 12 September 1916. P.H.L. Archives.

28. Sergeant W. Rumming, 2nd Bn Coldstream Guards. Diary, 15 September 1916. P.H.L. Archives.

29. Lieutenant Colonel R. C. Bingham, Lt, 3rd Bn Coldstream Guards. Diary, September 1916. P.H.L. Archives.

30. E. G. Bates, Lt, Northumberland Fusiliers (3rd Bn attached to 9th Bn). Letter, 25 September 1916. P.H.L. Archives.

31. Lieutenant Colonel G. B. de Courcy Ireland, Lt, King's Royal Rifles. Letter, 18 September 1916. P.H.L. Archives.

32. Major General W. A. F. L. Fox Pitt, extract from autograph letter 21 September 1916 by 2nd Lt W. A. F. L. Fox Pitt, Welsh Guards, to his father Lt Col W. L. Fox Pitt, Grenadier Guards. Original letter in Fox Pitt family archives, copy in P.H.L. Archives.

33. R. Tate, Dvr, Heavy Branch Machine Gun Brigade. Tape-recorded recollections. P.H.L. Archives.

34. Major General F. E. Hotblack, Capt, Heavy Battery Machine Gun Brigade. MSS recollections. P.H.L. Archives.

35. Guy Chapman, 2nd Lt, 13th Bn Royal Fusiliers. Diary, November 1916. P.H.L. Archives.

36. PRO WWO/95 3111 XC/H/045254 (research work made available to P.H.L. Archives by A.F.F. Froom).

37. See Douglas Jerrold, *The Royal Naval Division*, Hutchinson, London 1923.

38. E. G. Bates, source cited see note 30.

Chapter 5

1. B. G. Guy, 2nd Lt, 128 Battery, RFA. Diary for April 1917. P.H.L. Archives.

2. With regard to looting, S. G. Lloyd acquired a boxed Zeiss gunsight with a shell fragment embedded in the case and, quite remarkably, an officer from the overrun field battery concerned, met S. G. Lloyd in Argentina after the war, subsequently visiting him in South Wales where he saw on display the Welshman's souvenir, the gunsight from one of the German Officer's guns lost at Arras in April 1917. P.H.L. Archives.

2A From *My Grandfather's War*, W. D. Mathieson. Macmillan of Canada, 1981 pp. 116, 117.

3. C. E. Pullinger, 2nd Lt, 7th KRRC. Letter ND, but written April/May 1917. P.H.L. Archives.

4. Captain N. F. Humphrys, Capt, HBMGC. Letter, 17 May 1917, document per Col C. W. Clark. P.H.L. Archives.

5. Captain B. C. Hall, 2nd Lt, 1st Field Coy, Canadian Engineers, tape-recorded recollections and pp. 63/4 of *Round the World in Ninety Years*, privately published 1981. As it happens, Hall was then sent to the location of the two mines which had not exploded, but so damaged or destroyed were the headings that nothing could be done to revive the possibility of their explosion. One of these mines exploded in 1955! P.H.L. Archives.

6. E. C. Shepherd, L/Cpl, 13 Platoon, D. Coy, 9th Cheshires. October 1917 account. P.H.L. Archives.

7. John Terraine's *The Road to Passchendaele*, Leo Cooper, London 1977 may not be an easy book to digest, but is a much more useful one than Leon Wolff's *In Flanders Fields*, Longmans, London 1959, despite the glowing endorsement of the latter by the stimulating and prolific war historian and stern critic of Haig, Major General J. F. C. Fuller.

8. From the papers of Major T. S. Richards, Capt, 13 Welsh regiment. P.H.L. Archives.

9. V. E. Fagence, Pte, No. 11 Platoon, C. Coy 11th Bn Queen's Royal West Surrey Regiment. Typescript recollections. P.H.L. Archives.

10. Major E. Cooper, VC, Sgt, 12th (S) Bn KRRC. Tape-recorded recollections and papers. P.H.L. archives.

11. Reverend M. L. Couchman, Padre, 30 Division. Diary, 31 July 1917 and recollections. P.H.L. Archives.

12. Lieutenant General the Lord Norrie, Bde Major, 90th Inf Bde. Letter, 8 August 1917. P.H.L. Archives.

13. Colonel G. H. Brooks, Lt, F Bn HBMGC. Contemporary account. P.H.L. Archives.

14. Official History, 1917 vol. II, p. 331.

15. Sir Douglas Branson, Lt Col, commanding 4th Yorks and Lancs. Letters in October, November 1917. Branson's 24th birthday fell in July 1917. P.H.L. Archives.

16. Lieutenant Colonel J. Walker, Commanding 1/5th Duke of Wellington's Regiment. Copy of private note to Brig Gen Lewis. P.H.L. Archives.

17. Major General F. E. Hotblack, Major HQ, Tank Corps. Unpublished memoirs. P.H.L. Archives.

18. Captain J. K. Wilson, Capt, Tank Corps. Copy letter. P.H.L. Archives. 'When the leading tank broke down he walked out in front of the second tank and led it through the wire and enabled it to overcome several enemy machine-gun positions, thus largely contributing to the capture of the first two lines of enemy trench N of

19. Lieutenant C. Dillon-Kelly, RAMC. Letter, 24 November 1917 in papers of R. B. Marshall. P.H.L. Archives.
20. R. Tate, Cpl, Tank Corps. Tape-recorded recollections. P.H.L. Archives.
21. Major General H. L. Birks, Capt, Tank Corps. Tape-recorded recollections. P.H.L. Archives.
22. Captain J. K. Wilson, Capt, Tank Corps. Tape-recorded recollections. P.H.L. Archives.
23. Captain J. G. Hassall, Lt, Tank Corps. Tape-recorded recollections. P.H.L. Archives.
24. War Diary, Inniskilling Dragoons, December 1917. Copy held in P.H.L. Archives per Regimental Museum.

Chapter 6

1. J. R. T. Keast, Pte, 11th Bn AIF. Diary, November, December 1914. P.H.L. Archives.
2. W. M. Clark, Pte, 10th Bn AIF. Diary, January 1915. P.H.L. Archives.
3. G. C. Grove, Spr, No. 2 Field Coy, Australian Engineers, 1st Division, AIF. Diary, January 1915. P.H.L. Archives.
4. C. Parkes, Pte, 1st Bn AIF. Diary, November 1914. P.H.L. Archives.
5. I. T. Birtwistle, L/Cpl, 22nd Bn AIF. Diary, May 1915. P.H.L. Archives.
6. F. L. Goldthorp, Pte, 185 Coy MGC. Typescript recollections. P.H.L. Archives.
7. J. E. B. Jardine, Lt, 1st Bn Queen's Royal West Surrey Regt. Diary, October, November 1914. P.H.L. Archives.
8. Captain E. F. Wettern, Spr, 2nd Field Coy, RND Engineers. Letter, March 1915. P.H.L. Archives.
9. For *Manitou*, *Southland* and *Royal Edward* see *Men of Gallipoli*, P. H. Liddle, Allen Lane, London 1976 and for *Mercian*, *Cameronia*, *Aragon* and again *Royal Edward* see *The Sailor's War*, Peter Liddle, Blandford, 1985
10. W. R. Matthews, Capt, RAMC, Letter/Diary, July, August 1917. P.H.L. Archives.
11. Professor G. B. Harrison, 2nd Lt, 5th Bn Queen's Royal West Surrey Regt. Typescript recollections. P.H.L. Archives.
12. J. F. Alston, Lt, MGC. Typescript recollections. P.H.L. Archives.
13. Captain E. B. Hickson, Capt, RAMC. Diary, April 1915. P.H.L. Archives.
14. J. Grimshaw, L/Cpl, ASC. Diary, April 1917. P.H.L. Archives.
14A. W. Solden, Pte, Middlesex Regt. MSS recollections. P.H.L. Archives.
15. J. Parish, Pte, 2/1 East Lancs. Field Ambulance, RAMC. Letter, 17 August 1915. P.H.L. Archives.
16. T. H. W. Maxfield, Pte, 2nd Queen's Royal West Surrey Regt. Diary, November 1917. P.H.L. Archives.
17. H. E. Baker, Pte, 9th Bn Devons. Typescript recollections. P.H.L. Archives.
18. Brigadier G. E. R. Ince, 2nd Lt, RFA. Typescript recollections. P.H.L. Archives.
19. Major General D. G. Johnson, VC, Capt, 2nd Bn South Wales Borderers. Letters, September–November 1914. P.H.L. Archives.
20. Details taken from Government Gazette: British Administration – German New Guinea, vol. 1, No. 1.

15 October 1914 and from related papers of Col Basil Holmes, Lt and Aide de Camp (& son) to the officer in Command, Colonel W. Holmes. P.H.L. Archives. As it happened the occupying force was involved in a drama which had wider ramifications, the official flogging of a German found to have beaten a Methodist missionary.
21. L. P. Leary, Pte, 5th Bn Wellington Regt, NZR. Typescript recollections. P.H.L. Archives.
22. Sir Herbert Todd, 2nd in Command, Mandalay Military Police Expedition. Typescript recollections. P.H.L. Archives.
23. Doctor N. S. Deane, West African Medical Service, Medical Officer attached to West African Regiment. Diary, contemporary papers and recollections. P.H.L. Archives.
24. Doctor J. J. Fourie, Tpr, South African Defence Force volunteer. Typescript recollections. P.H.L. Archives.
25. H. Leith, Tpr, South African Defence Force volunteer. Typescript recollections. P.H.L. Archives.
26. Judge F. N. Broome, Tpr, Natal Carbineers. MSS recollections. P.H.L. Archives.
27. W. Whittaker, Gnr, Natal Field Artillery. Typescript recollections. P.H.L. Archives.
28. Marshal of the RAF, Sir Arthur Harris, Bugler, Rhodesian Regiment. Tape-recorded recollections. P.H.L. Archives.
29. C. Hordern, Military Operations: East Africa, vol. 1. August 1914–September 1916. HMSO, London 1941, p. 14.
30. C. Hordern, *opus cit.* note 29, p. 521.
31. Captain F. A. Archdale, 2nd Lt, 130th Baluchis. Typescript recollections. P.H.L. Archives.
32. T. N. Whitehead, Capt, ASC. Letters, June, July 1916. P.H.L. Archives.
33. Charles Miller, *Battle for the Bundu*, Macdonald & Jane, London 1974 (Purnell Book Services Edition, p. 68).
34. G. A. Pim, Lt, 130th Baluchis. Letter, 1 May 1915. P.H.L. Archives.
35. A. V. Groves, Spr, RE. Typescript recollections. P.H.L. Archives.
36. Doctor Q. Madge, Capt, RAMC. Letter, 3 November 1917. P.H.L. Archives.
37. P. Tozer, Gnr, 14 Bty RGA. Diary, 1916/17. P.H.L. Archives.
38. S. T. Whitty, Pte, RE (Dispatch Rider). Typescript recollections. P.H.L. Archives.
39. T. Smith, Pte, No. 6 Topographical Section, RE. Tape-recorded recollections. P.H.L. Archives.
40. Major General C. G. Phillips, Capt, 1st Bn King's African Rifles. Official Papers, 1914/15. P.H.L. Archives.
41. A. L. Messum, Sgt, British South African Police. Tape-recorded recollections, tape made by Rhodesia Broadcasting Corporation, 1973. P.H.L. Archives.
42. C. Shaw, Pte, 25th Royal Fusiliers (Frontiersmen). MSS recollections. P.H.L. Archives.
43. Lieutenant Colonel J. W. Watts, Lt, 2nd Bn Hampshire Regt. Brigade Staff Officer, Aden Field Force. P.H.L. Archives.
44. R. Graham, Officer with Aden Field Force detachment at Sheik Othman, 2 May 1916. P.H.L. Archives.
45. From the papers of Major F. B. Davies, 2nd Lt, RGA Aden Field Force. P.H.L. Archives.
46. A. C. Smith, 2nd Lt, 110/5 Bty RFA, Aden Field Force. Diary, September 1918. P.H.L. Archives.
47. Lieutenant the Hon Lancelot Bailey, Brecknockshire

Bn South Wales Borderers, Aden Field Force. Typescript of July 1915 Letter. P.H.L. Archives.

48. Lieutenant Colonel the Lord Glanusk, Brecknockshire Bn South Wales Borderers, Aden Field Force. Typescript of July 1915. Letter. P.H.L. Archives.

49. Philip Mason, *A Matter of Honour, An account of the Indian Army, its officers and men*, Jonathan Cape, London 1974 (Penguin Edition pp. 405–6).

50. Lieutenant Colonel O. D. Bennett, Lt, Khyber Rifles. Typescript recollections. P.H.L. Archives.

51. C. Pearce, Sgt, 4th Bn Duke of Cornwall's Light Infantry. Diary, November 1914. P.H.L. Archives.

52. Sir Olaf Caröe, Lt, 4th Bn Queen's Royal West Surrey Regt. MSS recollections. P.H.L. Archives.

53. C. J. Davies, Pte, 25 London Regt. Diary, June, July 1917. P.H.L. Archives.

54. F. J. Banks, Cpl, 25 London Regt. Contemporary account, 1917. P.H.L. Archives.

55. R. C. Morton, Capt, 2/6 Sussex Regiment. Diary, August 1918. P.H.L. Archives.

56. V. C. R. Yearsley, Cpl, 29th London Regt. Diary, June December 1918. P.H.L. Archives.

57. C. G. Wheeler, Lt, 252 Coy MGC. Typescript recollections. P.H.L. Archives. Colonel Springfield was much less enthusiastic about the boots than was Wheeler, Springfield reckoning that they slipped uncontrollably on hard-packed snow and were insufficiently warm.

58. Colonel C. H. D. O. Springfield, Capt, RGA. Typescript recollections. P.H.L. Archives.

59. L. W. Jacques, Pte, RAMC. Diary, 11/12 December 1918. P.H.L. Archives.

60. A. J. Goodes, L/Sgt, 2/10 Royal Scots. MSS recollections. P.H.L. Archives.

61. Major General D. A. L. Wade. Details taken from 'A subaltern in Italy' published in *The Fighting Forces* Vol. XIV, No. 4, October 1937 and supplemented by tape-recorded recollections. P.H.L. Archives.

62. Brigadier J. V. Faviell, 2nd Lt, RHA. MSS recollections. P.H.L. Archives.

63. Sir Louis Gluckstein, Lt, Intelligence Corps, GHQ Italy. Leaflet among his papers. P.H.L. Archives.

64. See note 62.

65. Colonel R. Macleod, Maj, RFA. Letters, January/June 1918. P.H.L. Archives.

66. G. E. Ramshaw, Pte, 18th Bn DLI. Official reports and MSS recollections. P.H.L. Archives.

67. H. P. Sherwood, 2nd Lt, 7th Bn Royal Warwicks. Diary, 15/16 June 1918. P.H.L. Archives.

68. W. J. Bradley, Sgt, 2nd Bn HAC. Typescript recollections. P.H.L. Archives.

Chapter 7

1. See for example *Home Fires and Foreign Fields*, edit. P. H. Liddle, Brasseys, London 1985; *Gallipoli 1915, Pens, Pencils and Cameras at War*, P. H. Liddle, Brasseys, London 1985; *Men of Gallipoli*, Peter Liddle, Allen Lane, London 1976; R. R. James's *Gallipoli*, Batsford, London 1965; A. Moorehead, *Gallipoli*, illustrated, Macmillan Company of Australia, 1975.

2. Personal note from Major General Sir Aylmer Hunter-Weston, CB, DSO, to each man of the 29th Division. P.H.L. Archives.

3. Captain G. N. Walford, VC, Capt, RFA. Brigade Major 29th Division Artillery. Letter, 21 April 1915. P.H.L. Archives. This was Captain Walford's last letter. He

was to be killed leading a storming party into the village of Seddul Bahr above 'V' Beach.

4. Official papers with the War Diary of the 1st Bn Royal Munster Fusiliers. PRO WO/95 4310 XK 976.

5. Report of 2nd Lt H. A. Brown, 1st Bn Royal Munster Fusiliers. PRO WO/95 4310 XK 976.

6. G. C. Grove, Spr, 2nd Field Company, 1st Aust Div, AIF. Diary, 24 May 1915. P.H.L. Archives.

7. C. H. Mapp, Tpr, City of London Yeomanry. Typescript recollections. P.H.L. Archives.

8. Captain J. R. Starley, 2nd Lt, 9th Royal Warwicks. Letter, 30 July 1915. P.H.L. Archives.

9. Official History, Military Operations Gallipoli, Brig Gen C. F. Aspinall Oglander, vol. II, Heinemann, London 1932, pp. 213–14.

10. A. Bayne, Bugler, 1st Bn Wellington Regiment, NZEF. Diary, 8 August 1915. P.H.L. Archives.

11. R. Davie, Pte, 1st Bn Wellington Regiment, NZEF. Post-war account published in a New Zealand newspaper. P.H.L. Archives.

12. Lieutenant General Sir Reginald Savory, 2nd Lt, 14th Sikhs. Letter, November 1915. P.H.L. Archives. The History of the 10th Princess Mary's Own Gurkha Rifles relates that the 2nd Bn had 447 cases of frostbite.

13. Lieutenant Colonel A. G. Brown, Cpl, Fife and Forfar Yeomanry. MSS recollections. P.H.L. Archives.

14. PRO WO/95 4310 XK 976.

15. Lieutenant Colonel D. B. Watson, 2nd Lt, 2/10 Middlesex Regt. Diary, December 1915; letter and official papers (Embarkation Order No. 4 by Major General Marshall 17 December 1915). P.H.L. Archives.

15a. Political/military argument as to whether the war could be waged more effectively from the eastern Mediterranean, outflanking the Central Powers, rather than according all priority to the Western Front.

16. Colonel G. H. Gordon, Capt, RFA. Letter, 1 November 1915. P.H.L. Archives.

17. R. C. McB. Broun, 2nd Lt, 6th Bn Dublin Fusiliers. Diary, December 1915. P.H.L. Archives.

18. Major General Sir Drummond Inglis, 2nd Lt, 38th Fld Coy, RE. Letter, 2 May 1916. P.H.L. Archives.

19. Brigadier Sir John Boyd, Capt, RAMC attached to 38th Wessex Fld Coy, RE. Sir John was subsequently posted to both Base and Mobile Bacteriological Laboratories and as Pathologist at No. 29 General Hospital. He has left a remarkable account of his medical research work in these appointments (held in P.H.L. Archives).

20. W. Battersby, Pte, 6th Dublin Fusiliers. Typescript recollections. P.H.L. Archives.

21. Weston Drury, Sgt, RAMC. Reminiscences published in *The Mosquito* (an Old Comrades' Association publication from which Tom Barker's recollections were taken too), and Divisional Commander's letter, July 1916. P.H.L. Archives.

22. W. D. Mather, Pte, 8th Ox and Bucks. Diary, September 1918. P.H.L. Archives, and 'Muckydonia,' Arthur H. Stockwell, Ilfracombe 1979.

23. T. Simpson, 2nd Lt, 26th Bn Middlesex Regt. Typescript recollections. P.H.L. Archives.

24. I. Davies, Gnr, 'Y' Bty 1st Trench Mortars. Typescript recollections. P.H.L. Archives.

25. Sir Thomas Harley, 2nd Lt, 9th Bn King's Own Royal Regiment (Lancaster). Letters, June, July, August 1917. P.H.L. Archives.

26. Lieutenant Colonel J. H. Young, Capt, 1st Bn Argyll

and Sutherland Highlanders. Account written in October 1916. P.H.L. Archives.

27. Colonel J. D. Milne, 2nd Lt, 1st Bn Royal Scots. Account written 14 October 1916. P.H.L. Archives.
28. T. F. Higham, 2nd Lt, 9th Ox and Bucks. Intelligence officer 67 Bde HQ. Official Report and related official papers, September 1916. P.H.L. Archives.
29. F. T. Mullins, Pte, 10th Devons. MSS recollections. P.H.L. Archives.
30. Official History, Military Operations, Macedonia, vol II, Capt. C. Falls, HMSO, London 1935, p. 291.
31. T. D. Cumberland, Capt, RAMC, attached 9th Bn King's Own Royal Regiment (Lancaster). Typescript recollections. P.H.L. Archives.
32. See The Report of the Mesopotamian Commission, HMSO 1917, Part XI, p. 97.
33. Major General H. H. Rich, 2nd Lt, 120th Rajputana Rifles. Typescript recollections. P.H.L. Archives.
34. I. Ferrier, Lt, 48th Bombay Pioneers. Letter, 5 May 1915. P.H.L. Archives.
35. Major W. W. A. Phillips, 2nd Lt, 24th Punjabis. Letter, 20 April 1915. P.H.L. Archives.
36. See note 33.
37. H. J. Coombs, Cpl, Royal West Kent Regt. Typescript recollections. P.H.L. Archives.
38. A. J. Barker, The Neglected War: Mesopotamia 1914–18, Faber & Faber, London 1967, p. 98.
39. Colonel T. E. Osmond, Capt, RAMC. Diary, June 1915. P.H.L. Archives.
40. J. E. B. Jardine, Capt, 5th Bn The Queen's. Letter, 21 January 1916. P.H.L. Archives.
41. A. Vanstone, Pte, Dorset Regt. MSS recollections. P.H.L. Archives.
42. Major General H. H. Rich, see note 33.
43. Lieutenant Colonel S. Van Buren Laing, Maj, 76th Punjabis. Letter, 11 January 1916. P.H.L. Archives.
44. A. J. Barker, The Neglected War: Mesopotamia 1914–18, Faber & Faber, London 1967, p. 137.
45. See note 43.
46. Captain C. R. S. Pitman, Temp Capt, 27th Punjabis. Letter, 15 March 1916. P.H.L. Archives.
47. Lord Hodson, Capt, 7th Gloucesters. Letter, 17 May 1916 and MC Citation. P.H.L. Archives.
48. See note 33.
49. F. S. Hudson, Bombardier, 86th Heavy Battery, RGA. Typescript recollections. P.H.L. Archives.
50. Captain J. Davey, A/Cpl, RE. Diary, February 1917. P.H.L. Archives.
51. Captain C. R. S. Pitman, Temp Capt, 27th Punjabis. Letter, 24th February 1917 and citation, and Lt Col D. G. Rule, Lt, 27th Punjabis. MSS recollections. P.H.L. Archives.
52. W. G. Gledhill, Sgt, 2nd Bn Norfolks. MSS recollections. P.H.L. Archives.
53. A. N. Stevenson, Pte, RAMC, 23 Stationary Hospital, Amara. Diary, February–November 1917. P.H.L. Archives.
54. See note 50. Diary, 11 March 1917. P.H.L. Archives.
55. G. P. T. Dean, Lt, 24th Punjabis. Contemporary account, 3 April 1918. P.H.L. Archives.
56. L. W. Jardine, Capt, 1/5 Queen's, contemporary account. P.H.L. Archives.
57. Sir Kenneth O'Connor, Lt, 14th Sikhs. Typescript recollections. P.H.L. Archives.
58. Brigadier J. Le C. Fowle, Capt, South Persian Rifles, from his 1916 diary. P.H.L. Archives.

59. Colonel J. Teague, Capt, 3/124 Baluchis. Typescript recollections. P.H.L. Archives.
60. Sir Ernest Goodale, Lt, 9th Royal Warwicks. Diary quoted in typescript recollections. P.H.L. Archives.
61. Lieutenant Colonel J. Haigh, Lt, 9th Royal Warwicks. Diary, September 1918 and typescript recollections. P.H.L. Archives.
62. See note 60.
63. Colonel W. Nash, Capt (Queen's Royal West Kent Regt), Staff Officer to General Malleson, quoting a Malleson Dispatch dated 17 October 1918. P.H.L. Archives.
64. Professor G. Wilson Knight, Cpl, RE (Dispatch Rider). Typescript recollections. P.H.L. Archives.
65. M. C. Evans, Pte, 1st Light Horse, AIF. Letters, December/January 1914–15. P.H.L. Archives.
66. K. Stephens, Tpr, Auckland Mounted Rifles, NZEF. Typescript, diary and recollections. P.H.L. Archives.
67. A. E. Joyce, Pte, 9th Bn AIF. Diary, 21 January 1915. P.H.L. Archives.
68. C. J. Walsh, Pte, 1st Bn Auckland Regt, NZEF. Diary, 2 April 1915. P.H.L. Archives.
69. A. Clennett, Sgt, 9th Bty Australian Field Artillery. Letter, April 1915. P.H.L. Archives.
70. G. C. Grove, Spr, 2nd Field Coy, Australian Engineers. Diary, notebook, 1915. P.H.L. Archives.
71. A. G. Jennings, Sgt, 1st Bn Wellington Regt, NZEF. Diary, 5 February 1915. P.H.L. Archives.
72. C.L.C. L/Cpl, 1st Bn Wellington Regt, NZEF. Account for 9 February 1915. See Official History of Military Operations, Egypt and Palestine, vol 1, p. 47.
73. M. Ward, Tpr, Dorset Yeomanry. Typescript recollections. P.H.L. Archives.
74. Major General G. W. Richards, 2nd Lt, MGC (Motor Branch) No. 2 Light Car Patrol, Western Desert, Egypt. MSS recollections. P.H.L. Archives.
75. Account taken from 'Sudan Notes and Records, Vol. XXII, Part 1 1939 Darfur 1916' by J. A. Gillan and Official History of Military Operations, Egypt and Palestine, vol. I, pp. 145–53.
76. P. G. Sneath, Lt, 1/4 Northants Regt. I/C Stokes mortars at Romani, July/August 1916. Typescript recollections. P.H.L. Archives.
77. Colonel Robin Buxton, I/C Camel Corps detachment in the Hejaz 1918. Diary, 1918. P.H.L. Archives.
78. C. Dawson, Tpr, Imperial Camel Corps detachment in the Hejaz 1918. MSS recollections. P.H.L. Archives.
79. Lieutenant Colonel D. B. Watson, Lt, 2/10 Middlesex. Diary, March 1917. P.H.L. Archives. Bracketted sections are abbreviated summaries of the original.
80. See note 79. Watson's Captaincy promotion came through on the day following this diary entry of 19 April 1917. He had been kept out of this attack initially as one of the 'ten per cents' normally withheld, but his keenness to be with his company enabled him to get permission to join them and, as it happened, a message had been sent back to bring him up as the officer in command of the company had been hit.
81. H. O. Bigg, Cpl, RE Signals, 54th Division. Diary, 19 April 1917. P.H.L. Archives. It might be mentioned that the 163 Bde referred to had 1,828 casualties.
82. See Official History, vol. 1, p. 339.
83. G. D. Breffitt, Cpl, RE. Letter, 23 September 1917. P.H.L. Archives.
84. Captain H. K. Hatrick, Lt, Auckland Mounted Rifles. Letter, 29 November 1917. P.H.L. Archives.

85. Official History, vol. 11, Part 1, pp. 58/9.

86. Brigadier Sir Kenneth Wills, Capt, 2/15th County of London Regt. Account written from notes made in 1919. P.H.L. Archives.

87. C. H. Perkins, Lt, Bucks Hussars. Typescript recollections. P.H.L. Archives.

88. Colonel E. C. Catford, Lt, RAMC, Yeomanry Mounted Division. Typescript of letters, November 1917. P.H.L. Archives.

89. Lieutenant Colonel J. H. Young, Maj and 2nd I/C London Scottish. Letter, 18 December 1917. P.H.L. Archives.

90. See Official History, Egypt and Palestine, vol. 11, Part 11, p. 423.

91. *The Romance of the Last Crusade*, Major Vivian Gilbert, D. Appleton & Co. London 1932, pp. 190/1.

92. *Imperial Camel Corps*, Geoffrey Inchbald, Johnson, London 1970, pp. 107 et seq.

93. 4th Cavalry Division Official Narrative of Events during operations, 10 September/15 October 1918. Among papers of Sir Godfrey Llewellyn, Lt, Montgomeryshire Yeomanry. P.H.L. Archives.

94. See note 88. Typescript of letter, September 1918. P.H.L. Archives.

95. See Official History of Australia in the War of 1914–18, vol. II, Sinai and Palestine, H. S. Gullett. Angus & Robertson, Sydney 1923, pp. 787-90.

Chapter 8

1. William Baynes, Lt, 2nd Bn Coldstream Guards. Letter, 17 December 1916. P.H.L. Archives.

2. Sir Geoffrey King, Capt, MGC, Letters, 10 June 1918 and 2 July 1918. P.H.L. Archives.

3. F. C. Pritchard, Capt, RFA. Letter, 5 January 1918. P.H.L. Archives.

4. Lieutenant Colonel A. C. Wilkinson, Lt, 2nd Bn Coldstream Guards. Letter, 12 December 1917. P.H.L. Archives.

5. His Honour, Judge J. B. Herbert, 2nd Lt, 5th Bn, attached to 2/4 Royal West Surrey Regt. Diary/Account, October 1918. P.H.L. Archives.

6. T. C. Gillespie, 2nd Lt, King's Own Scottish Borderers. Letter, 16 October 1914 in papers of J. W. Parr. P.H.L. Archives.

7. F. B. Denham, 2nd Lt, 1st Bn Worcester Regt. Letter, 17 March 1916. P.H.L. Archives.

8. W. Foster, Lt, 7th Notts and Derby. Letter, 5 May 1917. P.H.L. Archives.

9. Lord Norrie, Brigade Major, 90th Inf Bde. Letter, 6 December 1917. P.H.L. Archives.

10. E. G. Bates, Capt, 3rd Bn, attached 9th Bn Northumberland Fusiliers. Letters, 19 October and 5 November 1918. P.H.L. Archives.

11. M. W. Parr, Capt, 5th Bn HLI. Letter, 30 May 1918. P.H.L. Archives.

12. Doctor F. J. Blackley, Lt, RAMC. Diary, August, September 1915. P.H.L. Archives.

13. N. A. Turner-Smith, Lt, Staff Officer, 23 Div Signals. Diary, 24 March 1917. P.H.L. Archives.

14. Lord Norrie, Brigade Major, 2nd Bde Tank Corps. Letter, 2 April 1918. P.H.L. Archives.

15. E. Bowlby, 2nd Lt, 6th Bn E. Yorks. Letter, 20 April 1916. P.H.L. Archives.

16. William Baynes, Lt, 2nd Bn Coldstream Guards. Letter, 8 April 1916. P.H.L. Archives.

17. L. A. G. Boyce, Lt, 41st Bn AIF. From letters, October–December 1917. P.H.L. Archives.

18. W. G. Wallace, Lt, 2/3 London Regt. Typescript recollections. P.H.L. Archives.

19. Lieutenant Colonel G. de Courcy Ireland, I/C, 9th KRRC. Letter, 25 June 1918. P.H.L. Archives.

20. M. W. Parr, Capt, 5th Bn HLI. Letter, 22 June 1918. P.H.L. Archives.

21. W. G. Wallace, Lt, 2/3 London Regt. Official papers, January 1917. P.H.L. Archives.

22. Major General Sir Guy Salisbury Jones, 2nd Lt, Coldstream Guards. Diary, 7 June 1917. P.H.L. Archives.

23. W. A. R. Morrison, Rfn, 21st Bn KRRC. Letter, 30 August 1916. P.H.L. Archives.

23a. The best possible authoritative corrective to this view has recently been published: *Staff Officer*, the Diaries of Lord Moyne, 1914–18, ed. Brian Bond, Leo Cooper, 1987

24. R. Findlay, Petty Officer Hawke Bn RND. Diary, 13 June and 9 August 1915. P.H.L. Archives.

25. G. I. Larkins, 2nd Lt, 10th Bn W. Yorks. Letter to the author, 8 July 1982. P.H.L. Archives.

26. Captain J. C. Urquhart, Lt, 2/5 Lincolnshire Regt. Personal papers, poem initialled E.D.A. and dated 23 April 1918. P.H.L. Archives.

27. G. S. Atkinson, 2nd Lt, RE. Diary, 24 April 1918. P.H.L. Archives.

28. A. B. Waring, Lt, 1/8 Lancashire Fusiliers. Letter, 1 April 1917. P.H.L. Archives.

29. A. E. Bumpus, Lt, RE. Letter, 12 September 1915. P.H.L. Archives.

30. H. Innes, Pte, Pay Corps. 1 May 1918. P.H.L. Archives.

31. R. B. Marshall, 2nd Lt, 7th East Surreys. Letters, 9 July 1915, 22 July 1915. P.H.L. Archives.

32. Captain J. C. W. Francis, Lt, 19th Royal Hussars. Letter, 9 February 1916. P.H.L. Archives.

33. Captain A. B. Rowlerson, 2nd Lt, 9th Bn Lancashire Fusiliers. Letter, 26 March 1916. P.H.L. Archives.

34. A. G. Dutton, Pte, 1/20th London Regt. Letter, 3 October 1915. P.H.L. Archives.

35. Lord Norrie, Brigade Major, 2nd Brigade Tank Corps. Letters, 17/18 February 1918. P.H.L. Archives.

36. Doctor J. E. Mitchell, Capt, RAMC. Letter, 25 August 1915. P.H.L. Archives.

37. G. Venables, Pte, 3rd Bn Coldstream Guards. 18 November 1916. P.H.L. Archives.

38. P. A. Brown, AB, RNVR, RND. Typescript recollections. P.H.L. Archives.

39. His Honour, Judge J. B. Herbert, 2nd Lt, 5th Bn attached to 2/4 Royal West Surrey Regt. Diary/Account written October 1918. P.H.L. Archives.

40. Reverend A. L. Robins, Pte, 15th London Regt. Typescript recollections. P.H.L. Archives.

41. P. Room, Spr, RE. Diary, 5 August 1917 and 19 May 1918. P.H.L. Archives.

42. Canon M. Evers, Padre, 74th Bde. Letter, June 1917. P.H.L. Archives.

43. Brigadier F. P. Roe, Lt, Gloucester Regt. Staff Officer, VIII Corps HQ. Typescript recollections. P.H.L. Archives.

Chapter 9

1. The BEF in March 1918 had five fewer divisions than at the end of October 1917 and the 47 Divisions of the BEF were all well below their full complement. In Britain

there were more than 640,000 officers and men.

2. W. Foster, Lt, 7th Notts and Derby, Staff Officer 178 Brigade HQ. Letters, March 1918. P.H.L. Archives.

3. Captain G. D. Fairley, Capt, RAMC attached 7/8 King's Own Scottish Borderers. Diary, March 1918. P.H.L. Archives.

4. Frank Cunnington, Pte, 2/5 Notts and Derby Regiment. MSS recollections. P.H.L. Archives.

5. The 73rd Hanoverian Fusiliers for whom Gibraltar was a battle honour.

6. G. A. Fleet, Pte, 7th Bn Queen's Royal West Surreys. MSS recollections. P.H.L. Archives.

7. F. E. Starkey, Lt, Cheshire Regiment attached Army Cyclist Corps. Diary, April 1918. P.H.L. Archives.

8. B. W. Whayman, L/Cpl, RE Sigs, Field Survey Coy. MSS recollections. P.H.L. Archives.

9. *The Story of the 5th Australian Division* by Capt. A. D. Ellis, Hodder & Stoughton, London ND, p. 296.

10. Ibid, p. 298.

11. Brigadier C. Lawrence, Lt, 2nd Field Coy Engineers, AIF. Letter, April 1918. P.H.L. Archives.

12. Doctor G. I. Davies, 2nd Lt, Machine Gun Corps. Diary, 24 April 1918. P.H.L. Archives.

13. Major W. Tysoe, 2nd Lt, 7th Bedfords. Typescript recollections. P.H.L. Archives.

14. Doctor K. H. Cousland, Lt, RFA. Typescript account. P.H.L. Archives.

15. An officer's diary 4 July 1918 (ref. P.H.P.) P.H.L. Archives.

16. Lord Norrie, Capt, C. W. M. Norrie, GSO2 Tank Corps HQ. Letter, 11 August 1918. P.H.L. Archives.

17. D. Wilson, L/Cpl, 24th Bn AIF. MSS recollections. P.H.L. Archives. 'Possie' is of course 'position'.

18. An officer's diary, September 1918 (ref. P.H.P.) P.H.L. Archives.

19. Lieutenant Colonel J. C. Urquhart, Capt, and Adjutant 2/5 Lincolnshire Regiment. A document with his personal papers. P.H.L. Archives.

20. G. Scott, Cpl, RE 46th Divisional HQ Signallers. Typescript recollections. P.H.L. Archives.

21. Brigadier L. O. Clark, 2nd Lt, RE, No. 4 Section, 55th Field Coy. Typescript recollections. P.H.L. Archives.

22. A. Ellis, Cpl, 2/3 London Field Ambulance, RAMC 56 Division. Diary, September 1918. P.H.L. Archives.

23. Major General D. G. Johnson, Acting Lt Col I/C 2nd Royal Sussex. Letter, 8 October 1918. P.H.L. Archives.

24. War Diary, 1st Bn KRRC, September 1918. P.H.L. Archives.

25. *A Brief History of the King's Royal Rifle Corps 1755–1915* edit Lt Gen Sir Edward Hulton. Warren & Son, Winchester, ND.

26. Lieutenant Colonel A. C. Wilkinson, Capt, 2nd Bn Coldstream Guards. Letter, 6 November 1918. P.H.L. Archives.

27. Major R. B. Marshall, Maj, 7th East Surrey Regt. Letters, November 1918. P.H.L. Archives.

28. Major D. Gill, Maj, RGA. Letter, 12 November 1918. P.H.L. Archives.

29. Sir Charles Arthur, 2nd Lt, RFA. Letter, 10 November 1918. P.H.L. Archives.

30. Captain G. Eyston, Capt, RFA. Letter, 11 November, 1918. P.H.L. Archives.

31. F. A. R. Harvey, 2nd Lt, 3rd Bn York and Lancaster Regt. Field message, 10 November 1918. P.H.L. Archives.

32. Armistice documents: Unit Notification. P.H.L. Archives.

33. A. E. Buddell, 2nd Lt, 11th Bn Queen's Own Royal West Kent Regt. Unit Signal, 11 November 1918. P.H.L. Archives.

34. C. Birnstingl, 2nd Lt, RE Signals. Signal, 11 November 1918. P.H.L. Archives.

35. Reverend W. F. Browning, Cpl, RAMC. Typescript recollections. P.H.L. Archives.

Personal Experience Documentation

In assembling the names of all the people from whose papers evidence has been drawn for this book, I have followed the policy of this series of books by noting any rank held in retirement but not of cataloguing other distinctions or honours. By this means it is hoped to avoid giving cause for offence by error of omission or commission. Listed after the name is the year of the particular diary or letter used in this book (or of the period from which recall is made), the man's rank and unit at that time and the appropriate fighting front. On occasion, as with a particular battle, this additional detail is noted too.

Some men are mentioned several times; in these cases full details for each entry are given, but the reader must take care not to see this as a full military career biography – intervening stages may not have required recording for this book.

Unless specifically stated otherwise, all the material for the men and women here tabulated is held in my 1914–18 Personal Experience Archives.

Abbreviations

AB	Able Seaman
AFA	Australian Field Artillery
AIF	Australian Imperial Force
ALH	Australian Light Horse
ASC	Army Service Corps
Bde	Brigade
Bdr	Bombardier

BEF	British Expeditionary Force
Bn	Battalion
Brig	Brigadier
Bty	Battery
Capt	Captain
Col	Colonel
Coy	Company
Cpl	Corporal
CQMS	Company Quartermaster Sergeant
DCLI	Duke of Corwall's Light Infantry
Div	Division
DLI	Durham Light Infantry
Dvr	Driver
EEF	Egyptian Expeditionary Force
Fld Coy	Field Company
FP	Field Punishment
Gen	General
Gnr	Gunner
GOC	General Officer Commanding
HAC	Honourable Artillery Company
HBMGC	Heavy Branch Machine-Gun Corps
HE	High Explosive
HLI	Highland Light Infantry
I/C	In Command of
ICC	Imperial Camel Corps
KOSB	King's Own Scottish Borderers
KOYLI	King's Own Yorkshire Light Infantry
KRRC	King's Royal Rifle Corps
L/Cpl	Lance Corporal
Lt	Lieutenant
Lt Col	Lieutenant Colonel
Lt Gen	Lieutenant General
LRB	London Rifle Brigade
Maj	Major
Maj Gen	Major General
MGC	Machine-Gun Corps
MS(S)	Manuscript(s)
MT	Motor Transport
NCO	Non-Commissioned Officer
ND	No date
NZEF	New Zealand Expeditionary Force
NZR	New Zealand Rifles
OC	Officer in Command
OP	Observation Post
Ox & Bucks LI	Oxford and Buckinghamshire Light Infantry
Pdr	Pounder (gun)
PRO	Public Record Office
Pte	Private
QM	Quartermaster
RE	Royal Engineers
Regt	Regiment
Revd	Reverend
RF	Royal Fusiliers
RFA	Royal Field Artillery
Rfn	Rifleman
RFC	Royal Flying Corps
RGA	Royal Garrison Artillery
RHA	Royal Horse Artillery
RND	Royal Naval Division
RNVR	Royal Naval Volunteer Reserve
SB	Stretcher-Bearer
Spr	Sapper
2nd Lt	Second Lieutenant
Sigs	Signals or Signallers
TF	Territorial Force
Tpr	Trooper
UK	United Kingdom
VAD	Voluntary Aid Detachment
WAAC	Women's Army Auxiliary Corps

WAR	West African Regiment
W/F	Western Front

Name	Year	Details
Acland, Lt Gen A. N.	1914	Capt, 1st DCLI W/F, Mons retirement
Alston. J. F.	1915	Lt, MGC Troopship *Leasowe Castle*
Anderson	1914	Lt, Indian Medical Service Mesopotamia
Andrew, I. G.	1916	Pte, 6th Bn, Camerons W/F, Somme
Archdale, Capt F. A.		2nd Lt, 130th Baluchis East Africa
Armes, R. J.	1914	Capt, North Staffordshire Regt W/F Christmas Truce
Armstrong, Brig J. C.	1915	Capt, ASC
Arthur, Sir Charles	1918	2nd Lt, RFA W/F
Ashby, Capt A. B.		Lt, 5th Bn Queen's Royal West Surreys and Capt, Judge Advocate's Dept, Court Martial Office VIII Corps W/F
Atkinson, G. S.	1918	2nd Lt, 237 Fld Coy, RE W/F
Audrain, E.	1914	Pte, 1st Bn, Dorset Regt W/F Mons retirement and Givenchy
Bailey The Hon Lancelot	1915	Lt, Brecknockshire Bn, South Wales Borderers, Aden Field Force, Aden
Bain, Dr. C.	1916	2nd Lt, MG Coy, Officer 147 Bde, W/F Somme
Baker, H. E.	1917	Pte, 9th Bn, Devons, Troop train to Italy
Ball, A.	1914	Pte, Somerset Light Infantry UK
Banks, F. G.	1917	Cpl, 25th London Regt, India, Waziristan
Barber, H.	1916	Pte, 5th Bn, London Regt W/F Somme
Barclay, Brig C. N.	1914	Pte, London Scottish UK
Barraclough, Major W.	1918	2nd Lt, 11th Bn, West Yorks Italy
Barron, J. G.	1916	Pte, 2nd Bn, Tyneside Scottish W/F Somme
Bates, E. G.	1916	2nd Lt, then Lt, 3rd Bn, attached 9th Bn, Northumberland Fusiliers W/F Somme
	1917	Capt, 3rd Bn, attached 9th Bn, Northumberland Fusiliers W/F
	1918	Capt, 3rd Bn, attached 9th Bn, Northumberland Fusiliers W/F
Battersby, W.		Pte, 6th Bn, Dublin Fusiliers Macedonia
Bayne, A.	1915	Pte, 1st Bn, Wellington Regt, NZEF Gallipoli
Baynes, Sir William	1915	Ensign, 2nd Bn, Coldstream Guards W/F Loos
	1916	Lt, 2nd Bn, Coldstream Guards W/F
Bell, R. N.	1916	Pte, 15th Bn, West Yorks Regt W/F
Bennett, Lt Col O. D.	1914	Lt, Khyber Rifles India N/W Frontier

Bentley, W. G. | 1914 | Pte, 19th Bn, University & Public Schools Bn, Royal Fusiliers UK

Bertram, C. A. G. | 1917 | Lt, 2/5 Bn, Yorks and Lancs Regt W/F Cambrai

Betteridge, A. | 1916 | Pte, South African Scottish W/F Somme

Bigg, H. O. | 1917 | Cpl, RE Sigs, 54th Div, Egypt/Sinai/Gaza, Palestine

Billings, H. D. | 1915 | Spr, AIF (Engineers) Gallipoli

Bingham, Lt Col R. C. | 1915 | Lt, 3rd Bn, Coldstream Guards W/F (Loos)
| 1916 | Lt, 3rd Bn, Coldstream Guards W/F Somme

Bird, A. H. | 1916 | Sgt, Westminster Dragoons Egypt/Western Frontier Force

Bird, S. P. | 1915 | L/Cpl, RAMC Gallipoli

Birks, Maj Gen H. L. | 1917 | Capt, Tank Corps W/F Cambrai

Birnstingl, C. | 1918 | 2nd Lt, RE Sigs W/F

Birtwistle, I. T. | 1915 | L/Cpl, 22nd Bn, AIF Troopship Ulysses

Bishop, Lt Col G. | 1915 | Lt, Otago Bn, NZEF Gallipoli

Blackley, Dr F. J. | 1915 | Capt, RAMC W/F

Body, J. H. R. | | Pte, Meteorological Section, RE W/F

Bolton, E. F. | 1918 | Lt, 1/5 Queen's Royal West Surrey Regt Mesopotamia

Bowlby, E. | 1916 | 2nd Lt, 6th Bn, East Yorks Egypt

Boyce, L. A. G. | 1917 | Lt 41st Bn, AIF W/F

Boyd, Brig Sir John | 1916 | Capt, RAMC Macedonia

Bradley, Capt R. L. | 1915 | Capt, The Queen's W/F (Loos)

Bradley, W. J. | 1918 | Sgt, 2nd Bn, HAC Italy

Branson, Sir Douglas | 1915 | Maj, 4th Bn, Yorks & Lancs W/F
| 1916 | Lt Col, 4th Bn, Yorks & Lancs W/F
| 1917 | Lt Col, 4th Bn, Yorks & Lancs W/F 3rd Ypres

Breffitt, G. D. | 1917 | Cpl, RE Egypt/Sinai/Gaza

Brewster, Capt K. W. | 1915 | 2nd Lt, 6th Bn, Royal Fusiliers W/F

Bridgen, H. E. | 1915 | NCO RE Sigs W/F Loos

Brooks, Col G. H. | 1917 | Lt, F Bn, HBMGC W/F 3rd Ypres

Broome, Judge F.N. | 1915 | The Natal Carbineers German SW Africa

Brown, R. C., McB. | 1915 | 2nd Lt, 6th Bn, Dublin Fusiliers Macedonia

Brown, Lt Col A. G. | 1915 | Cpl, Fife and Forfar Yeomanry Gallipoli

Brown, P. A. | 1914 | AB, RNVR RND Antwerp

Browning, Revd W. F. | 1918 | Cpl, RAMC W/F

Buddell, A. E. | 1918 | 2nd Lt, 11th Bn, Queen's Own Royal West Kent Rgt W/F

Bumpus, A. E. | 1915 | Lt, RE Gallipoli

Buxton, Col R. | 1918 | I/C Camel Corps Detachment Hejaz

Cane, Maj A. S. | 1915 | Maj, RAMC Mesopotamia

Carew, E. H. | 1914 | AB, RNVR W/F (Antwerp)

Caröe, Sir Olaf | | Lt, 4th Bn, Queen's Royal West Surreys India

Cassidy, H. E. | 1916 | L/Cpl, RAMC Macedonia

Catford, Col E. C. | 1917/18 | Lt, RAMC Yeomanry MTd Div Palestine

Christison, Gen Sir Philip | 1915 | Lt, 6th Bn, Camerons W/F Loos

Church, B. H. | 1915 | 2nd Lt, RGA W/F

Clark, W. M. | 1915 | Pte, 10th Bn, AIF Troopship Themistocles

Clark, Brig L. O. | 1918 | 2nd Lt, RE W/F

Clayton Nunn, Lt Col T. H. | 1915 | (Royal West Kents) Staff Officer South Midland Infantry Bde W/F

Clennett, A. | 1915 | Sgt, 9th Battery, Australian Field Artillery, AIF Egypt

Coghlan, G. E. | 1918–19 | 2nd Lt, RE Sigs N Russia

Collins, A. J. | 1917 | Lt, Royal North Devon Hussars W/F Messines

Colvin, F. A. | 1915 | Pte, 2nd Bn, Royal Sussex Regt W/F Loos

Conville, Lt Col L. H. G. | 1918 | Capt, Indian Mountain Artillery Burma
| 1918 | Capt, Indian Mountain Artillery Aden Field Force Aden

Coombs, C. R. | 1915 | Pte, London Scottish W/F

Coombs, H. J. | 1915 | Cpl, Royal West Kent Regt Mesopotamia

Cooper, Maj E., VC | 1917 | Sgt, 12th(S) Bn, KRRC W/F 3rd Ypres

Couchman, Revd M. L. | 1917 | Padre, 30th Dvisiion W/F 3rd Ypres

Cousland, Dr K. H. | 1918 | Lt, RFA W/F

Chadwick, Dr N. E. | 1915 | 2nd Lt, 1/7 Essex Regt Gallipoli

Chance, Sir Roger J. F. | 1914 | 2nd Lt, 4th Dragoon Guards W/F

Chant, R. | 1914 | Pte, 5th Dragoon Guards W/F (1st Ypres)

Chapman, G. | 1916 | 2nd Lt, 13th Bn, Royal Fusiliers W/F Somme

Crabbe, Sir John | 1914 | Maj, 2nd Dragoon Guards (Royal Scots Greys) W/F

Craig, Lady | | Daughter of F. M. Lord Birdwood – re photos of Gallipoli

Crerar, A. H. | 1916 | 2nd Lt, 2nd Bn, Royal Scots Fusiliers W/F

Crew, G. | 1914 | Pte, Somerset Light Infantry UK

Cripps, Brig B. U. S. | 1915 | 2nd Lt, 2nd Bn, Welsh Regt W/F Aubers Ridge

Cumberland, T. D. | 1918 | Capt, RAMC attached 9th Bn, King's Own Royal Regiment (Lancaster) Macedonia

Cunnington, F. | 1918 | Pte, 2/5 Notts & Derby W/F

Davey, Capt J. | 1914 | Spr, RE W/F Christmas Truce
| 1916–17 | A/Cpl, RE UK & Mesopotamia

Davie, R. | 1915 | Pte, 1st Bn, Wellington Regt, NZEF Gallipoli

Davies, Maj F. B. | 1916 | 2nd Lt, RGA, Aden Field Force Aden

Davies, Dr G. I. | 1918 | 2nd Lt, MGC W/F

Davies, H. H. | 1917 | 2nd Lt, 21st Bn, Northumberland Fusiliers W/F

Davies, I. | | Gnr, 'Y' Batt, 1st Trench Mortars Macedonia

Davies, J. | 1917 | 2nd Lt, 8th Bn, Royal Fusiliers W/F

Davis, C. J. | 1916–17 | Pte, 25th London Regt India

Dawson, C. | 1918 | Tpr Imperial Camel Corps Hejaz

Dean, C. G. T.	1916	Capt, RGA W/F
Dean, G. P. T.	1918	Lt, 24th Punjabis Mesopotamia
Deane, Capt E. C.	1915	Capt, RAMC attached 2nd Leicesters W/F (Neuve Chapelle and eve of Loos)
Deane, Dr N. S.	1914–15	West African Medical Service attached to West African Regiment Cameroons
Denham, F. B.	1916	2nd Lt, 1st Bn, Worcester Regt W/F Somme
Dillon Kelly, C.	1917	Lt, RAMC W/F Cambrai
Dixon, E. H.	1915	Tpr Middlesex Yeomanry Egypt
Dod, O. A.	1918	Lt, 285 Fortress Coy RE Italy
Drury Weston	1916	Sgt, RAMC Macedonia (Concert Parties)
Dunlop, Lt Col C. A. M.	1915	Officer in the 41st Dogras, Indian Army W/F Neuve Chapelle
Dunn, W. L. P.	1916	Pte, 17th Bn, King's Liverpool Regt W/F
Durrant, A. S.	1916	Sgt, 18th Bn, DLI W/F Somme
Dutton, A. G.	1915	Pte, 1/20 London Regt W/F
Easton, H.	pre 1914	Tpr, 9th Lancers UK
Eldridge, Lt Gen Sir John		2nd Lt, 90th Siege Batt RGA W/F
Ellis, A.	1918	Cpl, 2/3 London Field Ambulance, RAMC 56 Div W/F
Evans, M. C.	1914–15	Pte, 1st Light Horse, AIF Egypt
Evers, Revd Canon M. S.	1917	Padre, 74th Bde W/F
Eyston, Capt G.	1918	Capt, RFA W/F
Fagence, V. E.	1917	Pte, 11th Bn, Queen's Royal West Surrey Regt W/F 3rd Ypres
Fairley, Dr G. D.	1916	Capt, RAMC attached to 2nd Bn, Royal Scots Fusiliers W/F (Somme)
	1918	Capt, RAMC attached 7/8 KOSB W/F
Faviell, Brig J. V.	1917	2nd Lt, RHA Italy
Fell, E. P.	1915	Pte, 1st Bn Essex Regt Gallipoli
Ferrier, I.	1915	Lt, 48th Bombay Pioneers Mesopotamia
Findlay, R.	1915	Petty Officer, Hawke Bn, RND Gallipoli
Fleet, G. A.	1918	7th Bn, Queen's Royal West Surrey Regt W/F
Ford, R.	1917	Gnr, RFA W/F
Foster, W.	1917	Lt, 7th Bn, Notts and Derby Regt W/F
	1918	Lt, 7th Bn, Notts and Derby Regt W/F
Fourie, Dr P. J. J.	1914	Tpr, South African Defence Force Rebellion in S. Africa
Fowle, Brig J. le C.	1916	Capt, South Persian Rifles Persia
Fox, A. S.	1915	2nd Lt, 2/6, North Staffs Regt W/F (Hooge)
Fox Pitt, Maj Gen W. A. F. L.	1916	2nd Lt, Welsh Guards W/F Somme
Francis, J. C. W.	1916	Lt, 19th Royal Hussars W/F
Fraser, A. T	1916	Sgt, 1st Border Regt W/F Somme
Fraser, Revd Dr J.	1917	2nd Lt, 7th Bn, Gordon Highlanders W/F
Friend, H. E.		Pte, 24th Bn, London Regt W/F
Frost, H. H.	1914	Pte, 2/21st London Regt UK

Gardner, Prof H. A.	1914	Pte, Queen's Westminster Rifles W/F Christmas Truce
Gates, W.	1917	Gnr, 10th Siege Batt, RGA
Geddes, Capt G. W.	1915	Capt, 1st Bn, Royal Munster Fusiliers Gallipoli (PRO Source)
Gill, Maj D.	1918	Maj, RGA
Gillan, Sir Angus	1916	Assistant Political and Intelligence Officer, Sudan Western Frontier Force Sudan
Gillespie, R. D.	1914	2nd Lt, 2nd Bn, Gordon Highlanders W/F Christmas Truce
Gillespie, T. C.	1914	2nd Lt, King's Own Scottish Borderers W/F
Gilpin, Brig G. R.	1917/18	Lt/Capt, RE Egypt, Gaza
Gitsham, A. H.	1918	2nd Lt, RAF W/F
'Gladys'	1918	No. 14694, WAAC UK
Glanusk, Lt Col the Lord	1915	Lt Col, Brecknockshire Bn, South Wales Borderers, Aden Field Force Aden
Gledhill, W. G.	1917	Sgt, 2nd Bn, Norfolks Mesopotamia
Gluckstein, Sir Louis	1917	Lt, Intelligence Corps, GHQ Italy
Godsell, Lt Col K. B.	1914	2nd Lt, RE W/F Mons, 1st Ypres
Goodale, Sir Ernest	1918	Lt, 9th Bn, Royal Warwicks Dunsterforce North Persia
Goodes, A. J.	1918	L/Sgt, 2/10 Royal Scots N. Russia
Goldthorp, F. L.	1916	Pte, 185 Coy, MGC Troopship *Berrima*
Gordon, Col G. H.	1915	Capt, RFA Macedonia
Graham, Brig H. L.	1915	2nd Lt, 6th Bn, South Staffs W/F
Graham, R.	1916	Officer, Aden Field Force Aden
Green, A. E.	1917	Capt, 2/5 West Yorks W/F
Grimshaw, J.	1917	L/Cpl, ASC Troopship *Cameronia*
Grossmith, W.	1915	2nd Lt, 1st Bn, Leicester Regt W/F (Loos)
Grove, G. C.	1915	Spr, No. 2 Field Coy, Australian Engineers 1st Div, AIF Troopship *Berrima* Egypt and Gallipoli
Groves, A. V.		Spr, RE East Africa
Guest, A. E.	1914	Gnr, 29th Bty, RFA W/F (The Aisne)
Guy, B. G.	1917	2nd Lt, 128 Bty, RFA W/F Arras
Gwynne Jones, A.	1916	2nd Lt, 1st Bn, Welsh Guards W/F Somme
Haigh, Lt Col J.	1918	Lt, 9th Bn, Royal Warwicks Dunsterforce N. Persia
Hakewill Smith, Maj Gen Sir Edmund	1916	Lt, 6th Bn, Royal Scots Fusiliers W/F
Hall, Capt B. C.	1917	2nd Lt, 1st Fld Coy, Canadian Engineers W/F Messines
Harbutt, Capt N. C.	1915	Lt, (Acting Capt) RE W/F 2nd Ypres
Hardy, F. W.	1915	Pte, 9th Devons W/F Loos
Harford, Sir James	1918	2nd Lt, Essex Regt W/F
Harley, Sir Thomas	1915	2nd Lt, King's Own Royal Regt (Lancaster)
	1917	2nd Lt, King's Own Royal Regt (Lancaster) Macedonia

Woodhead, S.	1916	Pte, 9th Bn, Duke of Welling-ton's Regt W/F
Woods, C. M.	1916	Rfn, 1st Bn, London Regt (Queen's Westminster Rifles) W/F Somme
Wray, F. R. & M.	1914	Rfn, 1st London Rifle Bde W/F Christmas Truce
	1915	Rfn, 1st London Rifle Bde W/F Loos
Yearsley, V. C. R.	1918	Cpl, 29th London Regt N. Russia

Young, Lt Col J. H.	1915	Capt, 1st Bn, Argyll and Sutherland Highlanders W/F (2nd Ypres)
	1916	Capt, 1st Bn, Argyll and Suther-land Highlanders Macedonia
	1917–18	Major and 2nd I/C London Scottish Palestine
Young, W. A.	1915	Pte, 87th Fld Amb, RAMC Gallipoli

Bibliography

As this book relies above all on personal experience testimony from sources which, with few exceptions, have not previously appeared in published form, it has not been thought fitting to provide here a comprehensive bibliography of First World War soldiering. Listed here, together with certain essential general works, are volumes from which either specific quotation has been made or valuable information gained. To the authors and publishers of these works a debt of gratitude is herewith acknowledged and sincere appreciation expressed.

General Works and Official Histories
Apart from the volumes of the Official History of Military operations on each of the main fronts and on East Africa and, for Gallipoli, the two-volume Australian Official History (the notes give specific detail where quotation was made from these volumes), the books of a general nature which were particularly useful were:
A Nation In Arms, eds. I. W. F. Beckett and K. Simpson, Manchester University Press, 1985
Ellis, J. *Eye Deep in Hell*. Croom Helm, London 1976
Falls, Cyril. *The First World War*. Longman, London 1960
L. Wilson, Trevor. *The Myriad Faces of War*. Polity Press, Cambridge, 1986

Monographs, Autobiographies and Biographies
Barker, A. J. *The Neglected War: Mesopotamia 1914–18*. Faber & Faber, London 1967
Baynes, J. *Morale: A Study of Men and Courage*. Cassell, London 1967
Bidwell, Brig Shelford. *Gunners at War*. Arms & Armour Press, London 1970
Bond, B. edit. *Staff Officer*. The Diaries of Lord Moyne, 1914–18. Leo Cooper, London, 1987
Campbell, P. J. *The Ebb and Flow of Battle*. Hamish Hamilton, London 1977

— *In the Cannon's Mouth*. Hamish Hamilton, London 1979
Carr, William. *A Time to leave the Ploughshares*. Robert Hale, London 1985
Dallas, G. and Gill, D. *The Unknown Army*. Verso, London 1985
Gilbert, Major V. *The Romance of the Last Crusade*. D. Appleton & Co., London 1932
Gwynne-Vaughan, Dame Helen. *Service with the Army*. Hutchinson, London, ND
Haber, L. F. *The Poisonous Cloud: Chemical Warfare in the First World War*. Clarendon Press, Oxford 1986
Inchbald, G. *Imperial Camel Corps*. Johnson, London 1970
Innes, J. R. *Flash Spotters and Sound-Rangers*. Geo. Allen & Unwin, London 1935
James, R. R. *Gallipoli*. Batsford, London 1965
Liddle, P. H. *The Airman's War 1914–18*. Blandford Press, 1987
— *Men of Gallipoli*. Allen Lane, London 1976
— *Gallipoli: Pens, Pencils and Cameras at War*. Brasseys, London 1985
Mason, P. *A Matter of Honour:* an account of the Indian Army, its officers and men. Jonathan Cape, London 1974
Mathieson, W. D. *My Grandfather's War*. Macmillan Canada, 1981
Mead, Brigadier P. *The Eye in the Sky*. HMSO, London 1983
Miller, C. *Battle for the Bundu*. Macdonald & Jane, London 1974
Palmer, A. *The Gardeners of Salonika: The Macedonian Campaign 1915–18*. Andre Deutsch, London 1965
Terraine, J. *White Heat: The New Warfare 1914–18*. Sidgwick & Jackson, London 1982
— *To Win A War: 1918 The Year of Victory*. Sidgwick & Jackson, London 1978
Uys, I. *Delville Wood*. Uys Publishers, Johannesburg 1983

Index

UNION OF SOUTH AFRICA

CANADA   NEWFOUNDLAND

GREENLAND

C A N A D A

QUEBEC TO LIVERPOOL 2,635

NEWFOUNDLAND

UNITED STATES

PORT

Bermuda

BAHAMA ISLANDS

W. INDIES

LEEWARD ISLANDS

BRITISH HONDUR

Jamaica

Barbados
WINDWARD ISLANDS
Trinidad
BRITISH GUIANA

GAM

SI
L

As

SOUTH
AMERICA

FIJI

NEW
ZEALAND

WELLINGTON TO LONDON 11,960 MILES

FALKLAND IS

South
Georgia

THE MEN OF THE EMPIRE; TH